Maine Speaks

AN ANTHOLOGY OF MAINE LITERATURE

D1441713

THE MAINE LITERATURE PROJECT

Maine Speaks

AN ANTHOLOGY OF MAINE LITERATURE

Published by the Maine Writers and Publishers Alliance

IN CONJUNCTION WITH

The Maine Council for English Language Arts

Special thanks to
The Maine Humanities Council and to Sun Savings and Loan
for making the Maine Literature Project possible.

First Edition

Design by Edith Allard.
This book was typeset by Maine Writers and Publishers Alliance on the Macintosh 512K, made possible by a grant from Apple Computer, Inc., Community Affairs, and on the Macintosh Plus.
Camera ready copy by G & G Laser Typesetting.

Published by Maine Writers and Publishers Alliance
19 Mason Street, Brunswick, Maine 04011.

Manufactured in the United States.

Library of Congress Card Catalogue Number: 89-060344

Library of Congress Cataloging-in-Publication Data

Maine speaks
        Includes index.
        1. American Literature—Maine. 2. Maine—Literary collections.
I. Fischer, Jeff. II. Maine Literature Project. III. Maine Writers & Publishers Alliance. IV. Maine Council for English Language Arts.
PS548.M2M33 1989   810.8'09741   89-8122
ISBN 0-9618592-1-0
ISBN 0-9618592-2-9 (pbk.)

Cover: Marsden Hartley, *Mount Katahdin*, 1941, oil on masonite, 22" x 28". Courtesy, Mrs. Paul J. Schrag.

Contents

Work

Nature

Communities

PREFACE

Maine Speaks is a sourcebook of Maine literature for the general reader as well as for students in the junior high and high school years, an invitation to Maine teachers to bring the writing of our state into their classrooms. It is the product of three rewarding years of collecting, reading, discussing, and sifting the wide range of literature created by writers whose lives have been touched by Maine.

It's hard to step back and see the whole when one has been obsessed with the details for so long, and I have often wondered, in the process of creating this anthology, just what vision of Maine it would present. The more the editorial group widened and deepened our knowledge of Maine literature, the more we came to realize that there is no single and unified vision of our state, but a chorus—and sometimes a cacaphony—of voices. Some delight in Maine's rich beauty; others complain of the long, bitter winter. Some sing in praise of the strength of small towns; others in anger at the deep social divisions they find in them. Every voice gives shape to its own vision of Maine, just as every voice is, in turn, shaped by place.

We see *Maine Speaks* as a place where readers can come to understand the close connection between the self and the environment that is so vital to literature, by examining the literature of a place near to their own experience.

Maine Speaks was compiled with several audiences in mind. To the general reading public we offer a volume that captures the sweep of Maine writing from her native American cultures to today's lively contemporary scene. For the school audience, we have had less the desire to provide a complete curriculum than to create a rich resource from which teachers can select the Maine writing that best suits their students. There is ample material in *Maine Speaks* to interest students in both junior high and high school English classes, as well as to provide a cornerstone for an interdisciplinary approach to Maine Studies.

Though the anthology is long, it does not pretend to be all-inclusive. Our apologies go out to writers whose work has been omitted through oversight, and to devoted readers who find their favorite authors or selections missing. Our choices were difficult. The factors we juggled in making our selections were complex; balancing geographical regions, ethnic groups, literary genres, accessible and difficult, traditional and contemporary pieces turned out to be a greater challenge than we expected. We hope, above all, that we were guided by literary quality and by consideration of our audience.

Our policy in using excerpts from longer works has been to select only those which can be enjoyed and understood in and of themselves, without need for lengthy explanation of what precedes and follows in the text. Thus, for instance, the work of Kenneth Roberts, difficult to excerpt, is missing here, though we do encourage students to read his novels. While we are proud of the breadth of our selections, we must acknowledge that *Maine Speaks* is only the tip of the iceberg. There is a lot of Maine out there, from the works of established Maine authors, to the wonderful surprises on the library shelves, to the poems and stories coming out today.

The authors' biographies in the back of the book, often in their own words, shed light on writers' origins: how this writer came to take up poetry; how that one found a story and made it her own. We hope that these personal stories, too, will inspire readers of the anthology to give shape to their own experiences in Maine, and out of them to make the Maine literature of the future.

We owe thanks for the generosity in time and in money given to the Maine Literature Project by many, many people who have expressed an enthusiasm for *Maine Speaks* from its inception.

For their financial support, we would like to thank the Maine Humanities Council, Sun Savings and Loan, the Maine Arts Commission, the Maine Council for English Language Arts, Bates College, the Maine Reading Association, Bookland of Maine, Waldenbooks, Down East Enterprises, The Maine Community Foundation, the Abelard Foundation, the Benjamin Wing Trust, Boise Cascade, the John Anson Kittredge Trust and the Institute of Financial Education.

Special thanks also to the Maine Department of Educational and Cultural Services; to Christine Macchi, Lee Murch, Pam Smith and Ben Swan of the Maine Writers and Publishers Alliance; to Gail Scott for selection of illustrations; to David Walker for help in the selection of poetry; to Beth Whittaker, Catherine Lattanzi, and Bates College; to Kathleen Ashley, Jere Daniell, Sandy Ives, Kathleen Lignell, Kate Barnes, Fred Bonnie, Robert Chute, Rebecca Cummings, Tom Fallon, Susan Hand Shetterly, Logan Johnston, Richard Rockefeller, Nancy Anderson, Anne Wescott Dodd, the Maine State Library, Richard Barringer, John Jacques, Ruth Moore, Eric Flower, Don Wismer, Stu Kestenbaum, Ronald Dow, Marilyn Emerick, Pamela Rolfe, Michael McCormack, Helen Thibeau, Connie Piper, Eleanor Tracy, Nancy Hutton, Fred Cheney, Joyce McCann, Phyllis Deringis, Carla Rensenbrink, July Hakola, Bill Richards, Elizabeth McClenahan, Carol Eisenberg and G & G Typesetting.

We would like to thank, too, the teachers and librarians who attended the first Summer Institute in Maine Literature at Bates College. We took to heart both their enthusiasm for and criticisms of the draft of *Maine Speaks* when creating the final table of contents.

Our deepest appreciation goes to the writers who have kindly granted us permission to use their work in *Maine Speaks*. They have been, from first to last, the purpose and the inspiration of our work.

Jeff Fischer, Director
Maine Literature Project

INTRODUCTION

Think for a minute about how much of your life is spent telling stories. The alarm goes off, you roll over, and in those first moments of consciousness think dimly, "Today I have to ..." and tell yourself the story of the day ahead. This personal storytelling is a rehearsal for living out the events of the day. When you daydream about the future, you are using stories to plan; when you reflect on the past, you are using stories to understand. You know who you are by the stories you tell yourself about yourself.

Much of what you know about the world also comes to you in the form of a story. A friend greets you: "You'll never guess what happened to me!" A favorite teacher launches into an explanation: "Think of it this way...." You pick up a newspaper or switch on the television. Your family gathers and begins to reminisce. Through hundreds of such small stories, you create both yourself and your world. In fact, your world is the sum total of all the stories you know about it.

As stories shape a person's identity, so too they shape the identity of a place. In our minds, that place is the sum total of all the stories that we know about it. No wonder, then, that this collection of stories about Maine—and by stories I mean many different forms of retelling including fiction, poetry, myth, legend, journal, essay—gives us a unique and powerful way to understand this place we call home.

This book is a prism of landscape, people and events. Turn it one way and you see the rockbound coast and icy sea; turn it again and you see the sweep of forest. One more turn for the potato fields of the north or the small farms and towns of the south. Much of Maine's identity is its geography; a northern outpost, isolated, facing the sea, the single state in the Union which shares a border with only one other state.

Further turns allow you to see Maine through the eyes of a hundred different people, from the makers of the Koluskap legends and early European travellers such as John Josselyn, through succeeding generations of in-migrants, the Franco-Americans, the Finns, the summer people from away who become year-round residents. You will see through the eyes of long-time settlers, whose lives are changed by these in-migrations and changed by the times themselves. You will see people at work—cutting ice on the Kennebec, logging in the northern woods, packing sardines, hauling traps, picking potatoes, working the family farm. You will see them rescuing and taking care of one another, entertaining one another, doing one another harm, trying to grow and struggling to work out the many complexities of human relationships.

Maine Speaks is a collage of voices—from anonymous storytellers to literary notables of the past such as Longfellow and Thoreau, and of the present, such as E.B. White and Stephen King. Through the words of all of them, you will hear many Maine voices. You hear colonial women struggling against the power of superstition, a nineteenth century "hayseed" humorist taking his first look at the great city of Portland; a modern-day teenager dealing with the meaning of winning and losing, as both a Franco-American and an unwilling long-distance runner. In the biographical section at the end of the book, you will also hear the voices of the authors themselves speaking about their lives and work.

Those of us who compiled this anthology did so because we believe in the power of story to focus and transform; and because there is no collection presently in print which brings together a range of voices and images to tell the story of Maine. Our aim was to include only work that we felt was exceptionally well-crafted and that represented a range of historical periods, geographical settings, literary genres and styles, and, most important, voices of Maine. It was not easy to choose among the many possibilities. We chose to include stories we knew some would find unflattering or controversial. We know that, in spite of our best efforts, readers are bound to feel there are gaps and omissions.

While we know that not all of these stories will relate directly to the experience of every reader, we feel it is important to let the many and varied voices of our state, past and present, speak for themselves. By doing so, we hope to make it clear that the stuff of storytelling is all around you. Believing this, we invite you to add your own stories to the many others that shape the identity of Maine.

Eileen Landay
Maine Council for English Language Arts
April, 1989

Isaac Simpson, Fourth of July Celebrants, Amity Maine, *photograph.*
Courtesy, Millard Simpson.

Identity

*"A boy's will is the wind's will,
And the thoughts of youth are long, long thoughts."*

Whale!

ELEANOR STERLING

On an afternoon in mid-August, a very large gray whale appeared up out of Casco Bay and swam between the rock ledges off Harpswell Island, scattering the perched seagulls to the winds, and washed ashore finally in little Dingley Cove; there it lay on its side like a stone half in and half out of the water, blowing lazily and dreamily through the opening in its head.

Now a great many things had come ashore at Dingley in the past: strips of old linoleum, spars, wooden crates and kegs, broken lobster pots, buoy markers, plastic bleach bottles, dead fish of all kinds, and once even a dead seal pup all fat and spotted, but never before a whale. Harley Perkins, who'd been fishing the incoming tide just off the ledges, immediately rowed for Harpswell Harbor and told the news that he'd seen a whale wash over. In fifteen minutes the Coast Guard at Seguin had been alerted, and half the Island was down to watch the whale die, for undoubtedly that was what it had come for.

The boy, Willan, was up-Island picking blueberries. He saw people driving down the dirt road to Dingley in an awful hurry, pick-ups and cars and a couple of jeeps, and he thought that maybe someone almost drowned. He was an island boy and in his ways he was as laconic as his ancestors' crayon portraits. As far as he was concerned someone was always and forever "almost drowning," especially summer people; his Mam told him that summer people could almost drown in a teacup.

Mam had the roadside Square Deal Restaurant on the Island. It was because she wanted to put blueberry pie on the menu early that Willan was out there picking, though not too many berries were ripe yet. Still, had he gone swimming or fishing he would have missed that whole thing about the whale altogether. As it was, the rush of people down toward Dingley finally poked at his curiosity enough to make him set his buckets aside and hurry down through the bay bushes to the cove too.

The first men into the cove had been the Quinn brothers, who'd been out that way site-ing for a new wharf and actually saw the whale float in. They'd slid down the rocky slope to the beach with caution; the whale was heaving its sides up and down, gleaming like wet slate with a slice of corrugated white on its underside. When the Quinns got down quite close, the whale suddenly snorted and spouted, a great spray rising up, and it watched them coming with the one eye on its side that lay upward out of the water.

Then more people arrived; the whale's eye rolled about, trying to watch them all coming from separate directions: Perley Doughty and his boy Phil, Marge Hapgood from the general store, the Moody boys home early from fishing, and the Coffins from the gas station. The whale's eyeball rolled and rolled. By the time Willan finally saw the whale, its huge head was surrounded by a bunch of ladies in pink raffia sunhats and high-heeled sandals, who were snapping pictures with their cameras and laughing pleasurably, and men with fat stomachs and walker-shorts and clean sneakers, who stood by helplessly, watching the ceremony of a whale's dying with all the involvement and compassion that might have accompanied another afternoon's activity.

"Well, will you looka there at ol' 'Moby Dick!'" someone was hollering. "He sick or somethin'? What's he doin' hea'?"

Nobody said anything. They were all watching the whale, fascinated by its mammoth size. Once again the whale blew lazily, a white spray rising sideways out of its head and blowing a hole into the place at the water's edge where the gravel began. People moved back, silent.

"Now who ever seed a whale hereabouts?" asked an old man in overalls of nobody in particular. "Who ever *seed* sich a thing?" he asked again, incredulously looking into the faces around him. Nobody met his old eyes, rheumy and shocked, and he began to circle through the crowd asking over and over, "Who ever *seed* sich a thing?"

The whale, about forty feet long, seemed to fill the small cove. It appeared to reach from one end of the gravel crescent to the other, its hulk gleaming smooth and slippery-dark, rising slightly on the incoming tide, the spade-shaped tail moving easily and powerfully back and forth in the low water. From the curve of its mouth and the way the mouth reached back along the whale's side some people thought the great creature was grinning—was, indeed, wounded or sick to the death, and in great suffering. Once it seemed to scream; the mouth opened slightly at the front and a sound came out, thin and piercing, and then the mouth closed down again and the whale rolled ever more to one side, spouting weakly.

"'E's a right whale, not a sperm," Thomas Quinn was announcing just as Willan scrambled to the scene.

"How come *you* know the difference?" Perley Doughty wanted to know. Along the Maine coast there had been few whalers, and knowledge of whales was not in the Harpswell Islanders' tradition. Other fish, yes; not whales.

"The head, see the head, how it's shaped? Now a sperm's got a big blunt head, but this fella's kind of flat-shaped and low to the front."

Nobody argued; nobody knew.

"We're going to have to nudge him down with a jeep and tow him out," said Mr. Coffin. "He dies here and it'll be a smell they'll know in Portland, ayeh."

Willan just stared. An artist was kneeling on the beach, sketching the whale in charcoal. A lot of little kids were there, and bigger ones who hadn't jobs that summer, and housewives in faded cotton aprons, men in hip-high boots, and lobstermen with faces as long and creased as bark, all just standing impassively there and watching.

Willan remembered Mam and the blueberries; Mam had to have them in time for the afternoon baking. Mam had taken care of Willan since his mother died the winter before; though Mam was good at being patient with a boy, and Mam was good at questions and answers, she hadn't even tried to give Willan the answer to why his mother was gone so soon. Willan had stopped his grievous asking. Instead they played the game that Willan was really Mam's own little boy. All they had in the world to be responsible to was each other and the Square Deal Restaurant; Mam did the cooking and the baking and whenever Willan could help, Mam pushed him into it, like gathering apples and slicing them for turnovers, and picking blueberries for pie. It was the blueberries that were really nudging Willan's mind just then.

He took one more look at the dying whale and the crowd of Islanders and Summer People watching it. Then he climbed back to where he'd left his buckets, going the long way to avoid the tumblestone edge of the Island cemetery where his mother and father both lay out of sight of the sea.

The buckets were full enough. He took them up to Mam in the Square Deal kitchen and she gave him a jelly sandwich. Mam had already heard about the big whale in Dingley Cove. She said she'd like to get down and see it but there was no time, what with the baking to finish. Then she said it was a crying shame, but what could they do except have the Coast Guard come and haul the big fish away?

"You wanta go back down and watch?" she asked, without turning from her pie dough. "Go now and I'll ask Billy to come for you later."

Billy was Mam's kitchen helper. He was Island and you had to "ask" him, you couldn't "tell" him anything; a paid salary would never alter that.

So Willan went back to Dingley, scuffing his sneakers down the long dirt road, and got there just as the small white Coast Guard cutter came in carefully between the ledges, its motor chugging and rumbling. Everyone in the cove and sitting up in the bushes on the rocky bank stood up and cheered when the cutter came about; their shouts made the whale rise up terribly and flail the water with flukes and fins until its body was enveloped in sea foam. It spouted, and a thin spray of blood came through.

Coming as rocking-close to the shore as they could, the Coast Guardsmen tried heaving ropes around the whale's mammoth body. Each line fell short or flicked right off the whale's skin, which looked to be as smooth as a piece of silk. The cutter lolled sideways in the trough of the waves.

Then Willan, looking almost idly out to where the rock ledges broke the sea, saw the whale's calf. It was swimming in a long, frantic ellipse, rapidly back and around and forward.

"A baby!" he shouted in spite of himself. People looked and saw and Phil Doughty said, "Well, I be damned, he ain't a bull-whale, he's a mother!"—which made a lot of them laugh. The whale, as though knowing her calf was coming dangerously close, increased her dying struggles. With repeated strokes of her flukes she worked her way a little off-shore, and then the ropes fell true and she was rapidly lassoed and secured. Again the watchers on the shore shouted. Willan noticed the whale's ears were little and lay far back on her sides. He wondered if she could hear her baby calf over the shouting and the beat of the cutter's engines and the crashing little waves that were running into the cove.

The whale was pulled slowly, slowly, farther from the beach. Willan kept one eye on the calf swimming near the ledges. It looked no bigger than Willan himself, pale as its mother was dark, and suddenly it turned and rapidly swam away; Willan lost sight of it completely, but there were other things to watch right then, for the ropes slipped and the whale cow wallowed back into the cove again, blowing weakly. The watchers groaned at the failure, and the cutter came in again slowly and lay off for another try.

Then Billy, Mam's kitchen helper, shouted "Willan!" Looking up, Willan saw Billy at the top of the cove waving a dishtowel, and he knew he had to come away. Dingley Cove was so jammed up by then that Willan thought there were more people than he'd ever seen on Harpswell Island, and the dirt road was parked solidly with cars and trucks, like a supermarket lot in town.

Billy was even older than Mam, too old and too long on the Island and too worried about getting Mam's dishes done to really care about the dying whale and her calf, so Willan walked silently with him. But as they went in the back way of the Square Deal, Billy spoke suddenly. "I saved you th' cherries from th' fruit salad," and gave Willan a grizzled, toothless smile; it was all right with folks like Billy, Willan thought, they understood.

That evening a lot of strangers came into the Square Deal, and Billy and Mam were kept on the hustle from kitchen to counter and back, with plates of lobster salad and fried clams and pie; most people had come over to see the whale and got hungry just standing there, so Mam said laughingly that maybe the whale was a good thing since business had been slow; when she saw Willan's face she changed her mind. No, she said, it wasn't a good thing. She was sorry for that poor big old Mam and her baby but for Willan not to worry; the baby would get on by itself, for that was the way it was with whales, she was sure.

Later, when the rush was over, Marge Hapgood came down from the store for a cup of coffee. She said the whale was still down there in the dark, higher up than ever now that the tide was on its way out. Willan wanted to know about the calf; was it still out there? he asked carefully. Marge didn't know, but she said she thought all the people had gone since it was too dark to see anything.

Willan waited and thought awhile, sitting under the electric light and listening to Billy's radio in the kitchen and the clash of dishes. Then he went out alone, picked a lantern off the shed door and lit it, turned the wick down, and started back to Dingley once more. He had to be careful on the road because he'd forgotten his sneakers and he wondered all the while that he was going at all; the night was black and silent and hung over the Island without a moon or a star, and the damp night wind was cold.

As Willan came down in the lantern-light through the trampled baybushes they lent their fragance to the wind, tarry and wild, but when Willan got to the beach where the whale cow lay high and dark the air was troubled by a strong, oily smell; the whale herself, Willan knew, and she was surely dead.

Nobody else was there. Raising the lantern wick he went up close, walking carefully on the wet, cold gravel, and the whale was so huge, so dark, and so terrible! He put his hand on the whale and she was fat-soft and icy, with crusts of barnacles along her fat lips.

Willan had once read that whales died heading into the sun, but this one had died in the night facing north, landward, and stirred up the beach for yards around it. The oily smell was thick in Willan's throat. He dropped his hand off the whale and, raising his lantern higher, he saw the calf, as he supposed he knew he would, lying half-submerged in the black shallows as close as it could get to its dead cow, pale and shining and desperate in the lantern light.

"Go away, baby," Willan called out softly, and the calf-whale stirred. "Go on, scram, git!" he called more loudly, swinging his lantern high in an arc, and his voice echoed back from the corners of the empty cove—go away, scram, git, scram git, scramgit.

Willan didn't know *why* he wanted the calf to go away. Partly it was because they'd made him go away in the wintertime, when Mam had come and gotten him and taken him with her too soon, before.... But it was too late here already, for this child had been there and known when it happened, had been with her all the time.

Willan began to cry silently. He set his lantern down and cried for the question that Mam couldn't answer; and when the crying was all done he let his face dry and stiffen in the wind. He picked up his lantern again and looked out at the whale-calf; it was there, Willan's terrible, sorrowing kin, and he whistled and called out softly to it, "All right you there, stay now, but you go later," and the calf stirred again in the dark water, spouting softly like a clear bell ringing in the lanternlight.

"It's all right, I say, but you take care in the morning, hear?" He swung the lantern toward the open sea. "You better go then, I'm telling you! Hear me?"

And there was one more thing, perhaps the thing he'd really come for.

"And listen," he cried out to the calf in the water, "there *ain't* no real reason, you hear? No real reason at all, not in the whole world, so don't you go asking questions!"

Then Willan was more satisfied. Dimly he sensed that his whale-calf kin had already been a part of a death larger and greater than most of the Islanders would ever, could ever, know. And when that calf-baby finally swam away, Willan thought to himself, then for him it would be all over. He lowered the lantern and started back, tired, up the dirt road to Mam.

Blueberry Boy

LEO CONNELLAN

I only wish I could have it just once more,
you go back and the place looks dull and
small in its mosquito biting green.

I was a Blueberry boy in that childhood,
the sun would flush my freckles out
from where winter hid them in the
sallow pale color of snow and I would
run the meadow for blueberries that
my aunt Madge would turn into muffins
I have longed for down the tripup of manhood.

Just a minute again, on my knees, picking
frantically with expectant watered tongue,
ignorant of what lay out of the woods.

A White Heron

SARAH ORNE JEWETT

I.

The woods were already filled with shadows one June evening, just before eight o'clock, though a bright sunset still glimmered faintly among the trunks of the trees. A little girl was driving home her cow, a plodding, dilatory, provoking creature in her behavior, but a valued companion for all that. They were going away from the western light, and striking deep into the dark woods, but their feet were familiar with the path, and it was no matter whether their eyes could see it or not.

There was hardly a night the summer through when the old cow could be found waiting at the pasture bars; on the contrary, it was her greatest pleasure to hide herself away among the high huckleberry bushes, and though she wore a loud bell she had made the discovery that if one stood perfectly still it would not ring. So Sylvia had to hunt for her until she found her, and call Co'! Co'! with never an answering Moo, until her childish patience was quite spent. If the creature had not given good milk and plenty of it, the case would have seemed very different to her owners. Besides, Sylvia had all the time there was, and very little use to make of it. Sometimes in pleasant weather it was a consolation to look upon the cow's pranks as an intelligent attempt to play hide and seek, and as the child had no playmates she lent herself to this amusement with a good deal of zest. Though this chase had been so long that the wary animal herself had given an unusual signal of her whereabouts, Sylvia had only laughed when she came upon Mistress Moolly at the swamp-side, and urged her affectionately homeward with a twig of birch leaves. The old cow was not inclined to wander farther, she even turned in the right direction for once as they left the pasture, and stepped along the road at a good pace. She was quite ready to be milked now, and seldom stopped to browse. Sylvia wondered what her grandmother would say because they were so late. It was a great while since she had left home at half past five o'clock, but everybody knew the difficulty of making this errand a short one. Mrs. Tilley had chased the horned torment too many summer evenings herself to blame any one else for lingering, and was only thankful as she waited that she had Sylvia, nowadays, to give such valuable assistance. The good woman suspected that Sylvia loitered occasionally on her own account; there never was such a child for straying about out-of-doors since the world was made! Everybody said that it was a good change for a little maid who had tried to grow for eight years in a crowded manufacturing town, but, as for Sylvia herself, it seemed as if she never had been alive at all before she came to live at the farm. She thought often with a wistful compassion of a wretched dry geranium that belonged to a town neighbor.

"'Afraid of folks,'" old Mrs. Tilley said to herself, with a smile, after she had made the unlikely choice of Sylvia from her daughter's houseful of children, and was returning to the farm. "'Afraid of folks,' they said! I guess she won't be troubled no great with 'em up to the old place!" When they reached the door of the lonely house and stopped to unlock it, and the cat came to purr loudly, and rub against them, a deserted pussy, indeed, but fat with young robins, Sylvia whispered that this was a beautiful place to live in, and she never should wish to go home.

The companions followed the shady woodroad, the cow taking slow steps, and the child very fast ones. The cow stopped long at the brook to drink, as if the pasture were not half a swamp, and Sylvia stood still and waited, letting her bare feet cool themselves in the shoal water, while the great twilight moths struck softly against her. She waded on through the brook as the cow moved away, and listened to the thrushes with a heart that beat fast with pleasure. There was a stirring in the great boughs overhead. They were full of little birds and beasts that seemed to be wide-awake, and going about their world, or else saying good-night to each other in sleepy twitters. Sylvia herself felt sleepy as she walked along. However, it was not much farther to the house, and the air was soft and sweet. She was not often in the woods so late as this, and it made her feel as if she were a part of the gray shadows and the moving leaves. She was just thinking how long it seemed since she first came to the farm a year ago, and wondering if everything went on in the noisy town just the same as when she was there; the thought of the great redfaced boy who used to chase and frighten her made her hurry along the path to escape from the shadow of the trees.

Suddenly this little woods-girl is horror-stricken to hear a clear whistle not very far away. Not a bird's whistle, which would have a sort of friendliness, but a boy's whistle, determined and somewhat aggressive. Sylvia left the cow to whatever sad fate might await her, and stepped discreetly aside into the bushes, but she was just too late. The enemy had discovered her, and called out in a very cheerful and persuasive tone, "Halloa, little girl, how far is it to the road?" and trembling Sylvia answered almost inaudibly, "A good ways."

She did not dare to look boldly at the tall young man, who carried a gun over his shoulder, but she came out of her bush and again followed the cow, while he walked alongside.

"I have been hunting for some birds," the stranger said kindly, "and I have lost my way, and need a friend very much. Don't be afraid," he added gallantly. "Speak up and tell me what your name is, and whether you think I can spend the night at your house, and go out gunning early in the morning."

Sylvia was more alarmed than before. Would not her grandmother consider her much to blame? But who could have foreseen such an accident as this? It did not appear to be her fault, and she hung her head as if the stem of it were broken, but managed to answer "Sylvy," with much effort when her companion again asked her name.

Mrs. Tilley was standing in the doorway when the trio came into view. The cow gave a loud moo by way of explanation.

"Yes, you'd better speak up for yourself, you old trial! Where'd she tuck herself away this time, Sylvy?" Sylvia kept an awed silence; she knew by instinct that her grandmother did not comprehend the gravity of the situation. She must be mistaking the stranger for one of the farmer-lads of the region.

The young man stood his gun beside the door, and dropped a heavy game-bag beside it; then he bade Mrs. Tilley good-evening, and repeated his wayfarer's story, and asked if he could have a night's lodging.

"Put me anywhere you like," he said. "I must be off early in the morning, before day; but I am very hungry, indeed. You can give some milk at any rate, that's plain."

"Dear sakes, yes," responded the hostess, whose long slumbering hospitality seemed to be easily awakened. "You might fare better if you went out on the main road a mile or so, but you're welcome to what we've got. I'll milk right off, and you make yourself at home. You can sleep on husks or feathers," she proffered graciously. "I raised them all myself. There's good pasturing for geese just below here towards the ma'sh. Now step round and set a plate for the gentleman, Sylvy!" And Sylvia promptly stepped. She was glad to have something to do, and she was hungry herself.

It was a surprise to find so clean and comfortable a little dwelling in this New England wilderness. The young man had known the horrors of its most primitive housekeeping, and the dreary squalor of that level of society which does not rebel at the companionship of hens. This was the best thrift of an old-fashioned farmstead, though on such a small scale that it seemed like a hermitage. He listened eagerly to the old woman's quaint talk, he watched Sylvia's pale face and shining gray eyes with ever growing enthusiasm, and insisted that this was the best supper he had eaten for a month; then, afterward, the new-made friends sat down in the doorway together while the moon came up.

Soon it would be berry-time, and Sylvia was a great help at picking. The cow was a good milker, though a plaguy thing to keep track of, the hostess gossiped frankly, adding presently that she had buried four children, so that Sylvia's mother, and a son (who might be dead) in California were all the children she had left. "Dan, my boy, was a great hand to go gunning," she explained sadly. "I never wanted for pa'tridges or gray squer'ls while he was to home. He's been a great wand'rer, I expect, and he's no hand to write letters. There, I don't blame him, I'd ha' seen the world myself if it had been so I could.

"Sylvia takes after him," the grandmother continued affectionately, after a minute's pause. "There ain't a foot o' ground she don't know her way over, and the wild creatur's counts her one o' themselves. Squer'ls she'll tame to come an' feed right out o' her hands, and all sorts o' birds. Last winter she got the jay-birds to bangeing here, and I believe she'd 'a' scanted herself of her own meals to have plenty to throw out amongst 'em, if I hadn't kep' watch. Anything but crows, I tell her, I'm willin' to help support,—though Dan he went an' tamed one o' them that did seem to have reason same as folks. It was round here a good spell after he went away. Dan an' his father they didn't hitch,—but he never held up his head ag'in after Dan had dared him an' gone off."

The guest did not notice this hint of family sorrows in his eager interest in something else.

"So Sylvy knows all about birds, does she?" he exclaimed, as he looked around at the little girl who sat, very demure but increasingly sleepy, in the moonlight. "I am making a collection of birds myself. I have been at it ever since I was a boy." (Mrs. Tilley smiled.) "There are two or three very rare ones I have been hunting for these five years. I mean to get them on my own ground if they can be found."

"Do you cage 'em up?" asked Mrs. Tilley, doubtfully, in response to this enthusiastic announcement.

"Oh, no, they're stuffed and preserved, dozens and dozens of them," said the ornithologist, "and I have shot or snared every one myself. I caught a glimpse of a white heron three miles from here on Saturday, and I have followed it in this direction. They have never been found in this district at all. The little white heron, it is," and he turned again to look at Sylvia with the hope of discovering that the rare bird was one of her acquaintances.

But Sylvia was watching a hop-toad in the narrow footpath.

"You would know the heron if you saw it," the stranger continued eagerly. "A queer tall white bird with soft feathers and long thin legs. And it would have a nest perhaps in the top of a high tree, made of sticks, something like a hawk's nest."

Sylvia's heart gave a wild beat; she knew that strange white bird, and had once stolen softly near where it stood in some bright green swamp grass, away over at the other side of the woods. There was an open place where the sunshine always seemed strangely yellow and hot, where tall, nodding rushes grew, and her grandmother had warned her that she might sink in the soft black mud underneath and never be heard of more. Not far beyond were the salt marshes and beyond those was the sea, the sea which Sylvia wondered and dreamed about, but never had looked upon, though its great voice could often be heard above the noise of the woods on stormy nights.

"I can't think of anything I should like so much as to find that heron's nest," the handsome stranger was saying. "I would give ten dollars to anybody who could show it to me," he added desperately, "and I mean to spend my whole vacation hunting for it if need be. Perhaps it was only migrating, or had been chased out of its own region by some bird of prey."

Mrs. Tilley gave amazed attention to all this, but Sylvia still watched the toad, not divining, as she might have done at some calmer time, that the creature wished to get to its hole under the doorstep, and was much hindered by the unusual spectators at that hour of the evening. No amount of thought, that night, could decide how many wished-for treasures the ten dollars, so lightly spoken of, would buy.

The next day the young sportsman hovered about the woods, and Sylvia kept him company, having lost her first fear of the friendly lad, who proved to be most kind and sympathetic. He told her many things about the birds and what they knew and where they lived and what they did with themselves. And he gave her a jackknife, which she thought as great a treasure as if she were a desert-islander. All day long he did not once make her troubled or afraid except when he brought down some unsuspecting singing creature from its bough. Sylvia would have liked him vastly better without his gun; she could not understand why he killed the very birds he seemed to like so much. But as the day waned, Sylvia still watched the young man with loving admiration. She had never seen anybody so charming and delightful; the woman's heart, asleep in the child, was vaguely thrilled by a dream of love. Some premonition of that great power stirred and swayed these young foresters who traversed the solemn woodlands with soft-footed silent care. They stopped to listen to a bird's song; they pressed forward again eagerly, parting the branches—speaking to each other rarely and in whispers; the young man going first and Sylvia following, fascinated, a few steps behind him, with her gray eyes dark with excitement.

She grieved because the longed-for white heron was elusive, but she did not lead the guest, she only followed, and there was no such thing as speaking first. The sound of her own unquestioned voice would have terrified her—it was hard enough to answer yes or no when there was need of that. At last evening began to fall, and they drove the cow home together, and Sylvia smiled with pleasure when they came to the place where she heard the whistle and was afraid only the night before.

II.

Half a mile from home, at the farther edge of the woods, where the land was highest, a great pine-tree stood, the last of its generation. Whether it was left for a boundary mark, or for what reason, no one could say; the woodchoppers who had felled its mates were dead and gone long ago, and a whole forest of sturdy trees, pines and oaks and maples, had grown again. But the stately head of this old pine towered above them all and made a landmark for sea and shore miles and miles away. Sylvia knew it well. She had always believed that whoever climbed to the top of it could see the ocean; and the little girl had often laid her hand on the great rough trunk and looked up wistfully at those dark boughs that the wind always stirred, no matter how hot and still the air might be below. Now she thought of the tree with a new excitement, for why, if one climbed it at break of day, could not one see all the world, and easily discover whence the white heron flew, and mark the place, and find the hidden nest?

What a spirit of adventure, what wild ambition! What fancied triumph and delight and glory for the later morning when she could make known the secret! It was almost too real and too great for the childish heart to bear.

All night the door of the little house stood open, and the whippoor-wills came and sang upon the very step. The young sportsman and his old hostess were sound asleep, but Sylvia's great design kept her broad awake and watching. She forgot to think of sleep. The short summer night seemed as long as the winter darkness, and at last when the whippoorwills ceased, and she was afraid the morning would after all come too soon, she stole out of the house and followed the pasture path through the woods, hastening toward the open ground beyond, listening with a sense of comfort and companionship to the drowsy twitter of a half-awakened bird, whose perch she had jarred in passing. Alas, if the great wave of human interest which flooded for the first time this dull little life should sweep away the satisfactions of an existence heart to heart with nature and the dumb life of the forest!

There was the huge tree asleep yet in the paling moonlight, and small and hopeful Sylvia began with utmost bravery to mount to the top of it, with tingling, eager blood coursing the channels of her whole frame, with her bare feet and fingers, that pinched and held like bird's claws to the monstrous ladder reaching up, up, almost to the sky itself. First she must mount the white oak tree that grew alongside, where she was almost lost among the dark branches and the green leaves heavy and wet with dew; a bird fluttered off its nest, and a red squirrel ran to and fro and scolded pettishly at the harmless housebreaker. Sylvia felt her way easily. She had often climbed there, and knew that higher still one of the oak's upper branches chafed against the pine trunk, just where its lower boughs were set close together. There, when she made the dangerous pass from one tree to the other, the great enterprise would really begin.

She crept out along the swaying oak limb at last, and took the daring step across into the old pine-tree. The way was harder than she thought: she must reach far and hold fast, the sharp dry twigs caught and held her and scratched her like angry talons; the pitch made her thin little fingers clumsy and stiff as she went round and round the tree's great stem, higher and higher upward. The sparrows and robins in the woods below were beginning to wake and twitter to the dawn, yet it seemed much lighter there aloft in the pine-tree, and the child knew that she must hurry if her project were to be of any use.

The tree seemed to lengthen itself out as she went up, and to reach farther and farther upward. It was like a great main-mast to the voyaging earth; it must truly have been amazed that morning through all its ponderous frame as it felt this determined spark of human spirit creeping and climbing from higher branch to branch. Who knows how steadily the least twigs held themselves to advantage this light, weak creature on her way! The old pine must have loved his new dependent. More than all the hawks, and bats, and moths, and even the sweet-voiced thrushes, was the brave, beating heart of the solitary gray-eyed child. And the tree stood still and held away the winds that June morning while the dawn grew bright in the east.

Sylvia's face was like a pale star, if one had seen it from the ground, when the last thorny bough was past, and she stood trembling and tired but wholly triumphant, high in the tree-top. Yes, there was the sea with the dawning sun making a golden dazzle over it, and toward that glorious east flew two hawks with slow-moving pinions. How low they looked in the air from that height when before one had only seen them far up, and dark against the blue sky. Their gray feathers were soft as moths; they seemed only a little away from the tree, and Sylvia felt as if she too could go flying away among the clouds. Westward, the woodlands and farms reached miles and miles into the distance; here and there were church steeples, and white villages; truly it was a vast and awesome world.

The birds sang louder and louder. At last the sun came up bewilderingly bright. Sylvia could see the white sails of ships out at sea, and the clouds that were purple and rose-colored and yellow at first began to fade away. Where was the white heron's nest in the sea of green branches, and was this wonderful sight and pageant of the world the only reward for having climbed to such a giddy height? Now look down again, Sylvia, where the green marsh is set among the shining birches and dark hemlocks; there where you saw the white heron once you will see him again; look, look! a white spot of him like a single floating feather comes up from the dead hemlock and grows larger, and rises, and comes close at last, and goes by the landmark pine with steady sweep of wing and outstretched slender neck and crested head. And wait! wait! do not move a foot or a finger, little girl, do not send an arrow of light and consciousness from your two eager eyes, for the heron has perched on a pine bough not far beyond yours, and cries back to his mate on the nest, and plumes his feathers for the new day!

The child gives a long sigh a minute later when a company of shouting cat-birds comes also to the tree, and vexed by their fluttering and lawlessness the solemn heron goes away. She knows his secret now, the wild, light, slender bird that floats and wavers, and goes back like an arrow presently to his home in the green world beneath. Then Sylvia, well satisfied, makes her perilous way down again, not daring to look far below the branch she stands on, ready to cry sometimes because her fingers ache and her lamed feet slip. Wondering over and over again what the stranger would say to her, and what he would think when she told him how to find his way straight to the heron's nest.

"Sylvy, Sylvy!" called the busy old grandmother again and again, but nobody answered, and the small husk bed was empty, and Sylvia had disappeared.

The guest waked from a dream, and remembering his day's pleasure hurried to dress himself that it might sooner begin. He was sure from the way the shy little girl looked once or twice yesterday that she had at least seen the white heron, and now she must really be persuaded to tell. Here she comes now, paler than ever, and her worn old frock is torn and tattered, and smeared with pine pitch. The grandmother and the sportsman stand in the door together and question her, and the splendid moment has come to speak of the dead hemlock-tree by the green marsh.

But Sylvia does not speak after all, though the old grandmother fretfully rebukes her, and the young man's kind appealing eyes are looking straight in her own. He can make them rich with money; he has promised it, and they are poor now. He is so well worth making happy, and he waits to hear the story she can tell.

No, she must keep silence! What is it that suddenly forbids her and makes her dumb? Has she been nine years growing, and now, when the great world for the first time puts out a hand to her, must she thrust it aside for a bird's sake? The murmur of the pine's green branches is in her ears, she remembers how the white heron came flying through the golden air and how they watched the sea and the morning together, and Sylvia cannot speak; she cannot tell the heron's secret and give its life away.

Dear loyalty, that suffered a sharp pang as the guest went away disappointed later in the day, that could have served and followed him and loved him as a dog loves! Many a night Sylvia heard the echo of his whistle haunting the pasture path as she came home with the loitering cow. She forgot even her sorrow at the sharp report of his gun and the piteous sight of thrushes and sparrows dropping silent to the ground, their songs hushed and their pretty feathers stained and wet with blood. Were the birds better friends than their hunter might have been—who can tell? Whatever treasures were lost to her, woodlands and summer-time, remember! Bring your gifts and graces and tell your secrets to this lonely country child!

from *Octavia's Hill*

MARGARET DICKSON

Thin like his mother, but brown-tanned and blond like Aldair Rowe, Marlowe Perry sat sweating in the hot, dark house on Octavia's Hill, reading to his mother from *Sartor Resartus*.

Lucy Perry had spoken to him sharply time after time that morning. "Marlowe, you're wandering! Pay attention, now!"

Fidgeting at the dining room table, Marl would feel bad and begin to read again, but it had been a long morning.

"'For the rest, how-however'—however?" Now he looked sideways at her. She sighed.

"Yes, yes, 'however.' Continue."

"'It cannot be un-unint —'"

"Uninteresting, Marlowe."

"'— that we here find how ear-ear —'"

"Early! You know that word!"

"'The significance —'" He pronounced it *sine-off-ants.*

"Marlowe!"

"'Of cloths —'"

"Clothes!"

"'Clothes —'"

"All right, all right, be done!"

It was what in all the world he'd been waiting for. He leaped from his chair and dashed through the house just to let off steam. He had no idea what the sine-off-ants of clothes was. The best and only thing about clothes that he could think of that hot summer morning was getting them off.

Of course, *Sartor Resartus* was too difficult for him. Often he went over whole paragraphs without understanding a single sentence. His mother made him read it to enlarge his vocabulary, she said. He wished she wouldn't bother.

But Marl forgave his mother; he had forgiven her long before. At age eight he knew already that she was scared, a woman bringing up a son alone, and not some backwoods country woman either. His mother was Octavia of Octavia's Hill and she wanted him to take after the Boston Marlowes for whom he was named.

She was always after him. His manner and his schoolwork had to be perfect. She made it obvious that there were two levels of achievement: one for Marl and one, considerably lower, for his classmates. Marl didn't let this bother him, or bother the other children either, for that matter. It was lucky he'd grown up in the schoolroom, he thought, so that he knew how kids were supposed to act, how to get along, for God's sake.

Marl squirmed through lunch, which he ate with his mother in the darkened dining room. They used silver, china, napkins, and all, because Lucy was bound that when her son finally made it to a place called Harvard, his manners would be impeccable. But Marl thumped at lunch, he rattled. He couldn't help it; he twisted in his chair restlessly until at last Lucy gave him an angry glance and let him go.

Often during the summer he was invited to other farms in and around Monson to visit and play, but today had not been one of those lucky days. For either of them, it seemed.

He stuffed deviled eggs into an old towel when Lucy wasn't looking and, with one last glance in her direction as she lay back wearily against her rocking chair with her eyes closed and her little wire spectacles sliding off her nose, he sneaked down off the porch.

It was no life for a boy, alone with his mother day in and day out. He knew it and she knew it, which was why she so often let him spend summertimes with his cronies. People in town approved of this. Octavia Perry, they said, was trying to bring her son up right.

But days like today were hard for them both. When Lucy looked at Marl, he knew she didn't see him exactly. She saw a piece of putty, and for some reason she was desperate to mold it into something she saw in her head. It was because she was desperate that Marl went along with it.

Now he scooted out across the field with the deviled eggs in a moist package under one arm, then doubled back to the road far down the hill out of her sight. He didn't want to risk her spotting him, which she could sometimes do, even in her sleep. Then he was free!

The first order of business, of course, was to take off his shoes and socks. These were required in Lucy's house, but all summer, far from her sight, Marl Perry had gone barefoot. In fact, he thought, as he stowed them by a big stump halfway down the hill, this pair of shoes would probably last him, for a change. He took out his package of deviled eggs, munching as he made his way toward what he thought would be bubbling water, a little tributary of the Branch that ran beside the road. It started at a spring about halfway down the hill. The water was clear and good to drink and Marl's eggs were salty, so he could hardly wait.

When he got there he saw the spring was bubbling all right—one bubble every five minutes. Marl stood and stared. Why, just the other day that brook had been a regular stream! Suddenly his whole body felt itchy and unclean; he was sweaty and decorated with the grime of half-ripe field grass, and he was thirsty.

He'd wanted to take off every last stitch of clothing, right down to the foolish underdrawers he had on. Lucy counted underwear, so he had to wear these at least a part of every day, but he hated them and tried to give them a maximum amount of wearage in a minimum amount of time. Lucy made his underwear herself, and the drawers were of an embarrassing variety, baggy, a yard of material to an inch of flesh, and held up not with an elastic, as Sears Trowley's were, but with—of all things—strings. Ribbons, practically. It made Marl blush just to think of it.

The particular underdrawers he had on today he'd worn all morning, which was long enough. He wanted to get them off, get all his clothes off, lie jaybird-naked in rippling water, and not go home until the sun was even with the Goulds' across the way.

He looked at the tiny trickle of water in the streambed and he was unbearably thirsty.

His mother was what he would call a doubtful cook. She made him strange things to eat, including what she called blonk monge, an evil, white vanilla pudding that she was apt to forget to stir. He would come into the kitchen and find her deep in some book or other while the pudding on the stove thrummed and hollered. Oatmeal was never the same two days in a row, one morning gummy, the next water-thin. On weekdays they often had meat sliced and cold, or Lucy would put it into what she called a chafing dish recipe, mixed with vegetables until it was a sticky and undistinguished mass. It didn't matter. Marl would have to eat it.

The deviled eggs were very salty. His mother had made lunch today as if she were having an argument with someone. She had wagged her head and talked under her breath while she cooked. "It is insupportable," Marl had heard her say, and then other long words. Talking to no one—the kitchen sink, maybe. But the eggs—oh, my. Marl, always hungry, burning all the fuel he could pack into his thin body, had eaten four of them by the time he reached the brook. He was very thirsty.

Dejected, he stared down into the mud. The beginnings of the spring were half-obscured by fallen twigs and grasses. It looked hopeless, but he took off his shirt to investigate, finding himself a pole and sticking it into a wide, flat piece of mudbed that was as shining and moist and brown as so much baked chocolate. On this pole he hung his shirt. The mud, he saw, extended for about four feet beyond where the tiny spring still bubbled feebly.

Without a shirt Marl felt better. There was no breeze, just pure air on his back. He could hear his mother now. "Marlowe Perry, how did you get so brown, have you been going without your shirt?" "Well, ol' Sears and I—" and then his mother would sigh. "Boys," she would say. "I don't pretend to understand them. But in my presence, Marlowe, you will wear a shirt." "Yes, Mother." He obeyed her, but the pure air on his skinny brown back was better than the shirt any day.

He put his bare feet into the mud. It oozed up through his toes nicely, and underneath the sun-warmed surface it was quite cool. It made, he decided, good footprints. Diverted for a moment, Marl paced with infinite care the length of the brown chocolate, until the soles of his feet were actually quite cool and the mud dotted with prints facing in various ridiculous directions. They were pretty good; he wished his friend ol' Sears could see them. But he was still thirsty, his tongue thick as a dry sponge.

He stooped over the spring source and gently pulled away what sticks and grasses he could, but it was no use. The source of the water was still obscured by a small grassy bluff and the roots of some bushes. There was only this little bubble, this inch-wide faint trickle, and now it was running muddy because of the stirring he'd given it.

Squatting, Marl waited. He stared out across the smoky blue of the horizon. Not a soul, it seemed, for miles. Idly, he wished again that good ol' Sears were with him. Him and Sears, boy, they'd dig out this old stream, he thought. Him and ol' Sears—the phrase had a satisfying ungrammatical sound. Him and ol' Sears, they'd find themselves some water! They liked to swim, in the farm pond in the Trowley pasture, if they had to, or down in the Branch, if no one knew about it. Sometimes Mr. Trowley took the whole family to Deer Pond, the local swimming hole, and then they had some fun. Oh, that cool water! Him and ol' Sears, yessir.

Marl sat beside the mudbed and watched the pitiful trickle of water, and in spite of himself began to fume. He began to fuss. Here he was, hottest day of the year, practically, so thirsty his eyes were hanging out, and all he could do was sit, and all he had was that tiny bubble of water, wouldn't fill a thimble.

After a while, however, the spring did run clear, and he stooped over and cupped the water as well as he could with his hands. He tried to drink, but it wasn't enough—it would never be enough, he felt. There wasn't enough water in the world. Suddenly it seemed obvious that in order to get a good solid drink, why, he was going to have to lie right down in that mud and put his mouth to that old water-run-through-your-fingers.

He never even hesitated; there was no one anywhere near. He skinned off the hot pair of trousers his mother had bought for him in Monson, then he took off the voluminous drawers. God, he thought, in full sail the things billowed out almost to his knees. Quickly he slung them up onto the dry, grassy bank, glancing around him again as he did so. In Lucy's household you grew up modest, even if good ol' Sears said what the hell did it matter anyways. Good ol' Sears. Just thinking of him made Marl grin a little.

"Yeah," he muttered to himself. "What the hell." (Lucy didn't allow swearing.) And then he lay down flat on the warm chocolate mud and put his mouth to the stream.

Thanks to Sears Trowley and his water hole, Marl was well tanned in places Lucy hadn't looked since he turned five; the sun on his back, buttocks, and thighs didn't bother him at all. He lay there, a pencil-slim arrow of heat in the warm mud, his tongue the nether tip. It was an odd feeling but a good feeling, hot from the sun, cool in the mud; the heat of his body and then, flowing in a line like the mercury in a thermometer, the narrow, cool trickle of that water down inside him as he swallowed.

In fact, that mud felt so good underneath his stomach and arms that when at last he had drunk enough, he continued to lie there, just worming his way down into that cool damp. With one hand he grabbed a chunk of mud and brought it to his nose. It had a peculiar smell, rotten but somehow friendly. Idly, he began to build a little wall, about a foot long by the time he finished it. And by that time he had made this discovery: if you dug down into the mud far enough, why, you got to water. Not clean water, course, he told himself. You couldn't drink it, hell, no. But it felt good when you dribbled it on your neck, around your ears, and in places where the grass chaff seemed to stick. It felt good on your face, too.

The implications were very far-reaching. If you dug enough, you'd have water to sit in! Marl began to work, heaping the mud to one side. A little messy, sure, but the mud was really pretty cold when you got down a few inches. Matter of fact, that nice cool mud underneath felt good on your back, which got awful hot stuck out in the sun while you worked. Every now and then Marl would reach up and pat a handful of that trickling aromatic black stuff onto his shoulders. "What the hell," he mumbled.

Pretty soon he had scooped out a basin about six inches deep and two feet long. Then he moved back and for a moment regarded his handiwork. Sure enough, the water had risen about an inch. Marl sat in it. Then he turned and eased himself into his mudbath the way a pig wallows, going down belly first and covering himself by rolling from side to side in the cool, damp grit. After a minute, he raised himself enough to make a pillow to lay his face on.

He rested. Then he turned and lay on his back and, inch by inch, while the muddy water coursed in a scarcely distinguishable rivulet around him, he covered himself up with mud until he looked like a root vegetable at the end of a long season. His head showed; the blond-white hair, however, was no longer shining. It was a gray and brown color that trickled down the sides of his face and into his ears, and it was drying at strange, stiff angles all over his head. From a distance it even had the faint greenish cast of worn-out vegetation.

"What the hell," he muttered, and settled once again. He closed his eyes, patted a little of the drier mud on them. Jeez, this was good. This was great. You could take a little nap.

Sure he was getting dirty, but so what? he wanted to know. Hell!

To date, Marl had never sworn so you could hear him except in the company of good ol' Sears. Now he practiced. "What the hell," he said tentatively, but that sounded a little too quiet. "Goddamnit, what the hell!" he roared.

After a while, however, he looked down his length and realized that it had turned a strange gray-brown all over. The old mud was drying, he guessed, getting pretty stiff. Time, he supposed, to move on. But he didn't, he thought, seem to be all that dirty, considering.

Once again he dug out the spring as well as he could and managed to wash his face after a fashion, not so much in the interest of cleanliness, but it was nice to be able to move your mouth if you wanted to. The rest of his body didn't feel too bad. Mostly it had a nice powdery smoothness. Here and there, course, a clump of dry mud; he scraped these off as well as he could, and trickled enough water onto his skin to make a kind of pattern that interested him. Black and gray, sort of like watermarks on his mother's silk dress. At last, however, he picked up his pants and moved toward the woods with them slung under his arm. The drawers he would not wear; he stuffed them into a pants pocket. The shoes and socks he forgot entirely, the shirt likewise. After a moment he turned off the road deliberately into ferns and underbrush and, coming up to an ancient stone wall—a fortress of other days—he sat upon it carefully because his bottom was bare.

The wall was lichen-covered, its crevices turned to rich humus and scratchy rock crystals that were almost like beach sand. It was in dark, comfortable shade, because this wall went right through the pine forest. Marl sat and stared off into the soundless, sun-dappled, fly-whirling woods and chewed a piece of sweet grass. He could have used his shirt now, maybe, to keep the bugs off, but he didn't care. The whole hill was his to play on, and he guessed he could go down and get that old shirt whenever he wanted to. He was happy. Under the wall, his old fortress, the hill breathed and moved with things to do on other days, but for now he was like a baby settled on its breast, so close to the heartbeat of it that it sounded like his own.

For a little while he thought about the men who had built this wall. They'd slung those old stones day after day to build these rock piles that meandered along the sides of their fields. Then they'd grown old or moved away and left the grass to turn into woods again. It was as if the hill knew something they didn't. Somehow Marl knew you had to listen to the hill if you wanted things to last.

Marl dug one bare foot into the crevice of a rock that was as familiar to him as his own skin. Someday this woods would be his. Ol' Sears's dad was a farmer, so were most of his other friends' fathers, and Marl had long ago decided for himself what his future would be. Oh, he would go along with his mother's fancy ideas for now, to keep the peace, but someday....

Just then Marl's eye was caught by something moving on the road. A horse and wagon—it was the Trowley wagon, and there was ol' Sears's father, Bill Trowley, and there, sitting right beside him and scanning the fields, was ol' Sears himself! What the hell!

Marl was immediately too excited to sit still. Ol' Sears had come to get him—oh, boy! He looked again through the woods at the wagon. There, sitting on the back, was thick-shouldered, square little Amy Trowley, age five, and beside her, her mother. Why, the whole family was out for a ride—no! They had a picnic basket with them! They were going on a picnic—and coming up onto Octavia's Hill first! Why, that must mean they were going on a picnic and they had come to get—of all people!—him! Marl Perry!

"Yahoo!" yelled Marl as he stood up and pulled on his pants. He raced across the soft pine-needle floor of the woods, with the pair of drawstring drawers flopping and flapping forgotten from his back pocket. It would take too long to catch up with Sears by going out to the road, so he took to the fields, skimming deerfleet over them. Why, the day wasn't lost after all, he was thinking. All that good mud, and now this!

In the distance across Octavia's Hill he could see the Trowley wagon pulling in at the farmhouse, and yes, there was his mother, still rocking on the porch. Marl's adventure with the mud couldn't have lasted more than an hour, then, although he felt he'd been gone for hours, all afternoon. No, the sun was still very high. There was Mother standing up on the front porch, and there was ol' Sears hopping down off the wagon and staring out toward the fields, his hand up to shade his eyes. Yes, there was Mother talking and nodding from the porch and there was Mrs. Trowley, with broad, square Amy on her lap, nodding and talking back. And then Marl was in the driveway and he was approaching the porch.

"Sears!" he yelled, a high-pitched, excited treble. "Hey! What you want me for? Hey, Sears!"

The adults turned toward Marl, then froze. What they saw was a little mud man about three and a half feet high, with blue eyes and gray-brown hair sticking out like the roots of a beet, in all directions.

"Oh, my Lord," said Lucy Perry. "My good Lord." And she sat down in her rocking chair quite suddenly.

Only Sears saw nothing out of the ordinary about his friend.

"Mackerel!" he yelled —-this was his name for Marl—and his brown eyes lit his whole broad, pink and white face. All of the Trowleys had a well-nourished look, and Sears was no exception. "Hey, Mack! We gonna go on a picnic! You wanna come? Goin' over to Deer Pond, and I made 'em come to get you."

"Deer Pond!" Marl cried. "Oh, boy! Just a minute, I'll get my bathing suit."

Turning from where he stood with one arm over Sears's shoulder, Marl grinned excitedly at the three too-quiet adults and at little Amy, who promptly hid her head in her mother's shoulder. What ailed her? he wondered. Perplexed, he looked from his mother, whose face combined shock, embarrassment, and shame, to Mrs. Trowley, who simply looked surprised. And her nose twitched a little, as if she smelled something she didn't quite like. As for William Trowley, Sears's father, nothing about him moved except his eyes, which winked and blinked. Come to think of it, Marl saw, his shoulders were shaking a little, too. "Why, Marl," he said gently, "been real busy today?"

"Oh, my Lord," said Lucy Perry, "I must apologize —" She sat forward a little in her rocking chair, then lay back again. "Marlowe Perry, I wasn't sure it was you!"

"Me?" said Marl uneasily. He was beginning to wonder if this meant he couldn't go on the picnic. "Course it's me!"

"I knew it was," said Mrs. Trowley loyally. But she was hanging onto Amy and rocking—with laughter, Marl saw. "Don't think Amy did, though." The little girl was still hiding in her mother's bosom.

"What is it?" cried Sears, now beginning to be anxious, too. "What's the matter?"

"Look at him!" Lucy cried. "Marlowe Perry, I am surprised! I am ashamed! Look at you!" She stood up and advanced upon Marl, waving her hands in little helpless gestures around his gray-dried hair, his mud-caked shoulders. "What have you been doing? Why, you look as if you'd been—lying in—in —" but she couldn't say "cow patty." It wouldn't have been proper, and it certainly wouldn't have been adequate. "Oh, Marlowe! No shirt! No shoes and socks —"

She circled him. Marl stood stock still. He was beginning to be alarmed. Sure, he was a little dirty, but for the life of him he couldn't see what all the fuss was about.

"Marlowe," his mother was raving, "you smell! You smell awful! You smell like a—a swamp! And what—what, why, your drawers! You haven't got on your—" Now his mother seemed to have forgotten herself completely. She pulled his underwear from his back pocket and waved it in the air accusingly.

"Them drawers," muttered Bill Trowley, "is the cleanest thing about him, if you ask me."

"Bill!" said his wife. "Now, Octavia—Miss Lucy—" Under the circumstances Mrs. Trowley didn't know how familiar she should get. "Don't let it get you down on our account! We seen bad's this and worse, you got to expect it from boys," and all the while she was wiping tears of laughter from her eyes.

Lucy was oblivious. "Marlowe Perry," she cried at him, sorely distressed. "Do you mean to tell me that you have no underwear on?"

This was serious. By now Marl was so afraid he wouldn't be allowed to go on the picnic that his thin, dirty frame began to quiver. But he told the truth. If you could depend on Marl Perry for one thing, it was that. "They're too big," he said briefly.

Behind him Bill Trowley snorted and let out a big "Haw! Haw!" Mrs. Trowley laughed, too. She'd never seen Octavia Perry so out of control. It was worth the price of admission.

Hearing the Trowleys' laughter, Lucy seemed suddenly to realize she was waving a pair of homemade underdrawers in the air. Quickly she rolled them into a ball and hid them under her apron, at the same time visited by a powerful rose-maroon blush that heated her face from dainty collar to hairline in one rich movement. After all, you wouldn't catch the Boston Marlowes raving in the driveway and flapping a pair of underdrawers in the breeze! "I am terribly sorry," she whispered to the Trowleys, who were by now weak with concealed laughter once again. "Please, forgive me."

"Oh, hell," said Bill Trowley, whose vast stomach rolled and trembled with mirth. "Get him on up here. We'll take him to the pond for a good swim, and bring him back clean as a whistle. It'll save you carryin' the bath water."

"Looks," said Mrs. Trowley, blowing her nose and wiping her eyes, " 's it would take quite a lot of carryin', too."

"Oh," said Lucy faintly. "How—how very kind. But he certainly can't go like this." She stared at Marl. "Merciful heavens, no. I couldn't allow it! No one in our family has ever —" As if for evidence, she looked down at her own spotless dress.

Marl was in agony. It looked like she wasn't going to let him go. In spite of himself, two tears fell down his cheeks, making their way like raindrops down a grimy window.

Mrs. Trowley saw the tears and realized it had all got a little past joking now. "Octavia—Miss Perry," she began, "please, he wouldn't want to miss a picnic. Would you, now, Marl?"

Marl shook his head somewhat pitifully and looked down at the gravel. Since he'd already cried, he tried to make as pitiful a picture as possible, mostly to hide the quick-leaping hope in his eyes.

"Oh, you let him come now," said Bill Trowley. "After all, got to give our best schoolteacher a rest from kids in the summer anyways. Why, you just set back up there on the porch and rock and we'll take care of this youngster."

"Oh, I couldn't," said Lucy, the blush still upon her. It came and went. "He's so filthy! And how could you sit beside him, considering how he—how he—"

"Stinks," said Bill Trowley. "Well, put him up here beside me. No, better still, put him on the tailgate. He'll be downwind all the way, we'll never smell a thing. Come on there, young Marl. Hop up! Five miles to Deer Pond!"

"But he has no bathing suit," said Lucy. Marl was already climbing up onto the tailgate.

"Oh, don't give it a thought," said Mrs. Trowley. "We've brought a bunch of clothes. We'll have something to fit him."

"You are too kind," said Lucy. "Marlowe, you be polite now! You remember to say please and thank—Oh, Marlowe! How could you?"

But Marl was happy. He was blissful. He and Sears sat on the tailgate with their arms over each other's shoulders and grinned for all they were worth. He waved at his mother while Bill Trowley turned the wagon around.

"We'll keep him overnight!" called Mrs. Trowley. "Save us a trip up the hill after dark. Don't worry, he'll be fine. We'll clean him up all right." Then they were off down the hill.

Inside Marl was singing. Deer Pond, a picnic, ol' Sears, and a night at the Trowleys'! And to top it all off, he realized as he watched his mother's neat little figure diminish in the distance, he'd managed to get away without the dadblasted underdrawers. Yessir, dirt and all, for once he was comfortable in his pants.

John and Emma Carpenter

GLENNA JOHNSON SMITH

They lived across from the church
in a square grey house
with tall narrow windows
lace covered
to keep the sun from fading things.

The back porch was secure
behind green shades.
The hard pine kitchen floor
was saved with varnish.
John pulled his boots off in the shed.
Emma said boots had never touched her floors.

Three times a day
at five, eleven, and five,
Emma
safe behind her high lace collar
and her starched percale apron
and John
bent, balding, sundried,
shielded by his clean stiff overalls
sat across from each other.
The food was plentiful and plain,
the words austere and sparse.

Sometimes on a summer afternoon
Emma plodded down the path
to the graveyard behind the church
(and sometimes John went alone and late at night, I've heard)
to the three little granite markers
near the broken fence.

When Emma bent,
careful not to soil her dress and apron,
to pull the weeds
from purple-flowered mounds,
something within her massive stillness
may have stirred.
But it never cried out.
Emma never let on.

Scobie

ELISABETH OGILVIE

Rhoda Randall came to see me yesterday afternoon. It was the first such afternoon in a good many years. It is strange how one can get out of the habit of closeness. There was a time, twenty-odd years ago, when Rhoda and I were inseparable, and therefore the butts of much slightly sarcastic family comment.

We are adults now and have husbands and children of our own. We live about ten miles apart, each as secure in her own universe as if we had never shared another one. But yesterday Rhoda came for the afternoon and asked an innocent question: "Do you remember Scobie?"

How tenderly she said it, and how bright her eyes became, so that suddenly she was the other Rhoda, who, with me, discovered Scobie. Rhoda at eight, in pink-and-white checks, with her flat, shining dark braids, her red cheeks, her freckles. And I, also eight, in blue percale and with a ginger-colored Dutch cut.

Our children are not so fortunate as we were. I see nothing in their childhood to make me feel cheated. They have movies on Saturdays, and comic books, and ice cream is a commonplace thing. If we don't have a television set—and we don't—they can always see Hopalong Cassidy at a neighbor's house. All their friends are the same age as themselves. They live in a world tailored to their size.

Rhoda and I grew up in a village where there were a general store, a filling station, a sardine factory, a fish-and-lobster buyer, and a fifteen-room hotel that catered for three summer months to artists and elderly people, who might have been very rich, but who looked like anybody else when they sat on the veranda and rocked through the sunny afternoons, watching the activity in the harbor. The artists, of course, did not look like anybody else. Anybody else in the village, I mean. There was a fascinating difference, apparent even to Rhoda and me. They were so happily immersed in their painting, so beautifully oblivious of criticism or ridicule.

We had Sunday-school concerts, Memorial Day with flags and lilacs, the July Fourth clambake, and the town Christmas tree; we had the harbor and the boats; in summer we had the summer people. Then, one year, we had Scobie.

At the time of Scobie, my father was the fisheries' warden for the district, and so he was often around the lobstermen's workshops. At the far curve of the harbor, away from the sardine factory and the big wharves, there was a regular settlement of lobstermen, who preferred to live in sight of the harbor and the moorings rather than in the town. Their houses, with neat white clapboards or silvery shingles, were sheltered by the spruce woods behind; the grassy ground sloped down to the shore, where their boats were hauled up for painting; and their traps were stacked against wildrose bushes and blackberry vines. My father spent a lot of time over there.

"Met a queer chap today," my father said one night over the fish chowder. "I don't know how long he's been around—you'd almost think he just materialized out of thin air." My father was not usually given to such fancies. "Probably it's just because I never happened to go as far as the marsh before."

"You mean where the old boats are hauled up?" my brother asked. He was fourteen and well traveled. "We call it the graveyard."

"That's right," said my father. "Well, this fellow—name of Scobie—has moved into an old pinkie."

This is where I came to life and thought of Rhoda. How she would relish this combination of rich words and facts. A queer man with a queer name, living in an old pinkie—whatever that was. I asked eagerly, and my brother said with disdain, "It's a sloop that's pointed both bow and stern, stupid." I didn't raise any hue and cry about the insult, being too excited about anyone's living in a boat on dry land.

My father went on. "He was cleaning fish on the beach, so I stopped to talk to him. He's homely as a hedge fence. Goes hand-lining and sells his fish to Job Carter." Father had to stop and eat some chowder then, and I waited breathlessly for him to go on. I don't know why I was so obsessed; it must have been because I was sure a man who lived in a boat ashore would be capable of all sorts of oddities.

"He invited me in," said Father, "or aboard, I should say. He's propped her up so she's not quite at a forty-five-degree angle, and the cabin's scrubbed so clean you can smell it. But what do you think he's got?" He looked around at us expectantly.

My mother said nothing, just waited. My brother said, "What?" But I, unable to contain myself any longer, leaned over my plate and said passionately, "Oh, Father, hurry up!"

"A pig," said Father. He measured about twelve inches with his hands. "A little white pig. I was sitting there on the bunk, and there was a scratching under the sink, and Scobie opened the cupboard door, and out came this little pig. 'You want to run around a bit, Barnaby?' he says, and the little fellow grunts. So Scobie takes him out and puts him over the side."

My mother said, "I've heard pigs can be real smart." My brother snorted. But I was too overcome to say a word. I was frantic to get away from the table and to Rhoda's house. A man in a boat—on dry land—and a pet pig named Barnaby. I could hardly stand it.

After I had wiped the dishes, I could go out for a while. I sped across lots to Rhoda. She had to go out in the yard and shut up the chickens for the night, and in the aromatic fastnesses of the hen house, I told her about Scobie and feasted on her reaction.

Surrounded by the comfortable bedtime conversation of the hens, we made our plans for the next day. We would go and see this for ourselves. It would have to be on the way home from school, and because the marsh was far out of the way, we would have to risk family censure for our tardiness. But we determined to risk it.

We had a hard time in school the next day, but Miss Winslow probably thought it was the spring weather that blew and glistened outside the windows; everybody was uneasy those days. At recess and at noon we withdrew from the game of Steal Eggs. On ordinary days we were savagely uninhibited players, but this was no ordinary day. We sat on the big granite boulder behind the schoolhouse and talked.

"Oh, Rhoda," I breathed, just as the bell rang, "what if he really did make himself out of thin air?"

Rhoda's dark eyes were deep and bright. She gave me a long, mystical look, and then we had to go inside.

After school we walked with the rest, though not of them, until we came to the crossroads. One road led into the town proper; the other led into enchanted territory. We took it. I am afraid I showed the worst manifestation of our new double life at that moment, because when somebody shouted at us, "Hey, where you goin'?" I replied, "I have to do an errand for my father."

We knew all the lobstermen's families, and they took us for granted when we went by. At length we were on the road to the marsh. When we looked across the harbor, the town was lovely and foreign under the budding elms. The harbor was a vast, restless stretch of bright blue-green between us and home, and we were struck silent, realizing with guilt the enormity of our adventure.

The woods thinned out and the marsh began, stretching to the other side of the point, a wide sheet of tawny grasses streaked with green. The spring wind blew cold here, and the water dashed noisily on the rocks. We felt very small, moving in an immensity of marsh, sea, and sky. "No Man's Land," said Rhoda.

We saw the old boats, lying on their sides at the edge of the marsh. And then, with the thrill of mariners making a landfall, we saw the pinkie with her masts against the sky. We were not smitten with shyness or sudden misgivings. I think our only fear was that Scobie might have disappeared back into thin air since yesterday. We walked past the disconsolate old boats without speaking, as if it were truly a graveyard, and stood hand in hand in front of the pinkie sloop.

There was no sound except the wind and water and a thin crying of gulls circling far overhead. Then, miracle that it was, there was another sound—the grunting voice of a small pig, who came hurrying around the boat on infinitesimal hoofs. We gazed at him with speechless delight, and he trotted up to us expectantly. He was beautifully clean from his pink snout to his pink curl of a tail.

"Barnaby," I said softly. "His name is Barnaby."

Like an echo, a man said, "Hey, Barnaby!" And there he was, looking down at us from the pinkie's deck. How can I describe him? And yet he is so clear to me, as if it were only this afternoon that I looked up and saw him against the brilliant clouds-and-blue of a spring day. In the next instant he was down beside us, scowling ferociously and saying, "Young ladies, is it? Shall we make them put for home, Barnaby?"

Rhoda's fingers tightened around mine, and we stared. He was short and had huge shoulders and long arms; his clothes were faded and patched, but we knew cleanliness when we saw it. He had a dark, long face, which I know now was almost simian in its sad and frowning furrows. His dark hair was cut close to his head, a fashion not familiar in the town then. His voice was raspingly deep, and he could have been either thirty or sixty. He was the ugliest man we had ever seen. He was Scobie.

After that first moment, we never knew an instant of fear. We never again thought he was ugly, either. How did he do it? He was not a charmer; he did not treat us as if we were adorable china figures. His chief concession to gallantry was to call us "young ladies."

That first day, after he gruffly put Barnaby through his paces for us, he didn't invite us aboard and we went hurrying home on the wings of our enchantment. My mother and Rhoda's were having a cup of tea together.

"Have you been looking for Mayflowers?" they asked kindly.

Rhoda said, "We didn't find any." It was not a lie. A deception, perhaps, but we were forced to it in order to guard our treasure. After that it was taken for granted that we were late coming from school because we were looking for Mayflowers. I suffer no remorse in saying that when we *did* find some Mayflowers one day, we took them to Scobie. Our mothers had the first Mayflowers other years; but this was the year of Scobie.

When we had visited him on the beach three times, we were invited aboard the pinkie sloop. It was a day of dense fog, and we were very damp. He had no other alternative than to boost us over the side and let us warm up in the cabin. It was a place to entrance two eight-year-old girls, it was so small, so compact, so scrubbed. A coal fire glowed in the stove, Barnaby was in his straw bed under the sink, and we sat on the bunk.

Scobie growled at us, "You should be spanked. What are you doing out here on a day like this?"

"We came to see you," Rhoda said placidly.

"And Barnaby," I added.

He shot me a glance from under his creased forehead. "Now, I can see some sense to that." He began to mix cocoa in two mugs for us. Our mothers disapproved of this method, but Scobie's cocoa that day, rich and dark, was nectar. "After all, Barnaby's the one you should come to see. He's the important one around here. I'm just an equerry."

"What's that?" said Rhoda.

"I stand between him and the world," said Scobie. "Keep off the rabble. Shelter him from the people." He poured boiling water into the mugs. "Of course, with a reduced staff, I have to double as his valet, too, but there's not much work to that. He's a tidy soul, is H.R.H."

"H.R.H.?" I asked. "What's that mean?"

"His Royal Highness, of course," said Scobie coldly.

This stopped us for quite a few seconds, during which we sipped the scalding cocoa, and Scobie began to mend socks as if he had said nothing strange.

"You mean," I offered at last, "that he's a royal pig? Like a prize pig?"

"I mean," said Scobie, "that he's royal, all right. But not in the way of being a pig. That's got nothing to do with it. He was royal before he ever was a pig. In fact—" Scobie's big, hairy hands plied the needle delicately—"in fact, it was because he was royal that he was turned into a pig."

I remember clutching the cocoa mug with both hands to control its shaking. My heart was pounding. Rhoda was pale under her freckles, her lips tight. How we ever endured that moment of discovery I don't know. We were both familiar with good and bad fairies and evil spells, but we had never expected to encounter the victim of such a spell right under our noses.

It didn't occur to us to doubt Scobie. He wasn't like Mr. Saunders in the store, always laughing and telling us fantastic stories that we knew for lies. Scobie, sitting there mending his socks in the tiny cabin of the pinkie sloop, hardly ever laughed, and he never talked to us as if we were children. So we knew he wasn't lying.

After the first shock, we asked questions, but Scobie wouldn't tell us too much. What country Barnaby was a prince of, or anything like that.

"I was connected with the royal household," he said. "And my father before me, and his father before him. It was a tradition in our family. Loyal to the death, we Scobies. So when events occurred—" he cleared his throat loudly, and we nodded to show we understood the significance—"it was only natural to give me the privilege of caring for H.R.H. and protecting him from harm."

We looked reverently at the little door behind which Barnaby slept. "You mean whoever put the spell on him would still want to hurt him?"

"You don't understand," said Scobie. "The spell was put on him to protect him from—er—factions that wished him out of the way. As a matter of fact—" again a portentous throat clearing—"I put him under the spell. That was what I meant about my privilege to protect him. My family have been sorcerers by appointment to the royal family for hundreds of years."

That was all he would say then. He told us to finish our cocoa and go, that it would be getting dark early. We hurried obediently, but we wanted to see Barnaby first. Scobie opened the door under the sink, and Barnaby awoke, snuffling and snorting, and lifted his pink snout to us. It seemed a little presumptuous to scratch a royal prince behind the ears, but Scobie said, "Go ahead. He's looking for it. While he's a pig, he likes what a pig likes. It's the only way for him to be happy."

When Scobie dropped us over the side, he didn't insult us by warning us to keep the secret. He did tell us not to come more than once a week. I suppose he had to make this ruling out of self-defense, or his life would have ceased to be his own. We did not suffer too much; we had our secret, and between visits we could conjecture endlessly on Barnaby's real name, his country, and the way he looked in his real flesh. We didn't have to conjecture about Scobie. He was a sorcerer, like Merlin. That made him, without excepting our fathers, the most remarkable man in the world.

With June the Hallidays came to their place on Lighthouse Point. Of all the summer people, the Hallidays meant the most to us, because of Kevin. He was nine that year and hadn't yet approached the point where he scorned girls as playmates. For two years we had been an inseparable triumvirate.

The Hallidays were considered advanced because of the way there were bringing up their children "in complete truth." That was the way they phrased it. We thought life must be rather barren for Kevin, without Santa Claus, the Little Lord Jesus asleep in the hay, and various delicious tales of horror we believed word for word, like *The Princess and the Goblins*.

But Kevin enjoyed playing Pirates and Explorers, so we were always busy, whether we were fighting or playing. He was a wiry, redheaded boy with intensely blue eyes, which were usually blazing with scorn for our puny female opinions.

This year we gloated about Kevin's arrival. This year the unbeliever was going to be shown, once and for all. We pictured the way his eyes would grow round, how his voice, already loaded with male arrogance, would be silenced by sheer force of astonishment. We had no doubt that he would be vanquished before the irrevocable fact of H.R.H.'s existence and Scobie's power over him.

For the first week of Kevin's stay we kept him in happy ignorance. No doubt he found us unusually pliable those days, consenting to be tied to trees as white captives, or doing all the hard digging for treasure while he, as Captain Kidd, stood elegantly by.

Then came the inevitable morning when the usual games palled, and we went to sit in a row on the end of the fish wharf.

Rhoda said suddenly into the bright stillness, "Let's go and see Scobie."

"Let's," I echoed.

Kevin looked down at his dangling bare feet and said in a blasé voice, "Who's Scobie?"

"Come with us and see," I said and got up. My voice must have been tense with meaning, because Kevin didn't argue, but got up, too.

It was a long walk, hot where the spruces shut off the wind. But we arrived at the marsh at last; in the summer, marsh rosemary spread a warm lavender sheen everywhere. Scobie had painted the pinkie sloop afresh, and it gleamed white beyond the wrecked, forsaken boat. Rhoda and I exchanged proud, secret looks about it. Scobie had already been out fishing and had come in. He was cleaning huge codfish down by the tide's edge. As we went over the beach to him, he scooped the entrails out of a fish and threw them to the flurrying, squawking gulls.

"This is Kevin Halliday," said Rhoda primly. "Kevin, this is Mr. Scobie."

Scobie nodded.

Kevin said, "How do you do," and stared hard at Scobie as if to discover his secret.

For a few minutes we watched Scobie and the gulls, and then I said with nonchalance, "Where's Barnaby?"

Scobie jerked his head toward the pinkie. "Up there."

"Can we go see him?"

"Sure."

"Come on, Kevin," we said.

He was polite enough to wait until we got away from Scobie before he said, "What's so special about him, except that he looks like the Piltdown man?"

"Who's that?" I asked, but just then Barnaby came rocking and grunting around the bow of the pinkie and raced toward us on his little hoofs. He was bigger than when we'd first seen him, but not too much, and he was still immaculate. We went through the usual greetings and back scratchings.

Kevin looked on, his hands in his pockets and his eyebrows knotted together. "And what's so special about a tame pig? You should see the zoo in Franklin Park, for heaven's sake."

"You don't believe in heaven, so you can't say 'for heaven's sake,'" said Rhoda. Her eyes took on their dark, mystic look. "Barnaby isn't just a pig, Kevin. That's the big thing about him. He looks like a pig, but he isn't."

"No," I said in a hushed voice. "He isn't. But we can't tell you the truth unless Scobie says so."

Scobie was coming up the beach, his huge shoulders bent, his great hands trailing fish.

I hurried to him. "Can we tell Kevin?" I begged. "He doesn't believe in anything—I mean, in anything he can't see. And he's always making fun of us."

Scobie almost smiled. "What makes you think this will convince him?"

"It has to!" I cried, amazed.

"Well, then," said Scobie, "tell him."

So I ran back and told him, without quailing before the fierce disbelief in those bright-blue eyes.

Rhoda added, "Scobie is a sorcerer. He was the one who did it. And any time he wants, he can make Barnaby a prince again."

Kevin burst into cruel laughter. "You're crazy," he shouted. "You're all crazy, only he's worse. There's no such thing as sorcerers and spells!" He was like a goblin himself, transfigured with unholy glee. "And that's just a plain old pig!"

Scobie's shadow fell over us, and Rhoda and I turned anguished faces to him.

"He doesn't believe it!" I cried. "He can't believe what he doesn't see with his own two eyes. He doesn't even believe in God."

"Then why should we expect him to believe in Barnaby?" asked Scobie.

"You can make him believe," said Rhoda fervently. "You're a sorcerer. You can show him."

"How?" said Scobie. He stood there, gently simian, looking down at us, the great, gleaming fish hanging by the gills from his fingers, and their fresh, cold smell in our nostrils. Barnaby rooted in the grass, talking to himself. "How can I show him?" asked Scobie. He looked gently at Kevin, and it seemed as if Kevin's bright-edged contempt began to dim. "Hide the sun, and spoil the day for fishermen? Scorch the marsh with a breath, and kill the rosemary? Bring down a gull out of the sky, when it's a far handsomer creature than I am, just to show Kevin?" He shook his head.

I felt vaguely ashamed, and Rhoda's cheeks had a quick blush. She said uneasily, "I thought, maybe, just for a minute, you'd bring H.R.H.

back."

"You thought that, did you?" Scobie's brow furrowed even more with astonishment. "Just for a whim, just for a little boy who thinks if he denies God that God will cease to exist?" Scobie laughed. It was the first time I had ever heard him laugh. It was a deep and rolling sound, and it went through me like the beating of drums. And suddenly I saw the foolishness of Rhoda and me, wasting this agony and rage over Kevin, as if we truly thought all our good things would cease to exist because Kevin had denied them.

Kevin was staring at his bare toes, wriggling them in the spongy black earth of the marsh. Then his red head canted slightly, and I knew he was looking at Barnaby. He looked for a long time.

Rhoda said in a clear voice to Scobie, "I guess maybe you're right."

"I know I'm right," said Scobie. "Now you'd better put for home, because I was up at daylight this morning, and Barnaby and I are going to take a nap."

"Come on, Kevin," I said. He didn't move at once, and I had to say it again.

His head snapped up, and he answered as if from a great distance. "Okay. Okay. Only—" He broke off and looked at Barnaby again; his eyes were cloudy with uncertainty.

We said good-by to Scobie and started away; but I, on some impulse, suddenly ran back.

He was putting the fish into a keg of brine and he looked at me without amazement. "What now?" he said.

He was bending over the tub, and it was easy for me to put my arms around his neck. I laid my cheek against this leathery, unshaven one. "Thank you, Scobie," I breathed. "Thank you forever and ever."

His hands were wet and scaly, so he couldn't hold me off. "For what?" he muttered, helpless.

"The prince is even more real now," I said. "No matter what Kevin says."

"He won't say much," said Scobie, "because he sees your faith, and it makes him wonder. You don't need to defend your faith. Just keep it, no matter what anyone says. For that's what makes you rich and whole and good. Now stop strangling me, and be off with you."

I kissed his cheek and ran without looking back. Kevin and Rhoda hadn't seen, for they were a good way ahead.

When we parted from Kevin at the foot of my street, he said, "See you tomorrow at the creek," and that was all. But he walked differently, as if his sight were still clouded with strange thoughts.

Three days later Rhoda and I were in my playhouse under the lilacs and weigela outside our dining-room window. We were hiding from the heat and from Kevin, who had been rather cranky of late. My mother was setting the table for dinner, and my father came into the dining room. We heard them talking. Out of habit we ignored them until a familiar name rang a bell in our ears.

"The man in the pinkie sloop—Scobie—has gone," my father said. "Guess the fish were playing out a little, and so he's moved on down the coast. That's the way with these transients."

My mother murmured something, but Rhoda and I didn't hear. We were numbed with this new, appalling hurt.

My father spoke again. "He'll turn up to the south'ard somewhere, like an apparition out of the mist," he chuckled. "Him and his pig."

The bands of shock loosened, and a delicious relief and exaltation spread through us. In the dappled shade under the lilacs Rhoda's eyes glowed like jewels, and mine must have glowed, too. We did not have to speak. We knew that we shared the same thought.

We knew far more than my father, or anyone else, about Scobie. He had gone farther to the south'ard than they had dreamed. He had gone a world away. We knew. He had taken his prince home to his own land at last.

My Lost Youth

HENRY WADSWORTH LONGFELLOW

Often I think of the beautiful town
    That is seated by the sea;
Often in thought go up and down
The pleasant streets of that dear old town,
    And my youth comes back to me.
        And a verse of a Lapland song
        Is haunting my memory still:
    "A boy's will is the wind's will,
And the thoughts of youth are long, long thoughts."

I can see the shadowy lines of its trees,
    And catch, in sudden gleams,
The sheen of the far-surrounding seas.
And islands that were the Hesperides
    Of all my boyish dreams.
        And the burden of that old song
        It murmurs and whispers still:
    "A boy's will is the wind's will,
And the thoughts of youth are long, long thoughts."

I remember the black wharves and the slips,
    And the sea-tides tossing free;
And Spanish sailors with bearded lips,
And the beauty and mystery of the ships,
    And the magic of the sea.
        And the voice of that wayward song
        Is singing and saying still:
    "A boy's will is the wind's will,
And the thoughts of youth are long, long thoughts."

I remember the bulwarks by the shore,
    And the fort upon the hill;

The sunrise gun, with its hollow roar,
The drumbeat repeated o'er and o'er,
    And the bugle wild and shrill.
        And the music of that old song
        Throbs in my memory still:
    "A boy's will is the wind's will,
And the thoughts of youth are long, long thoughts."

I remember the sea-fight far away,
    How it thundered o'er the tide!
And the dead captains, as they lay
In their graves, o'erlooking the tranquil bay
    Where they in battle died.
        And the sound of that mournful song
        Goes through me with a thrill:
    "A boy's will is the wind's will,
And the thoughts of youth are long, long thoughts."

I can see the breezy dome of groves,
    The shadows of Deering's Woods;
And the friendships old and the early loves
Come back with a Sabbath sound, as of doves
    In quiet neighborhoods.
        And the verse of that sweet old song,
        It flutters and murmurs still:
    "A boy's will is the wind's will,
And the thoughts of youth are long, long thoughts."

I remember the gleams and glooms that dart
    Across the school-boy's brain;
The song and the silence in the heart,
That in part are prophecies, and in part
    Are longings wild and vain.
        And the voice of that fitful song
        Sings on, and is never still:
    "A boy's will is the wind's will,
And the thoughts of youth are long, long thoughts."

There are things of which I may not speak;
    There are dreams that cannot die;
There are thoughts that make the strong heart weak,
And bring a pallor into the cheek,

And a mist before the eye.
    And the words of that fatal song
    Come over me like a chill:
"A boy's will is the wind's will,
And the thoughts of youth are long, long thoughts."

Strange to me now are the forms I meet
    When I visit the dear old town;
But the native air is pure and sweet,
And the trees that o'ershadow each well-known street,
    As they balance up and down,
        Are singing the beautiful song,
        Are sighing and whispering still
    "A boy's will is the wind's will,
And the thoughts of youth are long, long thoughts."

And Deering's Woods are fresh and fair,
    And with joy that is almost pain
My heart goes back to wander there,
And among the dreams of the days that were,
    I find my lost youth again.
        And the strange and beautiful song,
        The groves are repeating it still:
    "A boy's will is the wind's will,
And the thoughts of youth are long, long thoughts."

The State Meet

FRED BONNIE

Daniel had been sent to the state cross-country meet as an alternate after Ward twisted his ankle at practice just two days before the meet. All the way from Portland to Bangor, Daniel's stomach grew heavier as he sat in the reeling bus, his arms weak and limp, his eyes hot and sick in their sockets. Daniel tried to read. When he wasn't looking at the book, he stared out the window, watching the blank walls of pine that crowded close to the road. Every few miles, the road opened upon fields of tall grass where lone elms groped as if in retreat from the road, bare-limbed and gray and silent.

It was hard to read, though, with Eddie Murphy trying to distract him. Murphy was sitting in the seat in front of him. He turned and smirked at Daniel every few miles.

"Boucher's a Canuck," Murphy said loudly. "We oughta beat all them Frenchies with Boucher here. Ain't that right, Boucher?"

When Daniel ignored him, he reached back and tried to snatch Daniel's book. "I think he has a suggestive book or something back here, Father Paloski. He ain't talkin'."

Father Paloski's thin lips stiffened and he stared for a long moment before he spoke. It was a habit for which he was known as much as his Brooklyn accent. "Shuddup, Murphy. When's the last time you read anything?"

"I've read all the signs on this bus, Father."

One or two of the others laughed. Murphy was nearly a foot taller than Father Paloski. He ran with the cross-country team in the fall to get in shape for basketball. He was the best rebounder in the state, and his left hook was impossible to block. But he was inconsistent; some games he made thirty points, some games he made none.

Daniel sank closer to the window and continued to read. After a while, Murphy stopped gawking at him. Daniel thought again about the state meet and felt more strength drain from his limbs. He was on the team because Father Paloski was the algebra teacher and had intimated that the only way Daniel could rescue his ailing math grade was to run with the cross country team. No one truly thought Father Paloski would flunk someone for not joining the team, but it was widely felt that running could serve as an extra credit venture, capable of raising a grade of sixty-seven or sixty-eight all the way to seventy, the minimum passing grade. Running, according to Father Paloski, would clear Daniel's head of the distractions that Paloski had said eroded a young person's mathematical consciousness. A few miles a day might make Daniel want to study harder, retain more.

Paloski was also the sophomore geometry teacher. Almost every student passed through Paloski's clutches on the way to junior year. Significant was the fact that the cross-country team had only one senior, Sid Seamans, and one junior, Murphy.

"Cross-country," Paloski loved to tell them, "requires a special kind of detachment which can be found only in a state of exhaustion. And only when sufficiently detached can you demand of your body far more than your body can really do."

On the day of each meet during the long season, Daniel had felt as if he were carrying a lead vault in his stomach from the time he got up in the morning until he was actually running. He had one fear: to come in last.

In his first meet he had discovered that many of the runners could be beaten in the last half mile. He had come in twenty-seventh in a field of fifty. In the second meet he had come in twenty-first.

In the third meet he discovered the technique that allowed him to quell the fear of coming in last. At the starting line, Daniel had let everyone go before he began to run. Watching the sixty other runners jammed all together at the starting line, then surging away from him Daniel said to himself, *There. You're last. Now go!*

He began to catch and pass others in the long line which stretched itself around the football field and back toward the woods. With each runner Daniel passed, his pace grew quicker, and his breathing fresher, less taxed. In the last quarter-mile alone he passed sixteen runners, fifteenth. Had the race been longer, Daniel knew he would have continued to pass runners. He loved to pass the leggy basketball players. He was less than one inch over five feet, and weighed ninety-eight pounds. He could have easily run another three, or twenty-three miles. Paloski looked at him and said, "You don't punish yourself, Boucher. You might be good if you just once punished yourself. I've never seen you look tired after a race."

"I'm just in great shape, Father."

Paloski didn't flicker a smile, standing as always with his hands jammed into the pockets of his long, black coat, the visor of his black hat pulled low over his eyes.

Paloski suddenly sat down beside Daniel on the bus. Daniel had not seen him coming.

"Not to pry," Paloski said, "but what *are* you reading?"

"*A Short History of Mathematics.*"

Paloski glanced at the cover. "I think I'm going to faint."

"Like I told Murphy," Daniel said, smiling, "this book doesn't have any good parts."

"No good parts, eh? The history of mathematics is the history of science, and the history of science is the history of man, my boy."

"I think the history of agriculture has influenced the course of history more ...."

Paloski continued. "The history of agriculture is prehistory, Mr. Boucher. It's the story of simple-minded hordes capable of aspiring to nothing loftier than finding food and shelter. And propagating. Only when man got numbers did things start to move."

Daniel grinned and gestured with the book he held. "Sounds to me like you've read this one already."

"I've read this one and thousands like it. Fascinating, the world of numbers. The Pythagoreans worshipped numbers, you know."

"Yes, Father, you've told us that several times this year."

"Well, I can't say it enough. Getting back to the nitty-gritty," Paloski said, "don't think carrying that book on this trip has a chance of helping your math grade. If anything, it's damaged your grade. Better count on your running in the state meet today to get you through math this term."

Paloski got up and went to his own seat. The only runner on the team he'd ever heard Paloski praise was Ward, who threw up after each race. And once Paloski praised Michel Minard. Minard had led a race of forty people to within three hundred yards of the finish line before he caved at the knees and had to limp to the end, finishing twentieth. Daniel who had started the race as the last man finished twenty-first. Minard was gaunt, with a caved chest, bony legs, and thick glasses. He ran with pain burned into the squints and creases of his face and the set of his jaw. Michel had looked that way since first grade, Daniel recalled.

Michel Minard and Daniel had been forced to know each other all their lives. Their fathers were both foremen at the paper mill, and they often watched football together on TV. Each fall, as Michel's father began to come around on Saturday afternoons, Daniel's father began hinting to Daniel that he and Michel should become friends, that they would be good for each other.

Daniel had never felt an interest in Michel. Michel was funny looking and quiet.

"You two could speak French together," Daniel's father said.

"Wow, I can't wait."

The bus quaked over the shallow ruts and rocks of a stretch of road that was under construction. Daniel's teeth rattled him out of his thoughts.

"I'll bet the Canucks built this road," Murphy roared.

Daniel glanced once at Michel who was grinning foolishly toward Murphy.

"Don't invite abuse, Murphy," Father Paloski said. "Or we'll have to repeat your lobotomy."

Daniel's eyes dissected the back of Murphy's skull. He waited for Murphy to turn around and look at him with his flat, wide, freckled face. But already Murphy was distracted by something else. A story about himself in the newspaper. He'd just found it. And in the Bangor paper, not the hometown Portland paper. It was a preview of potential all-state basketball players. Murphy had made the second team. Murphy was a true athlete, an obsessive competitor. Only Murphy ran cross-country because he wanted to. The others ran for a strange variety of reasons. Carver ran because his brother had been captain of the team three years before, and his family expected him to run. Marcus ran because he wanted a letter in something, and he couldn't play football, basketball, baseball, hockey, or golf. Daniel didn't know why Michel Minard ran.

By the time the bus reached Bangor, the sky was grayer and colder. Rain seemed certain. Daniel hated running in the rain, with the paths muddy and the grassy fields like swamps. The drive from Bangor to the University field house was short. They arrived long before Daniel could accept being there. He was the last one to leave the bus.

They were shown a locker room to change in. Then they hung around the field house for about an hour. There were runners from nearly sixty schools. As a result, the competition was divided into two meets, one for the big schools and one for the small schools. The two groups gradually polarized to the two ends of the field house. After the runners had milled about for fifteen or twenty minutes, two assistant coaches from the university cross-country team came to lead the runners around the long course. The runners who expected to be near the lead stayed by the coaches and asked them questions. Daniel lagged behind. By the time they got back to the field house, a light mist had begun to fall. Having seen the course, Daniel felt sicker than ever. It was a longer and harder course than any in the high school league. There were hills and fields and a ravine. Part of the course followed a power line trail. It would be a difficult course for maintaining a steady pace. It was a good course for the kind of solitude that Daniel sometimes felt when he was running, but today there would be no solitude, he knew.

The runners from the small schools were taking off their sweatsuits and beginning to line up. Daniel's school was in the big school meet so he would have to continue waiting. He watched the small school runners stretching, grunting as they flexed their wiry, coastal bodies.

Daniel went back inside the field house and sat on the floor with his head between his knees until the dizziness went away. He felt drained and weak, and began to wonder if he would be able to get up for his own race. When the starting gun went off, Daniel heard the collective grunt of the runners and pictured the bright swish of their nylon running shorts. Daniel blocked his ears. His stomach tightened with hunger. The team had eaten breakfast but skipped lunch. He felt his tense thighs and calves and tried to massage them supple again, numb again. His legs looked thin and spindly to him, and he thought about Michel Minard.

Michel's entire family spoke French at home. Michel's grandmother had refused to learn English. Daniel's grandmother knew very little English, but that didn't motivate Daniel to learn French. To him, French wasn't a language to speak; it was the language your grandmother spoke. You answered in English. No one with any sense answered his grandmother in French.

His thoughts wandered back to the runners out on the course, clambering up the bank of the creek onto the power line trail, up that big hill through the apple orchard. He felt it in his thighs. "I hate this," he said aloud.

When he heard cheering outside, Daniel knew that the first runners must be coming into view, heading for the finish line. It was sooner than he expected and he realized once more that his own race was only a few minutes away. Anticipating a cross-country meet made him feel the same as if he were on his way to see the dentist.

He could not stop pacing.

Seamans appeared in the doorway. "Oh, there you are. Want to come watch?"

"Not really."

"What's the matter, Boucher? You all right?"

"Yeah. I'll be out in a second."

Seamans didn't move, so Daniel decided that he might just as well go ahead and watch. The dampness and the cold woke him up again as they crossed the field to a corridor of people that had formed along the final stretch. Across the wide meadow, Daniel could see the first runners winding through the tall grass. Three runners were visible and the crowd cheered whenever another runner came into sight. Daniel realized that he'd never watched a cross-country meet; he'd only run in them.

The leaders loomed closer. It would be a tight race. Days later, Daniel would read in the newspaper that the three runners leading the small school conference had created a much publicized rivalry that year. The state meet was to be their showdown.

As they came closer, Daniel realized that one of them was screeching, taunting the others like a crow. The crowd laughed.

"Dupont," someone said. "Dupont," the others echoed. "Paul

Dupont, il est fou celui-la." Everyone laughed.

They beat closer.

Paul Dupont, Daniel thought. Murphy was right. Most of the runners at least had French names. Daniel liked their names and the names of some of the schools: Lubec, Blue Hill, Mount Desert Island, Bonny Eagle. The runners were big lunks, too. "There's no money for football at most of these small schools," Paloski had told them. "Cross-country's the only fall sport. All the campus studs run."

Dupont was screeching again.

A man standing beside Daniel said, "He bedder shuddup an' run, dat one, before Fornier catch him."

The two lead runners seemed no more than an armstretch from each other, and Daniel studied their legs as he waited for their faces to come into view, the line of mouths and brows first, materializing out of the mist, then jaws and the creases of foreheads, only shadows for eyes. Dupont was dark and bent, a full step ahead of Fornier, whose face was frantic, both of them hammering at the ground and the mist with their feet.

"Yeeeeeech Yeeeeech...."

The crowd laughed again. Dupont and Fornier drew within a football field's length of the finish line. Their faces were as terrified as horses caught in a barn fire. Fornier, with a last yelp, lowered his head and surged past the other, flashing over the line just a few inches in the lead. The crowd roared, startling Daniel with its size and volume. He had never seen so many people watch a cross-country meet. At least five hundred people, he thought. The third runner finished, nearly unnoticed, and Daniel watched him collapse, heaving. A steady procession formed along the finishing stretch. Small clusters of two to five runners battled for position, each of them as if he were leading the whole pack. Daniel realized that he was watching more than one race, that he was watching eighty-seven races, each with its own agony. In his own race there would be two hundred and one agonies.

The cheering grew less regular, except when tight clusters ran hard. When individual runners crossed the line, most of the spectators only clapped.

Toward the end of the race, runners became more staggered. No one left the track, though. For over ten minutes, they watched the runners trickle back to the field house. The finish line was directly in front of a large bay door on the south side of the building, and as each runner finished, he went inside.

Daniel went inside to look at the runners who had just finished. Most of them pranced, hands on hips, lifting their reddened legs high to keep the muscles from tightening and freezing them into stiffness. Everywhere, Daniel heard the sound of deep, painful breathing. Some of the runners still lay collapsed on the ground several minutes after finishing. And still others went back outside to throw up. Daniel felt his own roiling stomach. He would not do this next year, he told himself. He would study harder, possibly get a private tutor for math, but he was not going to subject himself to this ever again.

Daniel went back outside. Far down the field, two more runners were straggling in, and he heard someone say these were the last two. These were the ones Daniel wanted to see. There was a lot of distance between them. The next to last runner continued to trot, although his limbs seemed to move in slow motion. But the last racer made no pretenses; he was walking. He was a stocky kid, and even at a distance Daniel could tell that his flesh jiggled as he walked. Most of the crowd began to move from the finish line back to the starting line on the other side of the field house, but Daniel stood transfixed, unable to take his eyes from this last man. His thick, black body hair was matted against his skin and marked by rivulets of sweat. One or two people clapped, but the idea of clapping sickened Daniel. To clap now would be to rub the guy's face in his own defeat.

But the guy was smiling. Daniel was stunned. How could he come in last with five hundred people watching and smile?

"Come on, Boucher," he heard someone say.

The public address system, which they had not managed to hook up in time for the small school meet, now came on to announce the beginning of the new race. Daniel was in a trance, thinking about the runners from the first race who were still pacing or lying, exhausted, on the ground outside the field house.

"Hey, Boucher!" Murphy shouted. "D'ja see that Frenchie win the last race? I bet he inspired you, huh?"

"Wake up, Boucher," Father Paloski said. He held several of his runners' sweatsuits over his arm. "Give us the duds."

Paloski then called the runners into a huddle.

"In the name of the Father, and of the Son, and of the Holy Ghost, amen. Oh Heavenly Father, we know we are nothing without thy continual love. Today, we beg thee for strength such as we have never known, and that in thy eternal kindness, thou shalt let thine only Jesuit representative in the state meet register a third or fourth place, in spite of our regular season record. In the name of the Father, and of the Son, and of the Holy Ghost, amen."

The amens echoed quietly.

When they stood up, Paloski slapped Murphy's butt. "I'm depending on you," he said gravely. Then he slapped Daniel's shoulder. "Boucher, try to stay right behind Murphy."

The runners were starting to line up. There were more than twice as many runners as for the small school meet, and Daniel felt dizzy as he looked down the long, chaotic line of colored running suits. The rain had quietly resumed.

"On your mark ...."

Daniel's stomach fluttered as he tried to concentrate on Eddie Murphy's feet, which were right in front of him.

"Get set ...."

Daniel started to sway as his vision blurred on the curtain of hairy legs in front of him.

"Go!" A pistol shot cracked and the runners thundered away from him, but Daniel stood dazed, sick, on the verge of fainting. Before his folding knees touched the ground, Paloski caught him by the arm.

"Are you all right, kid?"

Daniel snapped to. Whatever had made him dizzy now vanished as quickly as it had seized him.

"Yes. Let me go!"

"Don't run if you're sick, Boucher."

"I'm not sick, Father. Let me go."

Paloski released his arm and Daniel sped after the retreating runners. The moment his legs and arms were in motion, Daniel no longer felt sick. And being last caused him no panic; it was a familiar position, after all. In a few moments, he had crossed the field and entered the woods, where it was warm and quiet. He was ready to relax and try to catch someone, but the wet leaves on the path were slippery and he fell twice before he got to the creek bed. The sharp incline from the creek bed up to the power trail slowed him to a crawl, and he realized with the first inkling of desperation that he was already exhausted. At the top of the hill he regained his momentum and was once again ready to pass someone, but there was no one to pass.

He ran a little harder, knowing he'd catch up to someone soon. It had worked that way all year. But his old fear of coming in last began to gnaw at him in a way he had not known since the first race of the year.

As he topped one hill, he caught a glimpse of another yellow uniform, like his, topping the hill ahead of him. Steve Dennis, Daniel guessed. He'd just step up the pace until he caught Steve, then they could coast. He'd have someone to talk to, anyway. Steve had a sister who was a year younger than Daniel. Barbara Dennis was very cute, Daniel thought. Daniel had been cultivating a friendship with Steve Dennis since the beginning of the year because he wanted to be near the head of the line to ask Barbara out when she would be allowed to date the next year.

Daniel found himself going a little too fast down the backside of the hill, and he lost his feet and tumbled down a long stretch that was especially slippery with mud. Back in the woods again, he scraped his leg and arm on a broken branch. He was starting to get angry, but at least he no longer felt sick.

When Daniel finally caught up to Steve Dennis, it was not Steve Dennis; it was Michel Minard. Daniel caught him midway up the hill through the apple orchard. Michel's face brightened when he saw Daniel.

"I thought ... I was the ... last one," he said, breathing hard, his face a solid red. There was something else different about his face, but Daniel wasn't exactly sure what it was.

"You almost ... were. I started ... to black out at the ... starting line, but then ... I felt okay."

They ran together for a hundred yards or so, but then Daniel was conscious of having slowed down. He wanted to catch and pass someone else.

"Well ... see ya." He moved a few yards ahead and tried to speed up even more, but the sounds of Michel's feet didn't fade. He found it hard to believe he wasn't putting distance between himself and Michel, but Michel's breathing was so close behind him he began to think he could feel it on his neck.

Their momentum was disrupted by their descent into the ravine. The footing was tricky and they had to step carefully along the wet logs and rocks. Along the bank above them, the trees seemed to rock unsteadily on their exposed roots.

Michel was suddenly alongside Daniel. "Mean course, huh?"

His sudden presence startled and irritated Daniel, who had again begun to think he was gaining distance on Michel. As soon as the course uncurled into a flat path through the woods, Daniel sprinted to get away from Michel. Michel made Daniel think of a birthday party he'd had when he was little. Michel was there, and he had given Daniel a little book about turtles. The book was in French, and Daniel hadn't seen it since the day Michel gave it to him. They had always been together in school, and every year Daniel had expected Michel to flunk. His grades were terrible, even his French grades, but he managed to hang on through each year and squeak by to the next.

The path was padded with pine needles, so Daniel was especially surprised that Michel was still right behind him.

"You should come ... over and see my ... workshop sometime," Michel panted. "My dad and me ... we set it up."

Hearing Michel so close to him made Daniel feel drained and weak. Each leg sank heavily as he ran. He couldn't imagine where Michel was getting the energy to talk. Michel had edged alongside him again, and Daniel suddenly realized what was different about him.

"Where are ... your glasses?"

"I dunno," Michel gasped.

No wonder he's following me so closely, Daniel thought. He probably can't see a damned thing without those glasses of his.

They topped a final hill, and the athletic complex unraveled below them. They could hear the crowd beginning to cheer, and Daniel realized that the lead runners were nearing the finish line. The nearest runner was at least three hundred yards away. There was no hope of catching him. Daniel wondered if he shouldn't just slow down, but then Michel darted ahead of him. Daniel suddenly saw it was still a race to Michel.

Daniel surged a little harder. It was too soon to start sprinting, he told himself. But watching Michel start to put distance between them, Daniel realized with anguish that he'd better run or he would come in last. In moments, Daniel was running as hard and deliriously as he'd run all year. It took a monumental effort to catch Michel, and his lungs burned with pain as he tried to pass him. Michel's exertion showed, but not with the desperation Daniel now felt beginning to collect in his throat. Michel was only one step behind. The field house wavered at the end of the meadow.

Michel's voice seemed calm when he spoke. "When we ... get closer ... I'm gonna try ... and beat you, but ... thanks for staying ... back and helping me."

Daniel heard the words in a delirium. He was sure he had imagined them. But as Michel pulled alongside him once again, Daniel woke up.

"You are like hell!" Daniel lowered his body and his feet beat harder into the spongy grass. He no longer saw Michel exactly beside him, but he could hear the breathing inches from his ears.

Now the crowd saw them and began cheering. Daniel was humiliated to be in such a frantic race for nothing better than next to last place, but last place was simply unacceptable.

And Daniel could see that Michel felt the same way.

They were only the length of a football field away from the finish line. With every step, Daniel tried to surge. The wall of bodies that formed the corridor to the finish line seemed to close toward them as Michel's long arms flailed into Daniel's periphery. He felt Michel edging by him again.

No, Daniel told himself. The crowd was in an uproar as Michel gained an arm's length twenty yards from the finish line. Daniel lowered himself, closed his eyes, and heard himself cry out as he half ran, half leapt at the finish line, winning the race by only an outstretched hand. His legs gave, and he hit the dirt floor hard, rolling and rolling. His stomach and aching chest pulled him into a tight knot, and he was utterly certain he was about to die. He tried to move but couldn't.

Eventually the wavering din in his ears sorted itself into voices, and the voices became Murphy and Seamans.

"You *won*, Man," Murphy roared. "You came in *next* to last."

Daniel tried to roll away from them, but then Polaski grasped his wrists and pulled him to his feet.

"Good show, Boucher. That's the first time I've ever seen you run with conviction. But let's keep moving. Don't let your muscles tighten up."

Daniel felt unsteady on his feet, but he didn't think he was going to fall. He stumbled toward Michel, who grinned as he heaved, and wanted to shake hands. The loudspeaker boomed their names and the positions in which they finished. Daniel was amazed that Michel was willing to be friendly. How could you be nice to someone who made you come in last? He slapped Michel's back.

"Great race, mon ami. Hell of a race."

Michel nodded. There were tears in his eyes, but he wasn't about to start crying. Maybe later, but not now.

"Come on," Daniel said, nudging him toward the woods. "Let's go find your glasses."

The Bad One

GERARD ROBICHAUD

Father Joseph Lebois had a problem.

That was October of the year Thérèse was sixteen going on seventeen and expected to do very well in her last year at St. Michel's High School, and Laurent's marriage to Hélène Pelletier was just two weeks away. Father Lebois, recently of Berlin, New Hampshire, had just been assigned as the new parish assistant to Father Giroux at Sacred Heart Church in Groveton, Maine. And he came one night to the Martel apartment, with his problem.

Louis Martel had become fond of Father Lebois the very first time they'd met. This young priest, thought Louis, assumed that if you wanted to do the right thing for God and country, the Church, or to help people in need of help, everything would turn out the best possible way if only you had enough *savoir-faire* to have somebody else do it for you. It was a pleasure to see this priest work. His was, of course, the philosophy of a naive child, which the world needed, and the methods of a gang leader who could also quote the Latin. In any case, Louis mused, he doesn't mind getting his feet wet for our Lord.

Maman was delighted to see him. She had had her way, to some extent, in tightening up schoolwork in Sacred Heart parish. She was now at peace with its administration. In any case, a visit from the priest was always an honor. She promptly served him a cup of tea.

"Sugar? Milk?" she asked.

"A little dynamite?" suggested Louis.

"Ah, yes, a little dynamite," he said, "and thank you."

Father Lebois was tall, slim, well built. He looked like an athlete, and had been, at one time, sought after by "Les Canadiens" for a professional hockey career. He still was good at it, and on cold days he could be seen chasing the puck around on the ice with the choir boys. As a priest, however, he was still known as a hockey player: he could handle a stick well, he could and did bring the puck past the opposition, right up to the goal. He never shot a goal, however, for he was better known still for his ability to pass the puck to someone in a better position to score a goal. He was—well—a very good puck-passer.

Maman introduced him to Laurent, her oldest, Maurice, now

eighteen and very tall suddenly, to Félix, Emile, Marie, and Cécile. Thérèse was at choir practice. After his tea, Father Lebois took out his pipe, Louis handed him his own tobacco pouch, and soon both men smoked contentedly.

"What a grand family you have, Madame Martel!" the priest exclaimed.

"Thank you, Father," said Maman, "and they are doing well in school...."

Louis waited for the priest to show his hand, but there now came some polite talk with Laurent, soon to be married, and with Maurice who was part-time helper at the Exelsior Grocery Market. They talked about Thérèse who seesawed daily between becoming a teacher, like Maman, or a nun, or a movie star, and who never missed Rudolph Valentino whenever the Great Lover rode his white steed across the Empire Theater screen on a Saturday afternoon.

"Some movies are good," said Father Lebois, "and some movies are bad."

Yes, thought Louis, this hockey player, and priest, could also skate on both sides of the rink at the same time.

"Oh, yes," said Maman, "and we watch the movies they see. They are not allowed to see stories with ... you know ... where the leading lady acts like ... well ... a street girl...."

Father Lebois nodded quietly, and turned to talk. He spotted Félix and began to discuss with him baseball, boxing, autos, and, of course, hockey. Emile, Maman pointed out, would probably become a priest. Already he was an altar boy....

"And here," she said, "is Marie, who is six, and Cécile, who is our baby...."

"Ah," said Father Lebois, "Marie, and Cécile. And, Marie, what are you going to do when you grow up?"

Marie revealed a deep frown, and stared at the priest.

"A street girl!" she cried out in defiance.

Maman reddened. Father Lebois choked a smile. And Louis shrugged his shoulders. This too will pass away, he wanted to say, if only we make nothing of it. Maman went to the blackboard and put a red mark against Marie's name, and the latter frowned again.

"And you, Cécile?" the priest asked, fearing the worst.

Cécile hesitated, scratched her derrière and said nothing. Now, suddenly, Father Lebois seemed in a hurry. Maman told Laurent he was in charge. Then she invited Father Lebois to step into the *parloir*, and the priest smiled in appreciation of this distinct honor. Though muscular and tall, the young priest moved deliberately always, but after Maman had closed the door, and she and Louis were alone with him in the quiet of the *parloir*, he began to speak. He spoke so fast they could ask no questions. Before they knew just what the problem was, they were in the thick of it.

"She is an orphan," said Father Lebois, pouring his words without letup, "truly an unfortunate waif of fortune, the ill fortune of her parents. The father—he was Canadien—was killed in a street fight before she was ten and her mother died two months later. I knew her mother: truly she was a saintly woman, my own mother will testify to that. An aunt, a sister of her father, in New Hampshire, finally took the little girl into her house, but she is an unwanted child; there is no peace there for the child. And now this aunt says she can't handle her any more. She says that Sophia is a bad one, has gotten herself into bad company. The aunt does not want her in her house any more.... And right at the start of the school year...."

Louis turned to Maman. He was lost. What was this leading up to?

"It is a very sad story," said Maman vaguely.

"Right now," continued Father Lebois, "she is with the Sisters. In Berlin, but it is temporary. They have no place for her, really. Their shelter is for younger—much younger—girls. The Sisters have written to me—I was their priest for a while. There is no money, and no hope of money from the aunt. But I'm determined that she'll graduate fom high school, if she's to make a life for herself. Don't you agree, Madame Martel?"

"But, of course," agreed Maman vaguely.

"This aunt," shot in Louis, "is simply throwing her out?"

"It amounts to that," admitted the priest. "She is a sister of the father. It is a sinful thing she is doing...."

"It is, Father," said Louis, "but why tell us about this?"

"Yes, Father," asked Maman. "There are so many unfortunates, and so many sinful things ... why this one?"

"Ah," said the priest, "but this one I know personally. I have lived with these facts, in this special case, and the heart in such instances leaves the conscience no peace at all, and I must do what I can do...."

Louis, Louis Martel told himself, observe the technique of an expert. It is a pleasure to watch, but note well that you, or someone, is being set up for a long, long pass.

"Is there no family," asked Louis, "that will take her in?"

"An excellent question!" said Father Lebois. "And to it there is a sad answer. The aunt is the only relative, and she has never forgiven her brother for marrying somebody else but a Canadienne.... The mother of this poor little girl was Polish.... This child is unwanted. There is—well—some bad feelings...."

"Shameful!" said Maman suddenly.

Now, thought Louis, there should be some reference to the Sermon on the Mount, or a glowing picture of the virtues of this little orphan. This young Father knew his business. Now, watch....

"Of course," said the priest, lowering his head, "I must tell you, since you will want to know, and I must be absolutely frank with you, that Sophia is—well—reputed to be a bad one."

"Bad one?" snapped Louis. No, this smart man was taking the wrong approach. Who can sell a bad apple?

"The good Sisters," said the priest, "tell me she really is, as the aunt alleges, a bad one, a hard child to govern. Weeps all the time. Fights. Really fights with her fists. Sulks. Won't take care of her clothes. Won't do anything at all until she's good and ready to do it."

"I'm pained to hear this," said Louis, eyeing the priest. Now, Monsieur Lebois, what other maneuver will you pull?

"Poor little girl!" exclaimed Maman.

"What would you advise a young priest," said he, "in a situation like this? Frankly, Monsieur and Madame Martel, I have come only for this."

Louis gazed at his pipe. Now, that was real clever. Maman would fall for that. Here, here it comes.

"*Mon Dieu!*" said Maman. "She needs a good home."

"That's it," agreed Father Lebois violently, "and thank you!" Now he calmed down very quickly. "I have to find her, as you say, a home, a good home." He turned and fixed his eyes steadily on Louis. The counterattack was probably best.

"We're full up here," he stated firmly.

"Otherwise," added Maman, "we'd be glad to help."

"More tea," said Louis. Hell, I've got a houseful of kids right now. Perhaps for a few days, at most a week, to help out.

"It would be," continued Father Lebois implacably, "a matter of a few weeks only, at the most. The good Sisters in Berlin assure me that by that time they hope to find a place for her, somewhere...."

"Will you have more tea?" said Maman quietly.

"It wouldn't be so bad," continued the priest quickly, "if she had her diploma. Why, I could find her employment and a home right in Berlin, or elsewhere. But they don't want her at the high school either...."

"Nobody seems to want to help this girl but you, Father!" exclaimed Louis, getting irritated by all this.

"I know the Sister Superior in Berlin, and she is a high-booted Napoléon," the priest went on at high speed, "and if Sophia is a bad one, why, they feel they don't want her to agitate the others. Now, of course, if I could find her a home right here in Groveton, Father Giroux is the high-booted Napoléon at St. Michel High School...." He ended this with a quiet smile of power and then began to survey the *parloir*, probably looking for a spare bed, thought Louis.

He realized his pipe had gone dead and he lit it again.

"Well ..." he offered slowly, "we're full up here. All the bed space is taken up, two to a room as it is now, that is until Laurent marries. But right at this time, Father...."

The priest squared his shoulders and slowly enunciated the next sentence. Near the goal, after the series of smart stick-handling, he was now ready to pass the puck.

"To you who have so much," he said, "the Lord asks for just a little bit. Are we going to keep Him waiting?"

"At least two weeks," replied Louis swiftly.

Maman pursed her lips. She too was scheming, but if she weakened, he was lost too.

"This," she asked, "would be for only a week or so?"

"At the most!" announced the priest earnestly. "And if the good Sisters cannot find a place, why, we'd all have to trust to Providence...."

"And an extra bed," added Louis. "Now, let's see. If Laurent moves in with Félix and Emile, into their room until he marries—and that's two long weeks from now—and Maurice sleeps in the *parloir*, that'll give us an extra room, and an extra bed with this loveseat...."

"My loveseat!" exclaimed Maman, scandalized.

"...And," continued Louis, "if we can talk Thérèse into sharing a room with Marie, that would leave Cécile, alone in the little room.... This might make room for ... for this little girl...."

"Yes!" said Father Lebois, his mouth open. "That's good!"

"Good," agreed Louis, "but not wise. We've got to keep the boys away from the girls...."

"Oh," said the priest.

"Oh, yes," said Louis, "it is a fact of life."

He took a pencil and a used envelope, and drew a rough plan of his apartment. In the square now occupied by Emile and Félix he wrote in 10 and 12, the one assigned to Marie and Cécile he jotted down 6 and 4, in the square representing the room of Maurice and Laurent he wrote in 18 and 20, and in the room given over to Thérèse he scribbled 16. Then he began to erase all these figures. He moved Marie and Cécile out of their room and moved them into Thérèse's room.

"It's all right, Cécile?" he asked Maman.

"So far," she replied, frowning in concentration.

Louis then moved Maurice and Laurent to Marie's former room.

"They'll be crowded," commented Maman.

Then Louis moved Marie and Cécile into the room formerly assigned to Maurice and Laurent. Maman approved with a smile. Then he again moved Maurice into the room occupied by Félix and Emile, left Félix there, and moved Emile out.

"And where does Emile sleep?" asked Maman.

"In the *parloir*," said Louis.

"Where? On the loveseat?" asked Maman sadly. Her new loveseat!

"On the loveseat, where else?" asserted Louis. "After all, Emile might become a priest!" he added, and turned toward Father Lebois.

The priest nodded solemnly. Louis wrote 16 in the large front room and thus restored Thérèse to her old room.

"That," he concluded, "will make the boys' large bed available for Thérèse's room. It is a large double bed."

"For two weeks," said Maman, passing a loving hand over her loveseat. "And Emile is not a boy who's hard on things."

"And this little girl?" Louis asked. "How old is she?"

"Just seventeen," said Father Lebois sadly, "and already the boys chase her. It's a pity, but she's also very beautiful."

"At seventeen," Louis murmured, "everybody is beautiful!"

He wrote in 17 in the room now also assigned to Thérèse.

"Yes," agreed Father Lebois, studying the plan over Louis's shoulder. "It will be good for Sophia to share a room with someone her age."

"Now then," continued Louis, "when Laurent marries, perhaps we can make new arrangements, if she is still with us...."

"That's a good plan," said Father Lebois, beaming.

"And this will be good for Thérèse also," said Maman, "and if this little girl, Sophia, comes to our house, she'll be family...."

"That would be fine," said the priest, suddenly very calm.

"Subject to the same rules and regulations," snapped Louis.

"And to the same love," added the priest.

"That goes without saying," said Maman.

Louis suddenly frowned. When had he said he would do all this?

"Well, now, I haven't said yes yet," he objected. "I'm only thinking with my mouth open. As you see, Father, we are crowded...."

"Monsieur Martel," said the priest quietly, "that's exactly why I picked you. There's always room for one more child at the table of a good family."

"For," threatened Louis, "if Laurent weren't getting married...."

"Yes," said the priest soothingly, "and your son is marrying a nice Catholic girl of excellent parents—Hélène Pelletier. A fine family!"

"A fine family," agreed Louis, "and they'll have nice children, I know!"

"If it pleases God," added Maman.

"And if it weren't for that," continued Louis, "this business would be out of the question. I would say, 'No! Positively!'"

"And I wouldn't question your good judgment," added the priest emphatically.

"Because," continued Louis coldly, "to make room at the bottom, or in the middle, there's got to be movement at the top. If my children don't start moving out and into their own nuptial beds pretty soon, there won't be room in here for new ones to spring out of my own, including orphans."

"God provides," said Maman, suddenly delighted.

"Yes, Madame Martel," said Father Lebois, getting up to leave.

"God arranges all these things."

"If He does," Louis snapped, "why didn't you pass Him the puck?"

The priest, however, looked directly at Louis once more.

"And you'll make a home for Sophia?" he asked.

"Yes," he said firmly. "I don't give in easily, but when I do, I hold back nothing!" Now, he had said it. How could he be such an easy mark?

"Yes," added Maman, strangely excited by this turn of events, "this little girl is welcome to what we have to give."

"One more thing," said the priest in a low voice. "There is no money."

"There is no need," said Louis proudly. And there it was. He was now committed. Since when had his home become an orphan asylum? No matter. He would do his best for this little girl. A bad one, was she? He would see. Hell, two weeks at the most. It would pass quickly ... He'd been taken in, that was clear!

There was not much time to prepare the children for Sophia's arrival—less than a day and a night—but Louis and Maman did their best. Laurent was too busy getting ready for his own wedding to be overly concerned, as he and Hélène Pelletier had to paint and furnish their new apartment. Maurice and Félix took it all very calmly, though they spent a little more time than usual before the mirror combing and recombing their black hair. Emile looked forward to sleeping alone in the *parloir* and reading late at night.

Marie and Cécile were enthusiastic, but when Louis outlined his plan, Thérèse became moody, and when he was finished, she began to pout. She did not make any comment, nor did she join in the general fun and frolic of moving things from one room into another. When the large bed was finally set up in her room, which she was to share with Sophia, she suddenly spoke up.

"I bet she can't even speak French!"

"I bet," said Louis, "you can't even speak Polack."

"Polish!" corrected Maman quietly.

"I'm French," said Thérèse with sudden passion, "and the French language and French culture are the highest in the world!"

"They are very high, indeed," said Maman, "and you can be proud that you are of French blood, but Sophia can speak French and English and Polish too, but that does not make her better or worse than you, unless...." And Maman raised one index toward her.

"Unless what?" snapped Thérèse.

"Unless," continued Maman, "you prove yourself better before God—where it counts—with a little humility!"

"Isn't it better to be French?" Thérèse shot out.

"It's perhaps better," murmured Louis tenderly as he placed a rough hand over her silky black hair, "than being a Henglish haristo-crat, but it's no guarantee that the sun'll shine...."

"Papa!" Maman cried out in warning.

"...out of your derrière!" finished Louis.

"But she's a bad one!" raged Thérèse.

Louis cast a glance toward Maman.

"Why do you say that?" she asked Thérèse.

"Because ... because that's what they all say!"

"Who are they?" snapped Maman.

"All the kids!"

Maman looked toward Louis. It was going to be harder than expected. Oh, the terrible, terrible telegraphy of children, that spanned the long centuries, the barriers of countries and the walls of lan-guages.... Louis went up to Thérèse, put his hand under her chin that she might look him directly in the eye.

"And besides," he said evenly, in a low voice, "she's Polack!"

"Polish!" quickly corrected Maman.

"Let me tell you something," said Louis, "that I have pounded nails with Polacks...."

"Poles!" said Maman quietly.

"And Wops!"

"Italians," said Maman quietly.

"Italians," conceded Louis, "and Dutchmen and Swedes and Canucks...."

"French-Canadians!" said Maman haughtily.

"And all of them," continued Louis, "pray to the same Lord that you do, my precious future little nun, and they all do in their own lingo, and some of them are dumb as hell sometimes, and sometimes smart as hell, but all of them all the time are in God's heart and mind, like you and me!"

"I know that, Papa," answered Thérèse, near to tears.

"Do you, now, my pretty one?" he asked softly. "Maybe you think you do, at Mass, when your heart is full of Sunday-morning love and your tummy with flapjacks, but do you know it on Monday morning?"

Thérèse's mouth formed a quick answer, but she couldn't speak; her lips began to tremble. She turned toward Maman for support.

"Papa is right," said Maman firmly.

"And let me tell you something else," he continued, taking a deep breath. "Before I married your mother, when I was a lumberjack...."

"Oh, that story again!" Thérèse nearly screamed.

"Yes, that story!" said he in a firm voice. "When I was a lumberjack, one night, I stopped for a drink at a saloon, and an old Indian came in. He was from up North, and these Redskins never were known for their beauty. I must tell you that, without hesitation. This particular one was so ugly it made you want to sit down to compose yourself!"

There was some laughter, and he laughed also.

"Well," he continued, "this ugly-looking Indian—I tell you he had lost all the cheeks in his face—well, he wanted a drink. Just as I did, for, as you know, the great thirst assails all men, Indians too, just as does the great hunger of the stomach, and that other hunger of the flesh, the greatest hunger of them all...."

"Never mind, Louis!" snapped Maman.

"Anyhow," he continued, "Indians were not allowed to buy drinks at the bar.... Did you know that?"

"It made them wild," Maurice contributed quickly.

Quietly Louis turned toward him.

"It made them as wild," he asserted, "as it did any greenhorn who drank too much! Well, sir, this Indian, uglier yet because of his thirst, just stood there, two feet away from the bar, his mouth parched, his eyes fixed now on the colored bottles on the shelves, and now on anybody who would buy him a drink—you could do that, all right— and so I bought him one, and then another, and we conversed, man to man, and behind that long nose, and beady eyes, and dried-up cheeks, there was, I'm here to tell you, a smart brain, and do you know what?"

"What, Papa?" shot in Marie, admiringly.

"He gave me some of his secrets!"

"Secrets!" screamed Cécile in great wonder.

"Yes, mademoiselle! That night, we became friends, and the next day he took me into the woods and showed me exactly where to find the herbs and the plants that cure the maladies that mystify the doctors.... These herbs you boil, you see, and you drink the juice...."

"Ugh!" commented Maman, making a face of disgust.

"All right for you," said Louis, looking hurt, and turning toward Maman, "but it cured your backache when for weeks Dr. Lafrance could do nothing for you! But the point—the point of this—the moral, my children! This Indian had two beautiful daughters!"

"The ugly Indian?" asked Marie, breathless.

"With no cheeks?" screamed Cécile.

"Yes! It is a thing to remember that some of the most beautiful blooms emerge from the damnedest swamps! He had two lovely maiden daughters!"

"*Batege!*" exclaimed Maurice.

"What were their names?" asked Marie, enthralled.

"And I tell you," continued Louis, "I was introduced to them that very night...."

"So?" Thérèse asked very coolly.

"Papa, their names, plea-ea-se?" shouted Marie.

"Did they have cheeks?" screamed Cécile.

"Oh, yes," continued Louis, "and one fine day, both of them came softly walking through the village, in their moccasins and fine Indian dresses of many colors—both were slim, round-faced, dark-eyed, and graceful as elks.... And all the village sports came out of their hiding places, as if this was the circus, and went chasing after them...."

"I bet," said Maurice, biting his fingernails.

"But not one of them," said Louis, "could get a tumble...."

And Louis brought his right hand down sharply, like the sudden drop of the guillotine.

"Their names?" begged Marie.

"Oh yes!" And now Louis remembered. "The prettiest one, with the singing voice was Mockingbird, and the other, the frightened one, with the troublesome eyes, was called Moon Shadow!"

"Moon Shadow!" Marie whispered.

"Eh, *tonnerre!*" murmured Maurice.

"Well," continued Louis, "they were pippins, Indians or no, and I say that a pippin is a pippin in any country, and in that town I was the only fellow for which they would smile, they would talk to, whose jokes they found funny. Only Louis Martel! Only I could take them out, and I did, and that's a fact!"

"Both of them?" asked Laurent, his mouth open.

"One at a time," explained Louis. "That was before I met your Maman, and each in turn. I, Louis Martel, treated them both like princesses, which they were in manner and decorum, and I had them laughing, in stitches, all the time, and they made me a belt for to wear on holidays...."

"Yes, Pa," interrupted Laurent, "they were pippins, but in this case, what is the moral?"

"This!" And Louis took a deep breath. "If I had married either one of them, it is a fact that you'd all be beautiful Indian children!"

The younger children laughed in delight.

"We couldn't drink in a bar," countered Maurice thoughtfully.

Louis raised his right hand toward heaven solemnly.

"It could have happened!" he declared.

"But Papa, it didn't," said Thérèse coldly, "and we are not Indians, and that's a fact too."

Louis took a deep breath, frowned, sucked on his dying pipe.

"What Papa means," said Maman quietly, "is that Jesus stated: 'Suffer little children to come unto me!' He opened His heart to everyone. He didn't particularize!"

"That's it, damn it," barked Louis. "He didn't particularize whether they were Polacks...."

"Poles," said Maman.

"Or Wops...."

"Italians."

"Or colored, or Jews, or Canucks...."

"Or French-Canadians," said Maman impatiently.

"Or, for that matter," he concluded, "Protestants like Pete Young!" Maman said nothing.

"That's right," exclaimed Emile brightly. "He did not particularize."

"I know damn well that's right!" shouted Louis. "And furthermore, in this particular instance, I am putting down both feet on the floor in regards to this young girl who is to live in this house. I shall be very strict with the marks!"

"With Sophia too?" taunted Thérèse.

"With Sophia too," added Louis, "as with everybody else!"

Ah, the magic of that blackboard! How often, Louis thought, he should thank Cécile. For the mere mention of it seemed to calm Thérèse down immediately—and everyone else.

When Sophia Lewicka was brought to the Martel home, Louis Martel carried her two suitcases and one bundle of clothes into the kitchen where the entire family waited. He introduced her slowly to all. Maman came to her and gave her a nice, warm hug, but Sophia, slim, with blue eyes, blond hair, a fixed stare, stood near the door, her arms at her sides, not knowing what to do next.

As per previous instructions, Laurent and Maurice shook her hand and carried her bags into Thérèse's room, Marie, Cécile, Félix and Emile mumbled in turn that, yes, indeed, she was welcome, and Thérèse, without a word, showed her where the bathroom was and the room where she was to sleep, and then steered her back into the kitchen. Louis then excused himself and went out, and Maman went back to her stove, consciously tending to her supper. For an awkward moment, the children faced one another, and then turned toward Sophia, who still stood frozen near the door. At this moment, Laurent snapped his suspenders once or twice, and bowing slightly toward her, pointed toward a chair near the dining table.

"Please take a chair!" said Laurent. "My Papa says, when you are resting everything else, the tongue speaks easier."

The children laughed.

She moved toward a chair and Maurice quickly held it for her, and she sat down. Maman took one sly look toward her, and forced herself to continue with her supper preparations. The children stared hard at her blond hair. Now, thought Maman, the weather should come up for serious discussion....

"The weather," commented Laurent, "has been getting colder all the time." He sat down near Sophia and looked into her cold blue eyes. She said nothing.

"Yes, indeed," agreed Maurice, "the weather's been something," as he saw that Sophia was a real pip.

Marie and Cécile giggled toward Sophia and crowded near her at the table, and then everybody sat at the table also. Thérèse sat on the other side, facing Sophia. Sophia sat, her face still without expression, and stared at them with cold eyes, until suddenly she spotted the blackboard. At the bottom of the list of names, printed in letters equal in size to the other names, was her name: Sophia.

"What's that for?" she asked, a cloud of suspicion in her eyes.

That broke the ice. All of them competed with one another in words to tell her, and as quickly as possible.

"It's a peculiar idea of Maman," tartly concluded Thérèse. "Kind of silly, don't you think?"

"I don't know," said Sophia in a low voice.

"I think it's silly," said Thérèse finally. "As if we were all infants. Don't you think it's idiotic?"

"I don't know," murmured Sophia.

"I wish," Thérèse snapped, as she watched with one eye her Maman busily working at the stove, "that for once I was in a family without an idiotic blackboard! Just once!"

Cockily she glared at Sophia, and then turned sharply toward her Maman, but she only pursed her lips in great concentration on her supper preparations, and worked steadily, without hearing a word, it seemed, as if she had become suddenly deaf.

"Maybe," Thérèse hinted, looking sideways toward Sophia, "you can ask Papa to take your name off...."

"Why?" asked Sophia in sudden panic.

"Because..." said Thérèse. "Just because."

"No," said Sophia, in a low voice.

"You like it?" asked Marie hopefully.

"I don't know," said Sophia lamely.

"You'd like to win a bag of candies!" shouted Marie in triumph. Sophia turned toward Marie.

"No," said Sophia, "because if I ever won, I'd give it away. I don't like candies very much."

"You don't? " asked Cécile, deeply shocked.

Laurent cleared his throat, snapped his suspenders once, and when Cécile suddenly reached with her little hand into the large sugar bowl, he looked sharply at her, but she had withdrawn enough sugar for a mouthful and now she ate it smugly.

"I didn't like the blackboard once," he announced, "but as you grow older and begin to assume responsibility...."

"Well, well," purred Thérèse, "look at the little papa, all of you! He's not married yet, and already he's gone over to the opposition!"

"Yes," laughed Maurice, "just because you're going to live with a wife, this does not make you a patriarch, you know!"

Sophia turned toward Laurent. She cleared her throat. She was making a real effort.

"You are marrying soon?" she asked.

"Yep. In two weeks."

"God bless you!" she whispered.

"Thank you," he said. "I wish you, too, much happiness."

Sophia smiled a bit, and then there was a silence that lasted a minute or two. Cécile fidgeted, then turned a smiling face toward Sophia. Suddenly she got off the chair, picked up a broken-down doll off the floor—one arm was missing and her eyes were pushed in—sat down again near Sophia and then gave Sophia her doll. Sophia took it and made a pretense of looking at it and then being shocked at the wounded doll. Cécile giggled.

"I wish," Marie gasped suddenly, "I were getting married!"

"You're too young," said Thérèse.

"And I was wearing a long veil, and Maman cried because I was going away...."

"You'd make a nice bride," said Laurent, "and if it weren't that I'm already promised...."

"Hooked," said Maurice, "by a pair of dark eyes!"

"In any case," announced Laurent, "we'll have a blackboard in my house!" He looked toward Maman. This, she heard, and turned to look at him in turn. She nodded agreement. It was a victory that had been long in coming to her. Laurent, my first-born!

"Not in my house," said Félix, who at eleven was nowhere near marriage. Suddenly he was surprised. He'd gotten a word in edgewise.

Then there was a short pause.

"I don't know," said Thérèse, entranced by her indecision. "Maybe I would, and maybe I wouldn't."

"Maybe I would," repeated Marie, "and maybe I wouldn't!"

"I would," said Sophia suddenly.

"Why?" asked several voices.

"Did you have it in your house?" asked Thérèse pointedly.

"No," said Sophia.

"Then, how would you know?"

"I don't know," replied Sophia.

"That's it, you just don't know," said Thérèse with finality.

"I know this," Sophia replied, looking directly at her. "I like to be told where I stand. I like that. I like to know that!"

"Don't you know anything?" Thérèse asked sharply.

Sophia's blue eyes suddenly glittered.

"I know something you don't know," she snapped.

"No foolishness now," said Thérèse casually, "and what's that?"

Sophia suddenly brought up both closed fists forward.

"I know that you're lucky," she asserted, "and you're too stupid to know it!"

"Me!" screamed Thérèse.

Sophia held her two fists forward, ready to use them. Laurent and Maurice exchanged regards of admiration.

"Yes, you!" asserted Sophia.

Maman stopped working near the stove. She listened a minute, without looking, pursed her lips. Painfully, she then decided to go on doing what she had been doing. So long as they were both only exchanging hot words. Was the League of Nations doing any better?

"What do you mean?" cried out Thérèse, suddenly taken aback.

"I mean this," said Sophia, slowly lowering her fists, "that ... that it's nice to have your name on a blackboard. Somewhere. It's nice to know that what you do, good or bad, means something. To somebody. To anybody. That's ... all I mean."

"Right," agreed Laurent. He sighed and looked at Maurice. There would be no scrap, after all.

"It means something, all right," commented Félix.

"It means a bag of candy," argued Cécile.

"It means," said Laurent smugly, "that you know where you stand."

"Oh," said Maurice, throwing out his chest and flexing his muscles, "you know damn well where you stand."

He gasped at his own words and everyone turned toward Maman.

She put the ladle from the pea soup pot on the stove, peered anxiously into the large pot where steam was rising to the ceiling, wiped her hands on her apron and slowly walked up to the blackboard and quickly chalked a red mark against Maurice's name. Taken aback, he now gazed at Maman with cold eyes. In the silence that followed, Laurent smiled quietly, Félix smiled, Emile was noncommittal, Marie made faces at Maurice (and Maman did not see that!) and Cécile counted all the red marks and white marks with her outstretched finger and got all mixed up. Sophia looked up toward Thérèse and there was a message of peace in the barely perceptible curl of a snicker on their lips....

Louis returned then and put three large bottles of Moxie into the icebox, noticed that Sophia seemed to feel at home, and then turned toward Maman. Had his smart and decent children been smart and decent? No, Maurice had not. He looked at the blackboard, turned toward Maurice and looked at him as he pretended to study his fingernails.

"*Alors*, Maman?" he asked.

"Yes," said she.

Slowly now, Louis added up the plus and minus marks, and a deep silence crept into the kitchen. He shook his head. He picked up the eraser and at one stroke wiped all the red marks—and there was a short cheer. Next he picked up the white chalk and opposite each name he put one white mark, and one for Sophia too. Everybody cheered. And Sophia smiled for the first time and settled more comfortably into her chair.

Maman had prepared a supper of hot pea soup, boiled beef, home-fried potatoes, carrots, with a side dish of beets. For dessert there was ice cream, and tea and milk. After supper, and while the girls, and Sophia, cleared the table and washed the dishes, the men, that is, Louis, Laurent, Maurice, Félix and Emile sat around while Maman read in French, in her best teacher's diction, items from *Le Messager*, the local French-Canadian daily, and then, in English but with traces of hesitation, from the Groveton *Daily Herald*.

And then the girls were finished, and Louis served them each a tall glass of Moxie, and then he served the boys, and then he poured himself a shot of whisky, and lit his story-listening pipe. And Maman read them the story of young Adam Dollard, scieur des Ormeaux, whose selfless heroism and bravery and death, at Long Sault, with sixteen of his companions, saved the French colonists in the early days of French Canada against scalp-hungry Iroquois.

Maman read this epic, reminiscent of the Alamo, with vigor, rising intonations and dramatic pauses.... Once, Emile was seen to duck suddenly, as hundreds of Iroquois lunged screaming toward the fort held by the intrepid Frenchmen.... And Louis, holding to his pipe as a weapon, ducked and fought back, one with the defenders, as all of them, except one who managed to escape, were attacked, always by overwhelming numbers, and finally slaughtered to a man!

"And before going," Maman added, "they all had made their peace with God!"

It was past nine when the story was finished, and Maman kissed Marie and Cécile and Emile, and they in turn kissed their Papa on both cheeks, said their prayers and went to bed. Any whimpering meant a red mark and cheerful conformity meant an added squeeze from their Papa. At ten, Félix was bidden *"bonsoir"* and went through the same routine, and then Laurent, Maurice and Thérèse also. Maman now went to Sophia and took her in her arms. Sophia froze. But Maman hugged her, though her hands remained to her side. Now Maman kissed her on both cheeks.

"Bonsoir, Sophia," said Louis.

She nodded quickly at him and Maman escorted her to her bedroom.

Louis lit his pipe. Now, was she really a bad girl? What did anyone mean by bad girl? A bad girl was a girl, he had once heard, who went to bed with any lumberjack for the price of a brace of cordwood. Well Sophia was not *that* kind. Would Father Lebois permit her to sleep with sweet, pure, pestiferous Thérèse? No.

What other kind of bad girl was there? There had been his own sister. At seventeen, she had run away with a man, right after High Mass. Had she been a real bad girl? The man came from the brilliant world and his sister had been fooled. Was that real bad? If we think so in this world, may God forgive us in the next!

It's just that … a virgin of seventeen is a damn nuisance to some, and so is a boy of eighteen, and so is a keg of dynamite. But the greater pests are those who can see but a thin line between holiness and whoredom, and no pathway between…. The Creator Himself put the dynamite there. He expects explosions. Who are we to seek anything else?

O Lord, thank you that I'm no longer seventeen! Thank you that I'm spared from the frightened wisdom of those heavy in years who won't allow you in peace and comfort to make your own favorite mistakes—the ones they would like to repeat! Thank you to spare me now from those who remember not the hot cauldron that prevents the young from sitting for long anywhere at any time, who forget with what force unknown passions seek and must find outlets before one is ripe, who now remember in tranquillity only passions spent and misspent…. Thank you, Lord, and grant me humility.

Thank you, Lord, to remind me that you made parents out of people, and that from such can be born neither geniuses, nor criminals, nor idiots, but too often embarrassing hunks of ourselves. Thank you, Lord, and help me help this little bad one…. And while You are at it, help me help myself too!

He smoked his pipe and nodded in agreement with his own conclusions.

That next morning, Thérèse was commissioned by her Papa himself to take Sophia to St. Michel's High School and to register her. He warned Thérèse there might be difficulties.

"It is a task I don't envy you," he told her.

"Why?" asked Thérèse, suddenly alerted. "She's got as much right as anyone else. She's Catholic!"

"Sure," purred Louis, "but can you manage to get her in at this late date?"

"We'll see about that!" promised Thérèse firmly.

"Well," he hesitated, "I guess I'll have to depend on you, *mon amour!*"

After Sophia and Thérèse left together, he donned his work clothes, winked at Maman, and went to work, whistling. Sophia was admitted, of course, for Father Giroux, "the Napoléon of the school system," had been there before himself and greased the way. When the two girls came home that afternoon, Thérèse informed Maman that, yes, it had been hard, but she, Thérèse, had led her by the hand and Sophia had been admitted finally. Maman smiled and put a white chalk mark opposite Thérèse's name.

And then the two girls found that their clothes had been washed, and lay in a basket, damp-dry, to be ironed for the next day. Sophia picked up her clothes—Maman had emptied her suitcases—all the clothes she had in the world—then turned to Thérèse.

"I don't have to wash them," she announced. "See, they are all washed already!"

"Oh, yes," replied Thérèse casually. "Maman does all that," and she sat down royally in the nearest chair.

"You both do the ironing," said Maman calmly.

"I've never done that," said Sophia, hurt.

"Then you'll learn how," said Maman firmly. "Thérèse is very good, and she'll teach you."

"Maman!" Thérèse whined, but she did.

Supper time, once more, and though Sophia felt more and more at ease, she still spoke very little, and then only a few well-chosen words. After supper, and homework, Maman announced that this time she would read something different.

"Something peaceful, I hope," said Louis, lighting his pipe.

Slowly and distinctly, this time, Maman read the life story of a young girl, destined to become world famous, certainly not for great deeds as the world measures them, Maman explained, but for greater acts in the eyes of God. Thérèse Martin was born in France in 1873, the youngest of four sisters. Her family was well-to-do but average. When she was but five, her mother died of cancer. Early she resolved to give her life into God's service. "Heaven for me," she wrote later in her life, "will be doing good upon earth!" Félix yawned and slowly felt his pitching arm. Thérèse and Sophia were all ears. Cécile and Marie sat on their Papa's lap and listened.

As a young girl, Maman continued, and still in her very early teens, and yet convinced of her vocation, Thérèse pressed, against some of her family's objections, and against even those of a canon and a bishop, for permission to become a nun.

"Just a youngster!" protested Louis.

Thérèse decided, Maman continued, to petition Pope Leo XIII himself, and one day, when in his presence, she did. She begged permission to enter the Carmelite Order at the age of fifteen. Permission was granted and she became a Carmelite nun when she entered the Carmel of Lisieux in 1888. Too young to know her own mind, thought Louis, but then, at that early age, faith is at its purest, and the yearning to serve shines the brightest....

She underwent a rigid postulancy. Then she became very ill, and while a convalescent, she wrote her famous book, *Histoire d'Une Ame.* At twenty-four, she was dead of tuberculosis. "So young," said Maman, "and so beautiful, and so saintly, and hence why her impact was, is, and will be world-wide!"

Then Maman went on to explain why this was so. Not so much because of the miracles attributed to Thérèse, or because she prayed for snow when she entered the Convent, and that it snowed that day, or that she wrote a book that captured the hearts of many. No, said Maman, the world was now turning more and more to her, and the Pope was considering her beatification, and then eventually her canonization, now in 1923, because, perhaps, of Thérèse's way of life. "I shall spend my heaven," said Thérèse of Lisieux, "doing good on earth!"

Sophia stared straight ahead at the crucifix on the kitchen wall. Louis was sure the light in her blue eyes came from tears held back too long.... Thank God, he thought, I'm not seventeen, when you're no one and want to be everyone, when tears and laughter come for the same reasons and for no reasons that you understand, when you love and hate what you want and loathe, when the reality of what you see is deep, deep black and nothing but a great sacrifice, and the noblest deeds can square off the disquiet that haunts you for evils you have no memory of committing....

And now, they came, the tears down Sophia's cheeks, and her shoulders shook a bit and more tears came, and Maman looked up suddenly at her. Each, in turn, the children saw and then pretended not to see, for she wept silently. Louis stood up. Maman nodded to Laurent and he shepherded the others out of the kitchen. Louis took Marie and Cécile to bed.

"I don't know," he told them. "Something very sad hit her, all of a sudden, I guess."

That night, he slept in the *parloir* with Emile. He made himself a bed on the floor and Emile slept on the loveseat. Maman took Sophia to bed with her.

The next night, Maman read one of the adventures of Arsène Lupin, the great French detective, and held the whole family spellbound. One by one, again, all the children kissed their Maman and Papa. Almost casually now, Sophia kissed Maman on both cheeks. Suddenly she turned toward Louis.

"Good night, Monsieur Martel," she said, and smiled.

Louis looked up severely at her. He waved his index at her, indicating that she too should come and kiss him. Slowly, she approached him and pecked him quickly on the right cheek, and edged away.

"One moment, please," said Louis. "The left cheek? It will be lonely!"

She pecked at his left cheek and fled to her room, giggling.

When the children were all in bed, and quiet, Louis was relieved to be able to get back to his own bed. Still smoking his pipe, he flipped off his pants, and undershirt and underpants, grabbed his long nightgown and poked his head through the opening, puffing and blowing smoke all the while. He knelt by the bed, crossed himself, holding his pipe at a respectable forty-five degree angle from his mouth, and prayed intensely and briefly, quickly made the sign of the Cross and jumped into bed, yawning, still puffing on his pipe.

Maman had already put on her long, neck-high laced cotton nightgown and now, she too knelt near the bed for her prayers.

"It is going good with Sophia, *hein*?" said Louis.

"Good," said Maman curtly, not wishing to be disturbed during her devotions. She closed her eyes and lowered her head to concentrate.

"She's not a bad girl at all!" commented Louis.

"She's a good girl, yes, yes," agreed Maman, yawning, opening her eyes; she suddenly gave up, and rested comfortably on her knees by the bed. "Until last night," she added, "Sophia belonged to the bird kingdom."

"Now," said Louis, "what in hell is that?"

"The bird kingdom," insisted Maman. "Before, when I hugged her, did you notice how her arms remained by her sides? She wasn't accustomed to the hugging and the kissing. Didn't know how. She had no arms. Like a bird. No arms to embrace or to return a caress. Never had caresses and never gave caresses, until last night, or perhaps so long ago with her own mother, she had forgotten...."

"Yes," mused Louis, "the bird kingdom. No hugging, no kissing. It's enough to make anybody bad, your respectful servant included," he added with a laugh.

"Louis," she snapped, rising from her kneeling position, "that was a mighty short and sweet prayer you treated yourself to tonight. It seems to me your prayers are getting shorter and shorter every night."

"Getting older and older every night," said Louis, "and in many respects, this man, here, is not the man you married."

Maman slipped into bed beside him, settled herself comfortably against the small of his huge frame and sighed.

"However," she purred, "I notice that you still have an eye for the creatures at church every Sunday morning."

"I take notice," said Louis evenly, "that you take notice of that."

"It need not be taken notice of, particularly," she said, her head reared back in mock anger. "It strikes one's face that you scrutinize and analyze all the pretty legs that pass by everywhere...."

He sighed contentedly. He knocked his dying pipe against the shaving mug by his bedside table, and dropped the pipe into it. Then he raised himself on an elbow, bent his head near Maman's, kissed her ear and then tickled her in the ribs. Maman gurgled, giggled, and moved away.

"My dear Cécile," he said, with a chuckle in his throat, "my dear, dear *amie*, the best one any man ever had...."

He began to stroke her back gently, and she purred.

"On the left side, now," she begged.

"It is you I love," he continued, "and I love eternally, but when the day arrives that I stop gazing with fine appreciation at a passing pair of pretty legs, don't put me to pasture like an old horse...."

"No?" said Maman.

"No!" said he. "Shoot me!"

"Oh, you!" said Maman.

She sighed, turned toward him and put a sleepy arm around his neck.

"*Bonsoir*, Louis," she mumbled. Her head sought out and found the accustomed spot near his shoulder and rested there.

"*Bonsoir, mon amour*," he mumbled, yawning.

"It is you who is the bad one," she murmured gaily.

And then, slowly, they let go of all the burdens and the joys of the day and slept.

Sophia made out. Soon she had her first quarrel with Félix, and her first red mark, and their dramatic reconciliation. Soon also she and Thérèse shared secrets they shared with no one else. One week, she had the unenviable record of seven red marks. Once also, she got the bag of candy and promptly gave it to Cécile, as she had promised, and found out that this entitled her to two white marks for the following week.

Two weeks after Sophia arrived, Hélène Pelletier became the bride of Laurent at Sacred Heart Church, Father Lebois officiating. There was a breakfast and dance at Marceau's Dance Hall, and Louis danced with the bride and Maman danced with the groom, and the newlyweds went to Boston for their honeymoon, and when they returned their small apartment on Maple Street was ready.... And Emile moved out of the *parloir*. Nothing else changed, and the months went by....

Sophia made out. One Saturday night, she and Thérèse stayed outside the house, on a front porch, down the street, until eleven-fifteen. Louis was awfully mad at both of them.

"Papa," said Thérèse boldly, "we did nothing wrong. There were two new fellows we'd never seen before, and we talked...."

"We talked and talked," said Sophia. "Is that bad?"

"No," said Louis, "that is not bad...."

"Besides," she added, "we didn't know it was that late, and I have no watch...."

This stumped Louis a moment. He reached into his pants pocket and took out two one-dollar Ingersoll watches. First he listened to the ticking of one, and then of the other. Then he handed one to Sophia.

Both girls broke out into giggles, and Louis smiled also.

"Now," he stated simply, "we understand one another."

Another time, they gave themselves away. They found themselves talking excitedly before everybody about a movie they had seen. It was one Maman had forbidden them to see. Very specifically. Then and there she gave them both two red marks.

"Censorship!" cried out Sophia.

"No," said Louis. "Disobedience."

"Same thing!" cried out Thérèse.

"Don't press the point," warned Louis. How could Maman know if this movie was bad for the girls, for surely Maman had not seen it herself. Perhaps the priest had said so in church. Had he seen it himself? *Bonguienne*, concluded Louis, maybe he, Louis Martel, would have to see it, and decide this. After all, maybe it was a real whipper-snapper, and why miss it? But, in any case, children must obey their parents! And stay away from dynamite!

But Sophia did very well. She found the use of her arms. Twice she used them to push Maurice away when he got kiss-hungry and tickle-bent in the kitchen hallway. He never tried again. On the other hand— and Louis saw this himself by accident—the shy boy, once, who took her home after a school dance, found it very easy to hold her and kiss her in the hallway, near the door of the Martel kitchen.

"Don't break it up," he told the embarrassed pair, "on my account."

He smiled at them, as Sophia blushed and the boy quickly departed. It was only later that Louis remembered that it was Sophia who held the shy boy....

One fine day, she will graduate, thought Louis, and so will Thérèse, but something else will surely come up, for life is one damn thing after another, with young girls around the house, and young boys fully aware of it. One fine day, it should ease up, and parents could pick up their medals for conduct above and beyond the endurance of man.

One fine day, both she and Thérèse spent an afternoon shortening their skirts, and then rather brazenly came skipping into the kitchen where Maman was preparing onion soup.

"Not for Sunday Communion, I hope," she commented.

"What's wrong with them, Maman?" asked Thérèse with passion.

"They look 'fast' to me," said she, shrugging.

"But, Maman," screamed Thérèse, "all the girls are wearing them above the knees.... Yes, they are, Maman!"

"Yes, Maman!" screamed Sophia. She stopped short, aghast at what she had said. She put a hand over her mouth quickly.

Maman smiled.

"If you wish," she said simply.

Sophia flew into her arms.

"We can wear them?" she begged.

"No," said Maman.

About this time, Louis came in from work. Both girls turned to him as to the Supreme Court. He gazed judiciously at their legs.

"Nice legs both of you chickens have," he said. He put his hands under the kitchen faucet, lathered them and began to whistle an old song.

Thérèse, with this unexpected support, began to parade gingerly around the kitchen. Louis wiped his hands.

"However," he said slowly, "those skirts are just about the right size for Marie and Cécile."

"But, Pa!" implored Thérèse.

"Those skirts," he said, "are too short to be truly elegant."

"But, Pa!" said Thérèse. "The boys like to look at legs."

"Thérèse!" said Maman, her face very stern.

Louis slowly poured himself a shot of whisky, then raised his right arm, as he always did, on great occasions.

"That is true," he admitted, "but believe me, my little sirens, if you want the boys to keep looking, don't overexpose the merchandise!"

Sophia gurgled in laughter.

"Maybe he's right!" she exclaimed, and Louis bowed to her with a smile.

Sophia Lewicka remained at the Martels' nearly nine months. Both she and Thérèse, who were now inseparable, graduated from St. Michel's that June with honors. Thérèse got her first wrist watch, an expensive present by her Papa's standards. Father Lebois gave Sophia the same present, which he got at a wholesale price from a local jeweler. Maman gave them both a silver cross with a silver chain, and they were to use these at several dances that June at Old Orchard Beach. Maman liked the silver cross and chain so much herself that she expressed a wish for one too, and Sophia promised her one when she made her first money....

Late in June, Sophia left the Martels. Father Lebois took her to Boston where a job in a Catholic hospital awaited her. She wrote "home" every week for a year. She often spoke of a visit back to Groveton. Then she became a postulant nun in the order of the Sisters of Charity. Two years later, on their twenty-fourth wedding anniversary, "the bad one," as they still called her, sent "Maman" a new silver cross and chain, and to "Papa" an expensive pipe. A big one. "For story-listening," Sophia wrote.

They never saw her again. For Sophia Lewicka who, it seemed, had barely entered and passed through their lives, and yet somehow had found and given affection there, was now Sister Martha and attached to a hospital in the West. She would never come "home" again.

Each Christmas, and at each family birthday, there was always a cheerful note from Sister Martha, and the assurance of her continuing prayers and lasting love. First Maman, then Thérèse, then Marie—as the years went by—wrote to her, always on behalf of the entire family, and gave her the minutest details of their changing lives. And Louis, who listened to the letters as they were received, and as they were written in answer to them, never failed to add: "You should put in there also that the pipe she sent me is still a good pipe—never heats up—and that I put my arms around her and give her a big squeeze, even though she is a Sister, and all that folderol."

One night, Father Lebois came, and gave his report to the Martels.

"I have seen her!" he said. "The institution where she works—night and day—is for children with frightful diseases, children whom nobody but the good Lord Himself, or His servants on earth, look upon with love!.... You should see their eyes light up when she tells them her stories of laughter.... Or gives them a bath! Or feeds them! Monsieur and Madame Martel, I do believe she is a saint!"

"Perhaps," said Maman, "it all came about from reading the life of Sainte Thérèse, that night, long ago, when we wanted to love her and hoped that she would love us ...?"

"Perhaps," said Louis, "but something surely lit up in that little girl that night. Maybe we had the kindling, but no doubt God gave us the spark."

"Perhaps," said Father Lebois in quiet wonder.

Sophia's name was never removed from the list on the blackboard, even after she died suddenly at the age of thirty-two of an unknown disease. For one year, the family wore the conventional mourning, as if indeed they had lost a sister. But even before that, Father Lebois's report had caused Louis to think much about Sophia.

A saint? he wondered. Perhaps, and perhaps not. Surely not because a little forsaken girl needed a big job of giving and had found it.... Then all mothers with many children, and a big job of giving, were saints, without the benefit of brass bands. Yet, if Sophia was a saint, this had happened in his house.... That night, surely, Providence had caused the little girl to pause.... Father Lebois was a kind man who, perhaps, exaggerated....

However, if Providence had foisted this little troubled guest upon him, in all fairness, Providence perhaps had also decided to pay him off in this rare coin.... If this was so, how frightening the task, and how rewarding too the joy of the adult's blind groping to guide the young heart! Little Sophia Lewicka, an elect of the Lord? *Bonguienne!* If so, Messieurs, who else, these days, could say he'd been kissed by a saint?

"She was a bad one," he finally concluded for the benefit of his family, "the kind that gets and deserves a mezzanine box in Heaven for the big show." He lit his pipe and added: "I think she'll remember us all when we have to meet St. Pete, and save a few choice seats in the balcony for the likes of us."

Renascence

EDNA ST. VINCENT MILLAY

All I could see from where I stood
Was three long mountains and a wood;
I turned and looked another way,
And saw three islands in a bay.
So with my eyes I traced the line
Of the horizon, thin and fine,
Straight around till I was come
Back to where I'd started from;
And all I saw from where I stood
Was three long mountains and a wood.

Over these things I could not see;
These were the things that bounded me.
And I could touch them with my hand,
Almost, I thought, from where I stand!
And all at once things seemed so small
My breath came short, and scarce at all.

But, sure, the sky is big, I said:
Miles and miles above my head;
So here upon my back I'll lie
And look my fill into the sky.
And so I looked, and, after all,
The sky was not so very tall.
The sky, I said, must somewhere stop...
And—sure enough!—I see the top!
The sky, I thought, is not so grand;
I 'most could touch it with my hand!
And reaching up my hand to try,
I screamed, to feel it touch the sky.

I screamed, and—lo!—Infinity

Came down and settled over me;
Forced back my scream into my chest;
Bent back my arm upon my breast;
And, pressing of the Undefined
The definition on my mind,
Held up before my eyes a glass
Through which my shrinking sight did pass
Until it seemed I must behold
Immensity made manifold;
Whispered to me a word whose sound
Deafened the air for worlds around,
And brought unmuffled to my ears
The gossiping of friendly spheres,
The creaking of the tented sky,
The ticking of Eternity.

I saw and heard, and knew at last
The How and Why of all things, past,
And present, and forevermore.
The Universe, cleft to the core,
Lay open to my proving sense
That, sickening, I would fain pluck thence
But could not,—nay! but needs must suck
At the great wound, and could not pluck
My lips away till I had drawn
All venom out.—Ah, fearful pawn:
For my omniscience paid I toll
In infinite remorse of soul.

All sin was of my sinning, all
Atoning mine, and mine the gall
Of all regret. Mine was the weight
Of every brooded wrong, the hate
That stood behind each envious thrust,
Mine every greed, mine every lust.

And all the while, for every grief,
Each suffering, I craved relief
With individual desire;
Craved all in vain! And felt fierce fire
About a thousand people crawl;
Perished with each,—then mourned for all!

A man was starving in Capri;
He moved his eyes and looked at me;
I felt his gaze, I heard his moan,
And knew his hunger as my own.
I saw at sea a great fog bank
Between two ships that struck and sank;
A thousand screams the heavens smote;
And every scream tore through my throat.

No hurt I did not feel, no death
That was not mine; mine each last breath
That, crying, met an answering cry
From the compassion that was I.
All suffering mine, and mine its rod;
Mine, pity like the pity of God.

Ah, awful weight! Infinity
Pressed down upon the finite Me!
My anguished spirit, like a bird,
Beating against my lips I heard;
Yet lay the weight so close about
there was no room for it without.
And so beneath the weight lay I
And suffered death, but could not die.

Long had I lain thus, craving death,
When quietly the earth beneath
Gave way, and inch by inch, so great
At last had grown the crushing weight,
Into the earth I sank till I
Full six feet under ground did lie,
And sank no more,—there is no weight
Can follow here, however great.
From off my breast I felt it roll,
And as it went my tortured soul
Burst forth and fled in such a gust
That all about me swirled the dust.

Deep in the earth I rested now;
Cool is its hand upon the brow
And soft its breast beneath the head
Of one who is so gladly dead.

And all at once, and over all
The pitying rain began to fall;
I lay and heard each pattering hoof
Upon my lowly, thatchèd roof,
And seemed to love the sound far more
Than ever I had done before.
For rain it hath a friendly sound
To one who's six feet under ground;
And scarce the friendly voice or face:
A grave is such a quiet place.

The rain, I said, is kind to come
And speak to me in my new home.
I would I were alive again
To kiss the fingers of the rain,
To drink into my eyes the shine
Of every slanting silver line,
To catch the freshened, fragrant breeze
From drenched and dripping apple-trees.
For soon the shower will be done,
And then the broad face of the sun
Will laugh above the rain-soaked earth
Until the world with answering mirth
Shakes joyously, and each round drop
Rolls, twinkling, from its grass-blade top.

How can I bear it, buried here,
While overhead the sky grows clear
And blue again after the storm?
O, multi-colored, multi-form,
Belovèd beauty over me,
That I shall never, never see
Again! Spring-silver, autumn-gold,
That I shall never more behold!—
Sleeping your myriad magics through,
Close-sepulchred away from you!
O God, I cried, give me new birth,
And put me back upon the earth!
Upset each cloud's gigantic gourd
And let the heavy rain, down-poured
In one big torrent, set me free,
Washing my grave away from me!

I ceased; and through the breathless hush
that answered me, the far-off rush
Of herald wings came whispering
Like music down the vibrant string
Of my ascending prayer, and—crash!
Before the wild wind's whistling lash
The startled storm-clouds reared on high
And plunged in terror down the sky!
And the big rain in one black wave
Fell from the sky and struck my grave.

I know not how such things can be;
I only know there came to me
A fragrance such as never clings
To aught save happy living things;
A sound as of some joyous elf
Singing sweet songs to please himself,
And, through and over everything,
A sense of glad awakening.
The grass, a-tiptoe at my ear,
Whispering to me I could hear;
I felt the rain's cool finger-tips,
Brushed tenderly across my lips,
Laid gently on my sealèd sight,
And all at once the heavy night
Fell from my eyes and I could see!—
A drenched and dripping apple-tree,
A last long line of silver rain,
A sky grown clear and blue again.
And as I looked a quickening gust
Of wind blew up to me and thrust
Into my face a miracle
Of orchard-breath, and with the smell,—
I know not how such things can be!—
I breathed my soul back into me.

Ah! Up then from the ground spring I
And hailed the earth with such a cry
As is not heard save from a man
Who has been dead, and lives again.
About the trees my arms I wound;
Like one gone mad I hugged the ground;

I raised my quivering arms on high;
I laughed and laughed into the sky;
Till at my throat a strangling sob
Caught fiercely, and a great heart-throb
Sent instant tears into my eyes:
O God, I cried, no dark disguise
Can e'er hereafter hide from me
Thy radiant identity!
Thou canst not move across the grass
But my quick eyes will see Thee pass,
Nor speak, however silently,
But my hushed voice will answer Thee.
I know the path that tells Thy way
Through the cool eve of every day;
God, I can push the grass apart
And lay my finger on Thy heart!

The world stands out on either side
No wider than the heart is wide;
Above the world is stretched the sky,—
No higher than the soul is high.
The heart can push the sea and land
Farther away on either hand;
The soul can split the sky in two,
And let the face of God shine through.
But East and West will pinch the heart
That can not keep them pushed apart;
And he whose soul is flat—the sky
Will cave in on him by and by.

Past the Shallows

BETSY GRAVES

Imogene Larkin lay face-up on the wharf with her knees bent and her feet flat against the boards of the wharf. To shield her eyes from the noontime sun, she held at arms' length over her face her *Archie and Betty Comic Digest*, which she was also trying to read. The boards, warm from the sun, weathered, and curling up a little at the edges, felt good against her back, and the gentle motion of the water lapping against the sides of the wharf rocked her soothingly. She had pushed up her sweatshirt sleeves, but it was still breezy enough to keep the sweater on. She took off her glasses, rubbed her eyes and let them close, and then let the book drop to her chest so she could feel the sun on her face.

Glorious, cool June day, school out, and a whole week at camp, she thought. She felt lazy and content as a sleepy cat.

When she heard the sound of the motorboat, she got up. They were just rounding the point, she could see, when she replaced her glasses. She got up and waved her magazine at her oldest brother Pete and her grandparents Joe and Margaret. Her grandmother waved back, but Joe was shouting at Pete over the sound of the motor and didn't see her wave.

"They're here," she shouted up to the house, where her mother, Esther, and Buddy, her other brother, were getting lunch things ready.

Pete cut the engine thirty feet out and let the boat drift toward the wharf. He was more careful than usual, with Joe aboard. Joe was adamant about keeping all his boats unscratched and undented.

Esther, walking quickly and purposefully, came down from the house and called to Buddy to come too. He came out and trailed behind her, his hands stuck in his jeans pockets and his head down. He wore a ratty, too-large wool sweater that made him look even thinner than he was; Imo thought he looked droopy, like a houseplant someone had forgotten to water.

As the boat got closer, Imo caught the side of it and helped Pete keep it steady so that Joe and Margaret could get off easily.

"Hello, hello," Joe said jovially. "Put out the red carpet. We're here."

Imo helped her grandmother step from the boat to the wharf,

guiding her by the elbow. Dressed in a short-sleeved blue print cotton dress that puckered at the bosom and showed girdle lines about the hip, Margaret tried to climb up politely, keeping her sun hat steady on her head with one hand and holding her skirt closed around her knees with the other. She almost knocked Imo down. "You think I'd be used to that by now, after all these years," she said pleasantly, a little out of breath.

"Move out o' the way, Mumma," Joe said to his wife. He was short and barrel-chested, with close-cropped white hair and shining ice-blue eyes. He hoisted one thin leg over the gunnel and grunted as he stepped unsteadily to the wharf. Buddy moved forward and put his hand on the old man's arm to help him, but Joe pushed him away.

"I'm not feeble for Chrissake," Joe snapped.

The six of them stood on the wharf for several minutes, giving each other quick hugs and kisses, making exclamations about how everyone else looked; Buddy's height and Imo's new glasses got the most attention. They began to make their way toward camp, going one by one down the little runway that led from the wharf to shore. Bringing up the rear, Imo heard Pete mutter to Esther, "He's three sheets to the wind already."

"I can tell," she replied. "We'll just be nice for your grandmother's sake."

"Ya got some lemonade in there, Esther?" Joe yelled out. "I got quite a thirst."

"I think I can find some."

"Lemonade, made in the shade, stirred with an old man's wooden leg," he sang, tunelessly.

"Joe, we've all heard that one before," said Margaret.

He laughed. "So ya got t'hear it again. Lucky for you."

Imo caught up to her grandmother and took her arm. Margaret smiled at her. "The birches look nice, don't they?" Margaret said. "I've always loved them."

"Me too," Imo agreed.

"You'd best not be peeling off that birch bark for stationery," Joe warned her.

"The kids know it kills the trees," Esther said. "You've made that clear."

Imo remembered the time three or four years ago that she and Buddy had been pretending they were shipwrecked on a desert isle. Buddy had just torn off a piece of bark from one of the birch trees, planning to write on it a note that he could stuff into an empty Coke bottle and set adrift, when Joe caught him. Joe's lecture lasted for ten minutes and at the end of it Buddy was crying, though he tried not to show it.

"You'll want to put this steak in the fridge right away, Esther," Joe said, patting the brown bag he was carrying. "You don't want good meat like this t'spoil."

"No, we wouldn't want that," Esther said. She took the bag from him. "Let's go inside and I'll get you some lemonade."

Pete, Margaret, and Joe followed her into the camp.

Imo looked around for Buddy. He was down on the shore, watching a young waterskier skim the lake under the high sun. Imo ran toward him.

"Buddy, everybody's going inside now."

"Yeah, I know."

"They'll wonder where you are."

"I'll be up in a little while."

"We're gonna eat pretty soon, I think."

"I said, I'll be up in a little while."

She turned and ran back to camp, looking back once to see him skipping a flat stone across the surface of the shallow water near shore, letting it go with a hard jerk of his wrist.

Inside, in the dining room, Esther was arranging glasses on a tray, filling each one with ice cubes and lemonade. "Imo, there you are. Take these to Grammy and Grampa while I get the crackers out," she said.

"Ma, I think Buddy's upset."

"What's he upset about?" she asked, continuing to pour.

"I don't know. He's out there skipping rocks."

Esther didn't seem interested. "There," she said. "All ready. I'll be along in a minute." She went back into the kitchen.

Imo took the tray and found her grandparents sitting in the wicker chairs on the porch. Joe held binoculars up to his eyes to see more clearly the waterskier on the lake, and Margaret was sorting out photographs on her lap, handing them one by one to Pete, who was sitting on the floor beside her.

"That's really cute," said Pete, without conviction, looking at one of the pictures.

"What are they pictures of?" Imo asked, setting down the lemonade on the low table.

"Your cousins in California," Margaret replied. "These are pictures from last Easter."

"They have matching coats," said Pete.

"And hats, in robin's-egg blue," Margaret added.

Even though Imo could go for many months, happily, without looking at pictures of their Aunt Emily's daughters—identical twins with perfect features, long blond hair and beach tans, now ten years old and spoiled rotten—she sat down near Pete and looked through the pictures as if they were rare treasures. It was the look on her grandmother's face that did it. Margaret beamed as she told them the story behind each of the pictures, handing them carefully to Pete and Imo.

"There's Andrea with their cat, Fluffy—"

"She's down," Joe interrupted, gripping the binoculars and sitting on the edge of the wicker seat. "But that was a good run."

"And this is outside their church. That's your Uncle Dan in front of his new car."

Pete yawned. Imo nudged him in the arm with her elbow. "You still smell like fish," she whispered to him. He and Buddy had gone out to find some trout that morning.

Esther came out with a basket of crackers and a tub of spreadable cheese. "Here we are, Pete, why don't you start the grill outside and we'll get the steak going?"

He got up, handing the rest of the pictures to Imo. "I'll look at the rest of these later, Gram," he said. "Duty calls."

"You're a good boy," she said. "Now, Imo, you'll like this one. There's Alicia and Andrea in the playhouse their father built for them."

"They have a playhouse?" Imo said. "Wow."

"That's lovely, Margaret," said Esther.

"When are we eatin?" bellowed Joe. He shifted noisily in the wicker chair. "I didn't bring that steak all the way out here just to let the mice play with it."

Imo watched Esther, who sat, poised and controlled, like a cat. She didn't smile. "Joe, I just sent Pete out to get the grill going," she said calmly.

"Drink your lemonade," suggested Margaret.

"It's awful weak," he said. "You didn't put any vodka in it, did ya, Esther?" He laughed and winked at her.

"No," she said, "I didn't."

The front door opened and Buddy entered. He pulled up a chair and sat in it backwards, his long legs stretched out on either side.

"Glad you could join us," Joe said. "Where ya been?"

Buddy smiled. "Down there, watching the waterskier. You saw her, didn't you Grampa?"

The old man chuckled. "I sure did."

Imo heard something strange in Buddy's voice. It didn't quite sound like his. But then, he had so many voices he could do, it was hard to tell when he was just being himself.

"Curtis, how do you like school this year?" Margaret asked. She always called him by his given name.

"I love it Gram," he said. "The teachers are really wonderful, and the subjects are all interesting and applicable to real life."

Esther and Imo looked at each other, puzzled.

"You playin any sports this year, like your brother?" asked Joe.

"I thought I'd try out for the basketball team this winter."

"What?" Esther said, suspicious. "When did you decide this?"

"Ages ago," said Buddy. "When I got measured at school. I figure, nobody over six feet tall at the age of sixteen should forego a shot at a basketball career."

Joe squinted at him. He took a cigarette out of the pack in the breast pocket of his shirt and lit it with his flint lighter. "How are your grades?" he asked.

"Fine," Buddy answered. "How are yours?"

Joe took a drag on his cigarette, staring at Buddy. "You think you're pretty smart, don't'cha?"

Esther got up. "I think I'll see how Pete's going with the grill. How long do you think that steak will need to get done, Joe?"

He hacked. "Just keep cookin it and I'll cut it open when I think it's done."

"All right." She turned toward Buddy. "Why don't you take your grandparents out for a ride in the canoe?"

"That's a lovely idea," said Margaret, "but I think I won't go. It's awfully sunny and the doctor says I should watch my exposure. But Joe'd love it, wouldn't you Joe?"

He puffed on the cigarette. "I s'pose. How old are you now, Buddy?"

"Sixteen."

"Think you can handle that canoe?"

"I know what I'm doing."

Imo got up off the floor. "I'll go too," she offered.

"Why don't we all just go, then?" Buddy said, impatient.

"Buddy," Esther put a hand on his shoulder. He shook it off.

"OK, let's go. You ready, Grampa?"

"Ready as a forty-year-old virgin," he said, and laughed raspily.

Margaret blushed, but pretended not to hear him. She gathered her pictures into a pile on her lap. "I'll be glad to help you here, Esther. You just tell me what I can do."

They went off to the kitchen. Buddy led his sister and grandfather out the door and down to the canoe, a wide green wooden boat thirty years old, tipped over on its side atop a rack that kept it from touching the gravelly shore.

Joe walked unsteadily toward the boat. "Well, here she is. Ya gonna take me out or not?"

Buddy's face was angry, long. "Sure. I'm gettin it." He turned the canoe over and began to pull it off the rack.

"You sure you don't mind if I go?" Imo asked cautiously.

Buddy shook his head, not looking at her. Joe said, "The more, the merrier—but we won't be so light on the water now!" He laughed, dropped the cigarette on the ground and crushed it with the ball of his shoe sole. He walked to the edge of the water and began singing.

"Get your paddle, Imo," Buddy said.

"I'm paddling?"

"Well, what'd you think you were gonna do? He can't paddle," he muttered, nodding toward their grandfather.

"After the ball was over, Nellie took out her glass eye," sang Joe to the lake.

Buddy looked at Imo angrily. "Just get your paddle."

She ran up to the shed, picked out a three-quarter-size paddle from the rack and jogged back with it, panting.

Buddy was pushing the canoe into the water when she got back. It was heavy and broad and he strained to move it. Joe stood by. He wasn't allowed to do anything strenuous anymore, Imo remembered her mother saying. He shouted at Buddy, "Look at those muscles on ya! Almost as strong as your sister, are ya now?"

Imo felt a sharp sting in her chest, but checked it, taking a deep breath to calm herself. He always said stuff like that, she reminded herself, it didn't mean anything. Silent, Buddy pulled and pushed roughly at the canoe until it ploughed the water. He had to catch its stern before it floated away altogether with the force of his push.

Imo and Buddy held the sides of the boat so that Joe could get in.

"Take her out more! The bottom's gonna scrape if we get in here," he yelled.

"All right," Buddy replied evenly. He hauled it out a little farther, til he was about knee deep in the water.

The old man got in awkwardly and sat, like a king in his sedan chair, squarely in the middle of the canoe. Buddy held the boat steady for Imo and then swung over the side himself.

"Careful! Don't scratch it," said Joe. He turned around so that he faced Buddy in the stern.

They pulled out away from the shallows and past the wharf. The lake mirrored Burns Ridge and the barely clouded sky on its bright surface. Imo pointed out a loon and a kingfisher as they paddled. She liked being out on the lake, especially when she could sit in the front of the canoe and pretend she was head of an expedition.

"So how come you're not working this summer?" Joe asked Buddy when they had reached the middle of the lake and had turned toward the west end of it.

"Couldn't find a job."

"Couldn't find a job, my eye," said Joe. Imo heard him spit into the water.

"I couldn't. There's two thousand people in Willikeag, Grampa, and about five jobs."

"You can make your own jobs. I did, when I was your age."

"It was a little different then."

"Not much." He hacked up and spat again. "Watch where you're going. There's rocks over here."

Buddy swept the canoe along with determined strokes. "I've been up here a thousand times, Grampa. I know where they are."

"You don't know a damn thing!" the old man called back.

"Imo, keep up with me, will ya?" Buddy yelled at her. "Paddle on the right side now, for God's sake, so we won't go around in circles."

Her arms were getting sore but she paddled hard as she could. The sun was hot out here. She wanted to take off her sweatshirt, but she was afraid to ask Buddy to stop, so she could do it. He was paddling like a crazy man.

"Your father was the same way, at your age," Joe went on. "Lazy as hell. Couldn't get him to mow the lawn without a swift kick in the rear."

"Buddy's not lazy," Imo protested, but neither of them heard her.

"Pa's sure not lazy now," Bud said to his grandfather. "He works all the time. He's doing all right."

"If you call moving all around the goddamn country to go to work doing all right," Joe said.

"He's in construction. He has to move around."

"Why couldn't he have a job like Emily's husband?" Joe said. "Own his own something or other. So he could stay with his family where he belongs."

"Imo, we're turning around up here," Buddy yelled to her suddenly.

"Okay."

She held her paddle in the water while Buddy maneuvered the end around. Joe shifted his weight and the canoe rocked. "That was an awful short ride," he said.

"That's the way it is," said Buddy.

"You're awful sure of yourself, aren't you?"

Buddy said nothing. He slowed his pace on the way back. Imo turned to look back at him once and saw that he was sweaty and seemed tired.

They got back to camp and landed carefully, Buddy hopping out when the water was shallow enough. He stumbled and his grandfather laughed.

"Where's the food?" Joe yelled. Esther appeared at the top of the rise.

"Back so soon?" she called to them. "We're almost ready to eat I think."

They put the canoe away and walked to the camp. The picnic table under the cluster of birches was spread with a tablecloth and held stoneware plates, good cloth napkins, forks, knives, cups, a large bowl of potato salad in a bed of lettuce and a basket of rolls.

Smoke, and the gassy smell of lighter fluid rose from the grill where Pete was standing, red in the face, and sweaty from the heat. When Joe declared the steak done, Pete flopped it onto a serving tray held by

Esther.

"We can eat now," Joe announced.

Pete wiped his forehead with one end of the apron his mother had made him wear.

"I'm starving," Imo said.

"Everything looks delicious," Margaret observed.

Esther ran into the house and came back out with a plate that held three breaded pan-fried trout. "Surprise," she said, setting the dish in front of Joe.

"I bet I know who caught the skimpy one," he said, looking at Buddy.

Joe went into the house for a few minutes and let the screen door bang shut when he came back out. "Oh, what a beautiful day," he sang. "How the hell does the rest of that go?"

"Everything's going your way," offered Buddy.

They sat down. Plates and spoons passed from hand to hand. Joe presided over the steak slicing. His hand was unsteady, but everyone accepted, politely, the ragged slices of meat he gave them. Imo saw Esther check her watch. She knew what her mother was thinking; they would have to go home in a couple of hours, so that he could watch the news. They were halfway through the visit.

After he finished slicing, Joe said, "What's that notebook I found in the john, Buddy?"

No one spoke, or moved any utensils, for several long seconds. Then Buddy said, his voice no longer assured, "What notebook's that?"

"Looked like a notebook you might use in school, but it was kind of old lookin. Worn out. Had your name on the cover."

Buddy shifted in his seat. "Did you read it?"

Joe smiled. "What, ya got somethin juicy in there? Somethin I oughta see?" He laughed loudly. Imo, sitting beside him, smelled his sour breath as he laughed.

"No, Grampa. It's just—it's private." His face was red.

"Private?" Joe laughed again. "What do you have to keep private?"

Buddy's right hand gripped his steak knife and he rubbed the heel of his left hand, clenched in a fist, up and down his pantleg. Esther put her hand on Buddy's forearm.

"Joe," she said, barely containing her anger. "You shouldn't have looked at his notebook."

"Buddy's going to be a writer," cried Imo.

"A writer?" Joe said. "And what the hell's he gonna do for a livin?"

"Now, Joe," Margaret said.

"No wait," said Buddy. He put down the knife. "It's a good question. Deserves an answer. I don't know what the hell I'm gonna do, Grampa. Can you believe it? Even with you as a shining example of achievement through hard work, I, Curtis Elwood Larkin, don't know what I'm gonna do with my life."

"Buddy!" Esther said. "I think that's enough."

"Oh, let him go on," Joe said. "I always like to listen to talk from a kid who doesn't know anything." He laughed. "So you want to be a writer. You're gonna be poor. If you wanna go back to eatin potatoes and beans every day like my family did, then go ahead. There's no glory in it."

"Joe, what does all that have to do with anything?" said Margaret, worried. "Can't we just eat? Here we have good steak on the table that's getting cold, and you bring up beans and potatoes—"

"He's good at it," Imo interrupted. "Buddy, I mean. He's a good writer. He let me read a story he wrote once."

"Imo," said Buddy angrily.

"What? You are good."

"Thanks a lot."

"The trouble with you young people," Joe went on, waving away his wife's stern looks, "is that you take it all for granted. You don't know what it means to work hard, or work at all, for that matter."

"I think I do," said Buddy, raising his voice.

"Take it easy, man," said Pete. He had been eyeing the steak on his plate.

Buddy took a deep breath, and looked hard at his grandfather. "You remember that time you told me about when you were little, and your brother made you run all the way home from way out in the woods, without your pants on?"

"Of course I do. That goddamn Carl, he was a mean one."

"You remember how that felt?"

"Cold," quipped Joe, but no one laughed. "And like crap."

"Well, that's how I feel when I'm around you, Grampa. Cold. And like crap."

"Buddy!" cried Esther.

Margaret raised her napkin to her face and coughed into it. "Esther, I think I need to go into the house."

"Don't worry, I'm goin," said Buddy. He got up from the table. "Eat without me. I won't disturb you anymore. And Grampa," he added, "stay away from my journal, please. It is private."

He dumped his untouched steak onto Pete's plate, then placed his knife, fork, and napkin, precisely, in his now-empty one, and carried them from the table. His neck and face were flushed and his jaw tight, as he walked toward the front door, angry and dignified, without saying anything or looking back. He swung the screen door open noisily and disappeared inside.

Margaret placed one hand on her chest and breathed carefully. Esther got up, took Margaret's arm and helped her up the steps and into the house.

"Why don't the rest of you go ahead and eat," Esther said from the doorway. Strain showed on her forehead.

Imo, Pete, and Joe ate slowly, keeping their heads down. Imo looked up at Joe's face as he ate. His jaw shook as he chewed, and it seemed painful for him to swallow. He looked old and pathetic to Imo, and she felt sorry for him.

"He's got a mean streak," said Joe eventually, to break the silence. "Comes from my family. I passed it on to your father and your father passed it on to him." He looked up from his plate and glanced at each of them. "You got it too, both of ya," he added spitefully.

They continued to eat silently until Joe said, "What'd you do to this steak, Peter? It's tough as a pigskin."

Pete looked at Imo, unsmiling. She shrugged her shoulders and went back to playing with the potato salad on her plate. She didn't look up when Buddy came back outside, clutching his notebook, and took the long way around the picnic table toward the point.

When they were almost finished eating, Esther came back outside. "Margaret's lying down," she said. "She's not feeling too well, Joe. She says it's her asthma." She sat down in her place at the table.

"Her goddamn asthma." Joe forked the last piece of steak on his plate and dragged it through its juices. "So I suppose she wants to go home."

"I think that's best," Esther said, quietly. "Don't you?"

"I s'pose." He finished his lemonade.

"Imo and Pete, you help me get the dishes here."

They rose obediently and began clearing the table. Then the three of them went inside leaving the old man alone at the head of the table, watching the stillness of his lake.

Steady rain kept them inside for two days after the visit, and on the third morning Esther announced that they would be leaving the next day, a day earlier than they had planned. "It doesn't make any sense to finish out the week stuck inside, with nothing to do but play cribbage and read old magazines," she told them.

Imo knew that her decision also had to do with Buddy's unnerving silence. He had refused to talk to any of them in the two days since the visit, having had a long and angry argument with Esther that night. He seemed to have taken literally her request that he keep silent if he couldn't find anything positive to say, and instead communicated only to his notebook, in occasional writing jags. His family, in turn, ignored him.

On the day of departure, Imo awoke early, got dressed, and went down to the wharf by herself. Though it wasn't raining, Imo looked at the sky that was bright pink around the new sun and thought of the old rhyme, "Red sky at night, sailor's delight, red sky in the morning, sailors take warning." But the sky, to her, didn't look threatening at all.

On the calm flat water in the middle of the lake, Imo saw two loons swimming, hardly moving. They spoke to each other in long, mournful cries with a rippling sound like laughter at the end. She tried to imitate their strange call that sounded like laughing and crying at once, and the birds responded excitedly with their own more perfect calls. She tried again, stronger and more confident now.

"That was pretty good."

She turned, embarrassed. It was Buddy.

"You're talking."

"Yeah, I didn't want to lose my voice permanently."

She turned back toward the loons and called to them more quietly. Then she looked back at Buddy, who was still standing there, concentrating on some far off spot on the lake, wrinkling his forehead.

"Hey, do you know what time we're leaving?" she asked.

"Ma said in an hour or so."

"So we'll get home for lunch?"

"Do you always think about food so much?"

"For your information, no."

Buddy smiled.

"I heard her say we're gonna call Dad when we get home," he said.

"Yeah?" Imo got up. "That's great."

"Maybe." He began walking along the shore, away from her.

"Where ya going?" she asked him.

"Just down here a ways."

"To write?"

"Naw, just to walk."

"Can't I come?"

He stopped. "I'd sorta like to be alone."

"You've been alone for two days."

He thought for a moment. "Yeah, well. Come if you want, I don't care."

But he waited for her to catch up to him before he started walking again.

Silhouette

ABBIE HUSTON EVANS

The lamp flared in a quick gust.—"Yet," I said,
"You've had a full life, Sarah."—"That depends;
"If you mean busy, I suppose so. Yes.
"What with the old folks—and Aunt Jane—and Mandy."
She took her basket and got up to go,
Her hand a gaunt root wrapped about the handle.
"—Nothing ever took me off my feet.
"That's the whole story.—Well," she said, "good night."

I held the lamp to light her down the path.

The Ledge

LAWRENCE SARGENT HALL

On Christmas morning before sunup the fisherman embraced his warm wife and left his close bed. She did not want him to go. It was Christmas morning. He was a big, raw man, with too much strength, whose delight in winter was to hunt the sea ducks that flew in to feed by the outer ledges, bare at low tide.

As his bare feet touched the cold floor and the frosty air struck his nude flesh, he might have changed his mind in the dark of this special day. It was a home day, which made it seem natural to think of the outer ledges merely as some place he had shot ducks in the past. But he had promised his son, thirteen, and his nephew, fifteen, who came from inland. That was why he had given them his present of an automatic shotgun each the night before, on Christmas Eve. Rough man though he was known to be, and no spoiler of boys, he kept his promises when he understood what they meant. And to the boys, as to him, home meant where you came for rest after you had had your Christmas fill of action and excitement.

His legs astride, his arms raised, the fisherman stretched as high as he could in the dim privacy of his bedroom. Above the snug murmur of his wife's protest he heard the wind in the pines and knew it was easterly as the boys had hoped and he had surmised the night before. Conditions would be ideal, and when they were, anybody ought to take advantage of them. The birds would be flying. The boys would get a man's sport their first time outside on the ledges.

His son at thirteen, small but steady and experienced, was fierce to grow up in hunting, to graduate from sheltered waters and the blinds along the shores of the inner bay. His nephew at fifteen, an overgrown farm boy, had a farm boy's love of the sea, though he could not swim a stroke and was often sick in choppy weather. That was the reason his father, the fisherman's brother, was a farmer and chose to sleep in on the holiday morning at his brother's house. Many of the ones the farmer had grown up with were regularly seasick and could not swim, but they were unafraid of the water. They could not have dreamed of being anything but fishermen. The fisherman himself could swim like a seal and was never sick, and he would sooner die than be anything else.

He dressed in the cold and dark, and woke the boys gruffly. They tumbled out of bed, their instincts instantly awake while their thoughts still fumbled slumbrously. The fisherman's wife in the adjacent bedroom heard them apparently trying to find their clothes, mumbling sleepily and happily to each other, while her husband went down to the hot kitchen to fry eggs—sunny-side up, she knew, because that was how they all liked them.

Always in the winter she hated to have them go outside, the weather was so treacherous and there were so few others out in case of trouble. To the fisherman these were no more than woman's fears, to be taken for granted and laughed off. When they were first married, they fought miserably every fall because she was after him constantly to put his boat up until spring. The fishing was all outside in winter, and though prices were high the storms made the rate of attrition high on gear. Nevertheless he did well. So she could do nothing with him.

People thought him a hard man, and gave him the reputation of being all out for himself because he was inclined to brag and be disdainful. If it was true, and his own brother was one of those who strongly felt it was, they lived better than others, and his brother had small right to criticize. There had been times when in her loneliness she had yearned to leave him for another man. But it would have been dangerous. So over the years she had learned to shut her mind to his hard-driving, and take what comfort she might from his unsympathetic competence. Only once or twice, perhaps, had she gone so far as to dwell guiltily on what it would be like to be a widow.

The thought that her boy, possibly because he was small, would not be insensitive like his father, and the rattle of dishes and smell of frying bacon downstairs in the kitchen shut off from the rest of the chilly house, restored the cozy feeling she had had before she was alone in bed. She heard them after a while go out and shut the back door.

Under her window she heard the snow grind drily beneath their boots, and her husband's sharp, exasperated commands to the boys. She shivered slightly in the envelope of her own warmth. She listened to the noise of her son and nephew talking elatedly. Twice she caught the glimmer of their lights on the white ceiling above the window as they went down the path to the shore. There would be frost on the skiff and freezing suds at the water's edge. She herself used to go gunning when she was younger; now, it seemed to her, anyone going out like that on Christmas morning had to be incurably male. They would none of them think about her until they returned and piled the birds they had shot on top of the sink for her to dress.

Ripping into the quiet pre-dawn cold she heard the hot snarl of the outboard taking them out to the boat. It died as abruptly as it had burst into life. Two or three or four or five minutes later the big engine broke into a reassuring roar. He had the best of equipment, and he kept it in the best of condition. She closed her eyes. It would not be long before the others would be up for Christmas. The summer drone of the exhaust deepened. Then gradually it faded in the wind until it was lost at sea, or she slept.

The engine had started immediately in spite of the temperature. This put the fisherman in a good mood. He was proud of his boat. Together he and the two boys heaved the skiff and outboard onto the stern and secured it athwartships. His son went forward along the deck, iridescent in the ray of the light the nephew shone through the windshield, and cast the mooring pennant loose into darkness. The fisherman swung to starboard, glanced at his compass, and headed seaward down the obscure bay.

There would be just enough visibility by the time they reached the headland to navigate the crooked channel between the islands. It was the only nasty stretch of water. The fisherman had done it often in fog or at night—he always swore he could go anywhere in the bay blindfolded—but there was no sense in taking chances if you didn't have to. From the mouth of the channel he could lay a straight course for Brown Cow Island, anchor the boat out of sight behind it, and from the skiff set their tollers off Devil's Hump three hundred yards to seaward. By then the tide would be clearing the ledge and they could land and be ready to shoot around half-tide.

It was early, it was Christmas, and it was farther out than most hunters cared to go in this season of the closing year, so that he felt sure no one would be taking possession ahead of them. He had shot thousands of ducks there in his day. The Hump was by far the best hunting. Only thing was you had to plan for the right conditions because you didn't have too much time. About four hours was all, and you had to get it before three in the afternoon when the birds left and went out to sea ahead of nightfall.

They had it figured exactly right for today. The ledge would not be going under until after the gunning was over, and they would be home for supper in good season. With a little luck the boys would have a skiff-load of birds to show for their first time outside. Well beyond the legal limit, which was no matter. You took what you could get in this life, or the next man made out and you didn't.

The fisherman had never failed to make out gunning from Devil's Hump. And this trip, he had a hunch, would be above the ordinary. The westerly wind would come up just stiff enough, the tide was right, and it was going to storm by tomorrow morning so the birds would be moving. Things were perfect.

The old fierceness was in his bones. Keeping a weather eye to the murk out front and a hand on the wheel, he reached over and cuffed both boys playfully as they stood together close to the heat of the exhaust pipe running up through the center of the house. They poked back at him and shouted above the drumming engine, making bets as they always did on who would shoot the most birds. This trip they had the thrill of new guns, the best money could buy, and a man's hunting ground. The black retriever wagged at them and barked. He was too old and arthritic to be allowed in December water, but he was jaunty anyway at being brought along.

Groping in his pocket for his pipe, the fisherman suddenly had his high spirits rocked by the discovery that he had left his tobacco at home. He swore. Anticipation of a day out with nothing to smoke made him incredulous. He searched his clothes, and then he searched them again, unable to believe the tobacco was not somewhere. When the boys inquired what was wrong he spoke angrily to them, blaming them for being in some devious way at fault. They were instantly crestfallen and willing to put back after the tobacco, though they could appreciate what it meant only through his irritation. But he bitterly refused. That would throw everything out of phase. He was a man who did things the way he set out to do.

He clamped the pipe between his teeth, and twice more during the next few minutes he ransacked his clothes in disbelief. He was no stoic. For one relaxed moment he considered putting about and gunning somewhere nearer home. Instead he held his course and sucked the empty pipe, consoling himself with the reflection that at least he had whiskey enough if it got too uncomfortable on the ledge. Peremptorily he made the boys check to make certain the bottle was really in the knapsack with the lunches where he thought he had taken care to put it. When they reassured him, he despised his fate a little less.

The fisherman's judgment was as usual accurate. By the time they were abreast of the headland there was sufficient light so that he could wind his way among the reefs without slackening speed. At last he turned his bow toward open ocean, and as the winter dawn filtered upward through long layers of smoky cloud on the eastern rim his spirits rose again with it.

He opened the throttle, steadied on his course, and settled down to the two-hour run. The wind was stronger but seemed less cold coming from the sea. The boys had withdrawn from the fisherman and were talking together while they watched the sky through the windows. The boat churned solidly through a light chop, flinging spray off her flaring bow. Astern the headland thinned rapidly till it lay like a blackened sill on the grey water. No other boats were abroad.

The boys fondled their new guns, sighted along the barrels, worked the mechanisms, compared notes, boasted, and gave each other contra-dictory advice. The fisherman got their attention once and pointed at the horizon. They peered through the windows and saw what looked like a black scum floating on top of gently agitated water. It wheeled and tilted, rippled, curled, then rose, strung itself out and became a huge raft of ducks escaping over the sea. A good sign.

The boys rushed out and leaned over the washboards in the wind and spray to see the flock curl below the horizon. Then they went and hovered around the hot engine, bewailing their lot. If only they had been already out and waiting. Maybe these ducks would be crazy enough to return later and be slaughtered. Ducks were known to be foolish.

In due course and right on schedule they anchored at mid-morning in the lee of Brown Cow Island. They put the skiff overboard and loaded it with guns, knapsacks, and tollers. The boys showed their eagerness by being clumsy. The fisherman showed his in bad temper and abuse which they silently accepted in the absorbed tolerance of being boys. No doubt they laid it to lack of tobacco.

By outboard they rounded the island and pointed due east in the direction of a ridge of foam which could be seen whitening the surface three hundred yards away. They set the decoys in a broad, straddling vee opening wide into the ocean. The fisherman warned them not to get their hands wet, and when they did he made them carry on with red and painful fingers, in order to teach them. Once they got their numbed fingers inside their oilskins and hugged their warm crotches. In the meantime the fisherman had turned the skiff toward the patch of foam where as if by magic, like a black glossy rib of earth, the ledge had broken through the belly of the sea.

Carefully they inhabited their slippery nub of the North American continent, while the unresting Atlantic swelled and swirled as it had for eons round the indomitable edges. They hauled the skiff after them, established themselves as comfortably as they could in a shallow sump on top, lay on their sides a foot or so above the water, and waited, guns in hand.

In time the fisherman took a thermos bottle from the knapsack and they drank steaming coffee, and waited for the nodding decoys to lure in the first flight to the rock. Eventually the boys got hungry and restless. The fisherman let them open the picnic lunch and eat one sandwich apiece, which they both shared with the dog. Having no tobacco the fisherman himself would not eat.

Actually the day was relatively mild, and they were warm enough at present in their woolen clothes and socks underneath oilskins and hip boots. After a while, however, the boys began to feel cramped. Their nerves were agonized by inactivity. The nephew complained and was severely told by the fisherman—who pointed to the dog, crouched unmoving except for his white-rimmed eyes—that part of doing a man's hunting was learning how to wait. But he was beginning to have misgivings of his own. This could be one of those days where all the right conditions masked an incalculable flaw.

If the fisherman had been alone, as he often was, stopping off when the necessary coincidence of tide and time occurred on his way home from hauling trawls, and had plenty of tobacco, he would not have fidgeted. The boys' being nervous made him nervous. He growled at them again. When it came it was likely to come all at once, and then in a few moments to be over. He warned them not to slack off, never to slack off, to be always ready. Under his rebuke they kept their tortured peace, though they could not help shifting and twisting until he lost what patience he had left and bullied them into lying still. A duck could see an eyelid twitch. If the dog could go without moving, so could they.

"Here it comes!" the fisherman said tersely at last.

The boys quivered with quick relief. The flock came in downwind, quartering slightly, myriad, black, and swift.

"Beautiful—" breathed the fisherman's son.

"All right," said the fisherman, intense and precise. "Aim at singles in the thickest part of the flock. Wait for me to fire and then don't stop shooting till your gun's empty." He rolled up onto his elbow and spread his legs to brace himself. The flock bore down, arrowy and vibrant, then a hundred yards beyond the decoys it veered off.

"They're going away!" the boys cried, sighting in.

"Not yet!" snapped the fisherman. "They're coming round."

The flock changed shape, folded over itself, and drove into the wind in a tight arc. "Thousands—" the boys hissed through their teeth. All at once a whistling storm of black and white broke over the decoys.

"Now!" the fisherman shouted. "Perfect!" And he opened fire at the flock just as it hung suspended in momentary chaos above the tollers. The three pulled their triggers and the birds splashed into the water, until the last report went off unheard, the last smoking shell flew unheeded over their shoulders, and the last of the routed flock scattered diminishing, diminishing, diminishing in every direction.

Exultantly the boys dropped their guns, jumped up and scrambled for the skiff.

"I'll handle that skiff!" the fisherman shouted at them. They stopped. Gripping the painter and balancing himself he eased the skiff into the water stern first and held the bow hard against the side of the rock shelf the skiff had rested on. "You stay here," he said to his nephew. "No sense in all three of us going in the boat."

The boy on the reef gazed at the grey water rising and falling hypnotically along the glistening edge. It had dropped about a foot since their arrival. "I want to go with you," he said in a sullen tone, his eyes on the streaming eddies.

"You want to do what I tell you if you want to gun with me," answered the fisherman harshly. The boy couldn't swim, and he wasn't going to have him climbing in and out of the skiff any more than necessary. Besides, he was too big.

The fisherman took his son in the skiff and cruised round and round among the decoys picking up dead birds. Meanwhile the other boy stared unmoving after them from the highest part of the ledge. Before they had quite finished gathering the dead birds, the fisherman cut the outboard and dropped to his knees in the skiff. "Down!" he yelled. "Get down!" About a dozen birds came tolling in. "Shoot— shoot!" his son hollered from the bottom of the boat to the boy on the ledge.

The dog, who had been running back and forth whining, sank to his belly, his muzzle on his forepaws. But the boy on the ledge never stirred. The ducks took late alarm at the skiff, swerved aside and into the air, passing with a whirr no more than fifty feet over the head of the boy, who remained on the ledge like a statue, without his gun, watching the two crouching in the boat.

The fisherman's son climbed on the ledge and held the painter. The bottom of the skiff was covered with feathery black and white bodies with feet upturned and necks lolling. He was jubilant. "We got twenty-seven!" he told his cousin. "How's that? Nine apiece. Boy—" he added, "what a cool Christmas!"

The fisherman pulled the skiff onto its shelf and all three went and lay down again in anticipation of the next flight. The son, reloading, patted his gun affectionately. "I'm going to get me ten next time," he said. Then he asked his cousin, "Whatsamatter—didn't you see the strays?"

"Yeah," the boy said.

"How come you didn't shoot at 'em?"

"Didn't feel like it," replied the boy, still with a trace of sullenness.

"You stupid or something?" The fisherman's son was astounded. "What a highlander!" But the fisherman, though he said nothing, knew that the older boy had had an attack of ledge fever.

"Cripes!" his son kept at it. "I'd at least of tried."

"Shut up," the fisherman finally told him, "and leave him be."

At slack water three more flocks came in, one right after the other, and when it was over, the skiff was half full of clean, dead birds. During the subsequent lull they broke out the lunch and ate it all and finished the hot coffee. For a while the fisherman sucked away on his cold pipe. Then he had himself a swig of whiskey.

The boys passed the time contentedly jabbering about who shot the most—there were ninety-two all told—which of their friends they would show the biggest ones to, how many each could eat at a meal provided they didn't have to eat any vegetables. Now and then they heard sporadic distant gunfire on the mainland, at its nearest point about two miles to the north. Once far off they saw a fishing boat making in the direction of home.

At length the fisherman got a hand inside his oilskins and produced his watch.

"Do we have to go now?" asked his son.

"Not just yet," he replied. "Pretty soon." Everything had been perfect. As good as he had ever had it. Because he was getting tired of the boy's chatter he got up, heavily in his hip boots, and stretched. The tide had turned and was coming in, the sky was more ashen, and the wind had freshened enough so that the whitecaps were beginning to blossom. It would be a good hour before they had to leave the ledge and pick up the tollers. However, he guessed they would leave a little early. On account of the rising wind he doubted there would be much more shooting. He stepped carefully along the back of the ledge, to work his kinks out. It was also getting a little colder.

The whiskey had begun to warm him, but he was unprepared for the sudden blaze that flashed upward inside him from belly to head. He was standing looking at the shelf where the skiff was. Only the foolish skiff was not there!

For the second time that day the fisherman felt the deep vacuity of disbelief. He gaped, seeing nothing, but the flat shelf of rock. He whirled, started toward the boys, slipped, recovered himself, fetched a complete circle, and stared at the unimaginably empty shelf. Its emptiness made him feel as if everything he had done that day so far, his life so far, he had dreamed. What could have happened? The tide was still nearly a foot below. There had been no sea to speak of. The skiff could hardly have slid off by itself. For the life of him, consciously careful as he inveterately was, he could not now remember hauling it up the last time. Perhaps in the heat of hunting, he had left it to the boy. Perhaps he could not remember which was the last time.

"Christ—" he exclaimed loudly, without realizing it because he was so entranced by the invisible event.

"What's wrong, Dad?" asked his son, getting to his feet.

The fisherman went blind with uncontainable rage. "Get back down there where you belong!" he screamed. He scarcely noticed the boy sink back in amazement. In a frenzy he ran along the ledge thinking the skiff might have been drawn up at another place, though he knew better. There was no other place.

He stumbled, half falling, back to the boys who were gawking at him in consternation, as though he had gone insane. "God damn it!" he yelled savagely, grabbing both of them and yanking them to their knees. "Get on your feet!"

"What's wrong?" his son repeated in a stifled voice.

"Never mind what's wrong," he snarled. "Look for the skiff—it's adrift!" When they peered around he gripped their shoulders, brutally facing them about. "Downwind—" He slammed his fist against his thigh. "Jesus!" he cried, struck to madness by their stupidity.

At last he sighted the skiff himself, magically bobbing along the grim sea like a toller, a quarter of a mile to leeward on a direct course for home. The impulse to strip himself naked was succeeded instantly by a queer calm. He simply sat down on the ledge and forgot everything except the marvelous mystery.

As his awareness partially returned he glanced toward the boys. They were still observing the skiff speechlessly. Then he was gazing into the clear young eyes of his son.

"Dad," asked the boy steadily, "what do we do now?"

That brought the fisherman upright. "The first thing we have to do," he heard himself saying with infinite tenderness as if he were making love, "is think."

"Could you swim it?" asked his son.

He shook his head and smiled at them. They smiled quickly back, too quickly. "A hundred yards maybe, in this water. I wish I could," he added. It was the most intimate and pitiful thing he had ever said. He walked in circles round them, trying to break the stall his mind was left in.

He gauged the level of the water. To the eye it was quite stationary, six inches from the shelf at this second. The fisherman did not have to mark it on the side of the rock against the passing of time to prove to his reason that it was rising, always rising. Already it was over the brink of reason, beyond the margins of thought—a senseless measurement. No sense to it.

All his life the fisherman had tried to lick the element of time, by getting up earlier and going to bed later, owning a faster boat, planning more than the day would hold, and tackling just one other job before the deadline fell. If, as on rare occasions he had the grand illusion, he ever really had beaten the game, he would need to call on all his reserves of practice and cunning now.

He sized up the scant but unforgivable three hundred yards to Brown Cow Island. Another hundred yards behind it his boat rode at anchor, where, had he been aboard, he could have cut in a fathometer to plumb the profound and occult seas, or a ship-to-shore radio on which in an interminably short time he would have heard his wife's voice talking to him over the air about homecoming.

"Couldn't we wave something so somebody would see us?" his nephew suggested.

The fisherman spun round. "Load your guns!" he ordered. They loaded as if the air had suddenly gone frantic with birds. "I'll fire once and count to five. Then you fire. Count to five. That way they won't just think it's only somebody gunning ducks. We'll keep doing that."

"We've only got just two-and-a-half boxes left," said his son.

The fisherman nodded, understanding that from beginning to end their situation was purely mathematical, like the ticking of the alarm clock in his silent bedroom. Then he fired. The dog, who had been keeping watch over the decoys, leaped forward and yelped in confusion. They all counted off, fired the first five rounds by threes, and reloaded. The fisherman scanned first the horizon, then the contracting borders of the ledge, which was the sole place the water appeared to be climbing. Soon it would be over the shelf.

They counted off and fired the second five rounds. "We'll hold off a while on the last one," the fisherman told the boys. He sat down and pondered what a trivial thing was a skiff. This one he and the boy had knocked together in a day. Was a gun, manufactured for killing.

His son tallied up the remaining shells, grouping them symmetrically in threes on the rock when the wet box fell apart. "Two short," he announced. They reloaded and laid the guns on their knees.

Behind thickening clouds they could not see the sun going down. The water, coming up, was growing blacker. The fisherman thought he might have told his wife they would be home before dark since it was Christmas day. He realized he had forgotten about its being any particular day. The tide would not be high until two hours after sunset. When they did not get in by nightfall, and could not be raised by radio, she might send somebody to hunt for them right away. He rejected this arithmetic immediately, with a sickening shock, recollecting it was a two-and-a-half hour run at best. Then it occurred to him that she might send somebody on the mainland who was nearer. She would think he had engine trouble.

He rose and searched the shoreline, barely visible. Then his glance dropped to the toy shoreline at the edges of the reef. The shrinking ledge, so sinister from a boat, grew dearer minute by minute as though the whole wide world he gazed on from horizon to horizon balanced on its contracting rim. He checked the water level and found the shelf awash.

Some of what went through his mind the fisherman told to the boys. They accepted it without comment. If he caught their eyes they looked away to spare him or because they were not yet old enough to face what they saw. Mostly they watched the rising water. The fisherman was unable to initiate a word of encouragement. He wanted one of them to ask him whether somebody would reach them ahead of the tide. He would have found it possible to say yes. But they did not inquire.

The fisherman was not sure how much, at their age, they were able to imagine. Both of them had seen from the docks drowned bodies put ashore out of boats. Sometimes they grasped things, and sometimes not. He supposed they might be longing for the comfort of their mothers, and was astonished, as much as he was capable of any astonishment except the supreme one, to discover himself wishing he had not left his wife's dark, close, naked bed that morning.

"Is it time to shoot now?" asked his nephew.

"Pretty soon," he said, as if he were putting off making good on a promise. "Not yet."

His own boy cried softly for a brief moment, like a man, his face averted in an effort neither to give nor show pain.

"Before school starts," the fisherman said, wonderfully detached, "we'll go to town and I'll buy you boys anything you want."

With great difficulty, in a dull tone as though he did not in the least desire it, his son said after a pause, "I'd like one of those new thirty-horse outboards."

"All right," said the fisherman. And to his nephew. "How about you?"

The nephew shook his head desolately. "I don't want anything," he said.

After another pause the fisherman's son said, "Yes he does, Dad. He wants one too."

"All right—" the fisherman said again, and said no more.

The dog whined in uncertainty and licked the boys' faces where they sat together. Each threw an arm over his back and hugged him. Three strays flew in and sat companionably down among the stiff-necked decoys. The dog crouched, obedient to his training. The boys observed them listlessly. Presently, sensing something untoward, the ducks took off, splashing the wave tops with feet and wingtips, into the dusky waste.

The sea began to make up in the mountain wind, and the wind bore a new and deathly chill. The fisherman, scouring the somber, dwindling shadow of the mainland for a sign, hoped it would not snow. But it did. First a few flakes, then a flurry, then storming past horizontally. The fisherman took one long, bewildered look at Brown Cow Island three hundred years dead to leeward, and got to his feet.

Then it shut in, as if what was happening on the ledge was too private even for the last wan light of the expiring day.

"Last round," the fisherman said austerely.

The boys rose and shouldered their tacit guns. The fisherman fired into the flying snow. He counted methodically to five. His son fired and counted. His nephew. All three fired and counted. Four rounds.

"You've got one left, Dad," his son said.

The fisherman hesitated another second, then he fired the final shell. Its pathetic report, like the spat of a popgun, whipped away on the wind and was instantly blanketed in falling snow.

Night fell all in a moment to meet the ascending sea. They were not barely able to make one another out through driving snowflakes, dim as ghosts in their yellow oilskins. The fisherman heard the sea break and glanced down where his feet were. They seemed to be wound in a snowy sheet. Gently he took the boys by the shoulders and pushed them in front of him, feeling with his feet along the shallow sump to the place where it triangulated into a sharp crevice at the highest point of the ledge. "Face ahead," he told them. "Put the guns down."

"I'd like to hold mine, Dad," begged his son.

"Put it down," said the fisherman. "The tide won't hurt it. Now brace your feet against both sides and stay there."

They felt the dog, who was pitch black, running up and down in perplexity between their straddled legs. "Dad," said his son, "what about the pooch?"

If he had called the dog by name it would have been too personal. The fisherman would have wept. As it was he had all he could do to keep from laughing. He bent his knees, and when he touched the dog hoisted him under one arm. The dog's belly was soaking wet.

So they waited, marooned in their consciousness, surrounded by a monstrous tidal space which was slowly, slowly closing them out. In this space the periwinkle beneath the fisherman's boots was king. While hovering airborne in his mind he had an inward glimpse of his house as curiously separate, like a June mirage.

Snow, rocks, seas, wind the fisherman had lived by all his life. Now he thought he had never comprehended what they were, and he hated them. Though they had not changed. He was deadly chilled. He set out to ask the boys if they were cold. There was no sense. He thought of the whiskey, and sidled backward, still holding the awkward dog, till he located the bottle under water with his toe. He picked it up squeamishly as though afraid of getting his sleeve wet, worked his way forward and bent over his son. "Drink it," he said, holding the bottle against the boy's ribs. The boy tipped his head back, drank, coughed hotly, then vomited.

"I can't," he told his father wretchedly.

"Try—try—" the fisherman pleaded, as if it meant the difference between life and death.

The boy obediently drank, and again he vomited hotly. He shook his head against his father's chest and passed the bottle forward to his cousin, who drank and vomited also. Passing the bottle back, the boys dropped it in the frigid water between them.

When the waves reached his knees the fisherman set the warm dog loose and said to his son, "Turn around and get up on my shoulders." The boy obeyed. The fisherman opened his oilskin jacket and twisted his hands behind him through his suspenders, clamping the boy's booted ankles with his elbows.

"What about the dog?" the boy asked.

"He'll make his own way all right," the fisherman said. "He can take the cold water." His knees were trembling. Every instinct shrieked for gymnastics. He ground his teeth and braced like a colossus against the sides of the submerged crevice.

The dog, having lived faithfully as though one of them for eleven years, swam a few minutes in and out around the fisherman's legs, not knowing what was happening, and left them without a whimper. He would swim and swim at random by himself, round and round in the blinding night, and when he had swum routinely through the paralyzing water all he could, he would simply, in one incomprehensible moment, drown. Almost the fisherman, waiting out infinity, envied him his pattern.

Freezing seas swept by, flooding inexorably up and up as the earth sank away imperceptibly beneath them. The boy called out once to his cousin. There was no answer. The fisherman, marvelling on a terror without voice, was dumbly glad when the boy did not call again. His own boots were long full of water. With no sensation left in his straddling legs he dared not move them. So long as the seas came sidewise against his hips, and then sidewise against his shoulders, he might balance—no telling how long. The upper half of him was what felt frozen. His legs, disengaged from his nerves and his will, he came to regard quite scientifically. They were the absurd, precarious axis around which reeled the surged universal tumult. The waves would come on; he could not visualize how many tossing reinforcements lurked in the night beyond—inexhaustible numbers, and he wept in supernatural fury at each because it was higher, till he transcended hate and took them, swaying like a convert, one by one as they lunged against him and away aimlessly into their own undisputed, wild realm.

From his hips upward the fisherman stretched to his utmost as a man does whose spirit reaches out of dead sleep. The boy's head, none too high, must be at least seven feet above the ledge. Though growing larger every minute, it was a small light life. The fisherman meant to hold it there, if need be, through a thousand tides.

By and by the boy, slumped on the head of his father, asked, "Is it over your boots, Dad?"

"Not yet," the fisherman said. Then through his teeth he added, "If I fall—kick your boots off—swim for it—downwind—to the island...."

"You ...?" the boy finally asked.

The fisherman nodded against the boy's belly. "—Won't see each other," he said.

The boy did for the fisherman the greatest thing that can be done. He may have been too young for perfect terror, but he was old enough to know there were things beyond the power of any man. All he could do he did, trusting his father to do all he could, and asking nothing more.

The fisherman, rocked to his soul by a sea, held his eyes shut upon the interminable night.

"Is it time now?" the boy said.

The fisherman could hardly speak. "Not yet," he said. "Not just yet...."

As the land mass pivoted toward sunlight the day after Christmas, a tiny fleet of small craft converged off shore like iron filings to a magnet. At daybreak they found the skiff floating unscathed off the headland, half full of ducks and snow. The shooting *had* been good, as someone hearing on the mainland the previous afternoon had supposed. Two hours afterward they found the unharmed boat adrift five miles at sea. At high noon they found the fisherman at ebb tide, his right foot jammed cruelly into a glacial crevice of the ledge beside three shotguns, his hands tangled behind him in his suspenders, and under his right elbow a rubber boot with a sock and a live starfish in it. After dragging unlit depths all day for the boys, they towed the fisherman home in his own boat at sundown, and in the frost of evening, mute with discovering purgatory, laid him on his wharf for his wife to see.

She, somehow, standing on the dock as in her frequent dream, gazing at the fisherman pure as crystal on the icy boards, a small rubber boot still frozen under one clenched arm, saw him exaggerated beyond remorse or grief, absolved of his mortality.

exercise

LEE SHARKEY

focus on someone you love as much as you love your breath.
imagine yourself abruptly deprived of that relationship.   imagine
    your breathing.
imagine a world where everyone's lost their most precious
    possession,
and wanders helplessly.   now watch them disappear: each was
    someone's beloved
if only their own.   imagine mourning without mourners, voiceless
    dirges
stampeding across grasslands like bison before Massacring Buffalo
    Bill,
the tremors of earth, image and after image, settling into the absence
    of language.

Giacomo Gastaldi, La Nuova Francia, *1556, woodcut, 12¹/₂ "x 17",*
Courtesy, The Osher Collection.

Origins

"We are the stars which sing."

A Poem About the Red Paint People

SAMUEL FRENCH MORSE

Unfit for house or pasturage
But white with meadowsweet and haze,
This barren spot was sacred ground
When Sieur de Monts put in to shore
One of those windless August days
The sails fell idle like a sign
From God that he had come to found
The one true faith upon this rock;
Though as a soldier he must claim
The land for an ambitious king
So cold in his apostasy
He could not bless it. Oak and pine
And roses grew high up the slope
Above the naked outcrop where
The starving yellow hawkweed spread
In soil too thin to plant the cross,
If not the heavy sword he bore.
But other men had quarried here
Ten thousand years ago, and left,
In stiff repose, a hunter dead
Some weeks' hard travel from the place
Their own great gods inhabited—
Too long a journey for the soul.
The shaman smeared the body red
With ocher; then he filled the mouth,
Closed up the passage in the ears
And nostrils, set the fallen spear
Within the spirit's reach, and turned
The sealed eyes backward in the head.
Like any priest, he must have said
Some words to give the living pause
And keep the covert fox away.

Perhaps he gave the place a name,
Or left a mark the weather wore
As smooth as water long before
The Abenaki settled here.
But who they were and where they went
No Indian or white man knows,
Whose own untoward and bitter wars
Are shellheaps now and broken adze,
Not someone's half-remembered lies.
Whatever chance it was that kept
The shallow grave inviolate
So long, was all that laid it waste
One morning when a road crew turned
The thin soil over, and there burned
A moment in the summer sun's
Noon heat, the painted skeleton:
A moment only, while the air
Blazed into spirit, quick with rust.
Beyond all time and mere disguise
The body seemed, that was but dust,
A little handful of red bone
Outlasting any name we know
For men who kept a vigil here
Before our history began.

And who shall say what we have done?

Champlain Navigates the Penobscot River

SAMUEL DE CHAMPLAIN

5th September 1604 ... The same day we passed also near to an island about four or five leagues long. From this island to the main land on the north, the distance is less than a hundred paces. It is very high, and notched in places, so that there is the appearance to one at sea, as of seven or eight mountains extending along near each other. The summit of most of them is destitute of trees, as there are only rocks on them. The woods consists of pines, firs, and birches only. I named it Isle des Monts Deserts.

The next day, the 6th of the month, we sailed two leagues and perceived a smoke in a cove at the foot of the mountains above mentioned. We saw two canoes rowed by savages, which came within musket range to observe us. I sent our two savages in a boat to assure them of our friendship. Their fear of us made them turn back. On the morning of the next day they came alongside of our barque and talked with our savages. I ordered some biscuit, tobacco, and other trifles to be given them. These savages had come beaver-hunting and to catch fish, some of which they gave us. Having made an alliance with them, they guided us to their river of Pentegouet, so called by them, where they told us was their captain, named Bessabez, chief of this river....

As one enters the river, there are beautiful islands, which are very pleasant and contain fine meadows. We proceeded to a place to which the savages guided us, where the river is not more than an eighth of a league broad.... I landed to view the country and, going on a hunting excursion, found it very pleasant so far as I went. The oaks here appear as if they were planted for ornament. I saw only a few firs, but numerous pines on one side of the river; on the other side only oaks, and some copse wood which extends far into the interior.... We saw no town or village, but one or two cabins of the savages. These were made in the same way as those of the Micmacs, being covered with the bark of trees. So far as we could judge the savages on this river are few in number ... moreover, they only come to the islands, and that only during some months in summer for fish and game, of which there is a great quantity. They are a people who have no fixed abode, so far as I could observe and learn from them. For they spend the winter now in one place and now in another, according as they find the best hunting, by which they live when urged by their daily needs, without laying up anything for times of scarcity, which are sometimes severe....

[T]he savages who had conducted me to the fall of the river ... went to notify Bessabez, their chief, and other savages, who in turn proceeded to another little river to inform their own, named Cabahis, and give him notice of our arrival.

The 16th of the month there came to us some thirty savages.... There came also to us the same day the above-named Bessabez with six canoes. As soon as the savages who were on land saw him coming, they all began to sing, dance and jump, until he had landed. Afterwards, they all seated themselves in a circle on the ground, as is their custom when they wish to celebrate a festivity, or an harrangue is to be made. Cabahis, the other chief, arrived also a little later with twenty or thirty of his companions, who withdrew to one side and greatly enjoyed seeing us, as it was the first time they had seen Christians....

I directed the men in our barque to approach near the savages, and hold their arms in readiness to do their duty in case they noticed any movement of these people against us. Bessabez, seeing us on land, bade us sit down, and began to smoke with his companions, as they usually do before an address. They presented us with venison and game.

I directed our interpreter to say to our savages that they should cause Bessabez, Cabahis and their companions to understand that Sieur de Monts had sent me to them to see them, and also their country, and that he desired to preserve friendship with them and to reconcile them with their enemies, the Souriquois [Micmacs] and Canadians [New Brunswick Malacites] and moreover that he desired to inhabit the country and show them how to cultivate it, in order that they might not continue to lead so miserable a life as they were doing....

I presented them with hatchets, paternosters, caps, knives, and other little knick-knacks when we separated from each other.

from *An Account of Two Voyages to New-England*

JOHN JOSSELYN

Englishman John Josselyn travelled twice to New England, in 1638 and 25 years later in 1663. The second time he stayed for 8 years on his brother's plantation and did an extensive study of the plants and animals of New England, as well as of the native peoples. His account, first published in 1674, is considered one of the most valuable of our early descriptions of the natural history of the region. These excerpts give the flavor of what he wrote.

The people that inhabited this Countrey ... are tall and handsome timber'd people, out-wristed, pale, and lean Tartarian visag'd, black eyed, which is accounted the strongest for sight, and generally black hair'd, both smooth and curl'd wearing of it long. No beards, or very rarely, their Teeth are very white, short and even, they account them the most necessary and best parts of a man....

Their houses which they call Wigwams, are built with Poles pitcht into the ground of a round form for most part, sometimes square, they bind down the tops of their poles, leaving a hole for smoak to go out at, the rest they cover with the bark of Trees, and line the inside of their Wigwams with mats made of Rushes painted with several colours, one good post they set up in the middle that reaches to the hole in the top, with a staff across before it at a convenient height, they knock in a pin on which they hang their Kettle, beneath that they set up a broad stone for a back which keepeth the post from burning; round by the walls they spread their mats and skins where the men sleep whilst the women dress their victuals, they have commonly two doors, one opening to the South, the other to the North, and according as the wind sits, they close up one door with bark and hang a Dears skin or the like before the other. Towns they have none, being always removing from one place to another for conveniency of food, sometimes to those places where one sort of fish is most plentiful, other whiles where others are. I have seen half a hundred of their Wigwams together in a piece of ground and they shew prettily, within a day or two, or a week they have been all dispersed....

Their Diet is Fish and Fowl, Bear, Wild-cat, Rattoon and Deer;

dryed Oysters, Lobsters rosted or dryed in the smoak, Lampres and dry'd Moose-tongues, which they esteem a dish for a Sagamor; hard eggs boiled and made small and dryed to thicken their broth with, salt they have not the use of, nor bread, their Indian Corn and Kidney beans they boil, and sometimes eat their Corn parcht or roasted in the ear against the fire; they feed likewise upon earth-nuts or ground-nuts, roots of water-Lillies; Ches-nuts, and divers sorts of Berries. They beat their Corn to powder and put it up into bags, which they make use of when stormie weather or the like will not suffer them to look out for their food. Pompions and water-Mellons too they have good store; they have prodigious stomachs, devouring a great deal, meer voragoes, never giving over eating as long as they have it, between meals spending their time in sleep till the next kettlefull is boiled, when all is gone they satisfie themselves with a small quantity of the meal, making it serve as the frugal bit amongst the old Britains, which taken to the mountenance of a Bean would satisfie both thirst and hunger. If they have none of this, as sometimes it falleth out (being a very careless people not providing against the storms of want and tempest of necessity) they make use of Sir Francis Drake's remedy for hunger, go to sleep....

The Lobsters they take in large Bayes when it is low water, the wind still, going out in their Birchen-Canows with a staff two or three yards long, made small and sharpen'd at one end, and nick'd with deep nicks to take hold. When they spye the Lobster crawling upon the Sand in two fathom water, more or less, they stick him towards the head and bring him up. I have known thirty Lobsters taken by an Indian lad in an hour and a half....

They eat their broth with spoons, and their flesh they divide into gobbets, eating now and then with it as much meal as they can hold betwixt three fingers; their drink they fetch from the spring, and were not acquainted with other, untill the French and English traded with that cursed liquor called Rum, Rum-bullion, or kill-Devil, which is stronger than spirit of Wine, and is drawn from the dross of Sugar and Sugar Canes, this they love dearly, and will part with all they have to their bare skins for it, being perpetually drunk with it, as long as it is to be had, it hath killed many of them, especially old women who have dyed when dead drunk. Thus instead of bringing of them to the knowledge of Christianitie, we have taught them to commit the beastly and crying sins of our Nation, for a little profit....

The Pine-Tree ... is a stately large Tree, very tall, and sometimes two or three fadom about: of the body the *English* make large *Canows* of 20 foot long, and two foot and a half over, hollowing of them with an Adds, and shaping of the outside like a Boat. Some conceive that the wood called *Gopher* in the Scripture, of which *Noah* made the Ark, was no other than Pine. The bark thereof is good for Ulcers in tender persons that refuse sharp medicines. The inner bark of young board-pine cut small and stampt and boiled in a Gallon of water is a very soveraign medicine for burn or scald, washing the sore with some of the decoction, and then laying on the bark stampt very soft: or for frozen limbs, to take out the fire and to heal them, take the bark of Board-pine-Tree, cut it small and stamp it and boil it in a gallon of water to Gelly, wash the sore with the liquor, stamp the bark again till it be very soft and bind it on. The Turpentine is excellent to heal wounds and cuts, and hath all the properties of *Venice* Turpentine, the Rosen is as good as Frankincense, and the powder of the dryed leaves genereath flesh; the distilled water of the green Cones taketh away wrinkles in the face being laid on with cloths....

Of Beasts of the earth there be scarce 120 several kinds, and not much more of the Fowls of the Air, is the opinion of some Naturalists; there are not many kinds of Beasts in *New-England*, they may be divided into Beasts of the Chase of the stinking foot, as *Roes, Foxes, Jaccals, Wolves, Wild-cats, Raccons, Porcupines, Squncks, Musquashes, Squirrels, Sables,* and *Mattrises*; and Beasts of the Chase of the sweet foot, *Buck,* Red *Dear,* Rain-*Dear, Elke, Marouse, Maccarib, Bear, Beaver, Otter, Marten, Hare....*

The *Fox,* the male is called a dog-fox, the female a bitch-fox, they go a clicketing the beginning of the spring, and bring forth their Cubs in May and June. There are two or three kinds of them; one a great yellow *Fox,* another grey, who will climb up into Trees; the black *Fox* is of much esteem. *Foxes* and *Wolves* are usually hunted in *England* from *Holy-Rood* day, till the *Annunciation.* In *New-England* they make best sport in the depth of winter: they lay a sledg-load of Cods-heads on the other side of a paled fence when the moon shines, and about nine or ten of the clock the *Foxes* come to it, sometimes two or three, or half a dozen, and more; these they shoot, and by that time they have cased them, there will be as many; So they continue shooting and killing of *Foxes* as long as the moon shineth: I have known half a score kill'd in one night. Their pisles are bonie like a doggs, their fat liquified and put into the ears easeth the pain, their tails or bushes are very fair ones and of good use, but their skins are so thin (yet thick set with deep furr) that they will hardly hold the dressing....

The *Squnck* is almost as big as a *Racoon,* perfect black and white or pye-bald, with a bush-tail like a *Fox,* an offensive Carion; the Urine of this Creature is of so strong a scent, that if it light upon any thing, there is no abiding of it, it will make a man smell, though he were of *Alexanders* complexion; and so sharp if he do but whisk his bush which he pisseth upon in the face of a dogg hunting of him, and that any of it light in his eyes it will make him almost mad with the smart thereof....

The *Moose* or *Elke* is a Creature, or rather if you will a Monster of superfluity; a full grown *Moose* is many times bigger than an *English* Oxe, their horns... very big (and brancht out into palms) the tips whereof are sometimes found to be two fathom asunder (a fathom is six feet from the tip of one finger to the tip of the other, that is four cubits), and in the height from the toe of the fore-foot to the pitch of the shoulder twelve foot, both which hath been taken by some of my *sceptique* Readers to be monstrous lyes.... They are accounted a kind of Deer, and have three *Calves* at a time, which they hide a mile asunder too, as other Deer do, their skins make excellent Coats for Martial men, their sinews which are as big as a mans finger are of perdurable toughness and much used by the *Indians*....

The *Bear* when he goes to mate is a terrible Creature, they bring forth their Cubs in *March*, hunted with doggs they take a Tree where they shoot them, when he is fat he is excellent Venison, which is in *Acorn* time, and in winter, but then there is none dares to attempt to kill him but the *Indian*. He makes his Denn amongst thick Bushes, thrusting in here and there store of *Moss*, which being covered with snow and melting in the day time with heat of the Sun, in the night is frozen into a thick coat of Ice; the mouth of his Den is very narrow, here they lye single, never two in a Den all winter. The *Indian* as soon as he finds them, creeps in upon all four, seizes with his left hand upon the neck of the sleeping *Bear*, drags him to the mouth of the Den, where with a club or small hatchet in his right hand he knocks out his brains before he can open his eyes to see his enemy. But sometimes they are too quick for the *Indians*, as one amongst them called black *Robin* lighting upon a male *Bear* had a piece of his buttock torn off before he could fetch his blow....

The Countrey is strangely incommodated with flyes, which the *English* call Musketaes, they are like our gnats, they will sting so fiercely in summer as to make the faces of the *English* swell'd and scabby, as if the small pox for the first year. Likewise there is a small black fly no bigger than a flea, so numerous up in the Countrey, that a man cannot draw his breath, but he will suck of them in: they continue about Thirty dayes say some but I say three moneths, and are not only a pesterment but a plague to the Country. There is another sort of fly called a Gurnipper, that are like our horse-flyes, and will bite desperately, making the blood to spurt out in great quantity; these trouble our *English* Cattle very much, raising swellings as big as an egg in their hides....

English and Indians Have It Out at Pemaquid

JOHN GYLES

On the second day of August, 1689, in the morning, my honored father, THOMAS GYLES, Esq., went with some laborers, my two elder brothers and myself, to one of his farms, which laid upon the river about three miles above fort Charles, adjoining Pemmaquid falls, there to gather in his English harvest, and we labored securely till noon. After we had dined, our people went to their labor, some in one field to their English hay, the others to another field of English corn. My father, the youngest of my two brothers, and myself, tarried near the farm house in which we had dined till about one of the clock, at which time we heard the report of several great guns at the fort. Upon which my father said he hoped it was a signal of good news, and that the great council had sent back the soldiers to cover the inhabitants; (for on report of the revolution they had deserted.) But to our great surprise, about thirty or forty Indians, at that moment, discharged a volley of shots at us, from behind a rising ground near our barn. The yelling of the Indians, the whistling of their shot, and the voice of my father, whom I heard cry out, "What now! What now!" so terrified me (though he seemed to be handling a gun), that I endeavored to make my escape. My brother ran one way and I another, and looking over my shoulder, I saw a stout fellow, painted, pursuing me, with a gun and a cutlass glittering in his hand which I expected every moment in my brains. I soon fell down, and the Indian seized me by the left hand. He offered me no abuse, but tied my arms, then lifted me up and pointed to the place where people were at work about the hay and led me that way. As we went, we crossed where my father was, who looked very pale and bloody, and walked very slowly. Then when we came to the place, I saw two men shot down on the flats, and one or two more knocked on their heads with hatchets, crying out "O Lord," &c. There the Indians brought two captives, one a man, and my brother James, who, with me, had endeavored to escape by running from the house when we were first attacked. This brother was about fourteen years of age. My oldest brother, whose name was Thomas, wonderfully escaped by land to the Barbican, a point of land on the west side of the river, opposite the fort, where several fishing vessels lay. He got on board one of them and sailed the night.

After doing what mischief they could, they sat down and made us sit with them. After some time we arose, and the Indians pointed for us to go eastward. We marched about a quarter of a mile, and then made a halt. Here they brought my father to us. They made proposals to him, by old Moxus, who told him that those were Strange Indians who shot him, and that he was sorry for it. My father replied that he was a dying man, and wanted no favor of them, but to pray with his children. This being granted him, he recommended us to the protection and blessing of God Almighty; then gave us the best advice, and took his leave for this life, hoping in God that we should meet in a better. He parted with a cheerful voice, but looked very pale, by reason of his great loss of blood, which now gushed out of his shoes. The Indians led him aside!—I heard the blows of the hatchet, but neither shriek nor groan! I afterwards heard that he had five or seven shot-holes through his waistcoat or jacket, and that he was covered with some boughs.

The Indians led us, their captives, on the east side of the river, towards the fort, and when we came within a mile and a half of the fort and town, and could see the fort, we saw fire and smoke on all sides. Here we made a short stop, and then moved within or near the distance of three-quarters of a mile from the fort, into a thick swamp. There I saw my mother and my two little sisters, and many other captives who were taken from the town. My mother asked me about my father. I told her he was killed, but could say no more for grief. She burst into tears, and the Indians moved me a little further off, and seized me with cords to a tree.

The Indians came to New Harbor, and sent spies several days to observe how and where people were employed &c., who found the men were generally at work at noon and left about their houses only women and children. Therefore the Indians divided themselves into several parties, some ambushing the way between the fort and houses, as likewise between them and the distant fields; and then alarming the farthest off first, they killed and took the people, as they moved toward the town and fort, at their pleasure, and very few escaped to it. Mr. Patishall was taken and killed, as he lay in his sloop near the Barbican.

On the first stir about the fort, my youngest brother was at play near it, and running in, was, by God's goodness, thus preserved. Captain Weems, with great courage and resolution, defended the weak old fort two days; when, being much wounded, and the best of his men killed, beat for a parley, which eventuated in these conditions:

1. That they, the Indians, should give him Mr. Patishall's sloop.

2. That they should not molest him in carrying off the few people that had got into the fort, and three captives that they had taken.

3. That the English should carry off in their hands what they could

from the fort.

On these conditions the fort was surrendered, and Captain Weems went off; and soon after, the Indians set on fire the fort and the houses, which made a terrible blast, and was a melancholy sight to us poor captives, who were sad spectators.

After the Indians had thus laid waste Pemmaquid, they moved us to New Harbor, about two miles east of Pemmaquid, a cove much frequented by fishermen. At this place there were, before the war, about twelve houses. These the inhabitants deserted as soon as the rumor of war reached the place. When we turned our backs on the town, my heart was ready to break! I saw my mother. She spoke to me, but I could not answer her. That night we tarried at New Harbor, and the next day went in their canoes for Penobscot. About noon, the canoe in which my mother was, and that in which I was, came side by side; whether accidentally or by my mother's desire, I can not say. She asked me how I did. I think I said "pretty well," but my heart was so full of grief I scarcely knew whether audible to her. Then she said, "Oh! my child! how joyful and pleasant it would be if we were going to old England, to see you uncle Chalker and other friends there! Poor babe, we are going into the wilderness, the Lord knows where!" Then bursting into tears, the canoes parted. That night following, the Indians with their captives, lodged on an island.

A few days after, we arrived at Penobscot fort, where I again saw my mother, my brother and sisters, and many other captives. I think we tarried here eight days. In that time, the Jesuit of the place had a great mind to buy me. My Indian master made a visit to the Jesuit, and carried me with him. And here I will note that the Indian who takes a captive is accounted his master, and has a perfect right to him, until he gives or sells him to another. I saw the Jesuit show my master pieces of gold, and understood afterward that he was tendering for my ransom. He gave me a biscuit, which I put in my pocket, and not daring to eat it, buried it under a log, fearing he had put something in it to make me love him. Being very young, and having heard so much of the Papists torturing the Protestants, caused me to act thus; and I hated the sight of a Jesuit. When my mother heard the talk of my being sold to a Jesuit, she said to me, "Oh! my dear child, if it were God's will, I had rather follow you to your grave, or never see you more in this world, than you should be sold to a Jesuit; for a Jesuit will ruin you, body and soul!" It pleased God to grant her request, for she never saw me more! Yet she and my two sisters were, after several years captivity, redeemed, but she died ere I returned. My brother, who was taken with me, was, after several years' captivity, most barbarously tortured to death by the Indians.

My Indian master carried me up Penobscot river to a village called Madawamkee, which stands on a point of land between the main river and a branch which heads east of it. At home I had ever seen strangers treated with the utmost civility, and being a stranger, I expected some kind treatment here; but I soon found myself deceived, for I presently saw a number of squaws, who had got together in a circle, dancing and yelling. An old grim-looking one took me by the hand, and leading me into the ring, some seized me by the hair, and others by my hands and feet, like so may furies; but my master presently laying down a pledge, they released me.

We Are the Stars Which Sing

PASSAMAQUODDY LEGEND
J. D. PRINCE

Nilun pesēsmuk elintakwik
Nt'lintotēp'n k'p'sakh'nmâk'nuk.
Nilun sipsisuk skwu'tik
K'p'mitoyap'n pisokikw's;
K'p'sakh'nmâk'n p'sēs'm.

K't'lintowanen aut niweskwuk;
W't-aut K'tci Niweskw.
Kwitcimkononowuk nohowuk k'tonkewin'wuk
Nosokwat muwiniyul.
Nit meskw tepnaskwiewis
Meskw k'tonketitikw.
K't'lapinen pemteni'kok.
Yut lintowâk'n pemteni'kok.

We are the stars which sing
We sing with our light.
We are the birds of fire;
We fly over the heaven;
Our light is a star.

We sing on the road of the spirits;
The road of the great spirit.
Among us are three hunters
Who follow the bear,
There never was a time
When they were not hunting.
We look upon the mountains
This is a song of the mountains.

The Stars

PASSAMAQUODDY LEGEND

For we are the stars. For we sing.
For we sing with our light.
For we are birds made of fire.
For we spread our wings over the sky.
Our light is a voice.
We cut a road for the soul
for its journey through death.
For three of our number are hunters.
For these three hunt a bear.
For there never yet was a time
when these three didn't hunt.
For we face the hills with disdain.
This is the song of the stars.

January, 1724

ROBERT CHUTE

At Mekwas'que, moon when the cold is great,
we stood before the seashore chapel
after evening prayer. Sun low
over the islands. Sea mist, clouds,
glowing in red and yellows.
Spanish oranges, Persian melons,
a plate of smoky glass on a cloth
from Normandy.   The old man
swept his hand across the sky.
"Like that the deer split open
spills life and blood glistening
on the snow. The fat is soft
and yellow. The waves of gut steam."

It was bitter cold. The sea smoke rose
between us and the setting sun
but we stood there, Warramenset and I,
a little longer. Our hearts
were fixed upon the sunset. Warramenset
thrust his arm out, hand flat, palm down,
pointing to the last crescent of the sun.

"Where can we hunt?
Where can we fish?
The English stand
like sharp stones
and we must turn away."

La Dernière Lune

ROBERT   CHUTE

Nous sommes partis maintenant. Vers le nord
comme la neige de l'Amusswikizous
qui laisse derrière elle les larmes froides du printemps.
Personne, même pas les vieux, ne put suivre
le linceul de l'hiver dans sa fuite devant le soleil.
Nous aussi maintenant sommes rappelés
vers les terres blanches de nos pères.
Aucun Anglais, aucun Français, n'y sont.
Peut-être—on m'a dit—que nos âmes
iront au Paradis où vont les Robes-noires—
je ne sais pas. Mais nous, les Norrigwock,
sommes partis. Cherchez si vous voulez
le long des rivières, parmi toutes les îles
de la baie. Cherchez partout dans les forêts profondes.
Nous sommes partis comme fond la glace des lacs,
comme la neige fuyant vers le nord. Où sont les feuilles
qui sont tombées avant l'arrivée des Anglais?
Nous sommes partis comme se dispersent les feuilles.
Fondus comme la neige en fuite vers le nord.
Le pays n'est pas nôtre. Nous avons perdus nos prières.
La rivière ne coule plus vers la mer.

The Last Moon

ROBERT CHUTE

We are gone now. Gone north
like the Amusswikizoos snow
that leaves behind the cold tears of spring.
No one, not even the old ones, could follow
winter's shroud as it fled before the sun.
Now we too are drawn back
to the white land of our fathers.
No English, no French, join us there.
Maybe—I have been told—our souls
will be in Heaven where the Black robed
fathers go—I don't know. But we, the Norrigwock,
are gone. Search if you will
along the river, among all the islands
of the bay. Search all through the deep woods.
We are gone like the ice from the lake,
like snow fleeing north. Where are the leaves
that fell before the English came?
We are gone like the leaves are scattered.
Melted away like the north-fleeing snow.
The land is not ours. We have lost our prayers.
The river no longer runs to the sea.

The Coming of Glooskap

WABANAKI LEGEND
JOSEPH NICOLAR

Glooskap, The Man From Nothing, first called
the minds of his Red Children to his coming into the world
when the world contained no other man, in flesh, but himself.
When he opened his eyes lying on his back in the dust,
his head toward the rising of the sun,
and his feet toward the setting of the sun;
the right hand pointing to the north
and his left hand to the south.
Having no strength to move any part of his body,
yet the brightness of the day revealed to him
all the glories of the whole world:
the sun was at its highest standing still,
and beside it was the moon without motion
and the stars were in their fixed places
while the firmament was in its beautiful blue.
While yet his eyes were held fast in their sockets
he saw all that the world contained.
Beside what the region of the air revealed to him,
he saw the land, the sea:
mountains, lakes, rivers, and the motion of the waters;
and in it he saw the fishes.
On the land were the animals and beasts,
and in the air the birds.
In the direction of the rising sun
he saw the night approaching.

While the body clung to the dust
he was without mind,
and the flesh without feeling.
At that moment the heavens were lit up,
with all kinds of bright colors most beautiful,
each color stood by itself,

and in another moment
every color shot a streak into the other,
and soon all the colors intermingled,
forming a beautiful brightness in the center of the heavens
over the front of his face.
Nearer and nearer came the brightness toward his body
until it got almost to a touching distance,
and a feeling came into his flesh,
he felt the warmth of the approaching brightness,
and he fell into a deep sleep.

The wind of the heavens fanned his brow,
and the sense of seeing returned to him,
but he saw not the brightness he beheld before,
but instead of the brightness
a person like unto himself,
standing at his right hand,
and the person's face was toward the rising of the sun.
In silence he raised his right hand
in the direction of the rising sun,
passed it from thence to the setting of the sun,
and immediately a streak of lightning
followed the motion of his hand
from one side of the earth to the other.
Again he raised his right hand to the south,
passing it to the north,
and immediately another streak of lightning
followed the motion of his hand.
Immediately after the passing of the lightning over his body
a sense of thought came into him,
and the Great Spirit answered his thought
saying these words:

"Arise from thy bed of dust
and stand on thy feet,
let the dust be under thy feet,
and as thou believest,
thou shall have strength to walk."

Immediately strength came into him,
and he arose to his feet,
and stood beside the Great Spirit.

After this the Great Spirit moved
and turned half around
toward his right hand,
facing the sun.
Lifting both hands and looking up he said:

"Go thy way!"
and immediately the whole heavens obeyed.
The sun, moon, and all the stars
moved toward the setting of the sun.
The night coming slowly toward their standing,
when the Great Spirit sending up his voice, saying:

"Let us make man in our own image,"
and immediately dropped his two hands
and cast his eyes upon the land
and moved halfway around again toward his right hand
facing the setting of the sun
and passed his right hand from the north to the south.
The lightning followed the motion of his hand
from the north to the south,
and again passing his hand
from the setting of the sun
to the rising of the sun,
and when the lightning came upon the night which was
    approaching
it disappeared....

Gluskap Fashions the Animals

WABANAKI LEGEND
HORACE P. BECK

One of the first things Gluskap did was to fashion all the animals. As with the fish, his attempts were not totally successes. But Gluskap kept on until he had fashioned all the creatures and given them breath. He then went a little apart from the menagerie and made his favorite creature, man. To do this he gathered together a great pile of red sand and began to shape it into a figure that resembled himself. Since he had already made the fishes and the animals, he was skilled in his work and made an excellent model. First he made the head to the north, then the arms to the east and west, then the legs to the south. Finally he made the body, connected them all together, and breathed on his creation, which sprang up and became man. (To this day most Indians prefer to sleep with their heads to the north.) Where he had been lying sprang up a hill of corn. "That," said Gluskap, "is your food."

Next he decided to see what the animals would do to his newest creation, so he called them all together and said: "Man" and sat back to watch the results. At the dreaded word the animals all reacted as they should. The deer and the moose fled. The beaver and otter dove overboard, and the mink took to the ground. Birds flew away, and the wolf slunk off into the thickets. Only the squirrel, who was then very large, reacted badly. At the time he was a huge creature, and at the mention of "man" he went berserk. He dashed about biting down huge trees, throwing boulders, and making a terrible commotion, where-upon Gluskap called him to his side and soothed him and petted him. Each time the Master's hand stroked him the squirrel became smaller until, at last, he was the same size he is today. At the same time the petting curled his tail into the shape it now is instead of the straight tail he had formerly. Gluskap again said "Man" and again the squirrel reacted as before, but now, instead of biting down huge trees and throwing boulders, he could only snap off twigs and throw nuts and chatter harmlessly from the branches. Contented, Gluskap retired from the scene for a space, but once again he began to fret.

Again he called the animals to him and examined them. This time it seemed to him that the moose was far too large and might prove too dangerous for man to cope with, so he called the moose to him, held out his hand and said, "Push against this!" The moose did so. He pushed so hard he shortened his neck and compressed his shoulders. He pushed so hard that he broke his nose, but by that time he had been reduced to manageable size and Gluskap bade him desist. To this very day the moose has a broken nose, a short neck, and humped shoulders and, if you will look carefully, you will see in the fur between his horns the imprint of the Creator's hand.

Unfortunately, one moose appears to have escaped the pushing contest described earlier and retained its original size. This creature became a great burden to man, for he rushed through villages, knocking down wigwams and playing havoc in general. News of this finally reached Gluskap's ears, and he went in search of the creature, armed with his trusty axe and accompanied by his little dog, with whom he had previously made a contract that if man would feed Dog, Dog would serve him. After a lengthy search Gluskap found the moose and started him running. For four days and four nights the moose fled, and Gluskap raced in pursuit. On the fourth day the moose tired, but Gluskap came on apace, leaping valleys and vaulting mountains, as fresh as when he began, slowly gaining on his quarry. On the fifth day Gluskap caught up and swung the axe with terrible accuracy.

Being hungry, he dressed the great animal and threw the guts to his dog. Part of them fell on land; the rest went overboard. Dog devoured what lay on the land, but ignored what fell into the water, so Gluskap turned him to stone on the shore. The guts turned to white quartz in the water, and the fossil dog can still be seen looking at the fossil entrails at Cape Rosier. The rest of the moose Gluskap cooked in a pot and devoured. When finished, he overturned the pot, which became Mount Kineo at Moosehead Lake, and went home.

Koluskap and Wind

PASSAMAQUODDY LEGEND
WAYNE NEWELL & R. LEAVITT

The Indians believe in a great bird. They call him Wocawson, the wind-maker. He lives far in the north; there he sits on top of a big rock where the clouds end. Whenever he moves his wings, the wind begins to blow.

At that time when Koluskap still went around among men, often he too would go paddling in his canoe, hunting birds.

Once, long ago, the wind blew every day; it blew strongly. More and more the wind blew, until at last it gusted and brought on a storm. Koluskap could not travel about by canoe. He said, "Wocawson, this big bird who lives in the north, he is the one who is doing this."

He searches for him. He has to go very far before he finds him. He finds him sitting on a big rock—a huge white bird.

He says to him, "Grandfather, do you not have pity for your grandchildren? You are the one who has made the bad weather, the wind, the gusts. You move your wings too much."

In spite of this, the big bird continues yawning. "I was here at the very beginning. In distant days, before anyone spoke, I was the first one to be heard. I was the first to move my wings. And I will continue to move them as I please!"

At that point, Koluskap gets up. He is so powerful, he grows to the height of the clouds. He picks up this huge bird as if he were a duck. He holds him by both wings and throws him down into a crack between two rocks. There he leaves him.

From that time on, the Indians could travel about, all day long. It was always calm—for days, weeks, and months—until at last the water became foamy from stagnation. So thick was it that Koluskap could not paddle his canoe.

And then he remembered the great bird: he set out; he went to see him again. He found him just as he had left him—for Wocawson lives forever. He lifted him up, put him back again on the rock, and opened one of his wings. From that time one, it was not quite as windy as long ago.

Gluskap Goes to France

WABANAKI LEGEND
HORACE P. BECK

Once Gluskap saw boats sailing by. He walked out into the sea and picked one up and examined it carefully. He asked the crew who they were and they told him they were subjects of the King of France. This made Gluskap think, and as he went ashore he made up his mind that he should like to see Paris where the King of France lived.

"Grandmother, let us go to France."

"All right, let us go."

As soon as it was decided, Gluskap got some food together, and he and his grandmother went down to the harbor of St. John and picked out an island for their ship. They put some provisions aboard and made up a crew of squirrels because they were the best climbers around, loosened the island from the bottom, and sailed away.

After a long time they came to Paris and anchored their ship near the King's castle. It was almost dark when they dropped anchor, and the next morning the King looked out his window and saw an island with many tall trees in the harbor. Since the King needed some lumber he gave orders, saying, "Go send some soldiers out to cut down those trees."

Gluskap observed their coming and cried, "Look, Grandmother, the King of France is coming to see us." But the soldiers climbed aboard and started killing the squirrels and cutting down the trees. "What are you doing, cutting down my masts and killing my squirrels?"

"They are trees and squirrels and they belong to the King of France."

Then Gluskap became angry and thought to kill the soldiers, but his grandmother said no, that would not be polite. Gluskap put them in the boats and sent them to the King and told them to tell the monarch that Gluskap and his grandmother had come to see him.

When the King saw his soldiers and found they had not cut the trees, he was very angry. When they told him why, he was even angrier and sent the soldiers to bring Gluskap and his grandmother to him.

"Who are you?" asked the King. "Why don't you let the soldiers cut the trees on my island?"

"I am Gluskap and this is my grandmother, and the island is my boat."

This angered the King, and he ordered his soldiers to shoot Gluskap, but the latter just smiled and smoked his stone pipe and the bullets bounced off. Seeing this, the King realized that he had to think of some better way to dispose of these people, so he called his wise men. They said, "Put them in a cannon and shoot it."

The soldiers brought a great cannon and filled it half full of powder, and then shoved in Gluskap and his grandmother, and put a wad on top of them. When everything was ready the soldiers stood around, and somebody told the King, who gave orders to fire it. One man put a match to it and there was a terrible explosion.

After the smoke cleared away they discovered that the gun had blown up, killing a thousand soldiers. On the ground smoking their stone pipes and quite unharmed sat Gluskap and his grandmother. They got up and went down to their ship and sailed back to St. John, where they anchored and where the ship still remains.

However, Gluskap was so disgusted by his treatment at the hands of the white men that he and his grandmother went away somewhere far to the north where they still live. Before they left they promised the Indians that they would return and drive the white men from the land, when Gluskap had filled his wigwam to the very top with arrowheads, which he is still making.

When Koluskap Left the Earth

PASSAMAQUODDY LEGEND
WAYNE NEWELL & R. LEAVITT

At the time when Koluskap left the earth, he had scared away all evil-looking creatures. Giants, for instance, no longer wandered aimlessly in the forests. Kollu never again could bring darkness by spreading his wings. The great devil Cinu never again devoured people in the north. No evil beasts, devils, or great serpents could be found near where men live.

Once all the evil devils have been driven away, Koluskap tries to teach the Indians to live better lives. But he cannot please them. They cause Koluskap great worry; finally he can stay among them no longer. And so he gathers them for a feast along the shore at Minas Basin. All the Indians and animals attend.

At the end of the feast, he climbs into a great canoe. The Indians watch him until they can no longer see him. When they have lost sight of him, they still hear him singing on his way. His voice gets fainter and fainter as the distance increases. At last they do not hear him at all. There by the water's edge they all stand in a frightened posture.

And then something strange happens to them: creatures once understood one another—they had one common language. All of a sudden, they do not understand one another. They are so frightened they go crazy with fear. Then each one runs off on his own; that one goes one way and another that way. They will not gather again until Koluskap returns to them. He will bring them together again, and then the Indians will assemble peacefully. But now, he makes everything feel lonely.

It is said that when Koluskap left the Indians, the white owl went into the thick woods. And he will not return again until the day that he goes to greet Koluskap. There, even now, he can be heard deep in the forest. He says, "Kuhkuhu."

Koluskap's loons, his hunters, fly aimlessly all over the earth. They cannot find their master. Loudly they howl.

Many years before he left, he had given his loons a message. He had told them, "Whoever seeks me, I shall give one thing that he wants when he finds me, whatever it may be. Of course, it will be hard going, and very difficult to try, for the distance is very long. Those who try to find me will be the ones who endure great hardship and suffering."

It is said that three Indians made the attempt, one Maliseet and two Penobscots.

They travel for seven years, and at last they have almost reached him. Making their way along the trail is very difficult, and they encounter many hardships. Although they are still three months journey from where he lives, they can already hear his dogs barking. The closer they get to their chief's house, the louder his dogs bark. At last they find their great chief, the one who governs all men and animals.

He is very glad to see them, and he entertains them warmly. He asks them what it is they wish to have.

One, the oldest Indian, wants to know how to hunt. He looks trustworthy, but he is not respected among the people because he does not know how to hunt. He asks to be able to catch and kill animals. So Koluskap gives him a little whistle, a whistle with special powers. Everyone that hears it will like its sound. It has such great power that any animal will follow anyone who blows it.

The second Indian is asked, "What is it that you desire?"

"That women be fond of me."

Koluskap says, "How many?"

"It doesn't matter how many, just let it be enough."

When Koluskap hears him, he doesn't approve of the idea; nevertheless, he smiles warmly. He gives him a bag, tightly tied. He says to him, "Don't untie it until you get to your house."

The second Indian gives thanks, and then departs.

The third young man is quite handsome, but he has very little common sense. His heart is set on nothing but finding a way to make the Indians laugh.

He is asked, "And what is it you want?"

He says, "It would please me very much if you could find a way for me to make an odd noise, so that I can make the Indians laugh."

The strange noise he asks for is rarely heard in the Wabnaki territory. It can be heard only in a few huts far back in the great forest. There are now only a few fearsome *motewolons* or men with unusual powers who know how it is produced. It sounds so odd that those who hear it resounding have to laugh.

So Koluskap sends Nimaqsuwehs, the sable, into the woods to go pick a certain kind of root. When eaten, it will bring the strange effects that the boy wants. He is instructed not to touch it until he arrives at his house. If he touches it, it will not have a good effect on him. The young man gives thanks and departs.

It takes them seven years to make the return journey. Only seven days' journey is required when they make their way to the main path. Then each one goes toward his own village.

Only one makes it back to his house—this is the hunter. With his little whistle in his pocket, he has no worries. He walks about in the woods. As long as he lives, he will always have a good supply of fresh meat in his house.

That one who wanted to be loved by a woman, he doesn't even get a wife. He does not walk far before he unties the bag. Beautiful maidens come forth singing, looking like white doves. They surround him. Their eyes burn with desire and their hair blows about in the wind. They become wild. They hug him and kiss him.

They become more and more uncontrollable. Even though he sends them away, they do not listen. He tries to escape, but cannot. He gasps for air, suffocating. At last he dies. Those walking by find him, and he is already stiff. What happened to the maidens is not known.

The third Indian goes off by himself. He is happy. All of a sudden he remembers that Koluskap has given him something.

He does not even begin to think about what he was told: *Not until you arrive at your house do you eat this.* But right away he takes out the root. And then and there he eats it. Before he has finished eating it, he remembers that he will be able to make the strange noise: the strength of the magic root that he was given comes upon him. It makes a loud noise. The jesting devils are able to imitate it as it echoes from the high mountains, from the lowlands, and from the swamps. Eventually, the screech-owl answers him. He feels so proud, he struts along blowing. As he walks along, he is as happy as a little bird.

After a while, however, he begins to feel uncomfortable. When he sees a deer, he puts an arrow on a string. He begins to stalk it. Just when he raises his bow to aim, he can no longer hold the magical wonder-noise he was given. He really makes an evil sound. The deer jumps away. Then the young man curses.

When he arrives at Penobscot, he is half-starved. He is too pitiful-looking to arouse laughter. Those elder Indians are moved to laughter at first. They laugh hard. This makes the young man feel a little happier. But as the days go on, they think less and less of him, and he himself grows tired of living. He goes away into the woods to kill himself.

Then Cipelahq swoops down from the clouds and takes him to the lower world. The wondrous noise that was given to him he is allowed to use in the dark world. He is never again heard among men.

This story is ended.

The Witch of Harpswell

ANONYMOUS

A Tale of the Old Days when Maine was a Colony of Massachusetts

Nearly a century and a half ago when the Reverend Elisha Eaton, first settled preacher in Harpswell, ministered to the people in that town there existed among the fisher-folk an earnest belief in witchcraft. Strange stories of those early times have been handed down from generation to generation, but among them all there is none more dramatic than that of the burial of Hannah Stover.

This narrative is said to be based on facts, and at all events it is one of unusual interest in Harpswell.

The Witch of Harpswell

The feathery branches of the hemlocks that stood, tall and somber, beside the path along Harpswell Neck, soughed softly in the November wind; and the funeral train that wended its slow way, with frequent haltings, through the woodland track, might hear also the monotonous sound of the surf on the rocks out of sight, yet not far away.

It was a singular procession. Six brawny fisherwives carried the rude bier, on which rested a coffin unpainted and clumsy, while behind came a tall, pale girl, supporting the steps of a man who seemed too feeble for the task of walking at all. After these two mourners, to whose faces the effort of repressing emotion lent an expression of cold sternness, came a handful of women, who straggled irregularly forward, avoiding the rough places in the forest path with a half instinctive sense that comes from long familiarity.

Now and then the bearers were in silence relieved of their solemn burden, and with stolid impassiveness the train moved on. The quaint dresses of the women, the cold light filtered through the tossing boughs of pine and hemlock, the mournful bier, combined to produce a sad and strange effect. Even the stolid fisherwives who were thus accompanying Elkniah Stover's second wife to her last resting-place were not wholly unconscious of the wildness of the circumstances, and although they had few words in which to express their feelings, they now and then muttered half to themselves and half to each other, some comment which indicated the astonishment little short of stupefication of people used to the most common-place round of life who find themselves suddenly taking part in remarkable and startling occurrences.

The last century was not far past noon. Harpswell Neck, now a long cape, almost bare of trees, stretching out into Casco Bay with unattractive barrenness, was then still thickly wooded; and only a path through the primeval forest connected the fishing settlement at its end with the small village gathered about the graveyard and the old square church, still standing, where Parson Eaton, or, as the country people universally called him, Priest Eaton, broke the bread of life to his seafaring flock. There had been grave doubts how Priest Eaton might feel about performing the last rites over the body that the women, angrily deserted by the men of the settlement, were wearily bearing to her grave. Hannah Stover had not only been a Quaker, causing great scandal by refusing to be present at the services in the old square church, but there were afloat rumors of a wilder and darker character concerning her. To the stepdaughter, Mercy, who had been on the day previous to ask him, Priest Eaton had, however, given his promise, perhaps somewhat reluctantly, to over-look all shortcomings in view of the well-established godliness of Elkniah Stover's family, and her sorrowing husband hoped that no allusion to the religious wanderings of his dead wife might add to his pain.

While the women by their presence and by taking the office of bearers gave testimony to the worth of the departed, they were not without more or less conscious willingness that the occasion should be improved to their spiritual education by some contrasting of their own steadfastness in the faith with the errors of the deceased. They had labored zealously with her living, and their characters were too hardy to yield all opposition simply because Goodwife Stover could no longer reply. They had braved the anger of the husbands that had forbidden them to be present at the funeral of one to whom popular malignity gave the name of witch, a name in those days of terrible import; but righteousness, and perhaps especially feminine righteousness, is seldom unwilling to hear itself commended, even at the expense of the unanswering dead.

As the forest began to grow thinner, and there were signs that the village was near, a certain subtle air of expectation made itself evident by faint signs. The bearers walked with more alert step, the women behind drew their cloaks about them with an air half of protest and half of reproval, while Elkniah Stover's daughter held more firmly in her own the trembling arm of her aged father, as she vainly tried to repress the growing agitation that made her own limbs unsteady and her throat dry and parched.

At length, between the trees appeared the heavy eaves of the meeting-house, and in a moment more the rough palings of the enclosure in which it stood with the graves about it were brought in sight by the abrupt emergence of the path from a thicket of alders and arbor vitae trees.

Beside the churchyard gate the women saw Priest Eaton, his sombre robes of office blown by the chill November wind, and with a sudden surprise that made their hearts stand still, they saw, too, that he was not alone, but that around him in sullen groups were gathered the men of the Neck, whom their wives believed still at home in the settlement from which they had come.

For an instant the forlorn band of corpse bearers half halted and wavered as if to turn back; then, obeying the instinct that makes women in a supreme crisis so inevitably turn to the priest, they carried the bier quickly forward and set it before the black robed figure of Parson Eaton.

There was a moment of complete silence. Then Goodwife Mayo, with a deep-drawn sigh of fatigue, wiped her heated forehead upon the corner of her long, coarse cloak. The homely action broke the spell with which the strangeness of the situation had held them, and as if at a concerted signal, the men pressed forward. As they did so, a tall gaunt man, with weatherbeaten face and narrow eyes, spoke:

"Ye may take the witch-wife back," he said, with a roughness that was partly genuine and partly assumed to help him overcome some secret, lingering weakness. "Let her lie in some of the black places in the woods where she would foregather with her master, the Devil; but her wicked body shall never poison the ground where Christian folks are buried. No grave in consecrated ground for the likes of her."

A hoarse murmur of assent, like the distant roaring of the surf on the ledges of white Seguin, answered him from the men. The women half from a habitual fear of their husbands and half from superstitious dread of the possibility of contamination from the dead, began to huddle together, drawing little by little away from the bier. Their eyes appealed to Priest Eaton to speak for them and to direct their course in an extremity so far removed from their ordinary experiences.

The dead leaves, hurrying before the wind, rustled at their feet, while in the air as a vague monotone was the distant sound of the soughing boughs and the waves beating upon the inhospitable rocks.

"Ezra Johnston," the clergyman said in tones of solemnity, "who gave you the right to dictate who shall rest in consecrated ground? Are you the leader of God's people?"

"No," the other retorted, the angry blood flushing his swarthy cheek; "but when the leader of God's people would let the Devil's dam into the graveyard of our meetin'-house, it is time when any man may speak. This woman could never be made to go through that gate while alive; why should she be carried through it, now she is dead?"

The murmur of approval swelled again, louder than before; and little by little the groups shifted, until Mercy Stover and her white-haired father were left alone beside the rough coffin.

"You were always hasty of speech," Priest Eaton answered calmly, but with a certain stern dignity that belonged to his office in those days. "Who made you a witch-finder?"

"I do not need to be a witch-finder to know Goodwife Stover for a witch," was the stout reply. "I knew of her ways and her repute while still she lived in Freeport, and I warned Brother Elkniah against her. For that very thing she was hotly angered against me, by this token that my seine broke that same day I spoke as if every mesh in it were cut, and sorely hath she many times since tormented me with her witch wiles. Ask Goodman Haskell, here, if he was not on my boat when she bewitched my killock so that all my strength was not to move it until I made the sign of a cross on it. Ask—"

"I have heard," interrupted the minister, "of your popish practices before; but they are not to be boasted of in open day unrebuked."

Elkniah Stover's limbs had failed under him, as this strange colloquy went on, and he sank, a pathetic and broken figure, upon the handle of the bier. As he sat with one palsied hand, blue with cold, resting upon the head of his staff, and the other clasping tightly the wrist of Mercy, he lifted his hand with a gesture of despair and anguish.

"Was it for this," he wailed in a quavering voice of pain, "that the Lord gave me strength to rise from my bed and follow the body of my helpmeet to the grave when a grave is denied her? Ezra Johnston was greatly enraged, as we all know, that after his sister that was my wife died I should go to Freeport for a helpmeet, when he would have had me choose the sister of his own good wife. His killock caught under the thwarts. Waitstill Eastman can tell you that. But all that went amiss, Ezra would still lay at the door of my good wife; her that is here dead before ye, and ye deny her a grave away from the wolves."

"She shall have her grave, father," Mercy said, with an intensity of purpose that impressed even her angry uncle. "She shall lie by the side of my own mother if I have to bury her with no one to help me."

The fickle sympathy of the bystanders veered in her direction, and one or two of the fisher-wives that had formed part of the funeral train moved almost imperceptibly toward the spot where she stood, their action showing that the more merciful, at least, could not easily bring themselves to anything so horrible to their mind as to deny burial to a fellow creature. Before, however, the movement could be at all general, even before it was marked, Ezra Johnston, whose always violent temper was fast mastering him, broke out again:

"Oh, no doubt Waitstill Eastman knows, and I am a blind fool that cannot see when his killock is free on the thwarts. Perhaps Goodman

Eastman will say, too, that last Sabbath night I wasn't hailed in my sleep to the British bark off the point and dragged by the Devil's imps up and down the sides until I was bruised and aching in every bone of my body. And I might have been killed but that daylight drew on and with my own ears I heard Goodwife Stover say: 'Let him go, 'tis almost cock-crowing.' I knew her voice as well as I know my own, and that but two days before she died. What do you say to that, Elkniah Stover? What do ye say to that, Parson Eaton?"

A dozen voices broke loose into a sudden babble. The unseemly and cruel debate that had thus far been carried on by single voices was all at once taken up by the whole company. The first surprise and awe had now worn off enough to let the folks recover the use of their tongues, and men and women hurried now clamorously to deny or confirm Ezra Johnston's charges. The clergyman tried vainly to make himself heard. His words were lost in the growing tumult. The crowd became every moment more and more like a mob. Johnston grew more and more furious, and his anger infected the men who were most under his influence. The very name of witch roused all the superstitious fears of the simple fishermen, and all the fanaticism of their blood was appealed to.

"Come," Johnston cried out at last, struck with a sudden idea, "let us take the witch-wife to Devil's Den, and leave her bones to rot there. I warrant she has been there times enough before."

A shudder ran through his hearers. The Devil's Den was a rocky cave on the shore of Harpswell Neck, where more than one good boat had perished and more than one fisherman had seen straggling lights flitting about to cheat him to his destruction.

"Come," repeated Johnston, taking a long stride toward the bier, "take hold here, some of you."

But before he could grasp the rude handle, his niece sprang forward. Her eyes flashed; her simple hood fell back from her pale face, and her whole form quivered with excitement.

"Coward!" she cried. "Oh you coward, you coward!"

Her voice, shrill and high, rang upward toward the heavy gray clouds as it would call help down from heaven. The women shrank back in fear, and the men in astonishment, while with arm stretched out in an unstudied attitude of appeal, and with an energy the more impressive by contrast with her usually calm and almost shy manner, Mercy poured out her protest.

"What has my mother done," she demanded with a sort of sacred fury that stilled for the moment all murmurs, and brought tears to the eyes of more than one, half of pity and half of excitement, "what has my mother done that you would treat her dead body worse than that of a dog? She has been more than a mother to me, and how many times she has helped the sick and the poor! Oh, are you the neighbors I have lived among all my life, and that have been kind to me, that I must beg for a grave for my mother who was kinder and better than you all? And you, Uncle Ezra! Who saved your hand when it was frozen? Who doctored little Hope when she had the scarlet fever? You were glad enough to have her help when she was living, but now—"

Her self control gave way. She broke off in a burst of hysterical sobs, leaning her face on the shoulder of her trembling old father. Ezra Johnston, for a moment giving way before his niece's vehemence, covered his confusion with a sneer, and again attempted to seize the handle of the bier.

Before he could do more, however, a vigorous grasp caught his arm, and a stalwart young fellow drew him roughly back.

"Let be, Ezra Johnston," the young man said, in a deep voice, his strong white teeth showing angrily. "Let be, or it will be worse for ye."

Like a wildcat, Johnston turned to strike, but before the blow could fall, the clergyman sprang to catch the strong wrist of his angry parishioner.

"Stop!" Priest Eaton commanded in a voice of authority. "I warn you that you are going too far."

Enraged as Johnston was, he was still sufficiently master of himself to realize that it was not safe openly to defy the clergyman, and it is not improbable, too, that he could not himself wholly shake off the habit of obedience that was almost universal in the scattered parish.

With any ally less powerful than superstition, it would have been idle for him to set himself against the minister on any question; but the remote pulses of the wave of madness that shook Salem in 1648 was more than a century in dying away, and in Harpswell the belief in witchcraft was as perfect as the faith in religion. Even today, the superstition lives in many a remote New England village, and the air of the sea, laden as it is with mysterious sounds and influences, seems especially to nourish these delusions.

Johnston's whole stubborn nature was by this time aroused, and all his cunning bent on the carrying of his point. He felt instinctively that the tide of general feeling was turned against him, and with genuine New England shrewdness, he hit upon precisely the appeal that would most surely win the fickle crowd again to his views.

"Well," he sneered, falling back, "if Jacob Thatcher takes the matter up, of course we must all give way, even if he wants an accursed witch-wife buried in the same lot with all the Christian folks we come of. Everybody knows that Goody Stover bewitched him long ago to make him run after Mercy; and ye, Daniel Strong, have cause to remember the luck she gave him. But if he takes sides with the Devil, the two together may well be too much for the honest men of Harpswell."

The appeal produced an instant and powerful effect, and the angry retort of Jacob Thatcher was drowned in the cries of assent and approval that answered Johnston's words.

That Thatcher was the lover of Mercy Stover was well enough known in a community where a man was hardly able to keep even his thoughts to himself, and the reference to this fact impeached at once the sincerity and impartiality of his interference. By alluding, moreover, to an old rivalry that extended to boats, athletics, and all interests that the narrow life of Harpswell permitted, and that Thatcher was always victor in, Johnston had secured for himself a powerful support. Not only Daniel Strong, but the young men generally smarted under a secret sense of defeat, while the coincidence between the universal success of the winner and his fondness for the witch's daughter was exactly the sort of argument that appealed most strongly to the superstitious fisherfolk.

The crowd once more broke into speech, which was rather a babble than a clamor, and which became more angry as it swelled. The words of Priest Eaton were lost in the noise. Jacob Thatcher placed himself between the bier and his townsfolk, but even his stout shoulders seemed a slight enough barrier against sacrilege to the dead.

It was one of those chaotic and critical moments in the progress of a mob when it is broken into innumerable separate groups in angry dispute, and when it is idle to reach it as a whole until some striking incident unites once more its divided attention. It is usually true, moreover, that upon the first general impression that shall be exerted on a mob at such a crisis depends its action. It is at its most impressionable stage, and will readily take the stamp of whatever idea is strongly presented to it.

By this time the crowd collected at the churchyard gate included almost every human being in the village, and it had assumed the character of a genuine mob. The remonstrance of Priest Eaton, the entreaties of Elkniah Stover, the appeal of Mercy and the interference of Jacob Thatcher had all proved of no avail, and there seemed small hope but Ezra Johnston would carry his point, and that the body of the dead Quakeress would be cast in dishonor upon the jagged rocks of the Devil's Den.

Help at this desperate crisis came from an unthought of source. By one of these strange thrills that seem to reach the mind through some sense beyond the five, and to appeal to some faculty more subtle, the excited villagers became aware that something new had happened. A sudden hush spread over the wild company. Excited fisher-wives paused with open mouths in the midst of their haranguing, and stretched their necks toward the bier; the angry men broke off their noisy wrangling to turn their eyes in the same direction; even Mercy, who had clung convulsively to her father in the terror of seeing familiar faces transformed into strangeness before her eyes by superstition and rage, turned to look toward the coffin. It was only old Goody Cole, who had at this critical moment made her tottering way up to the bier and flung herself upon it. Lame and decrepit, weak and wandering in her wits, the poor old creature, whose stream of life had been so thin that for almost a century it had trickled on without draining even the ordinary measure of human existence, had only just been able to complete the journey from Harpswell Neck. All the long woodland track she had come to lay her blessing upon Goodwife Stover's grave.

In a wail that had in it the pathos of the sound of the wind in the forest, the wretched crone cried over and over, with heart-broken reiterance:

"Oh, but she was my life! Oh, but she was my life!"

The cry was so intense that it thrilled even the stolid fishermen of Harpswell Neck, perhaps for the time being rendered more sensitive than usual by unwonted excitement. The tension of their nerves became every moment greater, as they stood in unstudied groups, picturesque and strange. The November afternoon was darkening to its close, long lines of fiery light breaking the cold gray of the western sky. A few scant snowflakes were silently stealing through the air, falling upon the angry villagers, upon the tall form of Priest Eaton, with white locks and black gown, upon the strong, young figure of Jacob Thatcher, standing sentinel between his townsfolk and the dead, upon the pathetic group of father and daughter, and amid them all that withered, century-old figure of Goody Cole, repeating in shrill monotone: "Oh, but she was my life!"

They all understood that cry. There was no one there but knew well how long Goody Cole had been a pensioner on the bounty of Goodwife Stover. They might all remember, too, if they chose, that Goody Cole, whom they had left to the tender mercies of a woman they called a witch, was the widow of a man that had lost his life carrying help to a vessel on which were the fathers and husbands of people still alive and in this angry crowd. Goody Cole had been too proud to go on the parish, and her neighbors half a century ago had sworn that she should never come to want. Now, only the charity of this Quaker woman from Freeport had kept her from actual starvation.

"Oh, but she was my life!" quavered the trembling, aged voice over and over. "Oh, but she was my life!"

Pricked to the heart, two other women, almost young enough to be Goody Cole's grand-daughters, came out from the crowd and kneeled beside her, bowing their heads with sobs upon the coffin. There was a rustle and stir among the bystanders. They knew well enough what cause for gratitude these two had. Everybody knew all that happened on Harpswell Neck, and remembered now how to one of these women Goodwife Stover had come in the agonizing horror of child-birth, a saving angel; and how beside the bed of the second she had watched when a malignant disease kept every other woman on the Neck away.

"Oh, but she was my life!" shrilled Goody Cole, her voice rising in a thrilling strain which made the excited woman shiver as if with cold.

The crowd of fisher-wives wavered. Then Goodwife Mayo, whose stout muscles had out-tired those of all the other bearers on the long march from Elkniah Stover's cottage to the shadow of the square meeting-house in which they stood, strode forward again to the coffin. She set her arms akimbo and looked about her.

"And ye, Betty Hincks," she demanded, "who gave ye that cloak ye're wearing this very hour? And ye, Martha Hastings, who brought ye through the fever last fall? And ye, Andrew Cates, who nursed your wife in haying-time? If Hannah Stover was a witch, well would it be for Harpswell Neck if we had more of them."

"Oh, but she was my life!" came in the piercing cry of Goody Cole, like a refrain rising still higher. "Oh, but she was my life!"

"Take up the bier," Priest Eaton cried with a gesture at once of dignity and of command. "Bury her wherever these men will. The ground will be consecrated wherever her body lies. Take it to the Devil's Den," he went on, the occasion inspiring him with unwonted fire, "and I tell you the Devil's Den will be holy if Goodwife Stover's corpse comes there!"

A wave of sudden feeling swept over the people like a mighty wind. As if obeying a common impulse, they rushed forward, with sobs and broken ejaculations, to raise the bier.

But Goodwife Mayo waved them back.

"No," she said, "no man shall touch this bier. The women that have brought it so far in spite of their husbands' orders can carry it the rest of the way."

There was a murmur of mingled assent, contrition and remonstrance; but it was in the end as Goodwife Mayo said.

Followed by all the men, even to Ezra Johnston, who scowled but yielded to the tide of feeling he could not turn back, the women of Harpswell Neck bore the body of Hannah Stover to her resting-place in the consecrated ground of the old graveyard.

"We have buried a witch," Johnston muttered under his breath, as they left the sacred spot.

But in solemn rebuke Priest Eaton answered him: "We have made the grave of a saint."

Jack Downing's Visit to Portland

SEBA SMITH

In the fall of the year 1829 I took it into my head I'd go to Portland. I had heard a good deal about Portland, what a fine place it was, and how the folks got rich there proper fast; and that fall there was a couple of new papers come up to Downingville from there, called the Portland Courier and Family Reader; and they told a good many queer kind of things about Portland and one thing another; and all at once it popped into my head, and I up and told father, and says I, I'm going to Portland whether or no; and I'll see what this world is made of yet. Father stared a little at first, and said he was afraid I should get lost; but when he see I was bent upon it, he give it up; and he stepped to his chest and opened the till, and took out a dollar and gave to me, and says he, Jack, this is all I can do for you; but go, and lead an honest life, and I believe I shall hear good of you yet. He turned and walked across the room, but I could see the tears start into his eyes, and mother sat down and had a hearty crying spell. This made me feel rather bad for a minute or two, and I almost had a mind to give it up; and then again father's dream came into my mind, and I mustered up courage, and decided I'd go. So I tackled up the old horse and packed in a load of ax handles and a few notions, and mother fried me some dough-nuts and put 'em into a box along with some cheese and sausages, and ropped me up another shirt, for I told her I didn't know how long I should be gone; and after I got all rigged out, I went round and bid all the neighbors good bye, and jumped in and drove off for Portland.

Ant Sally had been married two or three years before and moved to Portland, and I inquired round till I found out where she lived, and went there and put the old horse up and eat some supper and went to bed. And the next morning I got up and straightened right off to see the Editor of the Portland Courier, for I knew by what I had seen in his paper that he was just the man to tell me which way to steer. And when I come to see him I knew I was right; for soon as I told him my name and what I wanted, he took me by the hand as kind as if he had been a brother; and says he, Mr. Downing, I'll do any thing I can to assist you. You have come to a good town; Portland is a healthy thriving place, and any man with a proper degree of enterprise may do well here. But says he, Mr. Downing, and he looked mighty kind of knowing, says he, if you want to make out to your mind, you must do as the steamboats do. Well, says I, how do they do? for I didn't know what a steamboat was, any more than the man in the moon. Why, says he, they go *ahead*. And you must drive about among the folks here jest as though you were at home on the farm among the cattle. Don't be afraid of any of 'em, but figure away, and I dare say you will get into good business in a very little while. But, says he, there 's one thing you must be careful of, and that is not to get into the hands of them are folks that trades up round Huckler's Row; for there's some sharpers up there, if they get hold of you, would twist your eye teeth out in five minutes. Well after he had gin me all the good advice he could I went back to Ant Sally's again and got some breakfast, and then I walked all over the town to see what chance I could find to sell my ax handles and things, and to get into business.

After I had walked about three or four hours I come along towards the upper end of the town where I found there were stores and shops of all sorts and sizes. And I met a feller, and says I, what place is this? Why this says he, is Huckler's Row. What, says I, are these the stores where the traders in Huckler's Row keep? And says he, yes. Well then, thinks I to myself, I have a pesky good mind to go in and have a try with one of these chaps, and see if they can twist my eye teeth out. If they can get the best end of a bargain out of me, they can do what there aint a man in Downingville can do, and I should jest like to know what sort of stuff these ere Portland chaps are made of. So in I goes into the best looking store among 'em. And I see some biscuit lying on the shelf, and says I, Mister, how much do you ax apiece for them are biscuit? A cent apiece, says he. Well, says I, I shant give you that, but if you 've a mind to, I'll give you two cents for three of 'em, for I begin to feel a little as though I should like to take a bite. Well, says he, I wouldn't sell 'em to any body else so, but seeing it's you I don't care if you take 'em. I knew he lied, for he never see me before in his life. Well he handed down the biscuits and I took 'em, and walked round the store awhile to see what else he had to sell. At last, says I, Mister have you got any good new cider? Says he, yes, as good as ever you see. Well, says I, what do you ax a glass for it? Two cents, says he. Well, says I, seems to me I feel more dry than I do hungry now. Aint you a mind to take these ere biscuit again and give me a glass of cider? And says he, I don't care if I do; so he took and laid 'em on the shelf again, and poured out a glass of cider. I took the cider and drink it down, and to tell the truth it was capital good cider. Then, says I, I guess it 's time for me to be a going, and I stept along towards the door. But, says he, stop Mister. I believe you haven't paid me for the cider. Not paid you for the cider, says I, what do you mean by that? Didn't the biscuit that I give you jest come to the cider? Oh, ah, right, says he. So I started to go again; and says he, but stop,

Mister, you didn't pay me for the biscuit. What, says I, do you mean to impose upon me? Do you think I am going to pay you for the biscuit and let you keep 'em to? Aint they there now on your shelf, what more do you want? I guess sir, you don't whittle me in that way. So I turned about and marched off, and left the feller staring and thinking and scratching his head, as though he was struck with a dunderment. Howsomever, I didn't want to cheat him, only jest to show 'em it want so easy a matter to pull my eye teeth out, so I called in next day and paid him his two cents. Well I staid at Ant Sally's a week or two, and I went about town every day to see what chance I could find to trade off my ax handles, or hire out, or find some way or other to begin to seek my fortune.

And I must confess the editor of the Courier was about right in calling Portland a pretty good thriving sort of a place; every body seemed to be as busy as so many bees; and the masts of the vessels stuck up round the wharves as thick as pine trees in uncle Joshua's pasture; and the stores and the shops were so thick, it seemed as if there was no end to 'em. In short, although I have been round the world considerable, from that time to this, all the way from Madawaska to Washington, I've never seen any place yet that I think has any business to grin at Portland.

Turnip Pie

REBECCA CUMMINGS

1907

Kaisa Kilponen's mouth watered in anticipation of the turnip pie she was making. Last Thursday, Hilja Kyllönen had given her three little blushing turnips, the first from her garden, and the thought of putting those sweet roots into a pie had been on her mind ever since. She was making enough so they'd have cold pie for Saturday supper, and since tomorrow was the Sabbath, enough for Sunday supper as well.

The sour rye-meal starter had been working overnight, and the bubbly sponge filled the wooden bowl. She mixed in handfuls of flour until she had a dough that was so stiff it wouldn't take any more and then kneaded it energetically, slamming it on the wobbly table top with a loud thump-thump. She cut off a big piece of raw dough, fit it into a pie tin, piled it high with slivers of boiled turnips, pork slices and lumps of fresh butter, and topped it with a crust. She rolled the remaining dough into fat round loaves, enough bread for the next week.

The bread her mother used to make back in the old country, in Finland, had a hole in the center so that the hard black loaves could be hung on a pole across the ceiling, but in America they didn't do it that way. A lot of things were different in America, but at least she and Matti, her husband of nearly three years, had turnip pie and *sauna*.

Turnip pie. Nothing like it. Now if Matti would only get home early enough, he could have some with her.

After breakfast that morning, Matti had rigged the horse and wagon and had gone to Scab Mountain where he would see about getting a pig. Not that going to Scab Mountain was an all-day journey, but Kaisa knew very well that Matti would probably stop by Erkki Suominen's, and then the two of them would go down cellar together. So it could be some time before she saw her husband again.

The large pie swelled in the oven and browned nicely. And oh, what a heavenly smell! Just looking at it was enough to make her hungry, but she didn't cut into it. She just left it on the table to cool. But didn't it look good.

As soon as the bread had baked and was beside the pie under a clean white cloth, she finished her inside work and then took her scrub brush and heavy broom to the *sauna* in order to give it a good scrubbing before lighting the fire. As she scoured the floor and wash benches with coarse sand and water, she thought more and more about the savory turnip pie. The more she thought about it, sitting on the table under the white cloth, the hungrier she got, and her stomach gnawed in impatience.

Finally she set a match to the kindling under the rounded mound of field stones. The fire would have to be fed all afternoon so that by evening there'd be a bed of white coals that would keep the *sauna* hot for hours. She then hurried from the small smoke-filled building, thinking about turnip pie. Just one piece. One little piece.

As she turned the corner to the house, she was surprised to see a sprightly black horse harnessed to a shiny buggy. Of course it belonged to George Pottle, their neighbor. He was the only one for miles who had such a showy animal. Sure enough. There was fat George Pottle standing in her open doorway. Now why wasn't Matti at home? Like most Finnish wives, Kaisa had never had any reason to learn English since her husband did all the talking for the two of them. But now here she was alone, and she'd be forced to say something. Gripping the scrub brush and broom, she approached him.

"There you are!" George Pottle bellowed at the small woman, so slight of stature that she was barely to his shoulder. "Where's Maddy?" He pronounced the name *Maddy* instead of *Mut-ty*, the way it should have been said. "Where's Maddy?" he again loudly demanded.

"No home! No home!" she said, shaking her head fiercely.

"No home?" George repeated. Then impatiently correcting himself said, "You mean he's not at home?" Although he was only a few feet from her, he continued to shout. He always shouted at his immigrant neighbors. He seemed to think that if he could only speak loudly enough, they'd understand. "That's a fine thing. Just fine." And he heaved a huge sigh. The bother in having to deal with these people. How did it happen that they had been able to get all these little farms in Edom? Now they were all over the place, and still more were coming every day. Each of them sending for sisters and cousins and uncles. There should be a law. Perhaps he should write his congressman. Or go to Augusta.

"YOUR COW!" he shouted in exasperation. "YOUR COW IS IN MY CORN AGAIN!"

"*Cow?*" Kaisa repeated, not understanding at all what he was making such a fuss about. Again she said the word. "*Cow?*"

George Pottle stomped his foot, a surprisingly small foot for a man of his great size, and let loose with a string of profanities which it was just as well that Kaisa, a church-going woman, did not understand. Again he sighed, much too loudly. It then occurred to him that if he mimicked the motions of milking, she might understand. Straining to keep from toppling over, he stooped and pulled vigorously at airy teats.

Kaisa nodded her head excitedly. She understood!

George puffed back to his feet—it seemed that he was finally getting somewhere—and jabbed his fat finger in the direction of his corn field.

Suddenly, Kaisa clapped her hands to her face. The cow was in George Pottle's corn! He had once warned that if it happened again, he'd keep the cow. Heaving aside the scrub brush but clinging to the broom, Kaisa whirled and started off through the field at a run.

George Pottle, with an air of righteous self-satisfaction, watched the small woman bob through the field, the white apron strings flapping against her long dark dress. He watched until he could no longer see the quaint maroon kerchief that covered her hair.

That cow of theirs had caused no end of damage. This was the third time it had strayed into his crops. And why wasn't the man of the house home to take care of it?

Strange, these folks, dressing like that and washing up in the queer way they did. He had seen the smoke pouring from the little shingled outbuilding when he drove in. He now knew that was where they took their baths. He remembered that the first time he had seen all the smoke, he had thought their building was on fire. And then he had thought that that was where they smoked meat. However, Albert Hayes had told him all about it one night at grange.

It seemed that Albert had even gone into one of those baths. He said it was like going into the jaws of hell, it was so hot. That served Albert right, being so friendly to these people and wanting to try everything.

It still angered George when he thought about the time he had passed by one evening last summer and had seen the husband and another man sitting outside that very bath house without a stitch of clothes on. For all the world to see! It was just as well that his Marjorie—bless her—was no longer with him to have to see such sights.

And the things they ate!

Perhaps it was the smells of the freshly baked bread and turnip pie wafting from the open doorway that made George Pottle think of what they ate. But suddenly, George could think of nothing but food. Not that the dark bread they ate had ever appealed to him. That tough-looking bread could never compare to the soft white bread his own mother had taught his Marjorie, as a young bride, to make for him. For a moment, it irked him that Marjorie had deprived him, by passing on, of the bread he had grown used to for over forty years. Life was unfair!

However, the thought of the unfairness of life dissolved as the sweet image of Rose Parsons flitted through his mind. He wondered whether she could make bread. This latest housekeeper he had hired had turned out to be nothing but a disappointment.

He had to admit that the smells drifting from the kitchen were mightily appealing. He stepped inside to look and lifted the corner of the white cloth. His nostrils twitched. Four loaves, all rounded and plump. But what was that strange-looking puffy thing? Because he had had to dash over, he hadn't yet taken the time to have his dinner, and he was a man who liked to eat at twelve sharp. He bent over the pie and inhaled.

To be fair, George Pottle truly felt that these people owed him something. Wasn't this the third time their cow had gotten into his corn? All that damage! Not to think of the inconvenience. He puffed in indignation. So, at the moment, he felt quite justified in helping himself to the turnip pie. Just recompense, he thought. They owe me for my trouble. It's small enough payment.

As he held the reins of the prancing horse, he hungrily eyed the pie. His huge stomach rumbled. At last, with one hand, he tore out a small chunk from the pie so that pieces of slippery yellow turnip slithered through his fingers. Although he had fully expected that he would be throwing the whole mess to his dog Satan because it would be so foreign, he did nibble the bit in his fingers. Not bad. Not bad at all. In fact, it was tasty enough that he took a more generous bite. The turnips, pork and freshly churned butter had all made a gravy inside the hard crust so that the filling was rich and moist. And what flavor! He had never had anything like it. As the buggy jostled down the rough gravel road, he greedily ripped off more, the juices drizzling down his plump hand to be stopped by his shirt sleeve.

Now if George Pottle had known better, he would never have eaten in a single afternoon a turnip pie that had been intended for two generous meals for two generous appetites. Never! Any Finn would have known better, especially if he had been planning, as George had, on finally asking Rose Parsons to become the second Mrs. George Pottle. Never! Anyone who has had turnip pie would have known better. But once started, George couldn't resist the pie, and he picked away at it all afternoon until it was gone.

As always on grange night, the street around the hall was lined with wagons and carts. Men, with their hair slicked back, milled outside in the warm evening air, smoking cigarettes and exchanging manly gossip. As George drove his buggy in, a small group disappeared around to the rear, most likely to share a covert flask.

Inside, the ladies, in their Saturday night finery, put out on the long cloth-covered tables, dishes of beans and pickles, cole slaw and hot biscuits.

George had no difficulty in finding Rose who, as always, was flanked by her two aging parents. George took a place across from the Parsons. Although he was not in the least bit hungry, to be sociable, he scooped a sizable helping of molasses-sweetened beans, a fair-sized portion of cole slaw and reached for two fluffy biscuits.

Adelaide Parsons commented on George's waning appetite and inquired whether he might not have a touch of the grippe that was affecting the area, but George denied any infirmity. "Just not much appetite," he claimed.

Adelaide looked knowingly at her husband.

Rose smiled up through distorting round eyeglasses. George Pottle might be nearly old enough to be her father and a bit more rotund than she had secretly dreamed her lover would be. But he was gentlemanly and would be a good provider. His was one of the largest farms around. She couldn't help but think of the future. There was no denying that her parents adored her, their only child, but time was marching on, and they wouldn't be able to care for her forever. She had thought of going to Lewiston or off to New Hampshire to work in one of the mills, but that thought frightened her.

When no one could take another bite, the ladies cleared away the empty serving bowls and platters, spent butter plates and pickle dishes, dirty silverware and water glasses. At last, they folded their aprons and hung the dish towels to dry. The gentlemen, who had been biding their time outside, smoking and discussing the new model of thresher, pushed back the tables to make room for dancing. The Stowe Brothers Four Piece Orchestra, in shiny black suits and dazzling white collars, arrived and mounted the stage.

George hurried across the noisy hall to Rose who waited with her anxious parents. Just as he asked the pleasure of her company for the first dance, he felt a twinge of distress, a knot in his lower regions that twisted and turned.

George's pink face flushed scarlet. Sweat stood out on his brow so that he daubed at his head with his huge linen handkerchief. The sounds of the orchestra tuning, the talk, the laughter jangled against his ears. A wave surged through him, rising and falling, ebbing and flowing, like the tides at Old Orchard Beach. Rose, chattering about next week's picnic, clung to his arm as though she would never let go.

"One-and-a-two...." Sammy Stowe directed from the piano bench.

The hall hushed.

The first notes of the Grand March resounded along with the gasses trapped in George's lower colon.

Rose gasped.

Harry Porter gibed, "Too many beans, George?"

Before Tom Record could say a thing, his wife Mavis jabbed her elbow so sharply into his side that he grunted.

Laughter broke loose.

The Grand March went on.

Rose fled for her wrap, insisting that her mama and papa take her home. George, however, bounded through the front doors out to the blessed relief of the cool night air.

As for Kaisa, when she finally returned home that afternoon wielding the broom behind the brown cow, she was as hungry as she'd ever been. After her cow was well tied, she went into the kitchen, prepared to cut into the turnip pie she had been thinking about all day. How surprised she was to find only the four loaves of bread under the white cloth. Am I getting feeble minded? she wondered. Did I only imagine making it? No, she knew she had made it, but it was no longer there. The door, she now remembered, had been left wide open. A peddler or a tramp? Could a wandering peddler have come in and helped himself? That had to be the explanation! What else could have happened?

Telling herself that the poor peddler must have needed the pie more than she—Or why else would he have taken it?—she appeased her hunger with a glass of cool buttermilk and a thick slab of rye bread, spread generously with good churned butter.

from *The Clear Blue Lobster-Water Country*

LEO CONNELLAN

Here living in among other
immigrants of Protestant New England,
it was better to clip and harden your name

to make it easy for other people who,
after all, would be your customers as well as
neighbors, people who weren't Irish to say

your name easily, not be annoyed and go buy
bread and milk some place easy to say the
owner's name, so my Grandfather dropped the O

and became bluntly Mike Dock easy to
say, to hear, to deal with, not
aggravating, not anybody thinking

you were putting on airs in this
new country using some
fancy-sounding name like

"O'Dock" which was your name, but
not here, not in the Protestant
New England clear blue

lobster-water country, not here where
you've come just to eat, to stay alive
away from where potatoes wouldn't grow

where potatoes wouldn't
grow even if Jesus
asked them to Himself.

Germaine

DENIS LEDOUX

"Don't be foolish," Louis said, patting Germaine's hands which she held tightly in the folds of her lap.

Across the road, *le rang St-Ignace*, the Jerseys, there were about twenty of them, continued to graze toward the stream. The big black one, *la grosse noire*, led as usual; her udder, empty now, would bulge and scrape against the rocks later when, at the end of the day, she led the herd back to the barn.

She and Louis and the kids would not be on *rang St-Ignace* for milking time. She didn't know where they would be. All of it was very strange to her who had never been more than twenty miles from the village. Later, in Maine, many years later, whenever she saw a black cow, she thought of *la grosse noire*. What had become of her? she thought in the way she sometimes was to wonder what had become of Mme Deshêtres or of Mme Boucher.

"We'll make out all right," said Louis. He gave Reine, the draft horse they were to leave at his brother's in the village, a gentle tug. The sun was rising over the rim of the valley. Reine walked toward the road and turned South. Slowly, she began to pull the heavy-laden wagon towards the village. St. Jude lay nine miles to the South and many hundred feet lower.

"Oh, I know," she said, turning to look at him. "I'm being foolish, but I can't help saying what I feel. I wish there were some means, some way, we could try for one more year."

To the right, across the valley, perched high on a range, the silver-painted roof of the church at Ste Hélène de Beresford shone brightly. How many times had she seen this roof shine in the morning—summer as well as winter—when she walked from the barn to the kitchen to get breakfast for the children!

When he had locked the door, this morning, she had said she was being locked out of her life. It wasn't fair to him, she knew, to say that. It had hurt him this morning as much as it had hurt her to walk about the empty house.

They crossed the stream. The water was low. For the second year, there had been too little rain during the summer and too little snow during the winter.

"No more lugging water," he said.

At that moment, she would have gladly hauled water all year long. Two years ago, the pipe leading to the kitchen pump had frozen in March. This was before Henri-Marc was born. They had to lug all their water in from the stream. The water did not flow in the pipe until the beginning of June. Many times, as she carried water to wash diapers, she had wished herself elsewhere. If only she could undo that wishing now!

After a straight course, about where the road began to climb between a double row of maples, they passed the schoolhouse. She turned to look at her children. They had begun to talk of the large school they would attend, of the many new friends they would make. Neither she nor they had any idea what it would be like down South in the States. She did not know much about schoolwork; she knew about other things, about gardening and herbs and sewing. She regretted not knowing more about schoolwork but there hadn't been time for that. There had only been time for the farm.

She sighed. How were they going to survive in a place where what they knew wasn't what you had to know?

"Germaine, we have to go."

"Yes, I know."

Jean Thibeau, the man who had wanted to marry her but whom she had refused for Louis, had become a prosperous farmer. He had received money from his father and had started in a big way. She would not be going now had she chosen differently. The very thought embarrassed her; it was disloyal to Louis. She loved Louis. It was only that the day, this day, was so difficult.

In the city, they would live in a tall building with many other people. The children would go to a large school. She herself would work in a factory with Louis. How much of this would be good for the children?

"Stop. Stop," she said to Louis.

He looked at her quizzically.

"It's Mademoiselle Lizotte!"

A young lady, dressed in a simple blue wool dress that swept against the sill, appeared at the doorway of the school. The building had been painted yellow when Germaine was a child at the school and, when she looked carefully, she could still see some yellow.

Mademoiselle waved and ran towards the road. She had the strong body of a Canadian farm girl.

"We'll miss you," she said. Already she had lost three families in one year. "The children were asking after you kids. You be good children and show those American kids how much we can learn in a Canadian school. I know you can do it if you want to."

"*Oui, Mademoiselle,*" they answered from the rear of the wagon. She was still their teacher, somehow, as long as they were in Canada.

They had been good neighbors. The *rang* would seem empty without them, said Mademoiselle.

Germaine began to cry. "Oh, Mademoiselle, if you only knew how much I hate being in my shoes. We tried everything."

"I know you did. Perhaps you'll see your way to coming back—or, perhaps you'll like it so much you won't want to come back." She tried to smile.

Above, on the school's weathervane, a last cardinal sat perched in its red splendour. It too would have to leave for the South. Already it had stayed too long.

They all three looked from one to the other, knowing that people did not come back to Canada. One thing led to another: the children grew older and found mates and did not want to return; the money was too good or not good enough, and so they would not be coming back.

"We'll miss you," she repeated simply.

Louis answered, "We have cousins who will help us. Perhaps we will like it so much we won't want to come back."

"You will be *un rich américain,*" she retorted laughing, forgetting for a moment the import of what they were doing. "You won't want to talk to us simple *canadiens.*"

"Oh, *non,* we will never forget our home, *jamais!*" Having said this, Germaine looked down.

A silence fell upon the group. Then Mademoiselle said, "*Non,* of course you won't. I must go back. The children are waiting for their lessons."

The windows were filled with children waving. Mademoiselle turned and walked down the weedy path and disappeared into the building. She was a good teacher.

"*Envoie, Reine.* Let's move on."

Slowly, Reine plodded up the long dirt incline. The fields were still green but soon the killing frosts would come.

"Oh, Mademoiselle," she had cried out, forgetting that Louis had said the more they talked about it the more painful the leaving would be. "And we will miss you," Mademoiselle had said.

To the right, closed, the porch beginning to sag, one of the dormers needing a window replaced, the Martineau house, the house where as a girl she had attended many *soirées,* showed to her what would become of their house. One day, they would come back to visit and their porch would be caved in. Some of the roof shingles would have come off and water have seeped inside, there to warp the wood walls and cause the ceiling plaster to fall.

She and Louis should have rented their house, of course. The Martineaus had wanted to rent their farm too but it was impossible to rent misery. Everyone was trying to get out. There were empty places all around them.

Her hands which she still held tightly in her lap were strong hands. They had not only baked and washed but shovelled and planted and milked. They had done everything. There was nothing they could do that would change things.

There was no money to go on. They had sold the harvest that otherwise would have gone into the root cellar. This sale had given them the cash for the trip. They had not yet gone into debt. They would have more money in the States because they would work in a mill. Every week they would receive a paycheck—whether there was a cold snap or not, whether there was rainfall or not. What was it going to be like, though, not to have a root cellar?

Oh yes, she was being foolish. She knew it was the right thing to do. Louis had tried his best. She had too. And the children. It had simply not been enough. Perhaps they could make a pile of money in the States and come back and get on top of things.

When she remembered this time later on, as she sat in her kitchen by the big American oil stove, looking out over roof tops to the mill where she had spent her days for more years now than she was old at the time it happened, she remembered it was at that point that she had broken down into abandoned crying, in front of the Martineau house, because the porch was sagging.

Reine continued to plod up the hill. They passed the Boucher place. A dog barked at them, a new dog, hardly more than a puppy. She had never seen it before. Already, things were changing.

Soon, too soon, they reached the crest of the hill. She knew that if she turned around she would be able to see their house. On many a cold Sunday as she had returned from the village, the sight of the house from the crest had warmed her.

"Look, children. *La maison.*"

They turned to look. The house was painted blue with a white trim. About two of the sides, the south and the west, ran a porch. Above the porch were two dormers. The children had slept upstairs. In back was the barn—a large wood structure with a cupola. The barn, as was the habit, had never been painted. Behind were the orchards and the gardens and the pastures.

Soon they could only see the second floor; that disappeared, leaving only the top of the barn. Then the cupola too disappeared.

There was nothing left.

History

ROBERTA CHESTER

I can thank the Czar
for the dirt between my toes,
the peas climbing the wire
and everything that grows
in spite of stones
on this piece of land
in Maine.
He took my grandfather's land away,
thick and heavy with trees,
in one of those occasional
pogroms.

Without his land
my grandfather had no reason to stay
and so he came here
with nothing to his name
except a woman,
who would live till she
was one hundred and three,
and a small son.
My grandfather searched the streets
for the gold of maple leaves
and paced the pavement
in his hiking boots.
I used to lace them up for him
beneath his eyes
dark as woods.

My grandfather lived
to thank the Czar
for kicking us out
of Europe's way

and over the sea.
My grandfather's eyes
look out from between the trees.
He knows how good the dirt feels
in the palm of my hand,
and how I shudder
at the white paper
in the marketplace.

Succoth

ROBERTA CHESTER

(Bangor, 1982)

After the last blast of the shofar
and the hard fast, the promises
and prayers for a good year,
it takes us by surprise
when we are in the season
of apples and honey cakes
and wine, when we eat in huts
open as birds to the stars,

it takes us by surprise
to see a swastika
drawn on the wall of the shul,
painted red and razor sharp
the women whisper,
there can be no mistake.
They know the sign.

It makes me think
we have been found out
although we've been here
for years, our candles shining
at the windows, the smell of challah,
the bittersweet sounds of Shabbos songs
escaping from out the windows and doors
and into the streets between the bridge
and the old brick church.

It takes us by surprise
and yet the trouble is so old
it echoes in my blood

with the sound of my grandfather
climbing the stairs of a building
on the lower east side
and pressed against the wall
by someone with a knife
who held the blade
against his neck and said,
"Swear, swear you are not a Jew,
and I will let you free!"

And from my grandfather who refused
just as they were both surprised
by an angel in disguise who opened a door
in that long, dark hall,
I learned never to be too much in love
with a roof over my head,
that houses are made of sticks and glass,
that they break like the works of our hands,
and that we should be ready to fly
up into the night with parcels and children
and scrolls under our arms
on the back of the wind.

Remembering The First "Newcomers"

MARGERY WILSON

"We stayed the longer in this place," writes James Rosier of Captain George Waymouth's voyage to the coast of Maine in 1605, "not only because of our good Harbour (which is an excellent comfort) but because every day we did more and more discover the pleasant fruitfulness; insomuch as many of our Companie wished themselves settled here, not expecting any further hopes or better discovery to be made."

The English soon learned, however, that their "good Harbour" was already inhabited by "a people of exceeding good invention, quicke understanding and readie capacitie." In brief, Native Americans, or in Rosier's terms, "Salvages." The English wasted no time bringing "them to an understanding of exchange...that they might conceive the intent of our comming to them to be for no other end." But exchange, Rosier's protestation to the contrary, was definitely not *all* they had in mind, for several days thereafter the English set a trap for the unsuspecting Indians and "shipped five Salvages, two Canoas, with all their bowes and arrowes." We can today only guess at what those five "Salvages" must have felt, taken by their captors to England and separated from their own good harbor.

We do not, however, need to guess about the next century of Maine's history, during which the English fought both the French and the Indians, offering bounties for the scalps of male "savages." The French survived. The Indians were decimated.

The conflict of Native and Newcomer doesn't end there, though. For a while the newcomers were the French Canadians, hired as loggers during the heyday of the lumbering industry; then they were the summer people, buying up acres and acres of the Maine coast, hiring the natives to cook the food, to weed the gardens, to drive the cars.

And now we have our Native-Newcomer conflict, begun fifteen years ago when young, middle-class urbanites came looking for their own good harbor. We found safety and clean air and water and acreage. And Natives. With the arrogance and insensitivity of the young and the educated, we were convinced that we were bringing what Waldo County had been waiting for; like Rosier, we were ready to trade knives for beaver skins, and we couldn't imagine why our neighbors were sometimes unhappy with the exchange.

For if there's one characteristic of the middle class, it's an unassailable conviction that its values and attitudes are far better than those of any other class. What we really wanted was the suburbs: only suburbs with 200-acre zoning ordinances. Now if we had been content to cultivate only our own gardens, perhaps we might have, in time, been able to harmonize with our environments and to live in harmony with our neighbors. But middle-class people are missionaries in Bean boots: we want to civilize the savages. So we decide that snowmobiling is noisy and noxious and we put fences across snowmobiling trails; we decide that hunting is primitive and violent and we post our land; we decide that dirt roads are romantic but ruin the front ends of our Japanese and German automobiles; we decide that selectmen can't possibly take care of the town indigent and ill, so we lobby for bureaucrats in Augusta to do it at our expense; and we decide that plumbers and horse pullers need lots of regulating—and we'll be willing to write the rules.

We speak up at town meetings, making fun of the "boys in the back row" with their caps and Dickies work clothes; and the cry of "just raise taxes" is heard in the land. Finally, we displace the selectmen and then we displace the school board directors, because if there's anyone who knows about rural education, it's people who went from kindergarten to twelfth grade in city schools.

So why should we be surprised when the natives express some displeasure at our implicit and explicit criticism of their way of life? We do not, as yet, belong here; we are from away; perhaps we feel as though we've found our good harbors, but what canoes have we swamped, what diseases have we spread, what exchanges have we taken advantage of along the way? Perhaps we should remember the newcomers of the Popham colony, which failed in 1608 because, we are told, "the colonists (were) generally lacking in those sturdy attitudes that such an enterprise demands." An observer at the time noted that if he and others were to succeed at all, "'there must go other manner of spirits' than were found so largely in the Sagadahoc colony."

We are Newcomers. Let us remember the manner of our spirits.

Micmac

SAMUEL FRENCH MORSE

The morning burns away like smoke.
The sunlight thickens. The salt pond
Glares through a haze of young scrub oak.
Caught in an alien dream beyond
His will to keep at bay, he leans
Against the battered yellow truck
He squandered more than money on
Before his hopes ran out like luck,

Then folds his arms like Samoset,
And squats beside the running board.
Fumbling for a cigarette,
He hears a car. The tourist's Ford
Blurs past. The locust's music whines,
The dry leaves of the alder spin.
He watches for a vagrant deer
To cross the blacktop. Sallow, thin,

He stares at nothing. Blue exhaust
And drying sweetgrass eddy, mix
Until, as in that future lost,
They fade and drift. How should he fix
On any meaning but the change
He cannot even understand?
Wrecked in a blind and rocky ditch,
He is a native of the land.

Lost Graveyards

ELIZABETH COATSWORTH

In Maine the dead
melt into the forest
like Indians, or, rather,
in Maine the forests shadow round the dead
until the dead are indistinguishably mingled
with trees; while underground,
roots and bones intertwine,
and above earth
the tilted gravestones, lichen-covered, too,
shine faintly out from among pines and birches,
burial stones and trunks
growing together
above the lattices of roots and bones.
Now is the battle over,
the harsh struggle
between man and the forest.
While they lived,
these men and women fought the encroaching trees,
hacked them with axes,
severed them with saws,
burned them in fires,
pushed them back and back
to their last lairs among the shaggy hills,
while the green fields lay tame about the houses.
Living, they fought the wild,
but dead, they rested,
and the wild softly, silently, secretly,
returned. In Maine
the dead sooner or later feel the hug of rootlets,
and shadowy branches closing out the sun.

Aye! No Monuments

RITA JOE

Aye! no monuments,
No literature,
No scrolls or canvas-drawn pictures
Relate the wonders of our yesterday.

How frustrated the searchings
    of the educators.

Let them find
Land names,
Titles of seas,
Rivers;
Wipe them not from memory.
These are our monuments.

Breathtaking views—
Waterfalls on a mountain,
Fast flowing rivers.
These are our sketches
Committed to our memory.
Scholars, you will find our art
In names and scenery,
Betrothed to the Indian
    since time began.

Marguerite Zorach, Old Mrs. Smith, *1932, oil on canvas, 42" x 30¹/₂",*
Courtesy, Norma B. Marin.

Work

"Work til the last beam fadeth."

The Logger's Boast

TRADITIONAL SONG

Come, all ye sons of freedom throughout the State of Maine,
Come, all ye gallant lumbermen, and listen to my strain;
On the banks of the Penobscot, where the rapid waters flow,
O! we'll range the wild woods over, and a lumbering will go;
>   And a lumbering we'll go, so a lumbering will go,
>   O! we'll range the wild woods over while a lumbering we
>   go.

When the white frost gilds the valleys, the cold congeals the flood;
When many men have naught to do to earn their families bread;
When the swollen streams are frozen, and the hills are clad with
    snow,
O! we'll range the wild woods over, and a lumbering we will go;
>   And a lumbering we'll go, so a lumbering we will go,
>   O! we'll range the wild woods over, while a lumbering we
>   go.

When you pass through the dense city, and pity all you meet,
To hear their teeth chattering as they hurry down the street;
In the red frost-proof flannel we're encased from top to toe;
While we range the wild woods over, and a lumbering we go;
>   And a lumbering we'll go, so a lumbering will go,
>   O! we'll range the wild woods over while a lumbering we
>   go.

You may boast of your gay parties, your pleasures, and your plays,
And pity us poor lumbermen while dashing in your sleighs;
We want no better pastime than to chase the buck and doe;
O! we'll range the wild woods over, and a lumbering we will go;
>   And a lumbering we'll go, so a lumbering will go,
>   O! we'll range the wild woods over while a lumbering we
>   go.

The music of our burnished ax shall make the woods resound,
And many a lofty ancient Pine will tumble to the ground;
And night, ho! round our good camp-fire we will sing while rude
    winds blow:
O! we'll range the wild woods over while a lumbering we go.
      And lumbering we'll go, so a lumbering will go,
       O! we'll range the wild woods over while a lumbering we
         go.

When winter's snows are melted, and the ice-bound streams are
    free,
We'll run our logs to market, then haste our friends to see;
How kindly true hearts welcome us, our wives and children too,
We will spend with these the summer, and once more a lumbering
    go;
      And a lumbering we'll go, so a lumbering we will go,
      We will spend with these the summer, and once more
        a lumbering go.

And when upon the long-hid soil the white Pines disappear,
We will cut the other forest trees, and sow whereon we clear;
Our grain shall wave o'er valleys rich, our herds bedot the hills,
When our feet no more are hurried on to tend the driving mills;
      Then no more a lumbering go, so no more a lumbering go,
      When our feet no more are hurried on to tend the driving
        mills.

When our youthful days are ended, we will cease from winter toil,
And each one through the summer warm will till the virgin soil;
We've enough to eat, to drink, to wear, content through life to go,
Then we'll tell our wild adventures o'er, and no more a lumbering
    go;
      And no more a lumbering go, so no more a lumbering go,
      O! we'll tell our wild adventures o'er, so no more a lumbering
        go.

from *Nine Mile Bridge*

HELEN HAMLIN

My grandfather was a game warden, my uncle is a game warden and I married a game warden. I first met Curly when I taught school at Churchill Lake, the headwaters of the Allagash River in the wilderness area of northwestern Maine. The settlement at Churchill was a lumberjack colony and was considered too wild and desolate for a woman teacher, but since I could speak French and had asked for a backwoods school, I became the first woman schoolteacher of Churchill.

I arrived at Churchill in October, after a four-hundred-mile drive with my family. We had followed a roundabout scenic route, down the colorful back road from Fort Kent to Ashland, through the Mount Katahdin region, Baxter State Park, Ripogenus Dam and Moosehead Lake. From there we drove over the Great Northern Paper Company's private road to the boundary and into Canada.

At the St. Zacharie Hotel I had my first taste of wilderness hospitality. The rooms at the hotel were small, close and stuffy, and the plumbing was antique—of the chain-pulling era. The table in the dining room was set with a fancy glass service and with a bowl of store cookies for a centerpiece. The proprietress was a little, fat old lady with one tooth in her head. She was either very well pleased with herself or thought we were very funny, because she smiled broadly and continuously. We grinned back and ate the centerpiece—the store cookies—while waiting for the salt pork and fried eggs she had promised us.

The next morning we drove sixty miles through numerous small Canadian towns, and at Lac Frontiere we recrossed the boundary into Maine.

As we skirted the wilderness I had a preview of the surroundings I had chosen for what was to be, though I didn't know it at the time, the background of my first years of married life.

The American customs officer at Lac Frontiere was not encouraging. "You're the schoolteacher for Churchill?" he asked.

"That's right," I answered.

"Ever been there before?"

"No."

He offered an unheeded warning. "That is no place for a woman."

We showed our permit to go over the private road, and started the forty-three-mile drive to Churchill. The change in scenery was delightful. Where the Province of Quebec had been cleared and open, here was a forest of trees. The few cabins and camps along the way were picturesque and mostly deserted. The morning was lovely and cool, and the lifting mist revealed the brown road, the red, yellow, orange, wine and golden tints of fall. Held to a slow pace by the narrow, rocky road, we saw many deer and partridges. Once a black bear jumped out of a ditch and galloped ahead of the car. His flying paws threw gravel and stones back on the windshield before he disappeared abruptly off the road and crashed away through the underbrush.

Because I lived in Fort Kent—farthest northern outpost—I had heard many lumbermen, cruisers and guides speak of the vast, unpopulated timberlands on the headwaters of the Allagash and St. John rivers. To the majority of people, including those who live in the St. John Valley, this forest area is still the mysterious "backwoods."

A map of the state of Maine shows a large area along the Maine-Canadian boundary that has no highways or towns. It is dotted with lakes and ponds strung along the thin, twisty lines of the St. John and Allagash rivers and their tributaries. There are no highways. There are no towns. There are a few lumber camps but these are not shown on the map. If they were they would be too minute to be noticed, and too temporary for a surveyor to locate, even if he found them. Some maps show the private road that runs from the boundary into Churchill Lake, in the very heart of this forgotten country. The road penetrates but a short way into ten million acres of forest land, the largest unbroken wild timberland area in private ownership within the confines of any one state. The area is approximately 15,600 square miles of woods and lakes, and nothing else.

Edward La Croix, a Canadian lumber king, had logging operations on the St. John and Allagash rivers. He built the road in 1927 to carry supplies to his numerous and far-flung logging camps on the lakes and rivers. He built the steel bridge across the St. John River in 1931. The bridge had once been in St. Georges in the Province of Quebec, but was discarded because its width allowed only one car to cross it at a time. "King" La Croix transported the bridge piece by piece to the St. John River, and rebuilt it to replace the ferry that had been used there for so long. This was the bridge at Nine Mile.

There are a few log camps at the St. John River crossing and a small settlement at Clayton Lake. Side roads at Umsaskis lead to two lumber camps on the lake, and there is a fairly large settlement at Churchill Lake, at the end of the road.

I was deposited at the company boarding house, and my trunk was carried up to my room under the eaves.

"You're sure you won't go back with us?" Mother asked before leaving.

"I'm sure," I said.

They left me eagerly looking forward to eight months of winter. I had picked a ringside seat for a view to the inside of the country.

Suddenly a gong on the back porch rang to call the men to dinner, and I walked into the kitchen just as a motley crew filed through the door at the opposite end and silently seated themselves at the table. They were French Canadians—tall and short, young and old—unshaven, weather beaten, long haired and ragged. This was their appearance at dinnertime.

At suppertime, their appearance was quite different, though equally amazing. Every man jack was neatly shaven. Unruly hair was combed, brushed and anchored with water. Water still dripped from the long, plastered locks. Socks were straightened over boot tops and shirttails were tucked out of sight.

I had taken a seat at the foot of the table, but was later moved to the head. There are social distinctions in a lumber camp. Clerks, scalers, blacksmiths, mechanics, tractor drivers and truck drivers are given precedence over the common herd—the lumberjacks who sit at the foot of the table. The blacksmith and I, the schoolteacher, held down the bench at the head of the table.

Pea soup was passed around and I ladled a generous helping into the battered tin bowl I found upside down in front of me. Pots of tea and coffee followed the pea soup on the tour around the table, but the omission of a cup and saucer caused me to glance at the bent heads of my dinner companions. The man opposite me seemed to be an American.

"What do we drink the coffee from?" I asked.

"Out of the bowl." He grinned and offered me his.

Joe Deblois, the man who had charge of the boarding house, interrupted by placing a cup and saucer at my elbow. I had committed a social error, and thereafter I ate pea soup in my plate and wiped it up with pieces of bread before the next course.

Food was good and plentiful. We had crispy roast beef for Sunday dinner, with little orange and yellow wheels of sliced carrots that were generously buttered and creamed. Golden potatoes were browned in meat gravy, and endless mounds of steaming, raised rolls kneaded and baked every day were appetizing enough for the most exacting gourmet.

The tables sagged under the weight of coffeepots, teapots, plates of apple pies, raisin pies, raspberry pies, sugar cookies, filled cookies and molasses cookies. The pea soup was the most delicious I have ever eaten. Whole peas were cooked in their own broth and were flavored with chopped green onion tops and salt pork. The rule was every man for himself—either grab what was passed down or grab what went back, with a real boarding-house reach.

All table service was unbreakable enamelware, with a sturdy knife and fork beside each overturned plate and bowl. Spoons were in small canisters, clustered about with salt and pepper shakers, a bottle of vinegar, jars of pickles or relish, bowls of sugar, bottles of catsup and a homemade spicy sauce for which Joe Deblois would never give the secret recipe. In addition to all this there were the inevitable small jugs of molasses that every Old Timber Wolf pours into his plate at the end of a meal, to mop up with pieces of bread.

Under the watchful eye of Joe Deblois, we ate in silence, the unwritten but rigidly maintained custom of the lumber camp. We finished in silence, silently carried empty plate, bowl, knife, fork and spoon to the sideboard, and filed out. I continued silently up to my room, properly awed.

When there were just a few of us at the table, we talked. Everybody spoke French, but there were some who could speak English.

"You like him here, Mademoiselle?" I was once asked.

"Yes, I like it here. You speak English?"

"Ho yess, hi talk him leetle bit."

"Where you learn him?" I asked, catching on this time.

"Hi take her Great Norden hon top huff Pittston." Meaning, I learned it when I was working for the Great Northern at Pittston Farm.

"You like Pittston?"

"Ho no, she no talk *français*. Hi come home. You got feller?"

"No, I have no feller."

"Me, hi ham nize feller."

I switched to French for the others' benefit. "You are not the only one here. You are all handsome gentlemen."

A snicker went around the table.

"Me hi talk hinglise. Pass the macaroni *s'il vois plait*."

"Yes, pass the macaroni to the sheik."

Laughter.

Joe Deblois called for silence. "Eat, Big Nose. You have a wife at home."

Uproar.

I spent most of my first day unpacking in my small room. The walls were painted a battleship gray and the floors a shrieking orange, as were all the walls and floors in the boarding house. But the room was cheery with its bright-yellow curtains at the window, yellow spread on the wide bed, and colorful braided rug on the floor. There was a washstand with its usual white pitcher and bowl. Hooks were behind the door and on the wall for my clothes.

After scattering a few books, doodads and knickknacks around and hanging up clothes and pictures, I began to feel at home. I was much too excited with the strangeness and newness of my surroundings to feel lonely.

My first view of Churchill was not impressive. It wasn't what I expected. Churchill was a commonplace-looking settlement and not a romantic colony under the shadows of giant spruces. The lake was ghostly. The shores were lined with dri-ki, the bleached, dead stumps of drowned trees. Some were still upright, but most of them slanted every which way and were ready to disappear—the shameful traces of a dammed and flooded lake. The gates in the dam were partly open, and water rippled and cascaded over a rocky river bed. A little shed on the bridge held the dynamo that generated the electric current for all the buildings.

Most of the houses were identical, one-and-a-half-story company houses that had once been painted white. There were a few log cabins in the settlement, a few hen houses, woodsheds, outhouses, garden plots, and pigsties. The boarding house was a long, barrackslike building.

On the other side of the river was the company office, a more elaborate building that was occupied by a bachelor clerk who kept a Pomeranian dog. Lombard tractors, dual-wheeled trucks and small caterpillar tractors were housed and repaired in the long garage. A storehouse was filled with barrels of molasses or salt pork, cases of canned goods, flour, sugar, salt, dried fruits, cereals, axes, rope, peaveys, tobacco, kerosene and almost everything imaginable, all to be sold by the company to the people living at Churchill, or to be used in the lumber camps.

Today was Sunday, and the settlement was quiet. Doors were open to let in the late fall sunshine. Children were playing outside—the customary hopscotch and skipping rope. Boys toured the mud pond on their log rafts and fell in. Men stood in groups, talking. Some were dressed in store clothes—brown or blue suits—but most of them were dressed in the regular loose-fitting and well-worn breeches and woolen shirts. Women could be seen standing in the open doorways with arms crossed under aprons. Very few cars drove into Churchill.

A car stopped beneath my window and I leaned forward curiously, my nose pressed against the windowpane. Out of the back seat of the car tumbled a man—or boy—these French Canadians were so small in stature, I have difficulty in knowing which is which. His long hair was matted with blood and fell over an almost closed black eye. One front tooth was missing. His white cotton shirt, a Sunday concession, was torn and bloody, and he was intoxicated beyond the point of belligerence. He had been well manhandled, when in the course of an argument he had threateningly brandished a small automatic.

There was much arm wagging—the punctuation to French conversation—before he was hustled into one of the houses to sleep it off. Someone looked up and caught me taking in the scene, and I drew back hurriedly, wondering if this colony was as tough as rumor claimed it to be. I didn't know it then, but this same follower of Bacchus was to be one of my bunk companions on a memorable night spent on McNally Pond, halfway to nowhere.

Such incidents were rare at Churchill and bore out the old Maine adage that I learned is still true: never believe anything you hear, and only half of what you see. I did see a few drunken lumberjacks during my stay there, but they were the exception rather than the rule.

Liquor was hard to obtain, and was strictly forbidden in the camps. The lumberjack does not drink while in the woods for the simple reason that he can't get it. When spring comes and he gets out, he celebrates. Even then he is not so pugnacious. Like other people, there are the good and bad, and the outstanding revelers have produced the impression that the lumberjack is a holy terror. The few drunken lumberjacks I have seen on their yearly benders were harmlessly merry or befogged with sleep.

I grew to like Churchill and all its drabness. The American customs officer at Lac Frontiere had been mistaken. There were several women at Churchill, mothers of large families and many girls who were no older than myself. There were a few English-speaking families scattered along the La Croix road and a definite majority of men—lumberjacks from a dozen camps around Churchill, likable, good-hearted and good-natured children of the forests.

On weekdays Churchill was a droning beehive. The storehouse was opened to the few customers. Sleds were loaded with supplies for a camp. The sawmill was in full buzzing swing, fragrant with freshly sawed pine and spruce. The noisy blacksmith shop was rosy with the glowing light from the forge. Hammers pounded and clanged all day as broken machinery was repaired or new logging chains and sleds were made.

Garage doors were open and the building reverberated with the muffled roar of a Lombard. The boardwalk to the office resounded to the heavy boots of lumberjacks going to and from the office. Tractors came down from the tote roads that branched out from Churchill. The muted hum of other tractors on hauling roads could be heard. Heavy trucks rumbled over the wooden bridge. The foaming water below the dam was never silent. The dynamo added its "watch-movement" throbbing.

At The Grave Of The Unknown River Driver

PAUL CORRIGAN

Hellbent bravado broke the jam
that busted your skull that spring.
No known kin, you signed the payroll X
and went by Bill or Joe.
Whitewater's thrill was seasonal.
When spikes were winter-stored
the river roared through dreams.
Your flophouse room was bleak. Mice crapped
in your teacup, chewed your new cantdog.

The day the jam let go, gnarled tons
of spruce caught you mid-current, napping.
You belleyed-up downriver, blond hair aglow
in foam and they bundled you in burlap,
mouthing bits of scripture so your luck
would lie down with you here.

Now loons spin comic hymns above
your bones. Boy Scouts shear new growth
that chokes you out each year
and paint your cross and white stave fence.
Men you might have known still mope
in nursing homes, arthritic remnants
of the rough and tumble, the river's
pounding strength a memory locked
in their old sinews, their shriveled arms.

from *Sign of the Beaver*

ELIZABETH SPEARE

In the spring of 1768, Matt and his father travel north from Massachusetts to become the first European settlers in a part of the Maine territory. After building a log house and planting a garden, Matt's father returns to Massachusetts to bring the rest of the family to their new home.

He leaves Matt behind to care for the land, promising to return in six or seven weeks. Soon afterward, a stranger steals Matt's rifle, leaving him no way to shoot game. Then a bear raids Matt's small supply of meal and molasses. Finally, while trying to take honey from a tree, Matt is severely stung by a swarm of bees.

Rescue comes in the form of Saknis, a native American, and his grandson Attean, who is about Matt's age. Though at first uncomfortable with one another, the two boys soon become friends. Attean teaches Matt to make a bow and arrow and to trap; Matt teaches Attean to read. The summer passes and Matt's family is overdue. It is time for the Beaver tribe to move and Saknis and Attean urge Matt to move with them. But Matt cannot give up the idea that his family will arrive soon. After accepting Attean's dog as a farewell gift and saying goodbye to his friends, Matt prepares to spend the winter alone.

Matt filled his days with work. He made the cabin trim. Where the clay had dried and crumbled away between the logs, he brought new mud, strengthened it with pebbles, and packed the spaces tightly. On the inside he chinked every tiny crack to make the room snug. The pile of logs stacked against the cabin wall grew steadily higher.

His meager harvest was safely stored away. The corn, the little he had managed to save from the deer and crows, had all been shucked. Sitting by the fire after his supper, he scraped the dried kernels from the cobs, remembering the many long evenings at home when he and his sister Sarah had been set to the same work with a corn scraper. Sarah would laugh now to see him rubbing away with an old clamshell like an Indian. Some of the ears of corn he had hung against the wall, by the twisted husks, as he had seen his mother do. She had said once they were like scraps of sunshine in the dark days. Overhead he hung strips of pumpkin on ropes of vine strung from wall to wall. They would be ready for his mother to make into pies.

In a corner leaned the old flour sack, overflowing with the nuts he had gathered, hickory and butternut, and even the acorns he had once thought proper food only for squirrels. On the shelf ranged birch baskets filled with dried berries and the wild cranberries he had discovered shining like jewels along the boggy shores of the pond. They were puckery to the tongue, but when his mother came she would bring sugar, and the stewed cranberries would make a fine treat with her bread of white flour.

Matt forced himself to eat sparingly of these things. The corn he regarded as a sort of trust. His father had planted it, and would be counting on it to feed the family through the winter. And some must be saved for the spring planting. Proud though he was of his harvest, Matt knew in his heart that it was far from enough. The hunt for food would be never-ending.

Hour after hour, with his bow, Matt tramped through the forest, the dog beside him. There was not much game to hunt these days. More often than not, his snares were empty. Soon the animals would be buried deep in burrows. Twice he had glimpsed a caribou moving through the trees, but he had little hope of bringing down any large animal with his light arrows. Once in a long while he succeeded in shooting a duck or a muskrat. The squirrels were too quick for him. Although the dog was certainly not much of a hunter, he did occasionally track down some small creature. But he also had to eat his share, sometimes more than his share, because Matt could not resist those beseeching eyes. Truth to tell, they were both hungry much of the time.

Luckily, they would not starve with the pond and creeks teeming with fish. Matt knew that for many months of the year fish filled the Indian cookpots. Luckily too, fish were easy to catch, though Matt had to be continually twisting and splicing new lines from vines and spruce roots. Mornings, now, he had to shatter a skim of ice on the pond. Soon he would have to cut holes with his axe and let his lines down deep. He shivered to think of it.

It was the cold that bothered him most. His homespun jacket was still sound, since he had had little use for it in the warm weather. But his breeches were threadbare. One knee showed naked through a gaping hole, and the frayed legs stopped a good five inches above his ankles. His linen shirt was thin as a page of his father's Bible, and so small for him that it threatened to split every time he moved. Even inside the cabin he was scarcely warm enough. The moment he ventured outside his teeth chattered. He thought enviously of the Indians' deerskin leggings. But a deer was far beyond his prowess as a hunter.

There were two blankets on his pine bed, his father's and his own. Why couldn't one of them cover him in the daytime as well as in the night? He spread a blanket out on the floor and hacked it with his axe and his knife, using his worn-out breeches as a pattern. From the leftover scraps he carefully pulled threads and twisted them together. He had seen the Indian women using bone needles, and he searched about outside the cabin till he found some thin, hard bits of bone. These he shaved down with his knife. He ruined three bits trying to poke a hole through the bone, before he thought to try a thin slit instead to hold the thread. Finally he managed to sew his woolen pieces together. He thrust his legs into the shapeless breeches and gathered the top about his waist with a bit of rope. He was mightly pleased with himself. He was going to be forever hauling them up, and they were sure to trip him if he had to run, but at least he could kneel on the ice and pull in his lines.

From two rabbit skins he made some mittens without thumbs. He had no stockings, and his moosehide moccasins were wearing thin. He decided he could stuff them with scraps of blanket or even with duck feathers. He remembered that once, in a downpour, Attean had shown him how to line his moccasins with dried moss to soak up the rain. Perhaps moss could soak up the cold as well, and there was plenty of it about.

His most satisfying achievement was his fur hat. For this he knew he must have more fur. In the woods Attean had once pointed out to him a deadfall, constructed of heavy logs so intricately balanced that they would fall with deadly accuracy on an animal that attempted to steal the bait inside. Beaver and otter were caught in such traps, Attean explained, sometimes even bear. Now Matt determined to make one for himself. Perhaps a small one. It would take a very large log even to stun a strong animal, and he had no wish to come upon a wounded bear. Much as he would like a bearskin, he would try for a smaller animal.

He felled and trimmed two good-sized trees. Setting the logs on lighter posts was a feat of delicate balance that took him hours of patient trial and error. Over and over they crashed down, threatening his toes and fingers. Finally, they held to his satisfaction, and gingerly he slipped three fish inside the trap.

To his astonishment, on the third morning he found an animal lying under the fallen logs, so nearly dead that it was no task to club it. It was smaller than the otters he had seen playing along the banks. A fisher, perhaps?

That night he and the dog feasted on crackling bits of roast meat. It was strong-flavored, and he knew the Indians did not care to eat it, but he could not be so choosy. Other strips he hung over the fire to smoke. There was also a scant amount of yellow fat. Used sparingly, a spoonful of that fat would make his usual fish diet taste like a banquet. The real treasure was the pelt, heavy and lustrous. He worked on it slowly, as he had watched the Indian women work. With a sharp-edged stone he scraped away every trace of fat and flesh from the skin, washed it in the creek, and for days, in his spare hours, rubbed and stretched it to make it soft and pliable. Then he set to work with his bone needle. He was enormously proud of the cap he fashioned. Saknis himself would have envied it.

Most of this work he had done by firelight. He longed for candles. He ate his supper by the light of split pine branches set in a crack in the chimney. They gave light aplenty, but they smoked and dripped sticky pitch, and he was always afraid he might drop off to sleep and wake up to find the log chimney afire. At any rate, after a day of chopping and tramping he was tired enough to go to bed with the dark.

So often, as he did the squaw work that Attean would have despised, thoughts of his mother filled his head. He imagined her moving about the cabin, humming her little tunes as she beat up a batch of corn bread, shaking out the boardcloth at the door—for of course she would not let them eat at a bare table. He could see her sitting by the firelight in the evening, her knitting needles clicking as she made a woolen sock for him. Sometimes he could almost hear the sound of her voice, and when he shut his eyes he could see her special smile.

He tried to think of ways to please her. She would need new dishes for the good meals she would cook. He whittled out four wooden trenchers and four clean new bowls, rubbing them smooth with sand from the creek. He made a little brush to clean them with from a birch sapling, carefully splitting the ends into thin fibers. In the same way, he made a sturdy birch broom to sweep the floor. Then he set himself a more difficult task, a cradle for the baby. With only an axe and his knife, the work took all his patience. His first attempts were fit only for kindling. But when the cradle was done he was proud of it. It was clumsy, perhaps, but it rocked without bumping, and there wasn't a splinter anywhere to harm a baby's skin. Sitting by the fire, it seemed a promise that soon his family would be there. When he had a few more rabbit skins he would make a soft coverlet.

For Sarah he made a cornhusk doll with cornsilk hair. He was surprised at how much he looked forward to Sarah's coming. Back at home she had been nothing but a pesky child, always following him about and pestering him to be taken along wherever he was going. Now he remembered the way she had run to meet him when he came home from school, pigtails flying, eyes shining, demanding to know everything that had happened there. Sarah hated fiercely being a girl and having no school to go to. She would be full of curiosity in the forest. She wasn't afraid like most girls. She was spunky enough to try almost anything. She was like that Indian girl, Attean's sister. What a pity they couldn't have known each other!

Matt stood looking up at the sky over the clearing. "It's going to snow," he told the dog. "You can feel it, can't you?" The dog lifted its nose, testing the promise in the air.

Matt reckoned he had been lucky so far. The heavy snows had not come. There had been flurries, thin and swirling, sifting through the trees. Many mornings he had waked to find a coating of white on the cabin roof, which would melt away under the noonday sun. Today everything seemed different. The sky was the color of his mother's pewter plate. The brown withered leaves of the oak trees hung motionless from the branches. Three crows searched noisily among the dry cornstalks. A flock of small birds hopped nervously under the pines.

"It's almost Christmas," he said out loud. He could not remember for sure how many weeks belonged to each month. Sometimes he was not even certain that he had remembered to cut a notch every day. Each day was so like the day before, and Christmas Day, when it came, would not have anything to mark it from all the others. He tried to put out of his mind the thought of his mother's Christmas pudding.

"We'd better get in extra firewood," he said, and the dog scrambled eagerly after him.

Late in the day the snow began, soundlessly, steadily. Before dark it had laid a white blanket over the trees and the stumps and the cabin. When Matt and the dog went outside at bedtime the chilly whiteness reached over his moccasins and closed around his bare ankles. They were both thankful to hurry inside again.

Next morning, in the darkness of the cabin, Matt made his way to the door. He could scarcely push it open. The bank of snow outside reached almost to the latch. He stared at it in alarm. Was he going to be a prisoner in his own cabin? With all his preparations, he had never thought of a shovel. His axe would be about as much use as a teaspoon. He set himself to hewing a slab of firewood to make some sort of blade. By the time he had dug a few feet of pathway, the sun was high. He stepped into a dazzling white world.

Now at last he could make use of the snowshoes that hung on the cabin wall. Eagerly he strapped the bindings about his legs and climbed up out of the narrow path he had dug. The snowshoes held him lightly; he stood poised on the snow like a duck on water. But with his first steps he discovered that he could not even waddle like a duck on land. The clumsy hoops got in each other's way, one of them forever getting trapped beneath the other. All at once he got the knack of it, and he wanted to shout out loud.

He tramped from one of his snares to another, waiting every few moments for the dog who floundered happily behind him. The snares were buried deep, and empty, and he set them higher, just in case some animal might venture out of its burrow. Then he tramped all the way to the pond for the sheer pleasure of it. Coming back through the woods he marveled at his own tracks, like the claw prints of a giant bird. Suddenly he realized that he was happy, as he had never been in the weeks since Attean had gone away. He was no longer afraid of the winter ahead. The snowshoes had set him free.

The cabin was warm and welcoming. He melted snow in his kettle and made a tea of tips of hemlock. He shelled and crushed a handful of acorns and boiled them with a strip of pumpkin. Afterwards, for the first time in weeks, he took down *Robinson Crusoe*. Reading by the firelight, he felt drowsy and contented. Life on a warm island in the Pacific might be easier, but tonight Matt thought that he wouldn't for a moment have given up his snug cabin buried in the snow.

Uncle George's Axe

ROBERT CHUTE

"Take her, Boy." The axe
hung heavy in my hands.
"Don't chop no stones. I've used
this axe for twenty years. She's had
six different handles
and three different heads."

Work

LURA BEAM

A boy coming around the corner of a barn at sunset with a milkpail in each hand was likely to be singing:

> Work for the night is coming,
> Work through the morning hours,
> Work while the dew is sparkling,
> Work 'midst springing flowers.
>
> Give every flying moment
> Something to keep in store,
> Work for the night is coming,
> When man's work is o'er.

This hymn, shouted by school children, chosen every week by young people at prayer meeting, harmonized in the parlor around the organ, was sung so much that everyone believed it.... "Work till the last beam fadeth ... fadeth to shine no more."

People were fanatics about work; they lived as if it were the bread of heaven. The countrymen came from the days when the word "covenant" was used in the indenture of an apprentice for three years. The master covenanted with his hand and seal to "truly and faithfully instruct and teach," and the apprentice covenanted to "truly and faithfully serve." Veterans of these indentures were still around in Town Councils, believing that all work was a kind of covenant.

Work was not for money or for possessions; it was for love, work for work's sake. Any old man too crippled by rheumatism to help on the farm would say, "Got to keep a-going," and shuffle off to saw wood for a widow or to tend the village cemetery.

The Yankee of this time and place was so serious a workman that as a spectator, he tended to identify himself not with the hero, but with substance and techniques. He was good at taking things apart and putting them together again and when his child came home from church he did not say, "How was the minister to-day?" He said "What was the topic of the sermon? What was the text? How many points did the sermon have?" He cared for the sermon apart from the speaker and he wanted the construction of it to build toward a conclusion.

People were on their own as workmen for sixty-odd years, beginning in their late teens and going on as long as health lasted, somewhere between eighty and eighty-five years of age. Before the work history began, children served a long time as helpers. They began to run errands and throw corn to the hens before they went to school, coaxed along on sayings like "If it is worth doing at all, it is worth doing well" and "Buttered bread does not fall into the mouth." Young workers began to be considered off their parents' hands except for shelter from the time they got their first job. At marriage, the parents might help to get them a house. After that, nothing more was given except the mother's help in illness.

An occupational census would have reported every man a farmer. Every man owned and worked a farm and sold produce. The psychology and bent were certainly of the farm, but all the young men and many of the others also worked "in the woods" for some months every winter. Two men were also sea captains at intervals; one man taught school when he could find a place; two had a slaughter house; one did painting, papering, and whitewashing; three or four worked around the sand and gravel holes when construction was going on in the town.

The occupational classification of farming does not give adequate credit to male ability in all kinds of work with wood and to a skill in handicrafts which could devise, make, and mend all the necessities of farm and home operation. Every man was "handy with tools" and was his own carpenter, painter, tinsmith, brick-layer, paper-hanger, fence-mender, and builder of stone walls. There was no community water supply, electricity, telephone, or plumbing. Whatever the needs of the day, the householder expected to improvise a way to meet them. He could dig a well, repair a road, make a bridge and a chimney, mend a stovepipe, a pump, a wagon wheel, a harness, a broken window. He often built a piece of his house: a bay window, a new roof, a poultry or carriage house.

The head of the family provided the fuel for his home. He either owned wood lots and cut his own land or he traded labor for the privilege of cutting on his neighbor's. The large and prosperous-looking black stoves were always yawning for wood. Cooking was done by wood every day in the year. All winter, a steady fire burned in the kitchen and sitting-room, at intervals two more in the parlor and one bedroom, and a fifth in the cellar only in the coldest weather. Beside each of these stoves a woodbox the size of a trunk gaped; it had to be filled up from the woodhouse supply night and morning.

Cords and cords of wood, sawed and split to stove size and piled to the roof, stood in the ell in a solid block as big as an ample ranch house of today. This hoard of wood represented man's slavery. When a man put a stick on the fire he was handling it for at least the eighth time. He had felled a tree in the woods, cut off the branches, loaded it as a log on a sled and brought it home, unloaded it, sawed it—either alone or as one of two men using a cross-cut saw—split it as necessary, piled it onto the wheelbarrow, trundled it to the woodshed, and stacked it systematically for winter. He or his children would carry it in his arms from the shed to the woodbox. The handsome birch he lowered into the flames might have been handled ten times. The expenditure of time and effort was so tremendous that it dwarfed any idea of small economies. Habit fed the fire with a lavish hand; there was no thought of saving wood or saving father.

A farmer was responsible for the strip of public land between the dirt road and his own property. If this strip were grassy upland, cows staked out could crop it short. If it were a seemly riot of wild roses and blackberries it could be left alone. But if the strip were fifteen feet wide and ran for half a mile, producing nothing but alders, he had to cut every tough green withe every year.

He had to thrash his grain with a flail and winnow the chaff in the wind. His large fields of peas and beans he picked by hand in a bushel basket and stored the yield in the barn; in a spell of bad weather he shelled them by hand. These phases of harvesting were barn occupations. Barns were the men's clubs. Soothed in the dark interiors with the haymows lost up under the roofs, men crouched on milking stools, mended and waxed leather, and talked.

Routine walking from job to job around the farm must have averaged two to three miles every day. Walking was so ingrained in the routine that it became a trance state or even a rest between jobs, like motorists in heavy traffic rest before a red light. Moving over familiar terrain, the walker became hazy in thought and feeling, only turning as a windmill turns. Women seldom "took" walks and they sent their children on errands, but it seemed to the woman that everything a child or man wanted of her was always half a mile away.

The weekly selling of farm produce in the town was calculated to give the seller prestige as well as money. He sold only his best. Girls sorted the potatoes, throwing aside for the pig or the hens the small rosy ones now served in city restaurants. Boys sorted the corn, keeping poor ears for the cattle; someone eliminated crooked vegetables and small fruit and berries. When the rounded measures were ready, thirteen units made a dozen and the specimens, handled one by one, were of a perfection.

The farmer counted on exchanging day labor with neighbors but he would not take odd jobs in the town. That would have been beneath the dignity of anyone except a boy just starting out. Unless he went into the woods in the winter, he was a self-employed man.

The man provided the shelter, earned the living, and held the initiative. He was always going, doing, lifting, repairing, deciding. Except as his wife planned the garden with him, he planned and executed the farm operations. He bought, sold, and tended the animals, bought and cared for the farm equipment. He remained tied to the daily and seasonal farm routine and taught his children how to fit into it, according to their age. As a citizen, unless he was below average in ability, he took his turn at helping manage the community. He helped choose the minister and keep the church in repair, leaving the music and the money-raising devices to the women. As a father, he looked after his sons' conduct, but wanted the mother to manage the girls.

The man operated in larger sweeps than the woman, just as the barn was bigger than the house. A man could build a doorstep or plow a field all day; one job at a time. As soon as a woman began to do anything, it split into a lot of unrelated brief operations, all requiring different skills. The demon of function seemed to bring it about that woman should work in a fog of complications. After the man had provided the house and major furnishings, the woman spent her life in getting the accessories, being responsible for upkeep and replacements, cooking, sewing, washing, churning, cleaning, raising children, nursing the sick, and satisfying everybody every day. For the farm she often took care of the pig and the hens, raised the chickens, perhaps milked one favorite cow.

Every woman was a housewife. In addition to being housekeepers four were teachers, two practical nurses, one a dressmaker, and one a working housekeeper.

To be in the fashion and keep up with the styles in household furnishings was costly in time and effort. Work began with the floor. Home-made rugs or store-bought carpets ran from wall to wall, over which rugs were then laid down as a second covering. Because of the cold, a kitchen might use a braided rug twelve by fifteen feet in winter. Carpet sweepers and vacuum cleaners were unknown; rugs and carpets were kept clean with a broom, with dampened tea leaves or newspapers, and by beating them in the dooryard.

The sofas had their cushions of silk or velvet, cut apart and pieced together again in a pattern. The chairs, plush or cane, had their crocheted tidies drawn through with satin ribbon. The mantelpieces were littered with vases, shells, dried grasses, and pottery; tables were covered with stereopticons, books, pictures, and plush photograph albums. If the walls had any pictures, they hung in every panel of space. The table at any meal had the same profuse details, as if the woman wanted to make work for herself; three kinds of pickles, two kinds of bread and pie. The tablecloths were so large that two feet of heavy damask hung down all around; to iron them while damp took heavy pressure from a hot iron.

A housewife served three hearty meals a day, since her husband and children came home for dinner at noon. She baked hot breads two or three times a day, cookies, cakes, and pies every other day, peeled vegetables and stewed sauces daily. In cold weather she fried dough-nuts—sugar, molasses, or cinnamon—weekly. Her kitchen utensils were often iron: the teakettle that hummed on the stove, the frying pans used for every meal, the deep kettles for soups and stews, the muffin pans. Heavy and hard to keep clean, they were washed separately and kept in a separate cupboard.

The housewife walked up and down cellar twice for every meal in summer when food was kept cool in the cellar on hanging shelves. For the rest of the year, it was stored around the first floor in the coolest spots; no ice and no refrigerator.

Winter food depended greatly on the woman's skill in canning, drying, preserving, pickling, and jelly making. In the cellarway above the stairs, or on the cellar shelves, jars stood in long rows: pint jars of strawberry and gooseberry jam, quart jars of string beans and peas, two-quart jars of corn. There were stone crocks of Bennington ware full of mincemeat and cranberries and boxes of dried apples. There were also stores of butter and eggs, salted and candled during the summer abundance, to use when the cows went dry and the hens did not lay.

The process of storing up food upset the household routine for days. For preserving highland cranberries, for instance, plans had to be made to get other work out of the way when they came on. The person who went after the cows at night would watch the pasture knolls where the cranberries were reddening and would announce when they were ripe. One or two children then walked two miles up into the woods and gathered a bushel at a time. On the next windy day, someone winnowed them in the breeze and then picked them over by hand. The first stewings were set away in crocks, some were spiced for eating with fish, some were made into jelly, a few were used in cranberry pies and tarts; in all, there were perhaps forty quarts. The last stage was when children set out carrying samples of everything to all the old relatives. The same process went on for bog cranberries, strawberries, raspberries, currants, gooseberries; blueberries were a final mass operation. Apples too were handled in quantity, cut into thin circles, strung on long sticks, and dried under mosquito netting in the sun.

Berrying and herb gathering were women's work, done while men were busy haying. Canning and preserving were solitary work, but berry picking was partly a social activity, especially the trips to distant blueberry barrens. Blueberries ran riot on any land which had been burned over in a forest fire from lightning. The landowner would then send around word that anyone might pick all the berries he wanted for home use. A hayrack left from a central point every afternoon and drove deep into the woods. Slow pickers brought back ten quarts by suppertime, fast pickers could bring twenty; fast or slow, everyone brought all the latest gossip.

Soft soap and yeast were made at intervals, butter twice a week during the summer. Dyeing cloth was a part of the process of re-making clothes and making quilts and other household furnishings. Young women used Diamond Dyes. Older women used copperas for yellow, indigo for blue, cochineal for red, and some kind of wood for black.

Washing and ironing were heavy because all the blankets, quilts, and rugs, which would today be dry cleaned, were washed by hand with soap and water. Gallons of water had to be carried around and emptied and the only labor-saving device was a wringer, found only in more prosperous homes. Clothes were cumbersome with frills, and the irons, heated on top of the stove, were heavy. The standard of accomplishment was to have the washing on the line as soon as possible after eight o'clock. Yet a woman doing a big washing or ironing would sing hymns all the morning, beginning with triumphant music like "Hark! the Herald Angels Sing," but becoming more reflec-tive as she grew tired, humming "I Love to Tell the Story."

Older women still held to making most of the family clothes, merely saying to protesting married daughters, "I don't have to run to the store every tack and turn." They had begun to sew as children of eight, making samplers, cross-stitching "Rock of Ages," "Jesus Lover of My Soul," and "God Bless Our Home" onto canvas. For a change they pieced quilts. Now they made tailored shirts, boys' suits, girls' coats, even overcoats. In summer, families bought several bolts of longcloth. As time permitted, the housewife made sheets, pillowcases, nightdresses, petticoats, drawers, and corset covers.

In the cold weather, women seemed never to stop making things: in the evenings they hemmed dish towels, made holders, fashioned curtains; knitted an afghan, hose, wristlets, scarves, earmuffs, or mit-tens; after several nights hard work at relining a coat, they would relax and make long newspaper spills to save matches—a holdover from Civil War economies. In the afternoons they settled beside their mending baskets. Among the younger women, there was a tendency to give up all this making and contriving, and sew chiefly at children's clothes and the mending.

The woman's functions still included acquaintance with medicinal herbs and the duty of night nursing for neighbors in cases of serious illness. She expected to look after her own family, and perhaps elderly relatives, in illness. The oldest women were usually the best in emergencies like croup and accidents. It was still a pre-aspirin age, but the knowledge of healing that country women used to possess was drawing to a close.

Herbs were collected in summer, dried and hung in the attic. Pennyroyal grew in every pasture, deliciously aromatic, with bees always cruising around the tiny lavender flowers. A dark brown brew of it was poured down every throat at the beginning of a cold. If the victim gagged at pennyroyal, he was sloshed with ginger tea: "a heaping teaspoon of powdered ginger in a cup of hot water, milk and sugar to taste." Hot water bags were not usual, but hot soapstones, hot irons, and hot hop bags were common substitutes. Hops were dried in the fall and sewn into many red flannel bags as big as hot water bottles. In case of a chill, a sprain, or a stomach ache, these bags were heated in the oven in relays and packed around the patient. Dried tansy, picked around old houses when the strong yellow blossoms were rank, might be used as well as hops; so also the dry blooms of "life everlasting." Tansy also relieved sprains, and was used for expelling worms in children.

The pale gray-green mullein in the pastures had large flannelly leaves at the bottom. When dried, these leaves had a slightly sedative and narcotic property. Red flannel bags of them were laid upon areas of pain, and were also used to check diarrhea. Sore throat was treated with a burning gargle of vinegar, salt, and red pepper. If the gargle alone could not be trusted, a bandage of salt pork rind and red pepper reinforced it.

Wild cherry bark made a drink for bronchitis, red currants a drink for fever, dandelions a stimulant for the kidneys. Thorn apple was a narcotic for asthma; burdock and elderberries were blood purifiers; sorrel was good for canker sores; tea from birch tree bark was a solvent for kidney stone. Bleeding from cuts was stopped with paper from a hornet's nest. A cold on the chest was treated with mustard laid on a flannel slathered with lard. Recovery from colds was coaxed along with home-made lemon and flaxseed cough medicine and a red flannel armor over chest and back, called a "chest-protector." Some unfortunates never got away from the chest-protector once it had been put on; it was yanked over the head night and morning, in addition to all the rest of the wool underwear. Boneset for fever and camomile for nervousness were other medications. Skunk's grease, figs and senna, sulphur and molasses, Scott's Emulsion, salts, castor oil, witch hazel, rubbing alcohol, arnica, spirits of nitre, and balm-of-Gilead buds in alcohol, were in every medicine cupboard. There was no medicine for a headache: the patient was told to take a walk and not read.

Since families were growing smaller and there was no longer an older child to look after every younger one, the mother's time had to go into looking after her children. Yet as she had time, the woman was supposed to provide cultural embellishments for the family. She taught the children to sing, and to memorize poetry. She advocated organ lessons and built the parlor fire so the child could practice. On winter nights she heard lessons in history and geography while the father taught arithmetic.

When the farmer and his wife had free time between seasons, they spent it in an indeterminate process known as "clearing up," an extension of cleanliness into orderliness. She had to "get at the wood chamber" and he needed to pick the annual crop of rocks out of fields. The woman also practiced housecleaning room by room and closet by closet, floor by floor and wall by wall, every spring and fall. Both house and barn had rules about "a place for everything and everything in its place." In the year's calendar, work passed in orderly line, varying only according to weather.

The working part of the man-woman partnership always appeared equal; both worked long and hard. The only sign of inequality was in the woman's voice. The man's voice was deep, easy to hear, calming. The woman's, thinner and ascending, sometimes carried a tone of complaint. Inner resistance to something in the life had gone on so long that it was part of her tonal texture.

Children realized early that work was the life-spring. They waked on Monday morning hearing that "tomorrow's Tuesday, next day's Wednesday, the week is half-gone and nothing done yet." To be late to school or church was very nearly a crime. To get to the railway station an hour ahead of time was better than getting there ten minutes early. The slow child was reminded that tardiness was "like a cow's tail—always behind."

By the time a child went to school he could drive the cows to pasture, feed and water the hens, fill the woodbox, and set the table, and of course run the family errands. Boys eight years old helped bed, feed, and water the cows, calves, and pigs, and began to ride and drive the horse around the farm. Girls at that age made beds and dusted, wiped the dishes; in two years more they could polish the steel knives and forks with brick dust, clean the silver, iron the towels, pillowcases and napkins, and be trusted with the care of the house, the fire, the younger children, and putting on the dinner the mother had left prepared for cooking.

Beginning at about the tenth year it was settled that children should do useful work in the morning. In the afternoons they played except during summer berrying and haying. A boy at ten could drive the horse while his father held the plow, could split kindling with an axe or hatchet. Boys and girls both had learned how to thin out carrots and beets, to weed the garden, pick slugs off the cabbage, tread and rake hay, and pick up potatoes following the man who dug them; girls were able to recognize and pick up some herbs and do most of the berrying. By the time they were twelve, the boy could plow under supervision and the girl was learning to cook, beginning with the food she liked best, cake, pie, and fudge. Cookery was hard to do because people teased about the results. Brothers were free with criticism, singing or whistling it so the grown-ups would not notice:

> She can bake a cherry pie, quick's a cat can wink his eye,
> But she's too young to be taken from her mother.

For the greater part of their sixty years of work history, the farmer and his wife subordinated their personality to working clothes, much as the British farm laborer wore the smock in an earlier century. When a woman got up she skewered her long hair into a quick "pug" at the back of the neck and drew on a long gray or black calico wrapper, the housecoat of the time. She got out of this uniform after doing the noon dinner dishes and coiled her hair on top of her head or in a "figure eight," but the man continued in the blue work shirt and overalls he put on when he got out of bed, unless he was going to town. Working clothes were a sign that the wearer was busy. To take too much of his time when he wore working clothes was an intrusion.

In the largest sense, the urgency about time and work must have come out of the climate. The three summer months raced by in preparation for the five winter months. Anyone tempted to relax too much was warned by the look of the sky and a sudden cold wind.

Almost nothing except the weather could interfere with an individual's plans, but he struggled against time as if every day were his last. Custom impelled him to be "fore-handed," to plan ahead, so that a man's thoughts of crops and a woman's of sewing were in terms of more than one season. Men wanted to get in the first plowing in the neighborhood, the first haying, to produce the first green vegetables. A man who had not even a watch, who came home to dinner by the sun, would complain if the meal were not on the table to the minute, so he could get back to the field. If he had the horse to consider, his noon hour would be as long as it took the horse to eat properly; if not he started back to his job the minute he got up from the table.

Still the element of choice must have helped mitigate the drudgery. The countryman of the 1890's lived in so large a setting that merely to work in his familiar place gave him a freedom we only have in vacation time. His motions were of the large body muscles, rather than the small ones of eye and hand. Whatever his eyesight was, he used spectacles only for reading. Carrying out his own plans, which had a long period of development, without an employer, without a train or bus to catch, or a watch to obey, he had an independence reserved in contemporary culture for scientists and artists.

Kennebec Crystals

ROBERT P. TRISTRAM COFFIN

The shopkeepers of Hallowell and Gardiner and Augusta had watched the January weather like hawks. They thumbed their ledgers and shook their graying temples at the lengthening columns of debit. The doctors had their eye on the sky as they felt of their lank wallets. Twenty miles deep each side of the river, farmers in small story-and-a-half farmhouses eyed their grocery-store thermometers at the side door, and bit more sparingly into their B.L. plugs. They chewed longer on their cuds too. In the kitchen, the wife was scraping the lower staves of the flour barrel. The big bugs in the wide white mansions along the river looked out of their east or west windows at crack of day to see the state of the water. Teachers in school grew short with their pupils who confused Washington's crossing of the Delaware with Clark's fording the fields around Vincennes. The mild weather continued. The river rolled on, blue in its ripples. Shopkeepers got short with their wives.

Then a sharp blue wind came up out of the northwest, the mercury in the thermometers tumbled. The pines roared on into the dark, the stars snapped in the sky like sapphires. Good weather for future soldiers, Napoleon once remarked. Napoleon be hanged! So thought the farmers along the Kennebec, who were up in history as much as they were down in their pork barrels. There were enough small pairs of pants running around their farms already. What they needed was nights to breed that life-giving ice which would keep the small thighs in the trousers going. Good freezing nights for starting the crop of the water.

The cold spell was a real one. Farmers had to beat their arms each side of their buffalo coats. Next sundown the wind fell. It got still as a pocket. You could hear the stars sputter over the valley. The shopkeepers sat sipping their evening's lime juice and gloated over their newspapers. "The Hudson Valley: continued mild weather, southerly winds, higher temperatures and showers for next week." It was a different story up here in Maine. The kitchen window panes had white ferns at their corners. A knife handle would have to be used on the water bucket in the morning. Down Hudson, up Kennebec! In the morning, there were no more waves running on the river. The water looked like a long, dark looking glass dropped between the hills. In a hundred sheds the grindstones were humming.

Then next day the January thaw came. Teachers went all to pieces as early as Wednesday in the week. Doctors used the whip on their horses as they clattered over the steaming ruts. Shopkeepers did not throw in the extra pilot bread but tied up the bags and bit off the twine. The big bugs behind the Ionian porticoes put aside the *Annals* of Tacitus and took down the *Magnalia Christi Americana* of Cotton Mather and Jonathan Edwards's *Sinners in the Hands of an Angry God*. Small boys lost their tempers and kicked the jackstraws their bachelor uncles had whittled out in the shape of oars and eelspears all over the floor. Farmers sat down to Indian pudding without any salt hake to season it off.

Young Timothy Toothtaker decided not to ask Susannah Orr a certain question until mayflower time or later. And he stopped spooling new rungs for her future bed.

The thaw lasted eight days. Somebody saw a robin. He didn't get any vote of thanks from his neighbors. A body could see his dead grandmother in such fog as there was. The graybeards by the barrel stove in Ephraim Doughty's grocery store at Bowdoin Center shivered in their shoes. Ephraim had said earlier in the evening, as he looked out at the weather glumly, "Open winter, fat graveyards." Active Frost cheated at checkers and got caught. Wash Alexander drank up all his wife's Peruna.

The only consolation in Kennebec county was the newspaper. It said it was raining all up and down the Hudson, from Saratoga to Staten Island.

February came in murky. But the trotting horses on the Kennebec barns swung round at last and headed north: the thermometer went below zero and stayed there. Everybody began to breathe again, and the grindstones started singing.

The Kennebec was gray glass again, next dawn and next and next. It grew blacker as the days went by. In the third night the drums began, a single stroke, now and then, low bass and far away, rolling and reverberating along the hills. Next morning there were white cracks on the dark drumhead to show where the drumsticks had struck. All at once, at four o'clock, the whole stretch of the river below the Augusta falls blossomed out with children in bright scarves, just out of school. A thousand young farmers and townsmen ground bark, cut figure eights, and yelled themselves hoarse at Ring-Leavo. Fat boys of six on their first skates stared wide-eyed at the green water weeds hanging still and going down into fearful darkness under their tows. At night bonfires ran down the river from bend to bend. Flame answered flame from Skowhegan to Swan Island. Everybody but those in slippers and those in the cradles was out on the ice. And next afternoon the horses had taken to the new ice highway that connected all the Kennebec towns. Men flew along behind them, mountains of robes in narrow sleighs. Their big mustaches smoked, and their breaths clung to them like mufflers straining out behind. Women swept past, little crepe bonnets cocked over the left eye and eyes like jets and blue diamonds. The ice was marked off into lanes, the racing sleighs came out. Horses came up the river, neck and neck, the flowers of their breaths festooned each side of them like garlands hung from high head to high head. Whips cracked, and shouts sent out long echoes each way. The chipped ice shone like splinters flying from a rainbow. Young men had young arms around waists of only eighteen inches, and young people started off on the road to matrimony on the thinnest of bright steel shoes.

But back up on the farms the men were grinding their picks. Women were laying out armfuls of gray socks with white heels and toes, piling up the flannel shirts, packing up bacon and ham and sausage meat and loaves. Boys were oiling harness and polishing the glass sidelights of headstalls. Chains were clinking, and sleds were being piled with blankets and bedding and victuals and extra whiffle-trees, cant dogs, picks, and feed for the horses.

Down along the river the doors stood open in the big ice-houses, with sides lined with sawdust, that for months had been shut in silence exept for the sharp, thin music of wasps. Men were clearing out old roughage and rubbing the sections of track free of rust. Machinery was being oiled. Gouges and scrapers were being looked over and as-sembled by the river's side.

The preachers and everybody else in Gardiner and Richmond, Hallowell and Dresden, went to bed that night praying for the snow to hold up and the red blood in the glass to stay down in the ball where it belonged. The river of Henry Hudson was still liquid as it went under the Catskills and down by the walls of the Palisades. God was in his heaven!

In the clear dawn next day, along a hundred roads that led down to the Kennebec, farmers were trudging, mustaches hanging down to the woolen mufflers like the tusks on the walrus. Brown mustaches, golden ones, black ones, gray ones, and white. But every one in front of a man. And behind them streamed their wealth, on its own feet. Tall, sinewy sons, out of school for good and on the doorstep of manhood and marriage, horses with hides like scrubbed horse chestnuts, big of hoof and billowy of muscle, fattened on corn, sharp shod, with long calks of steel that bit into the frozen ground. Here you could reckon up a man's prosperity in solid, tangible things, as in the days of Jacob and Laban. Goods with the breath of life in them. Like Job's. The richest man was one who had nine or ten strong men to follow the swing of his creasing trousers in ringing, ironed shoes. Or three or four spans of horses with the morning star in their forehead and the music of steel under their feet. So the wealth of the Kennebec came down to the harvest of Maine's best winter crop in the eighties.

Tramps, even, were coming. And all the black sheep of a hundred far away pastures, beyond Maine, were swinging off the sides of freight cars in the chill gray of the morning. Drifters from far beyond New England.

The men crowded into the river lodging houses of Hallowell and Gardiner, Pittston and Dresden. They unloaded and stowed their dunnage in their temporary homes for the next few weeks. They armed themselves with picks and gougers and saws. Each man had his favorite tool tucked under his quilted arm. They descended on the cold harvest floor with horses and sons in a great host.

Then the field of the harvest was marked off for the game of wealth to be played there. Men walked with gougers tracing the line their narrow plows made straight as a die across the river. After them came the horse-drawn gougers cutting a deeper double furrow. Another army of men took up the game at right angles to the others, crisscrossing the wide fields. And then the sawyers came, slow with their loads of shoulder muscle and woolen shirts. They set in their saws and began the cutting of the gigantic checkers from the checkerboard on the hard Kennebec. The men stood to their work with both hands on the handles each side of their long tools, going down, coming back, fifty men keeping time as they ate into the stuff that meant their life, bed, and board, and fodder for their cattle. It was a sight to see the gates-ajar mustaches swinging like pendulums, gold and dark, and the breath in them changing to icicles as they worked. Every so often the picks spoke, and the sawed lines lengthened ahead of the sawyers. Noon saw a dozen checkerboards marked out on the river. One notable fact about the tools of the ice industry on the Kennebec is this: they were the only tools that were good enough to remain unchanged from the beginning of the industry to the end of it.

Then the workers went to the shores and ate their cold ham and bread and broke the crystals in the top of their jugs and drank the sluggish milk. They built fires to toast their thick soles and sat on the leeward side chewing their quids of tobacco in the heat and haze of the smoke that made the tears run from their eyes. Fathers and sons broke into cakes and frosty doughnuts the wives and mothers had made. Apple pie with splinters of ice.

The afternoon saw the first great checkers of ice lifted from the checkerboards. With heaving of cant dogs and picks, the square crystals came up into the splendid sunshine, sparkling like emeralds shading to azure in their deep hearts, with sections of whole rainbows where the edges were flawed. Layer on layer of brightness, layers of solid winter to go into the hot heart of summer in faraway cities and scorching lands. Long canals opened up into dark water, and men poled the cakes down to the ends where other men caught them with cant dogs as they came, hoisted them up on the ice, slued them to the runways. Chains clanked, the hooks bit into them, and up they flashed along the high lines of steel and plunged into the icehouses.

Inside, men caught the thundering cakes and switched them, this one to the right, this to the left, to their places. The walls of cakes rose gradually, aisles of air spaces left between the walls of solid crystal. The workers here were in their shirt sleeves. They were the youngest of the men, sons more often than fathers. Their work made them glow inside like cookstoves. The sweat ran down their faces. They stood by the cataracts of ice and flung the bright streams each way, stepping as in a dance to keep clear of a blow that would shatter their bones. The work was like the thunder of summer in their ears, thunder all day long. And the house filled up with the cakes. Square cakes piled as even as the sides of a barn, true and deep blue in the steaming dusk. The men walked between walls of Maine's cold wealth.

And the steel-bright days went by. No thaws or rain came to erase the grooves in the checkerboards. The icehouses were filled to their eaves and the last tier roofed in the aisles between the cakes. Roughage was heaped over all. The doors were closed and sealed.

That year the Hudson did not freeze over til March. The betting of the Maine farmers had been three to one against its doing so. They won their bets. The rival river, the only rival the clear blue Kennebec had among the rivers of earth, had lean-kine stalls along its banks that year of our Lord. The Lord had been good. The Kennebec ice farmers heaped great towers of the harvest outside their houses and covered them with spruce boughs and sawdust, for extra measure. The Knickerbocker Ice Company lost nothing. For they owned most of the icehouses along both the Hudson and the Kennebec. All ice was ice to them. The Kennebec crop was better than the Hudson, in fact, for the water in the Maine river was clearer and purer. Kennebec ice stood at the head of all ice. It was the Hudson ice cutters who lost. But if Peter was robbed, Paul was paid. The Kennebec farmers went back to their hens and heifers with wallets stuffing out their trousers and their sons' trousers, after the $4-a-week lodging and eating bills had been paid. The grocers canceled whole tomes of ledgers. The schoolteachers kept their patience right up to "Horatius at the Bridge" in the Friday afternoon's speaking. New barrels of pork and flour came home to the high farms on the whistling runners of the horse sleds. And barrels of halibuts' heads and broken-bread. Active Frost stopped moving his checkers when his foreman turned to take a shot at the spittoon. And Timothy Toothaker asked the question when he brought his Susannah the first bunch of mayflowers. They were married and setting up housekeeping on new pine floors and in the spooled maple bed before the catkins were gone from the popples.

The geese were coming back early, up along Merrymeeting, that same spring, before the middle of April. And in late April that best day of all the spring on the Kennebec came, when the first boat arrived, the Boston steamer, with the star on her smokestack and her whistle tied down all the way from Swan Island to the Cobbosseecontee, waking the dead and the hills with her news of spring at last. There was not a church bell in the five towns that wasn't ringing. Women in bombazine waved handkerchiefs. School was let out for the day, and the hills were alive with children.

May saw the ice ships arrive and tie up at the docks. The icehouses opened their doors. The Kennebec crystals came down the runs, slithered across the decks of the four-masters and into the holds. When a number of the old hulls were loaded, which had once breasted the waves on the underside of the world, white under thunderclouds of sail, a tugboat steamed down-river on a neap tide, dragging the old veterans of the Atlantic back to the Atlantic again, below Popham.

And down in New York and Philadelphia prosperous citizens were getting down their ice-cream freezers. Children in Richmond and children under the shadow of the Blue Ridge were running starry-eyed behind high carts with letters frosted and dripping with icicles. The letters on those carts spelled "Kennebec Ice." And deep in Alabama and Mississippi pickaninnies ran with pieces of Maine's finest river in their black palms and heaven in their eyes. Farther south, the crystals of Maine touched the fruit of the Caribbees. Far down off the Horn and up the other side, ships with bones bred in Maine forests carried the Maine treasure to the Pacific. Trains plowed through the dusty cornlands of Nebraska and on to the Rockies, carrying Maine ice. And a whole nation knew the taste of the clear Kennebec. Half the world, too, England and France, and Holland.

But all that was in the twilight days of wooden ships, when Maine women still kept their neat houses moving around the world. That was when the wizards had not wakened new secrets out of electricity and steel. That was in the eighties and nineties.

Now the Kennebec icehouses are rotting and falling back into the earth. Their interiors are taken over by the wasps and the mice. The old piers are sinking into the water. No ships come up in tow of a tug through the first leaves of May. School keeps week after week, and there are no bells ringing out to greet the steamer that leads up the spring. The gougers and saws are rusted half away.

For the Kennebec crystals, last harvest of Maine's finest river, have joined the white pine and the spruce, the sturgeon and shad and salmon. The end is elegy. The day of natural ice is done. New men, outside New England, bring their sons in their strength to the work of refrigerating homes and factories. And the small farmhouses, back from the river, that once housed great numbers of young men and boys, are full of empty rooms where the swallows bring up their young, or they have only a few children who work at their tasks and never need turn their heads toward the river, where the strength of their fathers lay and their fathers' lives.

The other day my good Kennebec friend whose great house looks up the river and down, over a twelve-foot hedge of spruce, took me out and showed me the tools of the ice harvesters. They were dark with rust and covered with cobwebs. They had joined the flint arrows and the bows that once bent to bring life to the men along the ancient Kennebec. When we were coming back we passed a strange depression in the woods, grown up with lusty spruces. It was the refrigerator men of my friend's house used a hundred fifty years ago. It was the ruins of the earth cellar where they had stored their vegetables in summer and winter, to keep them from heat and cold. It was the Kennebec refrigerator his ancestors and mine learned how to make from the Indians when they drove them away into the everlasting dark from the bright blue river. That refrigerator was a ruin, and the Kennebec was as young and lusty as ever it hurried toward the sea. Someday our own sons' far great-grandchildren may find among the timbers of my friend's house the rusted shards of the electric refrigerator that serves the house today. And the Kennebec will be going down to the sea, as young and as fresh and blue as ever.

from *North of the C.P. Line*

JOHN MCPHEE

John McPhee, the author of this piece, received a letter one day from a game warden pilot in the North Maine Woods whose name was also John McPhee. John McPhee the game warden was writing to John McPhee the author because of some problems that their shared name was causing him. John McPhee, the author, had published a series of stories in a magazine, The New Yorker, *which were critical of Maine's policies concerning the North Maine Woods. John McPhee, the game warden, had also written some pieces about the North Maine Woods, but as an employee of the state of Maine, he was not allowed to be publicly critical of state policies. Given the unlikely possibility of there being two John McPhees who wrote about the North Maine Woods, people in Maine assumed that it was the game warden who had written the pieces in* The New Yorker, *and they weren't very happy about it.*

Fascinated that there could be two John McPhees who loved the Maine woods—and wrote about it—John McPhee, the author, wrote to his name twin, telling him of an upcoming canoe trip on Allagash Lake that the author had planned. The author was only a little surprised when, as he canoed on the lake, a float plane appeared above him, then landed beside his canoe. Out clambered John McPhee the game warden, to meet John McPhee the author. "North of the C.P. Line," from which this excerpt was taken, is the wonderful story of their fast friendship, and John McPhee the game warden's tales of the backwoods, as told to John McPhee the author. To avoid confusion, and because many other people did, the author called the game warden Jack.

Jack himself once had a compass fail him—long ago, when he was a ground warden assigned to a district in the southeastern corner of the woods. In a snowstorm in November of 1964, he and another warden walked for several hours trying to find a lost hunter in the woods of Princeton, near the St. Croix River lakes. They did not find a track. Now and again, they tried a rifle shot, but there was no response. Toward midnight, they sat down on a big rock, rested for a time, and decided to give up. In a technical sense, the wardens themselves were lost: they were depending on their compasses to get them out of the woods. "Well, let's go," one of them said, and they stood up, each with compass in hand, and walked away from the rock in opposite directions. Over their shoulders, they shouted simultaneously something like "Hey! Where are you going?" Holding their compasses side by side, they discovered that one had reversed. One compass was reading south for north. The magnetic poles of the earth itself have reversed at least twenty-four times in the past five million years. No wonder it could happen to a compass. But which compass? One was new. The other had been in use for a couple of years. If the wardens were to follow the wrong one, they, like the lost hunter, would spend a long, cold night in the woods. They had to make a choice, and shrewdly they chose the older compass. After a bit of sleep at home, they went out and found their man in the morning.

John McPhee's internal compass has always pointed north. As a pilot, he once felt drawn to commercial flying, but he let the impulse go, because—as he has explained—"there was no good way to be an airline pilot and live in the state of Maine." Earlier, as an undergraduate at the University of Maine, in Orono, he had studied electrical engineering, but had dropped it like a hot wire after the thought crossed his mind that an electrical engineer would almost surely have to live in a city. Shifting into a combination of mathematics, science, and English, he earned his bachelor's degree in education. ("I knew that as a teacher I could live in Maine and survive. I did not want to leave the state of Maine.") To fly in military service, he considered first the Air Force and then the Marines, but their sort of flying would not be relevant in civil aviation and would thus be useless in Maine. In the Army, he could fly Cessnas, de Havilland Beavers—the bush aircraft of the North. So he flew in the Army. Afterward, he tried teaching school for a time in Bath, on the Kennebec estuary. ("I liked the teaching but not the indoor environment. I had to get outdoors.") Born in Rhode Island, he had moved when he was in junior high school to his grandparent's town, Patten, Maine—next to Township 4, Range 7. His wife, Sharon, grew up in Patten, her father a fish-and-game warden in the North Maine Woods. When Jack gave up teaching to join the warden service himself, he started in Washington County, near Calais and Lubec and the Moosehorn National Wildlife Refuge—the easternmost county in the United States, and a fine landscape, but not for him (or me) the quintessence of Maine. His Maine of Maines is not the bold-headland coast, and not the drumlin farmland under maples that blaze in the fall. His Maine of Maines is north of the C.P. line.

If you enter Maine at Kittery, as most people do who are coming from the south, it's a couple of hundred miles to the C.P. line. People in Florida say that if you draw a line across Florida at the latitude of Daytona everything south of the line is Northern and everything north of it is Southern. By the C.P. line Maine is even more pronouncedly decided. The C.P. line is where the Canadian Pacific Railway, encountering the obstacle of northern Maine, overcomes the inconvenience by crossing the state—in one side (Jackman) and out the other (Vance-boro). When people of the north country use the term "downcountry," they are referring to everything south of the C.P. line. Above the line rise the Kennebec, the Penobscot, the Allagash, the St. John. Above the line is the Great North Woods. That is where Jack, as a new member of the warden service, hoped someday to be flying, and his chance came in 1967.

Since then, he has spent fifteen thousand hours above the North Maine Woods—hours equivalent to nearly two full years in the air. He will fly for a month and not once get into his car. Typically, he might land outside his home at noon, drink some coffee, eat a doughnut, take off, and return to the woods. Actually, he has two homes. One is a big cabin in leased land in the Allagash country beside a body of water variously called Allagaskwigamooksis and Macannamac and, on most maps, Spider Lake. By the dock at Spider Lake, near a rack of canoes, two airplanes are often parked nose to nose—his own and the state's, both Super Cubs. In his time off, he works as a flying woods guide, or fishes on his own, or roams the backcountry. Of the various canoes he has scattered through the north woods, one is on Peaked Mountain. It would not be unfair to say, I suppose, that only a McPhee would keep a canoe on a mountain. Walking back one evening after a visit to one of his canoes, he said, "Mother Nature has been good to us today, giving us three fish. For our part, we didn't do anything, particularly, except show perseverance."

His principal home, the airplane base in Plaisted, is on Brown's Point, in the lowest of the Fish River lakes. Sharon works as a dental hygienist in Fort Kent. Their two daughters are for the most part away now—one in college, the other working for a paper company as a chemical engineer. The base belongs to the State of Maine and consists of a three-bedroom house, a small barracks for the use of wardens, a garage, and a Butler hangar—all under birches and spruce on an acre that juts into open water, which in winter is capped with four feet of ice. He lands on skis, and taxis up the lakeshore to the hangar, where a power winch lifts his airplane while he spins it around with one hand. An eighteen-foot wood-and-canvas river canoe stands on end in the back of the hangar. "The rent isn't the cheapest," he said ruefully one evening as he finished closing the hangar and moved between high snowdrifts toward the glow of his house. He pays two hundred dollars a month.

Brown's Point is actually the delta of a small stream that enters the lake beside the hangar and spews nutrients to crowds of waiting fish. Boats collect in summer; and as soon as the lake is hard, fishing shacks arrive and remain through the winter. Fishing shacks tend to be heated, furnished, close to civilization, close to paved and numbered roads—shantytowns platted on ice, and clustered where fish are likely to be. In architectural style, at Brown's Point, they range from late-middle Outhaus to the Taj Pelletier, a ten-piece portable cabin with nearly a hundred square feet of floor space, red-curtained windows, cushioned benches, a Coleman stove, a card table, a hi-fi spilling country music, and hinged floorboards that swing upward to reveal eight perfect circles in the ice through which lines can be dangled from cup hooks in the ceiling. If the air outside is twenty below zero, the air inside will be a hundred degrees warmer, while men in shirtsleeves interrupt their cribbage to lift into the room a wriggling salmon. The principal participant in this enterprise is Melford Pelletier, of Walla-grass, Maine—as a sign above the door, by law, attests. He is a big, friendly man, a school math teacher, who grew up, with his three brothers, in the warden cabin at the Nine Mile tote-road bridge over the St. John River, one of the remotest places in the United States east of the Hundredth Meridian. Melford, hence, is an American Romulus, and his fishing shack is what he heard in the call of the wild. His brothers are wardens. His patriarchal father, Leonard Pelletier—the old war-den, father and grandfather of North Maine wardens—set up his own shack last winter on Square Lake (Township 16, Range 5), and we dropped in on him while we were flying ice patrols, but Jack did not check his license. A benign giant in insulated shoepacs and layers of thick red wool, he was the warm and voluble center of an otherwise gelid tableau, in a windchill so far below zero that its number had ceased to matter. Stinging needles of lake snow were blowing past his windbreak. Abundant cordwood was neatly stacked beside his shack. His axes, his pack baskets, his shovels, and his peavey leaned against the cordwood. All in the middle of the lake.

As we flew from fisherman to fisherman, lake to lake, we crossed a black-and-white world of bright light and long shadows. On St. Froid Lake (the nom juste if ever one has been chosen), a shivering woman said, "Hel- hel- hello, John," as Jack emerged from the plane. She had caught a seventeen-inch salmon, which he weighed and measured. It had no fin clips, which signified to him that it had not been stocked.

On Cross Lake, two men were much relieved that all we wanted was to see their catch. One said, "You had me worried. My brother is really sick. I told my wife if anything happened to call the warden. I thought it was an emergency."

Spread out radially from most of the fishing shacks were set lines called traps. On most lakes, five lines are permitted per license. Holes are dug with gasoline-powered augers that can penetrate in moments the four-foot hide of a lake. A spring-loaded flag is placed at each hole. When a fish gets on the line, the flag goes up and a fisherman comes out of the shack. Wind can trip the spring, sending up what is known as a wind flag, symbol of false hope. One of the many skills required of a warden pilot is an ability to taxi to a fishing shack without sending up a garden of wind flags.

"This ice fishing has a lot to do with the emotional stability of people in a place like this," he remarked over the intercom toward the end of one patrol. "Fifteen, sixteen years ago, people dreaded winters here. It was a terrible long haul after Christmas. They did a little smelt fishing in December, but that was all. They used ice chisels or hand augers. There were no power augers. Snowmobiles were just coming in then. Slowly, there was a changeover. Winter became less of a locked-in ordeal. Snowmobile clubs began to form. They made groomed trails. And soon there were interlocking networks of trails, involving one club with others. They started cross-country skiing. Always, it was a family affair—a big thing up here, under the heavy French influence. The fishing shacks are heated now. The snowmobiles have heated handlebars. People now say, when the winter comes to an end, 'I can't believe it's all over,' whereas fifteen years ago they could not wait for it to end."

Minutes later, coming in on final to land at the base, he found that he was on a collision course, descending toward a youngster on a snowmobile who was travelling over the lake ice in the same direction and—in the racket of the snowmobile's engine—had not heard, or looked around and seen, the plane. "Snowmobiles have done more than anything else to get people out and facing the hardships of winter," Jack had been saying. "They're a big thing up in this corner of Maine. Families with ten-year-old rattletrap cars will have three four-thousand-dollar liquid-cooled snowmobiles." Now he added some flap. "With this wind," he said, "I can slow the plane so that it will go slower than the snowmobile." It did. He waited to make his landing while the kid on the machine ran on in front of us faster than the flying airplane.

Work Piece

TOM FALLON

Eight hours: work:
in the paper mill.

At five paper machine:
at the rewinders:

What time is it:

Eight hours work:
pushing paper rolls.

Rolls, of paper:
off the paper machines.

All the machines:
the paper rolls push.

Match up roll sizes:
push the paper rolls.

To the lowerator:
lowerator downstairs:
push the rolls.

What time is it.
Wait: coffee break:
run the paper machines:
run the paper machines.

What time is it:
arrange the rolls.

Five paper machine runs
another set of paper:
five paper machine runs

another set of paper.

Pull rolls from floor truck:
pull rolls from floor truck.

What time is it:

Lowerator up: noise, noise:
what time is it.

Push matched up rolls:
from 9 paper machine:
2 paper machine: 4 paper
machine: 8 paper machine.

Noise continuous: keep
the machine running:
what time is it:
what time is it.

Keep the paper machines
running: pull: push:
wait: pull: push rolls.
What time is it.

Ha ha ha ha ha ha ha.
Noon, sandwiches. Eat.

What time is it:
8 hours: work:
this is the money.

The lowerator is up:
push on the rolls:
what time is it.

Wait: work: wait.
Run the paper machines:
run the paper machines.

Run:
drive: drive: drive:
drive:

from *Picking Up*

LUCY HONIG

At exactly six-thirty in the morning, April Devoe got out of her car, grabbed her basket and walked stiffly down the long furrow of potatoes to her section of field. The sun was not yet over the hill. Clumps of soil bearded and brittle with frost smashed to powder under her feet. The tractor was already halfway down the first long row, dragging the digger behind it, rattling and clanking. Where the digger had already gone lay two filament rows of potatoes on the dirt's surface. Here and there, huge coiled masses of plant tops had caught up in the digger and then been yanked out. More tops than potatoes, everyone grumbled this year. Every year.

Jean was already bent over and picking up. When April came near she stood straight, said hello, and dumped a full basket into her barrel. The potatoes bounced in with a rush of hollow thumps. At the next section, the one before her own, Freddy and Bea were just getting started; no hellos came from them. Their section seemed too short to April; her own looked too long, the far marker just barely visible. Freddy had probably moved her stake again, always giving her more section when he and Bea were feeling lazy or else shortening it up, sneaking that stake around behind her back, when they were greedy for more barrels and the picking was good.

April pulled on the gloves that were still damp and crusty with mud from the day before, yawned, and let her eyes stretch out for the last time this morning to the distant end of the field. And then she decided she'd finally better face it: the first bend of the day. She dragged a barrel over to the start of her section and tipped it on its side, then bent from the waist. It was done. She stifled a groan. Bullets of pain shot from her waist up and down the length of her body. Breakfast crouched in a cold heavy wad in her stomach. For an instant she was no longer blood and breath and bone and flesh but only pain. Then, since there was never any question of giving in to this agony, she forced herself into the rhythm of the day's work. First, her body arched over the tipped barrel, she flung potatoes into it with two hands at once. Then, swiveling it around as far as she could and flinging with wrist-flicks that astounded even the oldest and hardiest of pickers, she got that barrel half-filled from four rows across before she even set it upright. Then, "faster than the devil," they all said, with those wrists of hers on magic hinges, she threw potatoes into her basket like some crazy juggler, basket braced between her ankles, spuds flying into it from earth like rockets launched into space. Her basket full in seconds, she straightened up, ran to the barrel, and dumped in the potatoes. The second basket, filled even faster, finished off the barrel. She ticketed it with her number from a pile of tickets in her pocket and dragged over the next barrel. And then the next. One right after another so that even on the worst days with the smallest potatoes or rain muck or machinery breakdowns, she was barrels ahead of everyone else, even Charlie, who at the age of sixty-eight could not bend his back because the emphysema made him choke but could pick on his knees better than almost everyone else could pick on their feet.

She moved down her first set of rows like fire through dry brush. The sight of her line of barrels set off within her a small warmth of consolation that helped her maintain the frenzied momentum into the next row. She took a grudging pride in her work. Doing it well, doing it best, was what made it bearable. "Quite a worker, that April, quite a worker," people had always said, and always said twice as if unable to underscore the fact in any other way, even when she was a kid. "Quite a worker, quite a looker," is what some said now. Her features were large and lush and well-proportioned. Her long thick hair, red as fall maples, was pinned into a knot and tucked under a bandana when she worked. Her skin shone gold with freckles. She was tall, lean and solid with muscle. Carrying three children had not ruined her shape.

The morning began to warm. The frost vanished, earth dried pale. The trucks hummed and groaned behind her. One of them crept along the finished rows, picking up the filled barrels. From the back of the truck, Ernie, the year-round hired man, took the huge metal ring that was attached to the winch and threw it with a clunk over the rim of a barrel. "Aaa-yup!" Ernie's baritone floated out smooth as ice as the barrel was hoisted up off the ground with a screech of metal. When it reached the level of the flatbed, Ernie disconnected the ring and removed the picker's ticket, while another man swiveled the barrel into place with massive arms. Slowly the truck made its way down the row. Then, full, it turned back to the potato house to dump its load, passing the second truck as it went down the field with empty barrels. Two men on this truck threw off the empties, spacing them evenly along the length of the field—thud-plunk, thud-plunk, thud-plunk—they were timed, like pulse-beats, to fall regularly, precisely, one here, one there, thud-plunk, thud-plunk, until there were no more left, no matter what the difference was between the pickers' speeds and needs. April's neighbor on the far side, Edna, excruciatingly slow of body and mind, could barely manage a strip of field twenty feet long, yet each time the truck went by she got a few barrels, until the whole depth and breadth of her section, by the middle of day, was covered with empty barrels lying on their sides, while April and Jean and just about everyone else were a dozen rows ahead and crying for barrels; pacing back and forth with nothing to do, waiting, losing money, screaming at the fellows on the truck, "Give us more, you jerks! Can't you see?" And the fellows, as if deaf and blind or somehow convinced they were serving the interest of a higher, purer cause, gave them each two or three barrels, just like Edna, for an eight-barrel section.

"Edna, could I have one of your barrels?" April asked after lunch, smiling and trying to be friendly.

"Uh-uh," Edna answered, her face stony and grim. "I need it."

"Edna, you won't possibly be needing all those barrels before the truck comes back."

"Uh-uh."

"Edna," April said more sternly, with no smile left, "I've got to have more barrels. You've got more than any of us."

Edna wrinkled up her nose and held onto April with a long, hostile stare. Finally she said, "Take one from there," and pointed far behind her to the very first row. "Just one."

"Oh for chrissakes," April spit out, stomping away. "I'm taking two."

Each day there was at least one battle. She was growing to hate Edna. She could no longer feel sorry for the woman as she once had. With her children, April was very strict and forbade them to mock or belittle the kids in school who were retarded and slow. But as she dragged up the hard-won barrels from so far away, losing precious minutes, she grimaced derisively at the back of the dumpy, lethargic figure picking at each potato, one by one. Edna's very looks made April angry.

But anger kept her going. Except for moments now and then when the rhythm of her work maintained itself automatically, when there were no long waits or jumbles of tops to interfere, and her motions simply followed one another without thought, it was rage, not skill or even doggedness that propelled her. Anger at Edna. Anger at the voice of Edna's sister Annabel, a shrill whine that snagged on phlegm and snot as it drifted from the section beyond Edna's, wrangling with her husband's grunts. She was angry at the irrevocable order of pickers down the field, created on the very first morning by the sequence in which they arrived; they were stuck with each other all season so that Nelson the farmer could pace out and mark off their sections ahead of them as he started to dig each new field.

She got angry at the potatoes when they were so small and sparse she had to drag her basket halfway down the section just to fill it once, or when they were so diseased and rotten that her thumbs burst through them and the black, oozing gunk penetrated her gloves. She fumed at the truck crews when they were stingy and perverse with barrels. She seethed silently at Nelson when he slowed the tractor to talk or tinker with the digger, and they all had to stand by idly, waiting for him to dig the next row. She was angry at the pay that had gone up only once in the six years she had picked. They were paid by the barrel, yet it seemed rigged so she could never get ahead.

She grew enraged when, by late morning, the sun became so fierce that sweat poured from her in rivers. She had taken off her sweatshirt by eight, cold as the ground still was, then her sweater by nine, and the flannel shirt by ten. Now she was in her t-shirt. The men on the trucks liked to watch her strip and that made her livid, too. She got angry when the wind kicked up hard and the dry grit that was supposed to be soil got blown into her face. This afternoon the wind did not die down. Her eyes stung and blurred and she couldn't keep her speed. Nelson kept digging new rows and she got angrier. How did he expect them to pick? The grit coated her throat and rasped in her lungs. Finally, the tractor stopped near the road. Pausing, relieved, April squinted to watch as Nelson got off the tractor and walked across the next field toward the potato house. He went in. She bent to finish off her row, figuring it was the last. Five minutes later she saw Nelson come out of the potato house, walk back across the field, mount the tractor, put the goggles on over his eyes, start up the machinery, and begin digging the next row.

"Son of a bitch," April said to Freddy as they picked up the potatoes on each side of the stake. "It's nice that *his* eyes won't get dirt in them."

"Well what do you expect?" Freddy chuckled.

"Big deal, a little dirt," said Bea. "It won't kill you."

She got angry at Bea and Freddy, but kept on going crazy-fast. She thought suddenly of her wrists and saw how hard she was pounding the potatoes into each other in the basket and against the barrel. She was bruising them and she didn't care. Sometimes she must have had whole rowfuls of barrels of bruised potatoes, cut and smashed by the impact of her angry hurling, their skins scraped and dripping juice. Someone in the potato house must have noticed. They said they could tell whose barrels were whose, which pickers threw in rocks, who left the tops attached, who skimped at rounding off. Not that Nelson or anyone else ever said anything. What else could they expect from a bunch of dumb potato pickers, after all? No one ever said a thing about her bruised potatoes, either. For six years she had been waiting to get scolded or fired—just as every day she waited for Nelson to fish at her clumps of witchgrass and tell her to go back and pick up the potatoes she had missed in the heavy tangle of roots. She had trained herself not to bother with them. She knew he yelled at some of the others for the same thing.

Behind all the anger of this day she was fighting hard to keep from thinking about what she had learned the night before. Things are never so bad, her mother used to say, that they can't get a little worse. She had found out from her husband that he was cheating on her. It was not some little fling, either, but a full-scale affair with a woman from Boston he had met at one of those insurance seminars he went to all the time. Exciting, these big city women, she bet. None of them came home smelling of sweat and field rot and potatoes. The insurance woman moved to Augusta. Far enough away, one would think. But no, the two of them had managed back and forth. Try not to think of it, April told herself. She absolutely had to put it off for another three weeks, until the end of potato harvest. Seventeen or eighteen more days of work. Six or seven hundred more dollars. She had to have that money; there was just no more in sight for all the rest of winter if they were really going to close down the slab mill and that work was lost. She did not know what she would do, exactly. The car payments she might be able to manage, but the house! He had mortgaged it up to the rafters and now he didn't have a cent, or so he claimed. She and the kids would be out in a snowbank and he'd be sitting pretty in Augusta. She stomped her foot hard in the dirt and her toes stung against the sharp edge of a rock. Keep your mind on potatoes, she told herself. Don't think about the rotten goddamn, son-of-a-bitch and his fancy city lady.

She pulled over a new barrel and began shooting potatoes into it. Try not to think. Sure, just try. She laughed at herself. What was the big deal, anyway? So what if he had been seeing this woman for over a year? So what if he had probably had a hundred affairs before? It happened all the time. She heard about it from all the women. It was simply a matter of time; you just never knew what you were going to do about it until it happened.

But more than a year! She still cringed. And he had the nerve to laugh at her for taking so long to get suspicious. Right out loud, in the middle of *her* kitchen, he laughed. And she spluttered, "You've been lying to me all this time!"

"Lie!" he replied. "Why, I never lied to you!" He had that miserable mocking tone that he always used whenever he turned the tables back on her. "You just never *asked*!"

Last night she kicked him out. But deep down in her heart, below those first layers of hurt and shock, jealousy and resentment, she knew there was something far worse. She found she was beginning not to care at all. This hollowness to her feelings was more troubling than anything else. She tried to put it away, to save for that day she handed in her basket and left the field for good. But, like a giant hunger, it would not stop eating away inside of her, this emptiness.

At four o'clock she was done with her section. Down the field she saw others still rows behind, but she would not walk over and help them finish up. Always she used to, but not now. Someday she would get a cramp in her side and fall twenty rows behind, and then the others would all drive past at four o'clock, ignoring her, and she would have to work until midnight to finish. But she didn't care anymore. She counted up the tickets still in her pocket.

"How many you got today?" Charlie yelled as he went past.

"Sixty-six." Automatically she translated that into money: forty bucks.

"Not bad."

"You?"

"An even fifty."

"You get caught on that slope with the real bad ones?"

"Nope. Did about as good as any day."

She threw her basket into the back seat and got into the front of her Volkswagen. Woodie and Marge sidled up next to her in their car.

"You break a hundred today, April?" yelled Woodie, same as every day.

"Oh sure. Hundred and fifty even." She winked. "How'd you like that wind?"

"You think that was bad," said Marge. "Tomorrow we got russets to do, up on the dump road."

"Goddamn stinkin' peanuts," said Woodie. "Like marbles."

"They still don't irrigate up there?"

"No ma'am. I think it's time we asked for some money."

"Now you're talking."

"We'll see you tomorrow, April." They drove off in a spray of fine dust.

She set her mirror up on the dashboard. Her face was evenly coated brown with grit, dry and stinging. With the last of her drinking water she washed her hands. She took off her bandana and rewound her hair into a smooth, new knot, watching the crowsfeet around her eyes crack white and clean as she moved. Inside her satchel she found the damp towel she had wrapped up in the morning and carefully washed the dirt from her face and neck. Then she rubbed in lotion to soothe the sting. At no other time did she take such care of her face, but she was damned if she was going to let potato-picking dry her out and wither her up. She rubbed salve into her lips. She spread cream under her eyes and along the sides of her nose. She was *not* going to look like a shrivelled-up old potato before she hit thirty-five. Every year on the first day of picking she got a shock to see how much some people had aged. Marge had seemed to go gray in one season. Woodie had had his teeth all pulled out last summer, and before he got his new set the folds of skin drooped on his face, weathered dark like old clapboard, and made him look twice his own age. She was not going to let potatoes get the better of her, to cripple or mark her for life.

Her face was clean; it hurt less. She folded up the mirror and put a fresh shirt on over her filthy t-shirt. Then she drove off, past acres of potatoes still to harvest, past miles of rocky blueberry land, frost-tinged crimson, through woods still deep summer green with pine and hackmatack, and into the speck of town to pick up the kids.

Grandfather

GARY LAWLESS

come from Frankfort
just west of the Penobscot
farmland and marshland, hard rock.
quarried granite from Mount Waldo
lots of them left to work around Stonington,
Crotch Island and those other quarries.
I stayed on, got a foreman's job.
later had a little store down where
the road and railroad cross.
used to fish for salmon some too.
they used to swim up the river,
Indians would gill-net em
up around Passadumkeag.
one spring my son was settin a trapline
young and really didn't know—up in
the marshes.
Indians come along in a canoe,
showed him how to use a scent
for bait, and how to save it from
what he caught.
they'd go in their canoes down to Sandy Point
get clams and fish
nowadays no one comes around.
this day and the next are all the same.
one day yr. scrapin dirt, the next day
yr. in it.

A Mess Of Clams

ROBERT P. TRISTRAM COFFIN

The fields are high with all the Winter's snows,
But somewhere there is cawing and glad crows,
And ice upon bare birches feels the sun
And twinkles and is starting in to run.
An old, old man, with no tooth in his head,
Is walking fast, and Spring is in his tread
As he wades the snowdrifts of his farm,
His clam-hoe and clam-basket on his arm.
Down below him, all his bay is white,
But out towards sea the dark place overnight
Has widened, and blue waves are twinkling clear
Above the first and best clams of the year.

The March sun burns upon the man's bent bones,
His wife is lying where the slanting stones
Are hidden by the Winter. All his sons
Are begotten and have begot new ones.
He is alone, but he can go and bring
His mess of clams home in his eightieth Spring
As he could in his twentieth one, and he
Can pick his dinner up out of the sea
Just as well as any man alive
And think of things like young men fit to wive,
His head is high, and handsome as a ram's,
And life is good and tastes of sweet young clams.

Linn Goes Torching

DOROTHY SIMPSON

The good weather held, and in the next few days Linn hauled his traps without any interference from Randy. He was able to pay Norris Wade five dollars on the peapod out of each haul. Then one afternoon Wiley told him they would go torching that night, and Linn felt as if his cup were truly running over.

Not only Linn was pleased. At supper time, when he came in from the woodpile with his arms stacked high with spruce, Grampa was singing a hymn to himself in his soft high voice as he set out freshly baked beans and steaming squares of yellow johnny cake. He had brought a special jar of pickles from the cellar. Everything showed that he was in an exceptionally good mood.

As they settled down to eat he said, "So you are going for herring with Wiley tonight." Linn, his mouth full, nodded and the old man's eyes sparkled with satisfaction.

"That's good, good. Work hard and get the bait in. And if the herring are big ones, we will salt some away in kegs for our own winter eating." He wagged his head and began to eat with a good appetite.

Fishing from any aspect was a joy to the old man. Linn marveled sometimes at the way Grampa would pick up a herring and turn it over lovingly in his gnarled stubby hands. And now Linn had a chance to bring in bushels of the silver fish; no wonder Grampa was happy, remembering the days of his boyhood when a herring was as much the staff of life as bread. Grampa had gone fishing almost all his days; as a young man newly arrived from the Old Country, seeking a free life in America, he had signed onto a Grand Banks schooner. And from its deck, on the way to and from the Grand Banks, Grampa had seen a small island lying alone and self-sufficient in the sea, twenty-five miles from the mainland, and he had made up his mind that some day he would live on that island, an independent fisherman with his own land and his own boat.

He made many trips to the Banks and saved his money, until he was able to board the mail packet for Lee's Island. It was sparsely settled then, most of it was still in the hands of the Lee family, and they wanted young, vigorous, hard-working men to build it up. Carl Swenson suited them; they sold him a few acres and a bit of land on the harbor shore for his wharf and fishhouse. And here on Lee's Island he drove down roots like a young tree and became like a part of the island itself. For a wife he chose the daughter of another Scandinavian settler. They were all gone now, the Lees and the rest, except for Norris Wade.

It was not because Grampa was a Scandinavian, or old, that he was set apart from the rest. It was his attitude toward life. He had never forgotten his hard childhood and youth, and he had a deep reverence for the privilege of being able to work in freedom, for the things one wanted, and then to work to keep those things safe.

"Work is the poor man's blessing," he said often to Linn. "Your health, your strength, they are given to you for tools to labor with. *You must not waste them.*"

Linn understood what he meant, but sometimes he thought Grampa carried his doctrine to extremes. It had made the old man unpopular on the island, chiefly because he had never kept to himself his contempt for others who went at an easy pace. He could never pass a fishhouse where a group were yarning without stopping to shake his head.

"So you men have plenty of money," he would say silkily. "You are rich. You don't need to work!" And his bright dark gaze would move over the buoys waiting to be painted, the traps waiting to be patched. Some of the men would laugh, others were angry. Grampa wagged his finger ominously at boys who loitered around the wharf drinking pop at mail time. Grampa, meeting a woman getting water at the well, had been known to make little speeches about men who didn't tend the water pails but who were still late in getting out to haul.

"The grasshopper and the ant, it is more than a fable," he said.

"But Grampa," Linn tried to argue with him once. "Things are different now. Sure, you had to work hard every minute when you were in your prime; you had to haul your traps from your old sloop and it was slow going, and when you came ashore you didn't have a lot of daylight left to do your chores both at the shore and in the barn."

"So?" Grampa sounded dangerously silky. "Go on, please. Explain to your soft-headed old grandfather why it is no longer necessary to work to eat."

"But Grampa, George Kingman and Fred Mears and Bart Robinson and Wiley and the rest—don't *they* have enough to eat? Don't they have good boats, all paid for? Gorry, Grampa, just becase they aren't rushing around in circles all the time like ants when you mess up an anthill—that doesn't mean they don't get their work done!"

"So I have spent my life rushing around in circles."

"No, no!" Linn felt red and hot, he stumbled blindly on. "All I meant was—well, gorry, Grampa, everybody knows you did the work of *ten* men, but you were farming and fishing at the same time, and it was rough going then—no price at all for lobsters, and no wonder you had to keep hopping every minute to make a dollar! Nowadays, a fella with a good boat so he can range, and a couple hundred traps, he can make a hundred dollars or more in one haul, when the season's on!" In his mind he saw himself one of the lucky ones, standing at the wheel of a boat like Wiley's, heading far out over the endless blue plains of the ocean. He swallowed. "So if a fella wants to stand around talking a little on a pretty afternoon—I mean when he's doing well and doesn't owe anybody—and he's all baited up for the next day, well, what's the harm? He'll get his work done sooner or later."

His grandfather studied him for a long moment. "You make quite a picture," he said at last. "But tell me this. Is a man doing well when he spends his hundred dollars as fast as he makes it, with no thought for the days to come? What right has he then to stand around with his hands in his pockets, smirking and yarning like a rich man with no cares? With all his bills, he is as poor at the end of the day as you are."

Linn knew when he was beaten. The way the prosperous modern fishermen spent their money was another sore spot with Grampa, who could not believe any of them had anything laid by, at the rate they kept buying bigger boats and more expensive engines, and fine things for their houses, and always new clothes for their wives and children. The long visits to the mainland, where there were movies and meals in restaurants were especially distasteful to him. He would mutter dourly, "Throwing their money away on every hand, with never a thought for the rainy day."

It had taken him years of painstaking toil to accumulate a nest egg; then his wife's long illness had used up much of it. Sometimes Linn could understand the anger that burned in Grampa's eyes when he saw men hiring others to knit their trap heads for them, or paint their boats, or even build their traps; that they should willfully, *disgracefully*, pay out money for things they could do themselves in order to put that money safely away!

And for a man to go out and get his own bait, instead of buying it from the smacksman—that was fitting and good. No wonder he was happy on this night, when Linn was going out with Wiley after herring. As they ate, there was an unusual, though silent, harmony between the man and the boy.

The sunset light had faded by the time they had finished, and there was a rosy lavender glow in the western sky. There would be no moon, the sea would be calm; the best kind of night for torching. If the herring were schooling, then everything would be perfect. Linn's heavy boots seemed suddenly light as moccasins as he hurried into his jacket. Grampa reached for his; the dishes could wait on the table, he must get into the excitement of torching even if he could do no more than watch the men and boats depart.

They were halfway to the shore when Charles shouted from the road, "Hey, Linn, you got any rags for a torch? My mother says she hasn't got anything left—we've cleaned her out."

Linn glanced at his grandfather, who nodded. "Come, my boy." They went back to the house and into the woodshed. Linn followed the old man up the steep narrow stairs into the loft, where many boxes and barrels were stored under the eaves. From a barrel near the window the old man pulled forth pair after pair of trousers, blue and brown and gray, faded, threadbare, patched beyond wearing. But now they were valuable, for without plenty of rags for the torch bowl there was no sense in chasing the herring that schooled in the sheltered coves.

Watching his grandfather now, Linn was ashamed for a moment, remembering how many times he had thought his grandfather foolish to save these rags over the years. Why, there was enough here to keep many torches burning, and as he gathered the heap of old trousers into his long arms he felt warm and proud, not only would he be working his way tonight, but he would be contributing something essential for the work.

"Godfrey!" Charles gasped when he saw the clothes. "Where you been hoarding all that?"

Grampa gave a soft cough and Charles said hurriedly, "You're worth your weight in gold with all those rags, boy!"

Grampa sniffed and drawled, "Yes, it pays to take care of everything. It all comes in useful some day."

"I'll say. All Wiley could get Grace to give up was an old piece of blanket."

The two boys and the old man walked to the wharf where Wiley's boat lay with a big dory tied astern. Wiley stood in the dory, fastening the torch bowl to its side forward of the first thwart. Here he would stand with the great dip net ready for the herring when they came surging in a frenzy toward the blazing torch.

The boys stowed their oil clothes and water jugs aboard the powerboat and began tearing the old trousers into pieces. Grampa stood watching the proceedings, his hands behind his back, his dark eyes bright and intent; now and then he nodded as if in approval. Soon the dory was ready, the oars laid on the thwarts and the tholepins hung on their cords; the long handle of the dip net pointed far over the bow and the enormous fine-meshed bag lay in folds on the bottom, the kerosene for the torch was in a five-gallon can. Wiley looked around at the others, while he fished in his pocket for pipe and tobacco.

"Well, looks like we're all set," he announced.

Grampa stood on the wharf until the boat with the dory in tow was heading out of the harbor, the wake shattering the water's glassy surface. Then Linn saw him walking slowly back to the house.

The boat slid across the water with a soft powerful rush; Wiley was steering, his pipe clenched between his teeth, his hawklike face intent as he gazed ahead. Charles lay on the bow, looking over the side. Linn glanced astern and saw that a million phosphorescent fireflies danced in the swirling and bubbling water, and the dory behind them seemed to rush through a tumbling mass of liquid fire that increased in light and color as the darkness deepened.

"Where are we heading?" he asked Wiley.

"Think mebbe our best bet is to go around to Bull Cove. I imagine there's somebody with the same idea already."

Lee's Island bulked black against the starlit sky, and at Bull Cove the lights of two blazing torches moved slowly back and forth on the quiet water. Wiley was careful to give the other torchers a good berth as he steered in close to the mouth of the cove. Charles dropped the anchor, then came down to the cockpit to put on his oil clothes. Linn and Wiley put on theirs and the dory was brought alongside, and the three climbed in. Charles sat on the bow seat with his back to Wiley, who stood in the narrow space with the painter near his feet, the long handle of the dip net towering far above his head, his left hand clasped it while his right was free to motion whatever direction he wished them to go. Linn sat on the stern seat, facing the bow, where he could watch Wiley's hand whenever it should motion to the right or left. Charles pulled on his oars, and Linn pushed with his, but as he was also steersman, he held back or strengthened a stroke when necessary, whereas Charles pulled strongly and evenly all the time.

The two pairs of oars dipped the water; quietly the dory slipped away from the lobster boat. The oars felt good in Linn's hand. *I hope we do good tonight,* he thought, almost as if he were praying. It was not only because he needed the bait; but if they got a load of herring on his first night with them, they would say he brought luck with him and be glad they had asked him to join them.

Charles shipped his oars and put a handful of rags in the wire torch bowl that hung out over the side; he poured kerosene on them and then lighted the soaked mass. Instantly the torch was aflame, throwing up a great flaring light that illumined the dory, its occupants, and the surrounding sea in a wide bright circle. Close to the dory the water was a strange pale green, and the floating shreds of seaweed became mysterious.

The oarsmen rowed slowly, and Linn watched Wiley's right hand, which guided them. If he made a half-circling motion, Linn was to push harder with the right oar; if he waved his hand back it would be a deeper dig with the left oar. Charles, in the meantime, would row an even stroke and keep the torch bowl aflame.

All at once Linn saw the herring coming out of nowhere, it seemed. All in an instant they were crowding to the surface, drawn by the torch.

"Put your backs into it, boys!" Wiley yelled. The dory leaped ahead like a pony suddenly spurred in the flanks. The herring surged after the light in a boiling rush. The long handle of the net came up, the bag swung out in a wide arc and then swept down into the silver mass. Charles drew in his oars and turned to give Wiley a hand. Between them they pulled in the heavy, bulging net; into the dory the fish tumbled in a slippery, wriggling flood. They slithered aft and Linn rejoiced as the tide of herring reached his ankles. It wouldn't take many such dips to give the dory her first load.

Wiley had left a lantern burning aboard his boat, and when the dory was loaded the boys rowed back toward the soft glow and the accompanying yellow gleam of reflection in the dark still water.

"We're hitting them good," Wiley said with satisfaction. "If they'll only stick around. One minute they can be thick as sand and following the torch good and the next minute they're gone—just like that—"

"And you don't see 'em again, either," Charles added. "Well, so far, Linn isn't a Jonah."

"Wait till we go for the next load before you say that," Linn said. He laughed, but his heart was hammering with his fervent hope that he *wasn't* a Jonah.

Back at the big boat, Wiley set kidboards in place forward of the engine to make a pen, and Charles and Linn took turns with a small dip net bailing the herring aboard. They were good-sized, about eight inches long.

"Some of them would go good fried tomorrow," Charles said hungrily. "And corned later. Nothing like a good mess of corned herring and boiled potatoes. I guess the lobsters can spare us a few."

"Plenty for us and the lobsters too," Wiley drawled. "I figure we got about twenty-five bushel there, and if we have good luck we'll have that many more and then some before midnight."

Linn was no Jonah after all, and by midnight they returned to the boat with their last load. The pens fore and aft of the engine were filled, the dory was bailed dry and tied astern. Linn and Charles stretched their arms, groaning with pleasure and relief. They hadn't had Wiley's chances to rest. But Wiley was the best for dipping. You had to know what you were about when it came to poising the net and plunging it into the sea, or you might bring it up with no more than a handful of fish.

"How about some grub?" Charles demanded. "Seems to me I remember seeing some put down forward."

"Ayeh, it's there." Wiley sounded surprised. "I plumb forgot about eating while the fish were coming so good."

They squeezed into the small cabin and set the lantern on the little stove. Too hungry for talk, they ate sandwiches and cake and drank hot coffee from a thermos bottle. Linn was not only hungry, but rapturously happy. His thoughts flashed between the new double-ender lying at her haul-off, and this satisfactory companionship here in the cabin of the boat; the best companionship of all, when men rested and ate together after they had worked hard together.

Charles, having stuffed himself into a comfortable state, finally found speech. "Looks like we're ready for the minstrel show, boys! Come on, Wiley, give us a buck and wing!"

Wiley's teeth showed white in his sooty face, and Linn knew that he looked at the same as the others; the smoke from the burning rags had blackened their faces, accenting their teeth and the whites of their eyes.

The other torchers had gone long before, and as the boat headed homeward over the hushed waters the only light that showed anywhere, besides the stars, was from Bridges' Light, five miles to the southward. Wiley stood knee-deep in herring at the wheel. The bow of the boat cut through the black sea, curling it into waves that rolled and swirled astern where the dory rode high in the glowing wake; the water was alive with white and gold flame, so that the boat seemed to be setting the ocean ablaze as she moved through it.

No one talked on the way home; they were tired, and besides, this was no place for words. Linn gazed from the cold fire of the sea up to the stars and felt reverent. Why, this was just like one of the Psalms come to life! Maybe this was why Grampa liked reading them over and over.

Then Wiley was shouting at him. "Grab that mooring, Linn!" The engine slowed down and the boat slipped gently to her berth. Linn ran up over the bow and gaffed the buoy; Wiley shut off the motor and the following silence was so deep that it almost hurt one's heart. The harbor lay as black as the outer ocean, and the land was an even darker mass reaching toward the star-strewn sea.

Wiley and Charles unrolled a big canvas spray hood and spread it over the pens. "Keep the pesky gulls out as much as we can," Wiley grunted. "We'll bail these out first thing in the morning."

Charles poked Linn roughly in the ribs, stopping a big yawn. "You going to stand there all night? Come on, get into that dory unless you plan to stay here till morning. In that case we wasted our time dragging that spray hood over those herring. You could keep the gulls away."

Still yawning, Linn got into the dory, marveling how heavy his boots had become. Wiley took up the oars, saying, "You boys have rowed enough for one night."

The three parted behind Wiley's fishhouse, each taking his own path home. Each murmured, "See you early," and trudged away into the darkness.

The Night Charley Tended Weir

RUTH MOORE

Charley had a herring-weir
Down to Bailey's Bight;
Got up to tend it, in
The middle of the night.

Late October
Midnight black as tar;
Nothing out the window but
A big cold star;

House like a cemetery;
Kitchen fire dead.
"I'm damn good mind," said Charley,
"To go back to bed.

"A man who runs a herring-weir,
Even on the side,
Is nothing but a slave to
The God damned tide."

Well, a man feels meager,
A man feels old,
In pitch-black midnight,
Lonesome and cold.

Chills in his stomach like
Forty thousand mice,
And the very buttons on his pants
Little lumps of ice.

Times he gets to feeling
It's no damn use;
So Charley had a pitcherful
In his orange juice.

Then he felt better

Than he had before;
So he had another pitcherful
To last him to the shore.

Down by the beach-rocks,
Underneath a tree,
Charley saw something
He never thought he'd see;

Sparkling in the lantern light
As he went to pass,
Three big diamonds
In the frosty grass.

"H'm," he said. "Di'monds.
Where'd *they* come from?
I'll pick them up later on,
Always wanted some."

Then he hauled in his dory—
She felt light as air—
And in the dark midnight
Rowed off to tend weir.

Out by the weir-gate,
Charley found
An old sea serpent
Swimming round and round.

Head like a washtub;
Whiskers like thatch;
Breath like the flame on
A Portland Star match.

Black in the lantern light,
Up he rose,
A great big barnacle
On the end of his nose;

Looked Charley over,
Surly and cross.
"Them fish you've got shut up in there,
Belongs to my boss."

"Fish?" says Charley.
"Fish? In there?
Why, I ain't caught a fish
Since I built the damn weir."

Work   235

"Well," says the sea serpent,
"Nevertheless,
There's ten thousand bushels
At a rough guess."

Charley moved the lantern,
Gave his oars a pull,
And he saw that the weir was
Brim-belay full.

Fish rising out of water
A trillion at a time,
And the side of each and every one
Was like a silver dime.

"Well," says the sea serpent,
"What you going to do?
They're uncomfortable,
And they don't belong to you;

"So open this contraption
Up and let 'em go.
Come on. Shake the lead out.
The boss says so."

"Does?" says Charley.
"Who in hell is he,
Thinks he can set back
And send word to me?"

Sea serpent swivelled round,
Made a waterspout.
"Keep on, brother,
And you'll find out."

"Why," Charley says, "You're nothing
But a lie so old you're hoary;
So take your dirty whiskers
Off the gunnel of my dory!"

Sea serpent twizzled,
Heaved underneath,
Skun back a set of
Sharp yellow teeth,

Came at Charley
With a gurgly roar,
And Charley let him have it

With the port-side oar,

Right on the noggin;
Hell of a knock,
And the old sea serpent
Sank like a rock.

"So go on back," yells Charley,
"And tell the old jerk,
Not to send a boy
To do a man's work."

Then over by the weir-gate,
Tinkly and clear.
A pretty little voice says,
"Yoo-hoo, Charley, dear!"

"Now, what?" says Charley.
"This ain't funny."
And the same sweet voice says,
"Yoo-hoo, Charley, honey."

And there on a seine-pole,
Right in the weir,
Was a little green mermaid,
Combing out her hair.

"All right," says Charley.
"I see you.
And I know who you come from.
So you git, too!"

He let fly his bailing-scoop,
It landed with a *clunk,*
And when the water settled,
The mermaid, *she* had sunk.

Then the ocean moved behind him,
With a mighty heave and hiss,
And a thundery, rumbly voice remarked,
"I'm Goddamn sick of this!"

And up come an old man,
White from top to toe,
Whiter than a daisy field,
Whiter than the snow;

Carrying a pitchfork
With three tines on it,

Muttering in his whiskers,
And madder than a hornet.

"My sea serpent is so lame
That he can hardly stir,
And my best mermaid,
You've raised a lump on her;

"And you've been pretty sarsy
Calling me a jerk;
So now the Old Man has come
To do a man's work."

"Look," says Charley,
"Why don't you leave me be?
You may be the hoary Old
Man of the Sea,

"But I've got a run of fish here,
Shut up inside,
And if you keep on frigging round
You'll make me lose the tide."

Then the next thing that Charley knew
He was lying on the sand;
The painter of his dory
Was right beside his hand.

He could see across the bay,
Calm and still and wide;
It was full daylight;
And it was high tide.

"H'm," said Charley.
"What am I about?"
The oars weren't wet, so
He hadn't been out.

"Oh," he thought. "Di'monds,
Underneath the tree.
Seems to me I found some.
I better go see."

But he couldn't find any;
Not one gem;
Only three little owl-dungs
With the frost on them.

Factory Days

SUSAN HAND SHETTERLY

Two months after we moved onto our land, we ran out of money. For some reason, this astonished us. It wasn't that we didn't have enough for a winter's trip to Florida or a second car; we didn't have enough for a comb or a bottle of cooking oil. Laying aside my copy of Helen and Scott Nearing's *Living the Good Life*, I took a job at the local canning factory.

When there were fish to cut, the factory whistle blew. If the fish came from Canada, or southern Maine and not by boat, we always knew beforehand, because the factory trucks hurled themselves down the Pond Road in the dark. The Pond Road bears a certain resemblance to a subway tunnel. The trees on either side of it grow up onto the shoulder, and there isn't a curve in it.

Nothing hits this road like a truck with a sloshing belly of fish. It is as if the driver knows the road so well, he dismisses it. In his mind, he is already at the factory hardtop. We used to wake to the strain of metal and rubber, hearing them pushed toward another dimension. The air cracked with the roaring will of that truck to become a man's silent thought.

Women, not men, cut fish. Men unloaded the cold tanks, and bodies, wide-eyed with a surprise they no longer felt, ascended the conveyor belt that drummed down the length of the cutting room. Men heaved the cans into the trough above the belt. And men supervised the women's work.

Bullet was a supervisor. As we thrust our arms against the flow of fish and diverted a viscous school of herring onto our stainless steel sinks, as we cut the tails to resemble sardines, or sliced up to the gills for "fish steaks," our taped fingers holding scissors that had been honed to blades so sharp they could have shaved our legs, as we hurried to fill our cans and to fill our trays with thirty filled cans, Bullet prowled the aisles, making sure we did everything just so.

He didn't hurry. Ash built up on his cigarette. Like a Fourth of July snake, the ash bent but did not break. Occasionally, he leaned toward one of us:

"Put another few in this can, Grace."

"Them's too big, Ida."

Women were paid by piecework. Some, the fastest among us, had a rhythm—lunging, snapping, gutting, placing—every gesture blurring with the next. Their feet scraped a two-step against the cement floor.

My cutting style was slow. How far from the caudal fin should I cut this fish so it will look like a sardine rather than a herring's tail? Here? Well, how about here? A bell rang and the belt stopped for the morning break, my second day on the job. The women loosened their plastic aprons and walked over to sit on the benches by the Coke machine. One, as she passed me, hissed:

"They'll fire you, sure thing."

"Why?"

"You're too slow, dearie. You ain't worth their money."

My fingers ached. The stomach acids of the fish had peeled away the skin on my palms. It was exhausting to stand up hour after hour. But I couldn't afford to lose the job.

There was a cutter, well into her eighties, who wore a red nylon wig that always slipped over one eye as she cut, revealing dark sprouts of hair at the back of her head. Her legs were as muscled as a runner's. She never looked tired. If she can do it, I thought, so can I.

At the break, a few women would gather around my sink, engaging me in quiet, formal talk. As if they barely noticed what their hands were doing, they would finish cutting the fish to complete my tray. At first, I was ashamed. Some were twice my age. I murmured how they should be resting, how I could finish up.

"We don't have much else to do, dearie. And besides, I don't like to sit," one answered. Moved by their kindness, I almost cried.

Like most of the women in the cutting room, I would have liked to become a "sniffer." Sniffers were better paid. They worked in the dark sorting rooms, smelling cans that were ready to be boxed and sent. Sniffers hunted, like bloodhounds, for that stray whiff of leaking, soured fish. Or, I thought, closing the blades of my scissors so gradually through a herring that the swollen entrails nudged against its scales, maybe I'd like to be president of the company. I'd change a few jobs, first thing. I'd see how Bullet cuts a fish.

The herring along our shore spawn in summer in shallow water. Because the fish were being netted so intensely year-round, the vast schools that used to number as many as three billion individuals were smaller in size and there were fewer of them. Factory boats from other countries plowed beyond the two-hundred-mile limit. Our own boats, hounded by competition and a diminishing source, were picking up the fish on their spawning grounds.* They brought back in their holds herring that were swollen with eggs. When we cut into them, the eggs spurted out and clumped on our arms and aprons.

"I'm cutting up my daughter's job," commented one woman as she jabbed for another fish. By the end of the day, the eggs had dried into rubbery, itchy mats all over us.

No matter how the belt rattled and the cans clashed, the women talked.

"I seen him down there midnights, prowling about."

"And she shows her face 'round here."

"Yessah, don't care who knows it."

"Seems like her sister was just the same. And look how she turned out."

"He'll get his tail burned one of these days, fine and dandy."

"Did you know that Mabel's been up to the hospital?"

"No. What ails her?"

"Pains."

When the last whistle blew, late afternoons, most of the women piled into the yellow factory van to be driven home. Gulls keeled around the factory. The waves sparkled. There was always a brisk, salty wind. I walked through the screaming birds, letting the wind blow away some of the smell of fish. On the Pond Road, I stopped to pick blueberries. I pulled off my sneakers and lowered my feet into the icy water of a stream. As I sat within the hot-baked smell of the evergreens, my sore feet in the wintry water, things came clean again.

*This practice is no longer allowed.

In the Sardine Factory

KATHLEEN LIGNELL

There can be no other labor
like the slitting of dead fish into fillets,
no scissors so sharp
they miss and cut off chunks
of fingers and sometimes
missing altogether
you gash your partner at the bloody table,
rinsing pieces of flesh
with scales and fins.

You smile sardines.
The crease these scissors have worn
moves into your palm like a lifeline.
And more, your apron full of the stench
of fish, the torsos
packed into oil and canned,
bears your body home, smothered
in scales of pearls.

What you cannot see is your mother,
and hers, and all the other women in town,
waiting like fishwives
for the tide to turn into weirs
turning into hogsheads of silver herring.
In my dream I see you bending at your sink,
not knowing where or who you are,
becoming part of some awful whale,
cold-blooded, you grind
fish bones into fertilizer.

You do not see yourself
as someone you scarcely know,
working your shift, day after day,
among the hundreds of women
who rise each morning, automatic,
to the factory whistle.

Maine

PHILIP BOOTH

When old cars get retired they go to Maine.
Thick as cows in backlots off the blacktop,
East of Bucksport, down the washboard
From Penobscot to Castine,
they graze behind frame barns: a Ford
turned tractor, Hudsons chopped to half-ton
trucks, and Chevy panels, jacked up,
tireless, geared to saw a cord of wood.

Old engines never die. Not in Maine,
where men grind valves the way their wives grind axes.
Ring-jobs burned out down the Turnpike
still make revolutions, turned marine.
If Hardscrabble Hill makes her knock,
Maine rigs the water-jacket salt: a man
can fish forever on converted sixes,
and for his mooring sink a V-8 block.

When fishing's poor, a man traps what he can.
Even when a one-horse hearse from Bangor fades
away, the body still survives:
painted lobster, baited—off Route 1—
with home preserves and Indian knives,
she'll net a parlor-full of Fords and haul in
transient Cadillacs like crabs. Maine trades
in staying power, not shiftless drives.

Neil Welliver, Osprey's Nest, *woodcut, 31" x 33",*
Courtesy, The Maine Savings Bank Collection, Portland, Maine.

Nature

"Stones are the sheep of these hillsides
And fog is the wool of these stones."

The Wreck of the Hesperus

HENRY WADSWORTH LONGFELLOW

It was the schooner Hesperus,
    That sailed the wintry sea;
And the skipper had taken his little daughter,
    To bear him company.

Blue were her eyes as the fairy-flax,
    Her cheeks like the dawn of day,
And her bosom white as the hawthorn buds,
    That ope in the month of May.

The skipper he stood beside the helm,
    His pipe was in his mouth,
And he watched how the veering flaw did blow
    The smoke now West, now South.

Then up and spake an old Sailor,
    Had sailed to the Spanish Main,
"I pray thee, put into yonder port,
    For I fear a hurricane.

"Last night, the moon had a golden ring,
    And to-night no moon we see!"
The skipper, he blew a whiff from his pipe,
    And a scornful laugh laughed he.

Colder and louder blew the wind,
    A gale from the Northeast,
The snow fell hissing in the brine,
    And the billows frothed like yeast.

Down came the storm, and smote amain
    The vessel in its strength;

She shuddered and paused, like a frighted steed,
    Then leaped her cable's length.

"Come hither! come hither! my little daughter,
    And do not tremble so;
For I can weather the roughest gale
    That ever wind did blow."

He wrapped her warm in his seaman's coat
    Against the stinging blast;
He cut a rope from a broken spar,
    And bound her to the mast.

"O father! I hear the church-bells ring,
    Oh say, what may it be?"
"'T is a fog-bell on a rock-bound coast!"—
    And he steered for the open sea.

"O father! I see a gleaming light,
    Oh say, what may it be?"
But the father answered never a word,
    A frozen corpse was he.

Lashed to the helm, all stiff and stark,
    With his face turned to the skies,
The lantern gleamed through the gleaming snow
    On his fixed and glassy eyes.

Then the maiden clasped her hands and prayed
    That savèd she might be;
And she thought of Christ, who stilled the wave,
    On the Lake of Galilee.

And fast through the midnight dark and drear,
    Through the whistling sleet and snow,
Like a sheeted ghost, the vessel swept
    Tow'rds the reef of Norman's Woe.

And ever the fitful gusts between
    A sound came from the land;
It was the sound of the trampling surf
    On the rocks and the hard sea-sand.

The breakers were right beneath her bows,
    She drifted a dreary wreck,
And a whooping billow swept the crew
    Like icicles from her deck.

She struck where the white and fleecy waves
    Looked soft as carded wool,
But the cruel rocks, they gored her side
    Like the horns of an angry bull.

Her rattling shrouds, all sheathed in ice,
    With the masts went by the board;
Like a vessel of glass, she stove and sank,
    Ho! ho! the breakers roared!

At daybreak, on the bleak sea-beach,
    A fisherman stood aghast,
To see the form of a maiden fair,
    Lashed close to a drifting mast.

The salt sea was frozen on her breast,
    The salt tears in her eyes;
And he saw her hair, like the brown sea-weed,
    On the billows fall and rise.

Such was the wreck of the Hesperus,
    In the midnight and the snow!
Christ save us all from a death like this,
    On the reef of Norman's Woe!

A Stay at the Ocean

ROBLEY   WILSON, JR.

On the sixth day of his vacation in the old house on Perkins Point, Stephen Bell woke, as usual, at five-thirty. The sun was on the wall opposite the small window of the bedroom, though the room was still chilly. Birds in the meadow behind the house made unintelligible conversation, and the remoteness of the ocean's noise suggested that the tide was out.

He got up and dressed. His wife, Clarice, was snoring becomingly in the big bed, and he paused on his way to the kitchen long enough to look into his daughter Linda's room and see her curly blonde hair nestled into the corner of one elbow. He felt a strong possessiveness toward both his women, and a kindness; he did not wake them.

In the kitchen he quietly poured himself a glass of orange juice, washed a vitamin pill down with it, then set out on his customary walk down to the sea.

The summer place, a modest white building the Bells had rented through an agent in Damariscotta, had been built in the 'Twenties nearly at the tip of the point. From its upper windows it provided a view of the Atlantic in three directions, and while the Point had very little sandy beach—only a strip of some hundred feet along the south-west edge—it had nearly three-quarters of a mile of shoreline along which Stephen could stroll in the early light. Rocks and split black ledges met the thrust of the sea with a kind of stubbornness, and brief reaches of lowland were strewn with coarse stones the ocean was rounding into its own toys. At the tip of the Point was something fairly worth calling a cliff; at high tide it dropped off five or six feet to the water; at low tide it became nearly impressive.

It was to the edge of this overhang that Stephen walked each day, to look at the sea and to assemble his private thoughts—this morning no different from any other. He noticed that the tide was remarkably low. Rocks he had never seen before had risen up off the end of the Point; his cliff plunged down not to green water, but to an unfamiliar shelf of darker stone which sloped gradually toward open sea. This morning the nearest tidal pool was so far away that it took all his strength to throw a stone hard enough to reach and ripple the smooth surface. Thrumcap Island, nearly a mile out, was an unaccustomed high shadow in the morning fog, and a few yards out from the tiny beach the blue rowboat which had come with the house sat aground on damp sand; the rope from its bow looked ridiculous, as if the boat were anchored somewhere under the earth.

"What's going on?" Stephen said, half to himself, but loud enough to startle a single gull overhead. The gull, which had appeared out of the fog, glided back into it. Stephen threw a last rock after it and returned to the house.

He found Clarice getting breakfast; Linda, in pajamas, had just poured a bowl of dry cereal and was now spilling a pitcher of milk over and around it.

"Did you get your pill?" Clarice asked.

"First thing." Stephen sat at the table across from his daughter. "You ought to see how low the tide is."

"The moon's full," his wife said. "It was low yesterday."

"I know, but this is *really* low. I've never seen anything like it."

Clarice set a plate of eggs before him. "Coffee's coming," she said. "Lin, please honey, eat over the bowl."

"You could walk halfway to Thrumcap," Stephen said.

Linda looked up from her cereal.

"No kidding, Lin. Halfway to Thrumcap."

"What do you suppose it is?" his wife said.

"Don't know," his mouth full. "What you said, I guess. The moon."

"Daddy, does the moon make tides?"

"So they say. Clarice? It's so low I can't throw a rock to the nearest water. And the boat's high and dry."

"How does the moon make tides?" Linda persisted.

"Gravity," Stephen said. He winked at his daughter. "But you know what I think? I think this tide is too low for the moon to take credit for. I think the ocean is just a gigantic swimming pool, and somebody's draining it."

"Mother, *is* the ocean a big pool?"

"I think your father's teasing you." Clarice poured two cups of coffee and brought them to the table.

"*You* swim in it, don't you?" Stephen said.

"Everybody does."

"There you are. It's a pool, and somebody's draining it, and now we can walk halfway to Thrumcap."

Clarice frowned at him. "Drink your coffee, and stop feeding misinformation to eight-year-olds," she said.

Stephen patted his mouth with a napkin and pushed his chair back. "You think I'm making it all up," he said. "You come on and I'll show you."

By the time Stephen had jogged down to the Point, the two women trailing after him, the fog had begun to burn away and Thrumcap Island stood monumentally ahead of them. The sea had receded still further: now over the mile between the Point and the island only a few round pools of water were left. All else was a waste of gray sand and flattened black weed. The island looked as if it had been lifted onto a plateau of sand, rimmed with twisted tree-roots.

Clarice stopped short. "Oh, Steve," she said. "Oh, Steve; my Lord."

"Is that something?" Stephen felt oddly as if he were taking credit for the phenomenon.

"Look at all the lobster traps!" Linda shouted.

Stephen looked. Where his daughter was pointing he saw a line of a dozen or so lobster pots mired in the channel about fifty yards out from the old shoreline. He started down the slope to the small beach.

"Let's have some lobsters," he called back.

"Steve, no. They belong to Paul Dunham."

He faced his wife. "But they'll just die, won't they? They won't be any good to anybody."

"Paul will get them."

"How? You can't run a boat through the sand."

"Then he'll walk. Stop showing your criminal side."

Stephen shrugged and came back.

"Aren't we going to have lobsters?" Linda said.

"We'll buy some, honey," Clarice told her. "Steve? Isn't this awfully strange?"

"I'll go along with that."

"I mean, this couldn't happen, could it? Are we just all having a dream?"

"You want me to pinch you?"

"Be serious, Steve." She sounded ready to cry.

He hugged her lightly. "I don't know, Clar. Yes, it's strange. It's impossible."

"Is it bad when the water goes so far away?" asked his daughter.

"No, Lin, it's just very funny. Very unusual and crazy." He looked at Clarice. "What do you want to do?"

"I don't know."

"Hey, I do. Let's all walk out to Thrumcap and explore. We've never done that before."

Linda danced. "Yes, let's."

"What if the tide comes back in?" Clarice said.

"Then we'll be marooned on the island and we'll hail a passing lobster boat."

"But if this is low tide—" Clarice hesitated. "What will high tide be like?"

"Slow. And we'll see it coming and run back to the house before it gets us." Stephen started down the beach. "Come on," he yelled, and his family followed after.

It was something like walking the edge of a usual beach, the sand packed hard, and the footprints of the three of them spreading into patterns of dryness as they walked. Except that there seemed no end to the beach. The sand was remarkably clean, Stephen noticed, with only random patches of seaweed beginning to dry in the sun, and here and there a mussel shell or a black crab half-buried. The sensation of actually walking to Thrumcap Island was eerie. He had never landed on Thrumcap—not even by boat. When they reached the island, he had to climb up to it, hand over hand, along and through the exposed roots of a tall pine, then reach down to pull Linda and Clarice ashore with him.

"It would be lovely to build a cottage out here, and just be isolated from everybody," Clarice said as they crossed the island.

"Would have been," Stephen agreed.

"Why say it that way?"

"I think the tide won't come back in. I think the ocean must be drying up, or changing its basin, or something."

"Are you serious?"

"I don't know. It doesn't make sense that this is just some fantastically low tide." They were standing on the far side of the island, facing southeast. "Just look," he pointed out. "You can't even *see* the ocean."

He felt his wife's hand find his and squeeze hard. "I'm scared, Steve."

He put his other hand over hers. "Freak of nature," he said. "Let's walk back and see what's on the radio."

By the time they had started across to the Point, other figures were moving out from the old shore—men and women, and a few children; some of them were carrying picnic hampers. Dogs pranced around family groups or clawed and nosed at objects half-submerged in the sand. Not far from his own beach Stephen saw a lone man plodding toward a lobster trap, pulling a high-sided wooden child's wagon behind him.

"There's Paul," Clarice said. "Why don't you see what he knows about this? I'll take Lin up to the house and try to get some news."

They separated. Stephen caught up with the lobsterman. "Morning, Paul."

Dunham nodded to him. "Morning, Mr. Bell." He was a thin, fortyish man, needed a shave, had watery-gray eyes that looked out under a long-billed yachting cap. He had pulled on hip boots over his clothes; in the wagon Stephen could see a few lobsters moving sluggishly against each other.

"What's happening, Paul?"

"Can't say." He had come to the next of his string of traps, and had stooped to open it, drawing out a single lobster. He measured its carapace, then turned a perplexed look toward Stephen. "Don't know what to do with the damned thing," Dunham said. "Too small, but there's no place to throw the critter back to." He replaced the lobster in the trap and stood up.

"What's happened to the tide?" Stephen repeated.

Dunham gazed westward. "Man up the coast told me it's gone out close to fifteen mile," he said. "Lives up on Pine Ledges. Owns a telescope."

"Will it come back in?"

Dunham picked up the handle of the wagon. "I got my waders on," he said.

Stephen made an awkward gesture of parting. "Happy fishing," he said, stupidly.

He met his women near the beached rowboat. "Anything?" he asked.

"There's nothing on the radio but bad music," Clarice told him. "We should have brought the little TV with us. What do you want to do?"

"Look what some people are doing, Daddy."

"Steve, they're driving cars out there," Clarice exclaimed.

It was true. Stephen could see a half-dozen automobiles moving out toward Thrumcap, and the Schumanns—whose cottage was a few hundred yards northeast of theirs—had actually piled into their truck-camper and had just now driven off the beach, threading between two grounded sailboats toward the east.

"Let's do that," Stephen said.

"Drive out *there?*"

"Why not? Obviously it can support the weight."

"It would be fun," Linda said.

"Of course it would. Let's pack a lunch and get into the car and go."

"But go where?" Clarice wanted to know.

"To the ocean," Linda said.

"Right. That's what this vacation is all about. We'll drive to the ocean."

Clarice finally agreed, and in an hour the Bell car, a white compact station wagon, was packed for the outing. Clarice had made sandwiches and filled a thermos with coffee. Stephen had put in a six-pack of beer, along with some hamburger and a carton of milk—all of it packed with ice in the metal chest. Linda had gathered together a careful selection of comic books and dolls. Almost as an afterthought, Stephen loaded the Coleman stove, and a five-gallon can of gasoline he had bought the day before for the outboard motor—explaining to his wife how unlikely it was that they would be able to find either firewood or a gas station on the ocean floor.

"All set?" They were in the car, Linda curled in the back on a thin plaid mattress.

"All set," the women chorused.

Stephen was pleased that everything was turning out so well—that what might in some families have become a fearful time, a kind of domestic disaster in the face of the unexpected, was now resolved into one more vacation side-trip. Even Clarice seemed relaxed, though commonplace misgivings still plagued her.

"Do we have enough gas in the tank?"

"I filled it yesterday," he reassured her. "Cruising range up to 500 miles."

"I hope nothing breaks down."

"Not a chance," Stephen said.

"Well," said his wife reluctantly, "just don't drive too fast."

It was easy to disobey her, Stephen discovered. The surface he drove on was unbelievably smooth, and though he once in a while was obliged to go around upjutting rocks or to avoid genuine islands that rose ahead of the car, the experience was very much like that of crossing a shopping-center parking lot—every destination reached by the straight-line distance, with no attention paid to lines painted by developers or highway commissioners. And the ride itself was luxurious; no bumps, no curves to speak of, the tires against the gray sand making a sound like skis on dry snow. The further he drove, the fewer the obstacles became; even with the speedometer needle swaying between 70 and 75, Clarice made no protest.

Several cars passed him—none of them closer than ten yards—and the occupants of each car waved joyously and called out to the Bells.

"It's certainly a free-for-all," Clarice remarked.

"They're excited," Stephen said. "Nobody ever did *this* before."

"You couldn't even do this on television!" Linda shouted.

At the end of an hour-and-a-half of driving, Stephen was surprised to see a great number of cars—thirty or forty, he guessed—lined up about a mile ahead. They were stopped; the people in them had gotten out and were milling around.

"What's that all about?" Clarice asked.

"Maybe the road's washed out," Stephen suggested. He winked at his wife.

"You're so damned funny," she said.

"I bet it's the ocean," Linda said.

"Hey, I'll bet you're right." He slowed down and eased the station wagon to a stop between two of the parked cars. "Okay," he said, "everybody out."

But it wasn't the ocean. Walking in front of the car, the three of them found themselves at the edge of a steep bluff.

"Wow!" said Linda. "Look how far down it is."

It was more than 200 feet to the bottom of the bluff—not a perpendicular drop, but at a perilously steep angle from where they stood down to what appeared to be a limitless dry plain. The cliff consisted primarily of coarse rock, partly bare, partly encrusted with green and white shell-things. Deep crevices between the outcroppings of stone were filled with sand. The plain below seemed entirely of sand, and looked flat as a table top.

"We'll never get down there," Stephen said. He heard a touch of awe in his own voice.

"Quite a sight, isn't it?"

The words startled him: he turned and found himself facing a stranger—a middle-aged man with rusty hair and plump chins.

"Incredible," Stephen agreed.

"There's a couple of guys down the line say they're going to try and drive a Jeep down to the valley. I say they're batty."

Stephen nodded soberly. "I should think so."

"Me and the wife, we're going to head south from here."

"Why south?" Clarice was asking the question.

The stranger hesitated and put out his hand. "Excuse me, folks," he said. "The name's Allen. We're out here from Des Moines."

Introductions were exchanged. Mrs. Allen, a dowdy facsimile of her husband, joined them.

"We met this gentleman from New York," Allen told them, "says he used to study geology in college. He claims that if you drive a couple of hundred miles south—down near Cape Cod, he says—and then head straight east, you won't have to run up against this particular cliff. I don't know, but he claims he does."

"That's interesting," Clarice said.

"Says you can drive right out on this Continental Shelf he used to study about," Allen added.

Stephen looked at his wife. "Want to try it?"

"Are you and Mrs. Allen going to do that?" Clarice asked.

"Oh, yes; we surely are."

"What for?"

"Curiosity, mostly," Allen told her. He seemed reluctant to say more.

"And the treasure," Mrs. Allen put in.

"Treasure?" Linda was suddenly interested.

"Oh, well, yes, we sort of thought we'd look around for a little sunken treasure." Allen shuffled uneasily as he spoke. "You know, all those old ships that went down—oh, hundreds of years ago—and up to now nobody's been able to find 'em. We thought we'd keep an eye out. You saw that old hulk on the way here?"

"No, we didn't," Stephen said.

"Oh, we drove past it. Half-buried thing. No way to get inside it."

"But we've got shovels in the pickup," Mrs. Allen said.

Allen began drifting away with his wife. "We'd better get started," he told Stephen. "Have a safe trip."

"Steve? Does that make sense? Finding sunken treasure?"

He gave a small, noncommittal gesture with his arms. "At this point, I'll believe anything. How about eating? It's way past noon."

"But we haven't seen any old hulks," Clarice said.

"True, but it stands to reason there must *be* some. There ought to be a lot of Second World War shipping scattered around somewhere, too."

"We haven't seen anything, not even any dead fish, or those strange underwater plants you see pictures of. Why is that?"

He passed around sandwiches. "I suppose everything got buried under silt or swept out clean. This was some tide, you know."

They ate. Stephen sat on the fender of the car, the sandwich in one hand, a beer in the other. As he gazed out over the edge of the bluff he marveled at how far he could see, and how little was to be seen. The horizon—how far away? Twenty? Thirty miles?—was as unbroken as the rim of a plate. God knew where the ocean was, what it was doing, how long it would recede from them. He shook his head, as if to wake himself up. Off to his right, a young couple in white deck shoes was gingerly climbing over the edge of the cliff. He leaned forward to get a glimpse of the precipitous slope. The couple was picking black, withered plants out of a thin river of sand. They climbed back up, obviously delighted with what they had done. Off to his left, a small boy was sailing bottlecaps far out and down to the plain; the caps glided like odd birds. Where were the gulls and cormorants? he suddenly wondered. Following the elusive sea?

"Let's take that drive south," he said to his wife.

"Should we, Steve?"

"We won't get lost. I'll move in so we can see the shore on the way down."

"We ought to go back to the house first, don't you think? Maybe we should get the tent, and some more food."

"No," he said, "let's be really adventurous. There's food enough for breakfast, and we can sleep in the car if we have to."

It occurred to him as he backed the car around and set a course for the southwest that he had to go as far as he could—as if something in him insisted that he find the ocean. He rationalized the insistence in two ways: first, the ocean was what he had left Cleveland for, and he refused to be deprived of it after fifty weeks of slaving over his drafting board; second, he certainly wanted to be able to tell his friends, firsthand, what that Great Tide business had been all about. *I was there,* he could say. *I was part of it.*

"Now there's land in front of us," Clarice was saying.

He had been driving for two hours since lunch, making good time as before, except that there had been considerable cross-traffic to keep him alert—cars, campers, motorcycles, all moving madly east. He had kept the New England coast in sight most of the way—*the old coast.*

"Let's go ashore and see where we are," he said.

What he had in mind was to stretch his legs in some kind of normal place, to find restrooms and buy gas, to keep his ears open for any news sifted in from the larger world. The landfall turned out to be the Gloucester peninsula, and Stephen was able to drive up out of the ocean bottom across a pebbled beach not far from a paved highway. In the nearest town he pulled into a gas station. Reading a road map while a sullen young man filled his tank, Stephen concluded that the town was Rockport, and he tried to estimate—referring to a sun that was by now halfway down the sky—which direction to set out in to avoid driving into Cape Cod Bay.

In twenty minutes they were on their way southeast; the attendant had refused to honor his credit card—another driver at the station had complained loudly—and Stephen had paid what seemed an unusually high price for the gas. *Frightened,* Stephen decided; *taking the cash while he can.*

He drove casually and fast; he was getting used to this sort of travel, to the experience of other cars strewn as far as the eye could see in every direction.

"It's something like an old-fashioned land rush," he said to Clarice.

"I suppose," she said. "Did you hear any news at the gas station?"

"Rumors, is all."

"Well, like what?"

He pursed his lips. "Silly things. Some guy told me he'd heard most of Europe was under water."

"My God, Steve."

"Oh, come on, Clar. That's hardly likely, you know."

"I *don't* know." She slouched into the corner by the door. "The water must have gone somewhere."

"Believe anything you want. Maybe it's Judgment Day."

His wife kept quiet.

Of course it was possible—that wild story about Europe. It was strangely logical, Stephen admitted. Still, fantastic. How could you explain it? A shift in the magnetic poles, maybe. Or a meteor—something huge—hitting the earth with incredible force. But wouldn't there have been earthquakes? He mused, scarcely thinking about his driving—not needing to. There were no obstructions, nothing to slow down for.

"I can't say much for the scenery," he said.

"Daddy, my stomach hurts," Linda complained.

He glanced at his watch. It was after six o'clock, he was amazed to notice; he had lost track of time since leaving Rockport, and surely his daughter had a right to be hungry.

"Be patient, honey," Clarice said in a tone part soothing, part mocking. "Daddy will stop as soon as he finds a nice shady spot."

He smirked. "Now *that's* funny," he said, yet almost at once he was startled to see something black on the horizon. He pointed. "What do you suppose that is?"

"I don't know," Clarice said, "but let's stop there."

Closer, he identified the object.

"There's our first shipwreck," he said. It looked, as he drew toward it, to be a modern ship—metal hulled, at any rate—stern up as if it had dived sharply to the bottom. Second World War? Victim of a submarine? Its enormous square plates were deep red with rust, and its unexpected presence made the miles of sand around it all the more desolate. Circling to the ship's shady side, he saw that two other cars were already parked alongside it.

"Company," he said.

"That's good," Clarice decided. "You'll have somebody to talk to while I get supper."

Stephen parked and got out. People from one of the cars had spread a cloth under the lengthening shadow of the hulk. A man appeared on top of the wreck and peered down over the crusted railing, hanging on to keep his balance against the rake of the deck.

"Looking for the ocean?" he called down to Stephen. "It's all in here." He pointed toward the submerged bow. Leaving the women to fix the hamburgers, Stephen walked around the ship and made his way precariously up the steep deck. "I think it must have been a tanker," the man above him said.

"Torpedoed?"

"I expect so?" The man wore Bermudas and a Hawaiian shirt; he grinned at Stephen. "Makes you feel like Davy Jones, doesn't it? I looked into that hatch down there. Couldn't see anything, but I could hear water sloshing. Bet there's a lot of bones rolling around in there; poor bastards."

Stephen nodded. He didn't feel like talking, but stayed on the ship, bracing himself against a ventilator. To be above the ocean's floor was pleasant; the air was warm and windless; he even enjoyed the difficulty of keeping his balance, after hours of cramped driving.

Certainly this had been the most remarkable day of his life—of all their lives—and filled with small wonders. The lobsterman pulling his coaster wagon. The foolish couple from Iowa with their shovels and dreams of treasure. The boy and girl at the cliff, acting like honeymooners picking edelweiss in the Alps. And the ocean. The ocean he had grown used to in summer after summer of holidays in Maine— suddenly turned into a desert. Still—He felt a faint shiver of apprehension. If there was water in the hold of this broken tanker—

He edged his way to the open hatch, a gaping black hole in the rust and scale of the deck-plates, and tried to see inside. It smelled like ocean, he thought. He listened, and could hear the water. *Why should it be moving?* Stephen stepped off the hulk and looked around. Nothing—but was that fog, far off to the east?

Stephen called up to the man in Bermudas. "Do you hear anything?"

"No," the man said. Stephen noticed a car, about a mile away, headed west. "Wait a minute," the man said. "I do hear something."

It was the sound of the tide he had awakened to that morning—of the tide, far, far out.

"By George" the man said, "I think we've found her at last." He stumbled down from the deck. "We've caught up with her," he said, and went to tell his family.

Stephen walked back to the women.

"Not ready yet," Clarice said. "Why don't you open a can of beer?"

He took a deep breath. "Listen, I think we'd better start back. It's about a hundred-and-fifty miles to the Cape, but we ought to be able to get there just after dark."

Clarice tensed. "What is it?" she said.

"I just think we'd better go. It's been a long day."

His wife turned off the stove and dumped the meat onto the sand. "Linda, get in the car."

"Don't we get to eat anything?"

"Linda, honey, don't quibble with me." She glanced around. The two neighboring cars were gone. Other cars appeared from the east and sped past.

"I'm going to put that spare gasoline in the tank," Stephen said, "just so we won't have to stop."

As he worked, he could hear the soft, incessant whisper of waves at his back. He made a botch of pouring the gas. *Steady,* he told himself. *It's your own damned fault.*

When he finished, the women were inside, waiting. He tossed the gasoline can away in a high, tumbling arc, and hurried to get into the car. The sea noise behind them was by now so loud that he could hear it even above the engine as it burst into life. He shifted into first gear and skidded forward.

"Tides come in gradually, don't they?" Clarice said in a tight voice.

"Usually," Stephen said. He threw the shift lever into second; again the rear wheels of the station wagon spun, as if the sand under them were getting wetter.

"I just can't believe any of this," his wife said. She leaned her head against the back of the seat and closed her eyes.

Now he was in high gear. The engine was turning over smoothly and the speedometer needle stood unwaveringly at seventy miles an hour. Ahead of him the evening sun was sliding down to the horizon; he kept the car headed toward it, squinting across the enormous reach of gray sand. *What a queer thing,* he thought. *What a devil of a way to finish a vacation.* He was aware all around him of other cars, other drivers, all racing west on this incredible aimless track. One car passed him, then another, and he pushed the accelerator down. He overtook a white camper and swerved around it; the station wagon fishtailed slightly.

"What's the matter?" His wife opened her eyes.

"Nothing's the matter."

"We won't run out of gas now, will we?"

"Not a chance." He watched the needle slide past eighty. The sand was glistening ahead of him, water seeping to the surface. The tide must be racing in behind them. Could they swim free? Where would they swim to?

"Daddy!" The scream startled him. "Daddy, I can see it! I can see it coming after us!" Linda wasn't crying. In the rearview mirror he could see her face, half-turned in his direction, her eyes vivid, her mouth working desperately to make more words. Out the back window he could make out a low gray wall that seemed to be gaining on him. Under his wheels he could hear water splashing, see spray flying. He switched on the wipers.

He reached over and squeezed his wife's hand. *At least we're all together,* he thought. Off to the right he saw an overturned car, two men and a woman out trying to turn it upright. The sun was almost at the horizon and its light cast back a hundred rainbows through the wakes of a hundred cars. A pale, pebbly mist began forming on surfaces inside the car. The roar of the impossible tide was deafening; it seemed now to be all around him, and the deepening water drummed like hammers against the metal under the car. He was thinking irrelevantly of how quickly the salt sea would rust out the fenders and rocker panels when he heard Clarice for the last time, shrieking:

"Drive, Steve, drive. For pity's sake, drive, drive, *drive!*"

The Day The Tide

PHILIP BOOTH

The day the tide went out,
and stayed, not just at Mean
Low Water or Spring Ebb,
but out, out all the way
perhaps as far as Spain,
until the bay was empty,

it left us looking down
at what the sea, and our
reflections on it, had
(for generations of
good fish, and wives fair
as vessels) saved us from.

We watched our fishboats ground
themselves, limp-chained in mud;
careened, as we still are
(though they lie far below us)
against this sudden slope
that once looked like a harbor.

We're level, still, with islands,
or what's still left of them
now that treelines invert:
the basin foothills rock
into view like defeated castles,
with green and a flagpole on top.

Awkward as faith itself,
heron still stand on one leg
in trenches the old tide cut;
maybe they know what the moon's

about, working its gravity
off the Atlantic shelf.

Blind as starfish, we
look into our dried reservoir
of disaster: fouled trawls, old
ships hung up on their mon-
ument ribs; the skeletons
of which our fathers were master.

We salt such bones down with self-
consolation, left to survive,
if we will, on this emptied slope.
Réunion Radio keeps reporting
how our ebb finally flooded
the terrible Cape of Good Hope.

Lakes and Ponds: Some Blue Spots on the Maine Highway Map

KATE BARNES

There's Blunder Pond and Bluffer Pond, Molasses Pond and Bean;
There's Scraggly Lake and Ragged Lake; there's Silver, Clear, and
    Green;
Bear Pond, Caribou, Beaver, Mink; Moose Pond and Eagle Lake.
White Horse Lake and Spider Lake; Panther Pond and Snake;
Hound and Otter, Togue and Salmon; Loon, and Swan, and Duck.
There's Hot Brook Lake and Cold Stream Pond; there's White Pond
    and there's Black;
Lobster Lake and Bean Pot Lake; Shin Pond for a stew;
(Toddy Pond will make you cheerful, Brandy Pond will too,)
Hay Lake, Harrow Lake, Chain of Ponds; Buttermilk and Mud;
White Oak, Cedar, Seven Tree, Elm; Mill Pond, Meadow, Flood;
Meddybemps and Pocomoonshine; Simsquish, Skitacook,
Syslodobsis, Nahinakanta; Ugh Lake and Ticook;
Indian Pond and Soldier Pond; Polly Pond and Jim:
Round Pond, Square Lake, Corner Pond; Cut Lake and Old Stream;
Endless Lake and Desolation; St. Froid in the snow;
Flying pond and The Enchanted, its haunted stream below;—
Blue spots on the road map with their blue names printed by,
Many words for "water," many eyes that see the sky.

The Passing of the Hay-Barn

ABBIE HUSTON EVANS

When we reached the bend of the road and came on the roar
And the small crackle under, we stopped short in our tracks.
The roof had fallen in; the frame stood up
A blazing crate of timbers still untilted,
Flagged all along with tatters of flame blown sideways.

The old white-chimneyed house under the elms
Stood in the glare unharmed. The morning-star
Was fabulous. Out of the darkened west,
Low, reddened to its setting, the full moon
Looked in like a great melancholy eye.
The dead of night was round; meadows below
Gave up their chill; dew wetted down the stubble.
No breath of wind was stirring, no sound but the fire's.

The little crowd of neighbors stood round watching
The bright malignant thing that reared its head
Thus without warning in their silent fields.
That brash display and flicker of fangs the land
Repudiated; turned its back; and slept.
The fields had other business at that hour
Of night; relinquished small concerns to men ...
There was nothing to do but let it burn out.

That night I hardly slept for having caught
A glimpse of the universe under a north light.
Hay-barn or planet—does it signify?
An ancient inmost frame gone down the wind,
Become a puff of smoke; given back; at one ...
Seeing the frame of anything consumed
Is solemn business when you come full on it:
Annihilation getting in its work

At top-speed, unmasked, is no sight for children.

All night under sleep I bore the brand of a grid-shape
Far-gone. Saw girders consuming. Not of a barn.

Fire

WILLIAM CARPENTER

This morning, on the opposite shore of the river,
I watch a man burning his own house.
It is a cold day, and the man wears thick gloves
and a fur hat that gives him a Russian look.
I envy his energy, since I'm still on the sunporch
in my robe, with morning coffee, my day not
even begun, while my neighbor has already piled
spruce boughs against his house and poured
flammable liquids over them to send a ribbon
of black smoke into the air, a column surrounded
by herring gulls, who think he's having a barbecue
or has founded a new dump. I hadn't known what labor
it took to burn something. Now the man's working
at such speed, he's like the criminal in a silent
movie, as if he had a deadline, as if he had
to get his house burned by a certain time, or it
would be all over. I see his kids helping, bringing
him matches and kindling, and I'd like to help out
myself, I'd like to bring him coffee and a bagel,
but the Penobscot River separates us, icebergs
the size of small ships drifting down the tide.
Moreover, why should I help him when I have a house
myself, which needs burning as much as anyone's?
It has begun to leak. I think it has carpenter ants.
I hear them making sounds at night like writing, only
they aren't writing, they are building small tubular
cities inside the walls. I start burning in the study,
working from within so it will go faster, so I can
catch up, and soon there's a smoke column on either
side, like a couple of Algonquins having a dialogue
on how much harder it is to destroy than to create.
I shovel books and poems into the growing fire. If

I burn everything, I can start over, with a future
like a white rectangle of paper. Then I notice
my neighbor has a hose, that he's spraying his house
with water, the coward, he has bailed out, but I
keep throwing things into the fire: my stamps,
my Berlioz collection, my photos of nude people,
my correspondence dating back to grade school.
Over there, the fire engines are reaching his home.
His wife is crying with relief, his fire's extinguished.
He has walked down to the shore to see the ruins
of the house across the river, the open cellar,
the charred timbers, the man laughing and singing
in the snow, who has been finally freed from his
possessions, who has no clothes, no library, who has
gone back to the beginning, when we lived in nature:
no refuge from the elements, no fixed address.

New England

CONSTANCE HUNTING

Stones
are the sheep of these
hillsides
and fog
is the wool of these
stones

Dry Summer

MAY SARTON

1

That summer
We learned about water—
The long suspense,
Dry winds, and empty sky.
The village parched
Slowly,
Till leaves began to shrivel
On the tallest trees.

The Indians would dance.
We had no rite. No refuge.
To wait, endure, listen
To the weathervane creak
Through the tense, hot night,
And, waking to a new sickness,
Turn the word "rain"
In our mouths
Like a cool pebble,
As one well after another
Went dry.

2

The time came for me.
My rich well,
Fed by three springs
Of clear cool water,
Deeper than I could touch
The bottom of
With a long pole—
The never-failing well
Was milked out.

The pump rattled on
Like a broken record
Repeating one word,
Water,
Water.
But when I shut it off
I heard the silence,
The dry silence of
No water,
No water,
No water.

3

One morning
The great leaves of the squash
Had fallen, wrinkled,
Round the raw brown stems.
I hid from the curse
Like a goddess
Who has lost her power
To keep life alive.
"This," said the Egyptians
In the time of drought,
"Is the taste of death."

Weather Prophet

EDMUND WARE SMITH

Once I came up in February because I had to see how the lake country looked under snow. Steve Ireland met me at Mopang, and we started for Privilege in the pung, with a northeaster building steadily behind us. Steve yelled into his turned-up collar: "Travel eight hundred miles to spend one day in a blizzard. Jesus!"

"Maybe it'll clear."

"Doc Musgrave says it'll hold northeast for two days. He don't often miss."

Whenever Steve mentioned Dr. Delirious Musgrave, there was a note in his voice of troubled fascination. I had always wanted to meet the doctor. His personality seemed to weigh on Steve's mind. I wanted to hear Steve talk about him now, but a quickened bitterness of the storm made talk an effort.

We were crossing the wake of an old burn where the blown snow towered around us, and the wind struck sharp. When at length we came into the shelter of the spruces, the wind seemed far away. You could hear it roaring in the branches, and the snow swept down like spilled veils, but the storm was at arm's length, momentarily.

Steve lifted his chin above his collar, and said:

"He claims the day he does he'll die."

"Does what?" I asked, my wits half numbed.

"Figures wrong on the weather."

"Oh, Doc Musgrave?"

"Yuh," said Steve, resettling his chin.

We put a blanket on old Chub in the Privilege stable, fed him his oats, and floundered up the hill above the lake to Steve's cabin. It was nice inside. You could smell peeled spruce, oakum chinking and wood smoke. The wind sent the fine snow hissing against the windows, reminding us of our comfort within.

"This time of year," Steve said, as he primed the pump, "there ain't much doin', only ice fishin'."

"I don't mind. I got to dreaming about winter on the lake, and had to come and see."

"You're seein' it, all right. You better stay over a few days."

"I can't do it. I'll have to go in the morning."

I opened the bottom draft of the stove, and the fire woke up and made the chimney roar. "Maybe if the storm holds, I'll be snowbound."

"He claimed it would," Steve said. A gust rattled the stovepipe in its guy wires, and Steve added: "Listen to that."

We ate fried salt pork, pickerel and tea. Steve inquired for all my friends he had guided. I asked about Uncle Jeff Coongate, Neilly Winslow, the Iron Duke and Jim Scantling. Steve said they were all smart, and let it go at that, but when I mentioned Peter Deadwater, the Indian, he perked up.

"Say! Peter's wife's goin' to have a kid."

"Honest?"

"Fact, so help me. Talk about a happy Injun."

"I thought Peter and Sadie couldn't have any kids."

"Well," Steve said, "they thought there wa'nt no hope, an' so'd everyone. They been wantin' one twelve years."

"When's the baby due?"

"Peter figures apple-blossom time. He's been poundin' ash, an' got a cradle built, an' a basket, an' a doe-skin suit with pants to it, soft as silk. It's a caution, the way that Injun works. Changed his whole character. He ain't touched a drop of lemon extrac' nor essence of pep'mint, not for five-six months. Just works, an' tends Sadie, an' lays plans for that kid."

"That's wonderful, Steve."

"It's the Lord's mercy. Let's wash the dishes."

We cleaned up, and got out the ice-fishing equipment. We were ready to start for the lake, when Steve spotted a gap in the chinking. A fine spray of snow had blasted through, building a hard white mound on the floor. Steve got a mallet and caulking iron and closed the gap with a twist of oakum. "Some storm, to find a hole that small," he said.

"Steve, didn't you say you drove Doc Musgrave's buggy for him, when you were little?"

"Yuh. We was good friends in them days."

"Aren't you now?"

"It's mighty queer, but he don't care for me now, me nor anyone at all."

A moment later we were out in the blizzard, toting our fishing gear down to the lake. I was more than ever determined to meet the doctor some day; but now his prophecy of weather was of direct concern. We chiseled our holes in the lee of Genius Island, but shelter was scant. The snow gave visible shape to the turbulence in the sky, and my forehead ached with cold.

The tip-ups were active, but we couldn't hook a trout. "They're slapping it with their tails," Steve said. "You can watch 'em do it, if you lay still over a hole."

I tried it, shading my eyes with my hands. Down there in the deep clear water, you could see the togue swimming along slowly in single file. They would bump the bait with their noses, and, as they swam by, bat it with their tails.

"Can you see 'em?" Steve asked.

He was kneeling on the opposite side of the hole, facing me. I glanced toward him, but my answer froze. Just behind Steve, and to one side of him, stood Peter Deadwater, the Indian. He was wearing snowshoes—the long, narrow Cree model for open travel. Suspended from a thong in his left hand were two lake trout of about six pounds. Steve saw my astonished expression, and turned.

"You ghost," he said to the Indian.

"No." Peter made an up-and-down motion with his free hand.

"Heard us chiseling," Steve explained to me; and the Indian grunted.

I stood up and brushed off the snow. "Hear good news, Peter," I said. "Congratulations."

Peter grunted again.

"How things with Sadie?" Steve asked.

Peter shrugged. While we took up our sets, he stood perfectly still in the exact spot where we had first seen him. Steve kept glancing at him curiously, and, when we were ready to go, said:

"Peter. You come my cabin. Get warm. Tea. Pickerel chowder."

Peter declined with a headshake and held out one of the lake trout, saying: "Namaycush."

"Come help eat," Steve said, taking the trout.

"I go home. Sadie hot. Crazy talk."

Steve looked quickly at me. "He means Sadie's sick." Then he turned to Peter. "How long Sadie hot? How long talk crazy?"

"Morning."

"This morning?"

Peter Deadwater nodded, his eyes vacant.

"She got pain some place?"

Peter touched his forehead, then put his hand down over his stomach, groaned, and stared at Steve.

"You go home. Take trout to Sadie. I get doctor. See?"

Peter moved away a few steps, turned on his long webs, and came back. "Doctor cross lake to Injun Village in storm?"

"Yes."

"Tell him open water Leadmine Point. Spring-hole. Tell him very danger spring-hole."

"I know," Steve said. "I tell him."

Peter started off, the snow blowing shoulder high around him. Ten steps and he had vanished. It was six miles, due southwest across the lake to the Indian Village. In the falling dark, even with the northeast gale full on his back, it would be a bitter journey.

Steve and I hid our tackle on Genius Island and went straight in to Privilege. I had to stop behind a shed at the public landing to get out of the wind for a minute. I thought my forehead was frozen, but it wasn't. Steve drew off a mitten and blew on his knuckles. "You're goin' to get a hell of a start," he said. "Doc Musgrave talks like he wasn't there at all."

"What? How do you mean?"

The shed trembled in a gust. In the dark you could still see the snow-shapes racing. Steve said: "Well, he don't say 'I done this,' nor 'I done that.' You'll think he's talkin' about someone else that ain't anywheres around. Once, when I was a kid, he told me why. Thought I'd forget, p'raps, but I didn't. He told me it was his other self he is talkin' about—the man he might of been, he said. But all the time it's really him, because he ain't no one else. But you got to talk to him like he was."

"Are you going to drive him across the lake tonight?"

Steve put on his mitten. "You can't work a horse on the lake. Four bad reefs in the ice between Genius Island and Caribou Rock. He'll go on snowshoes."

In the back room of Sam Lurch's barbershop in Privilege, we found Dr. Musgrave. He was a man in his early fifties. He sat on the wood box, a bottle between his knees, apparently entranced by the gleaming nickel stove-rail. The air in the room was hot and foul, but Musgrave wore a heavy sheepskin coat. The lamplight showed the birthmark which spread from his right temple over his entire right cheek to his jaw. His upward glance was too swift for me to see his eyes. With no sign of recognition for Steve, whom he had known since boyhood, he resumed his staring at the nickel rail. Steve had told me what to expect, but no warning could have prepared me for talking face to face with a man who not only dreamed he wasn't there, but demanded that others honor his unreality.

"Well," Steve said to him, "he said it would hold northeast for two days."

"Yes," said Musgrave. "He is an authority on the weather, as well as on rum, axe wounds and obstetrics."

Outside, the wind rose shrieking. You could hear the hard snow batter the walls like shot. As if at this corroboration of his prophecy, Musgrave grinned and leaned closer to the stove.

When the gust had spent itself, Steve said: "Would he cross the lake tonight to tend a sick woman in the Injun Village?"

After a long silence, Musgrave said: "He would think hard during such a trip—think himself into a stupor."

To see the man actually sitting there, yet talking of himself as if he were absent, gave me the shivers.

"He would have his coat collar up," he went on, "and his face wrapped to the eyes. He would keep the wind dead fair on his back, and—"

Steve moved toward the doctor nervously. "He would want to keep the wind heavy on his right shoulder. That would bear him inside of the open spring-hole off Leadmine Point."

Dr. Musgrave took a small drink from the bottle, replaced it between his knees, and, as if Steve had not spoken, resumed:

"—his thoughts would keep him company, and he would hum. His humming, and the cadence of his steps, would make him forget the night."

"But," said Steve, his voice rising, "he would want to keep his mind on that spring-hole. If the wind backs into the north, it would veer the doctor off course. He would walk right into *open water* in the dark."

"He stated that the wind would hold northeast," said Musgrave, complacently. "And it will."

"Even so, he'll pass within two hundred yards of the spring-hole!" Steve took a radium-dialed compass from his pocket and held it out to Musgrave in his open palm. "The snow is blowing so he won't even see his feet," he went on, his voice growing unsteady. "Wouldn't he take this?"

"Does a prophet need a compass?"

The man on the wood box seemed to ignore our presence as well as his own, and, while we humored his strange conceit, the purpose of our visit had been obscured. When I could bear the suspense no longer, I began speaking to him, unnaturally, in the third person:

"Is he equipped to take a six-months baby from the wife of Peter Deadwater? While the men discuss the weather, the Indian's woman lies out of her head with fever."

"He has performed Caesareans in this country under strange conditions," Musgrave answered, "and with strange instruments. Once he cauterized an amputation with a heated abutment spike. And he did a transfusion with the quill of a goose."

"But the Indian woman has been delirious since morning," I said. "The man with Steve Ireland thinks it may be emergency."

"Ah, yes, no doubt," replied Musgrave, blandly, "but the doctor hates cold—cold and terror, they are the same." He picked up the rum bottle and held it to the light. As near as I could judge, he had drunk half the contents. He removed the cork, took another swallow, and said: "Northeast for two days."

"Maybe the Indian's woman will die," I said, "and they are all here, talking."

"Maybe," said Musgrave, rising.

In the act of buttoning his coat collar to the throat, he turned toward us, and I saw him full face in the light. I knew why Steve Ireland both feared and pitied him. Above the doctor's straight, merciless mouth, were the eyes of a child; and I saw in these features the evidence of a man divided. You looked into his wide child's eyes, and pitied. You remembered his mouth, and shrank from him.

Steve went to him, begging: "Would the doctor please take a friend for company tonight? The friend that used to drive the buggy for him?"

"No."

Musgrave jerked his snowshoes from a peg, and kneeled to tie their lampwick lashings. Whether Steve was driven by a superstition about putting on snowshoes indoors, or by his dread that the wind would shift, I do not know. But when Musgrave stood up, Steve clutched him by the shoulders, and shook him, saying:

"If he walks into that spring-hole, *both* of him will go under the ice together—the one he is, and that other one, too!"

For an instant, as Steve backed away, the child part dominated Musgrave's face. He seemed touched that anyone should go to such lengths to warn him away from danger; and, in the only natural sentence I heard him speak, he said: "That's all right, Stevie—I'll be there in two hours."

He put on the pack which I assumed contained his instrument bag, and we followed him out into the blizzard. At the lake shore, he said: "He will go on from here alone." He hesitated for just a moment, then turned away, and walked off in the dark.

For two or three minutes after he had vanished, we stood looking out over the howling blackness of the lake. Then we turned wearily up the hill to Steve's cabin.

The warmth, the smell of broiling trout, and the leaky kettle's hiss could not remove the spell of Dr. Musgrave. Steve kept glancing at the black windows. It was as if he thought he might actually see the wind's direction.

"Steve," I said, "how wide is that spring-hole?"

"Better than a quarter-mile, when I last saw it."

After we had eaten, I lay in my bunk; but, despite my snow-burned face and eyes, there was no drowsiness. And there was none for Steve. He looked at his watch, and said: "It's thirty-eight minutes, now."

"Where would he be, about?"

"Mouth of Hardwood Cove."

Presently, as if Musgrave were with us in the cabin, we began to talk his way. To Steve Ireland, whom I had known fourteen years, I said: "The men lay in comfort wondering if the wind would change."

Steve got up, opened the door, and looked out into the whirlpools of the sky. He had to use his strength to close it, and the cold wind drove in a spray of snow and tore the ammunition-company calendar from its hook. "One of the men knows the wind is changing," he said.

"Where would he be now?"

Steve answered so quickly that I knew he was with Musgrave almost step for step: "Forty-three minutes—off Bear Trap Landing."

"They thought of how, in summer, they had paddled often across the six miles to Peter Deadwater's shack."

Steve got out his compass and set it on the table. He looked again at his watch. "The men couldn't rest good."

"No," I said. "They were thinking of the other man, counting on the wind to hold him on course, and the wind veering him toward the open water, and the Indian waiting, and his wife hot and crazy talking."

"For Chris' sake!" Steve cried. "I'm goin' outside and see for certain."

When Steve came in again, his face looked numb. His hair, powdered white with snow, made him seem prematurely old. He went to the stove and sat on the deacon seat, his back to the warmth. He kept looking at his watch, while the snow melted, glistening in his hair.

"Well?" I asked.

"The wind's due north—changed, with never a lull to warn him."

Steve got a lumberman's blueprint map of the lake, and spread it on the bench beside him. With a pencil he drew a straight line due southwest from Privilege six miles to the Indian Village on the far shore. Along that line he marked various points, and the times he estimated it would take Musgrave to pass them, at a speed of three miles per hour. Hardwood Cove, 38 mins. Bear Trap Landing, 43 mins.

At Caribou Rock, an hour and five mins., Steve drew a gradual curve on the map. The curve bore left—southward, as the wind veered into the north. A mile south of Caribou Rock, he drew in the spring-hole off Leadmine Point. Then he looked at his watch again, and said: "Munson Reef—an hour and twelve minutes."

"My God, Steve! How many, many times we fished that spring-hole in hot weather when the trout were deep."

Steve made a dot on the penciled line which curved and then straightened toward the open water. He sat tense, his watch under his eyes, his pencil poised.

"Sometimes," Steve said, "when we was makin' calls away out somewheres away from the villages, he was mighty nice. He was kind. He would tell me to stop the buggy by a field of daisies, or hockweed. Them things made him happy. If he saw a doe deer on the lake shore, that would make him happy, too, or a loon callin'. It was the same with insects, any livin' thing, or anything that was pretty to look at. He could explain them things. I thought the world was flat, till he told me why it ain't. He said I was the only one he could talk to, or that could talk to him. I was eleven years old, then...." Steve's pencil point touched the map, as he checked the time. "Little Mopang Bar—hour an' eighteen minutes."

"Steve! How close is he to it—now?"

"Seven minutes."

Steve brushed his hand over his damp hair, and wiped the wet palm on his thigh. "It was when I got older that he changed toward me. But I guess he thought 'twas me that changed. He wouldn't talk to me no more, nor he didn't want me 'round. He said people was not good after they stopped bein' children. But *he* was good, them times with me, when I was a boy. There wa'nt a thing he wouldn't do for people that was ailin'. But outside of for that, he wouldn't go near no one."

Steve got up from the bench, took off a stove lid and stirred the fire. A furious wind-blast drew back down the stovepipe, and the fine ash rose in the room.

"Big Mopang Bar," Steve said, "hour an' twenty-three minutes."

"That leaves him three minutes!"

"Two … I wonder how Peter's woman's makin' out?"

"But he knows the lake, Steve. Maybe, when he got out there alone, with the storm, and the darkness—maybe he remembered what you said, and kept the wind heavy on his right shoulder. That would save him. He would pass Leadmine Point inside the spring-hole."

Steve looked intently at his watch. I saw his lips move, as he checked over the last minutes. Then he stopped counting. He was so quiet it was as if he had stopped breathing. After a long time he folded the map, put the watch back in his pocket, and stood up.

"Well," he said, "I liked him, just the same. It's like I'm with him out there tonight, right beside him the whole way, till he drowned. Only nothin' I could do to help him, like watchin' a blind man walk off a cliff, an' your voice gone."

"Steve, I can't believe it!"

"That's 'cause you don't want to, an' I don't, neither."

Steve crossed to the table and turned down the lamp. He stood there with the dim light on his face, until I had stretched out under my blankets. "All set?" he said.

"Sure—maybe he made it all right."

"Maybe." Steve blew out the lamp and we lay in the dark, listening to the long-drawn fury of the storm.

Morning broke clear with a light north wind. Steve had the bacon frying. The cabin was warm, and bright sunlight streamed through the windows. I looked out, and saw the lake stretching white and lovely below us. That view, so peaceful now, so immaculate, made the night seem unreal.

"Steve, how do you feel this morning?"

"Frisky," he said. "That was bad last night."

Yet in Steve's voice there was uncertainty. I felt it, perhaps in his very cheerfulness. When we had eaten, and were on our way down to the stable, Steve said: "Would it trouble you if I got Jim Scantling to drive you to Mopang this mornin'? I want to cross the lake."

"No, Steve, of course not. I'd stay and go with you, if I could."

"Well, I just got an awful hankerin' to make it across," Steve explained.

Jim and Steve hooked up, and old Chub's breath blew white in the cold. We climbed to the seat, and I reached down to shake hands with Steve. "Let me know about things, will you?" I asked.

"Sure. I'll write you a letter. So-long."

I looked around once to see Steve striking off across the white-glaring lake toward the Indian Village.

Dere frend,

I seen from his drifted tracks right where it begun to change on him near Caribou Rock. I followed the curve of them until I dassent go no closer the open water, where his tracks run off I seen one of his mittens layin on the ice where he tried to claw back on but that is all so I swung back and went to the Peter Deadwater shack and the priest was there. Peter's woman was dead and the baby was dead.

Well my good frend I must close now as there is a diver comin from Eastport to dive for him and I am to lay a boom on the ice for him to work off of, but they will never find him as the currents will draw him under, as ever your frend Steve Ireland.

P.S. I told Peter how we tried to get the doctor to him and he said all right.

This Is a Night

ELIZABETH COATSWORTH

This is a night on which to pity cats
hunting through dripping hedgerows,
making wet way
through grasses heavy with rain,
their delicate stepping
tense with distaste,
their soft and supple coats
sodden, for all their care.
This is a night
to pity cats which have no house to go to,
no stove, no saucer of milk, no lowered hand
sleeking a head, no voice to say, "Poor kitty."
This is a night
on which to weep for outcasts, for all those
who know the rain but do not know the shelter.

Winter Splendor

ELIZABETH COATSWORTH

This is a day to be compared with lions
if one considers the yellow-maned, round-faced sun,
or with an eagle for its icy glare;
or with a stag for something tense and proud
(and perhaps the antlered thickets enter in).
If men were chosen, I'd choose Charlemagne
for what was Northern in him, haughty, clear;
horns would find here their cold and proper echoes;
"magnificent" is perhaps not quite the word
but I can come no nearer. Such a day
towers above its fellows, passing by
with chargers, ermines, pennons, and with spears.

Poem for St. Francis

SYLVESTER POLLET

At 10 below
thinking to help the birds survive
we increase the dole of seeds—
look out to see a fat jay
pinned by a hawk.

In this cold even death moves slowly
there is time for much crying
and flapping of wings
but the hawk holds
and things calm down again.

The woods are silent:
two movements only—
the hawk's beak to the jay's breast,
and the bits of fluff
blown over snow crust.

We have helped a hawk survive.

Great Horned Owl

SUSAN HAND SHETTERLY

As steady as a metronome, the roof leak kept its time, even though the rain had stopped. Outside, the wind gusted in the branches of the red maples. We opened a window, and a breath of cold air entered the room, buffeting the flame in the kerosene lamp on the kitchen table. The sky had cleared and a gibbous moon glinted through the trees. On spring nights such as these, our house was a frail refuge, besieged by weather and dark miles of trees.

"Listen," I said to my husband, "there's a mourning dove cooing outside." Moaning rose from somewhere beyond the maples and the ring of spruces beside the field.

"The pitch is too low," Rob said after a pause. "Anyhow, doves don't coo in the dark."

"It's a dog," I decided. We opened the kitchen door to a deep howl. I pictured the animal, its neck outstretched, its mouth, as it cried, forming the letter "O." It sounded far away ... chained, perhaps, and longing to be free at thaw-time.

It was, in fact, a great horned owl. Another bird soon hooted from the woods. And the first, from the neighboring field, returned the sonorous call.

We took down our volume of Edward Howe Forbush's *The Birds of Massachusetts*. "The great horned owl," we read by lantern light, "is the most morose, savage and saturnine of all New England birds. We can hardly wonder that certain Indian tribes regarded this fowl as the very personification of the Evil One. If he ever be moved to affection for any living creature, except, perhaps, for his mate, with whom he is accustomed to pair for life, the existence of such emotion is certainly not betrayed by any outward sign."

We read on, the dry pages of the book rustling like mice over fallen leaves. Outlaws were stalking the darkness beyond with a skill and cunning we did not possess.

"A farmer brought me a great horned owl one winter day that had killed his pet tom cat.... The cat was out walking in the moonlight ... when the farmer heard a wail of mortal agony, and opening the door saw Mr. Cat in the grasp of the owl. Before he could get his gun and shoot the bird the cat was no more. Its vitals had been torn out."

"Our cats!" I whispered.

I plunged down the path to the garden, calling, the flashlight making a thin stab at the night. If it crossed my mind that my pets were predators like the owls, I wasn't inclined to dwell on it. I had become—provoked by the voice of a bird—one of those Americans who like their wilderness, but like it tame.

Working on my hands and knees along a row of cabbages one day that summer, I turned to see a great horned owl perched in a tree at my back. As I leapt up, it rose—wraithlike—and with one flap of its wings, disappeared. Sometimes at night when I walked through the high, wet grass to the garden, my cats would appear suddenly, their hair pearled with a dew like a spider's orbed web at dawn. I would pick them up and carry them inside because I was afraid of the owls. But more often, the cats ignored my calls at night. I would find them when mist hung above the garden in the first light and the summer driveway was dry, trotting leisurely up to the house, satisfied with their time in the dark, it seemed, sure of themselves and their place here and their place out there.

There was an ice storm the following January. Alone in the house, Rob tended the fire in the cookstove and read by the lamp. The cats lay curled in their favorite chairs. At midnight, Rob rose to check the build-up of ice on the deck. He leaned out the door. Something yelped, brushed against his face, and beat away from the doghouse roof. He fell back as if punched. One of the owls had been waiting in the sleet and the wind, driven from the safety of the conifers by the prospect of cat.

Great horned owls claim territory and, unless driven from it by hunger, live all year within it, extending or reducing the boundaries depending on the abundance of prey. In February, the least likely month to start anything new in Maine, these owls begin their courtship, filling the night with whoops and hollers. The male, the smaller of the two, shuffles after the female. Alighting on a branch close to her, he clicks his beak and bobs his round, wide-eyed face, pressing it close to hers. Then, stepping back and forth along the branch and fanning out his tail, he performs a choreography as stiff and mechanical as a break-dancer's. She does what so many female birds do: she ignores him. But this lack of enthusiasm only spurs his passion. He hurries off to return with a tidbit—a mouse perhaps, or a small bird. Daintily, she accepts the morsel from him and swallows it in one large gulp. She draws her eyelids down and raises them dreamily. Like an aphrodisiac, the food takes effect. She bobs and weaves along the branch as avidly as he, and they mate.

Great horned owls are not nestbuilders. They will settle into the ragged stub of a tall, dead tree or help themselves to squirrels' nests—

and to the squirrels. They may usurp an old nest of the red-tailed hawk, the red-shouldered hawk, or the crow, and have even been known to preempt the rampart of the bald eagle. Since they breed early, before almost all other birds, they can take their pick.

On February, after a storm, I found a nest in a lightning-injured pine. The setting owl wore a cape of snow on its shoulders and head; snow wreathed the nest. Biologists believe that early nesting is necessary because incubating the eggs and raising the owlets takes so long. Not until October do the young wander from their parents' territory to begin independent lives. Also, winter affords the parent owls a choice of nests and a clean panorama—no deciduous trees or bushes curtain the activities of hares, squirrels, or wandering skunks.

The female great horned owl lays two or more eggs and begins brooding immediately after laying the first. Her nestlings are born consecutively.

If food is scarce, the youngest and weakest perish. Usually only one fledgling survives into the second spring.

The down of a newly hatched owlet is fluffy and white like cotton plucked from a cotton boll. In three weeks the eyes lose their milky blue and begin to show that bold, yellow cat color. At this time, the first real feathers appear. But unlike fledgling hawks, which exercise their wings at the nest's edge and then launch themselves into short, ungainly flight, young owls have not practiced when they tumble from the nest at about six weeks of age. Though they look lost, they aren't; the adults continue to feed their owlets, calling to them, coaxing them up onto logs and into the safety of bushes. It is here— on the ground— that the young learn to overcome the fear of other creatures. They rehearse catching insects and holding food in their talons and ripping off pieces with their beaks. They jump and coast short distances, and eventually, they fly.

Owls, like most birds of prey, regurgitate compact, cylindrical pellets of indigestible fur and bones called castings. Those of the great horned owl are two or three inches in length. A close examination of the bones and beaks packed within the castings reveals what prey is most abundant in their territory at that time of year.

Great horned owls are opportunistic feeders. Almost any animal is fair game. Weighing between two and a half and three pounds, great horned owls have been known to attack seven-pound Canada geese. Though rodents and hares are the staple fare, weasels and skunks are common prey, as are hawks and other species of owl.

The owl's strength is in its short, feathered legs and its oversized feet. From the four toes of each foot curl sharp, tapered talons just under two inches long. When an owl hits its prey, the legs buckle, the tendons tighten, and the feet close like fists. Double ice tongs, the feet cinch around the prey. The only way to loosen a great horned owl's grip when it is determined to hang on is to forcibly straighten its legs. I have held a recuperating great horned owl on my arm and felt the talons lock as the bird settled onto the glove—a grasp one does not quickly forget.

Once I cared for a great horned owl that had attempted to kill a porcupine. I am quite sure it never ate its victim, for there were quills in its feet and chest; its face sprouted quills. Even its tongue was peppered with black quill stubs. The veterinarian who anesthetized the bird and removed the quills stopped counting after eighty.

Most people who have worked with great horned owls describe them as sullen and ugly-tempered. This one only snapped and hissed half-heartedly when I lifted it into a cage. How long it had lived like a pincushion, unable to eat, able to stand only after breaking off the points of the quills that stuck out of its feet, too weak to hunt, and, at last, too weak to fly, I have no idea.

I bent my head close to the owl's and made what I hoped were friendly sounds. I reached my fingers through the feathers of its head, between the feather tufts we call "ears," and massaged the loose, papery skin. The owl's eyes closed. Then, leaving it three defrosted mice with antibiotics down their throats, I latched the cage.

It feasted on mice, it preened, it healed. In a week, I moved the owl to a large cage where it could stretch its wings. I had no flight cage for it, and for reasons I can no longer remember, I was uneasy about flying it on a tether—jessing it. Its strength increased. Clearly an aggressive bird, it spoiled for a fight. It hissed long, sibilant expletives that reeked of damp mouse fur. Old Mouse Breath, we called it.

On a glimmering late winter day, I hauled it back to the woods where it had been found. Holding its legs in my glove, I let the owl look around, let it flap. It seemed strong.

I released it. The bird took to the air, beautifully plumaged, the colors of tree bark, of sunlight against the bark, and of shadows thrown by a spray of twigs. But it slid downward, landing on a fallen tree. It raced and stumbled over the snow crust and bounced up on a stump, then puffed out its feathers and snapped. The owl was only fifteen feet from me but I could get no closer.

The muscles of its wings must have weakened from its time in the cage. It wouldn't fly. If I chased it, it would thrash over the maze of downed trees just fast enough to keep ahead of me.

I sat in the melting snow under its gaze. Outraged, bellicose, it clung to the stump anticipating my attack as if I could lunge at it across two piles of brush. I unwrapped the last wet package of mice and laid them in the snow in a semicircle before the bird as if to appease an irritable god. I wanted the bird to live.

A moth flew between us. The wrong time of year for a moth, and the sun going down. A thread of light caught on one of its wings, which the owl and I noticed, before the moth flew off and the sun did go down.

In the dusk I heard the owl hop from the stump and move along the underbrush. But those sounds mixed with the wind in the trees and soon I could not tell where the owl was anymore. It seemed as if the woods were all owl or all the bare, snapping branches of the trees.

An Unseen Deer

JOHN TAGLIABUE

An unseen deer through seen shadows leaps through my
    heart
A seen deer through unseen songs leaps through winter
And spring, the shadow on the cold dawn, the green
    beginning,
Ending, leaping, singing, all are in his luminosity.
The King quietly sees us, his eyes swift stars in the leaves,
Blesses us with his power, and then the forest hides him
    and sings.

How to See Deer

PHILIP BOOTH

Forget roadside crossings.
Go nowhere with guns.
Go elsewhere your own way,

lonely and wanting. Or
stay and be early:
next to deep woods

inhabit old orchards.
All clearings promise.
Sunrise is good,

and fog before sun.
Expect nothing always;
find your luck slowly.

Wait out the windfall.
Take your good time
to learn to read ferns;

make like a turtle:
downhill toward slow water.
Instructed by heron,

drink the pure silence.
Be compassed by wind.
If you quiver like aspen

trust your quick nature:
let your ear teach you
which way to listen.

You've come to assume
protective color; now
colors reform to

new shapes in your eye.
You've learned by now
to wait without waiting;

as if it were dusk
look into light falling:
in deep relief

things even out. Be
careless of nothing. See
what you see.

from *Year of the Big Cat*

LEW DIETZ

They set forth in the chilly predawn before the others were astir. Crossing the brook, they picked up an overgrown logging road that quartered the slope. The thin frosty rime of snow that had stiffened in the night crunched under their boots.

John McLaren swung off on a trail that went straight up through the black growth. He stopped and spoke for the first time. "It's light enough to begin hunting, Ben. You hang behind me thirty paces or so. And we're *deer* hunting. Let's get that straight."

"Yes sir."

Ben knew his father wasn't satisfied, for his eyes remained on him, troubled. "A mountain lion makes a business of staying out of man's way. Don't expect to see that cat, boy."

"He's here, Pa," Ben said. "I know he's here."

"You can't know, Ben. That's foolish. You know it's foolish. A deer can smell a cat. But you don't have that good a nose. Do you? *Do* you?"

"No sir."

His father swung off. Ben waited until his father had a lead, then began moving softly in his wake.

Soon the trail petered out. They were climbing straight up over boulders and ledges, taking handholds on juniper roots when they offered. The morning light came on strong as they hit the open hardwoods; maples, yellow birch and stalwart stands of great bear-scarred beech. A few squirrels scurried about in the sere leaves. A nuthatch began a dreary beeping.

They had a hasty lunch on an open glade where reindeer moss cushioned the rocks. As he ate, Ben looked down at the river far below. Trees and more trees marched on and on to the edge of the world. They slung on their packs and began climbing again. Ahead was the nether world of blowdowns.

Ben was gripped by a feeling of awe. Great prone and uprooted trees lay every which way, much as if some giant had gone raving mad and spent his rage upon the forest.

Up ahead, he saw his father stop suddenly. Ben moved up quickly and looked down where his father was pointing with the toe of his boot.

The splayed track of a buck deer, the largest he had ever seen in his life, was punched deep into the crusted snow.

"That was made this morning, Ben. We could have jumped him."

Ben dropped to his knees and examined the track closely. The loose crystals of snow had annealed. They hadn't jumped that deer and his father knew it.

John McLaren nodded, grudgingly. "All right, Ben. It was made maybe an hour ago, just before light. The deer wheeled and ran. He wouldn't have panicked at the smell of the likes of us. He would have eased off."

"You've seen a cat track, Pa?"

"No. But that don't mean he's not here. A cat will cover his scats, travel on ledges and in brook beds. He'll leave little trace, if that's his wish. What else you see, Ben?"

The boy's eyes moved in a slow circle. His gaze caught. He stepped to his right and found the heart-shaped print.

"The big deer is traveling with a doe."

John McLaren nodded. "The doe will head downslope for cover. Old Ironsides has headed for high ground. He'll want to use his eyes. He's using them now." He pointed. "See that rock ledge to the left of those Jack spruces? That's where he's watching us right now."

The boy stared ahead, heart pounding. "I don't see him. I don't see a thing."

"Nor do I. But that's where he'll be. I doubt if we can fool that old-timer, but we can try."

Ben waited and his father said softly, barely moving his lips, "You swing down the mountain, then work back, bearing behind and to the left of that nubble. Keep the wind in your face and take care not to break brush. Find a spot with some cover and a clear opening. I'll hold his eyes and try to pin him down. I'll give you fifteen minutes, then I'll start moving up on him. He'll hold his ground until I'm all but up on him. He'll break then. And you be ready."

Ben wanted his father to have the shot. What if he missed? But his father had turned away to fix his eyes on that nubble and Ben knew he had to go.

He slipped away and soft-footed it down the slope, then circled back, easing carefully so as not to loosen a rock or break any brush. He found a spot in a nest of loose rocks shielded by junipers. He broke off a few branches and made an opening. Then he rested the rifle down just so, with his left hand under the barrel and his right hand at the trigger guard.

The wind had begun to honk down the mountain. It brought tears to his eyes and he began shaking from the cold. Ben waited, hoping that big deer would come his way and afraid at the same time that the animal would come and he would miss.

There was no warning when the big deer came. It was as if the spot was a picture frame. The deer walked right into it, filling the space. He came with his great head held high and yawing from side to side. Ben saw his swollen neck arch back. His nostrils flared, and he blew. He blew again, pawing the reindeer moss with his sharp hooves.

Then the big deer wheeled and was gone. And it was only then Ben realized that he'd made no move to raise his gun. Through the haze of his anguish he saw his father pushing towards him through the thicket. John McLaren's expression was quizzical.

"I didn't hear any shots, Ben."

He had never before lied to his father. It was as if something ugly and alien had crept in and buried itself close to his heart. "I never saw him, Pa," he said. "I heard him blow and raised my gun, but never saw a hair of him."

"No matter," his father said.

His father said no more nor did he find much to talk about on the long downhill trail. The boy, walking with his own joyless thoughts, felt more alone than ever in his life.

The men, gathered about the stove, looked up as the two stomped in. John McLaren, wordless, set his gun in the rack, then shook out his jacket. He poured hot water from the kettle into a basin and began washing up.

Sam, stirring a stew on the stove, said irascibly, "Why does a man need to be so confoundedly exasperatin', John?"

John McLaren smiled a little as he toweled off. "He just naturally's got to be born that way, Sam. He was too smart for us, if that's what you want to know."

Ben felt relief come back into the room and, with it, ease. The men settled into chairs and the bottle was passed. Will chuckled suddenly. "There'll come a day. By Judas, there'll come a day!"

Ben, watching outside the circle of hunters, saw Jim viewing his father through veiled eyes. "Let's have it, John. The game's moved out. What is left is so spooked none of us have got within a half mile of a shot. We know the Big Cat's here. You might as well talk."

His father shrugged. "Ben says the cat's here. I think you'd better take his word for it. There'll be no trouble so long as he keeps to rabbits and young deer. We can expect a hue and cry for his skin if he comes into the farms and kills stock or breaks into a logging-camp hovel and rakes a horse or two. There'll be a price on his head. Last time there were a hundred men ring-hunting for him and that many dogs, all shouting for the blood of one big cat. I say we let him be ... and wait."

Sam Heard nodded slowly. "Yes, if he sticks to the rules and stays out of my clearin', I'll leave him be, John. But maybe you best tell my old lady that that cat has rights like you and me. I don't relish the idea, Johnny."

"A lot of things a man don't relish to do, Sam. We'll head home by the woods in the morning, the boy and I. I want to check by at my camp. You drop off my canoe on the way downriver, will you, Jim?"

"You're cutting the boy's first trip off early, aren't you, John?"

"I expect I am," John McLaren agreed, "but now that he's had his chance the same as the rest of us, he's joined the club. There'll be another year."

Ben and his father took the trail with rifles and backpacks after breakfast in the morning. They were across the burn and on the ridge trail when Ben broke the long and oppressive silence.

He said as he looked at the earth, "I saw that big buck, Pa. I saw him plain."

John McLaren nodded and kept on his loping stride. "I know. He's a real beauty, now, isn't he?"

"You knew?"

"You don't lie too good, Ben. Nor do the others. You should have guessed. They're all a pack of liars. They've been lyin' for years. Not one of them that couldn't have laid that big buck low one time or another."

Ben, a long way from understanding, slowed his pace. His father turned back and slung off his pack. He looked up through the dappled light to the sky. "You're asking why they were lying, Ben? I expect it's because they are hunters, bred and born. They and their fathers before them have been a part of the woods, as much as the cat and the hawk. And like the animals and birds, they have hunted for food and have given no quarter. I guess they all hate to admit that they are just men after all and given to sentiment."

"And you too, Pa?" Ben asked, still not quite understanding. "You let that big buck go?"

His father smiled. "Yes, but for a different reason, maybe. If I'd shot that deer they might never have hunted with me again and never told me why."

"But what if I'd shot that deer?"

"They would have blamed me, not you. There's not a boy alive who doesn't dream of bringing down a big buck deer. A man who's a man doesn't require that to feel like a man."

Ben said very softly, "It's the Big Cat I want, Pa. Nothing else. Nothing else in the world."

John McLaren went on chewing a twig. "Ben, it's not good for anyone, man or boy, to want something that bad."

First Deer

PAUL CORRIGAN

In that thicket of creaking firs,
my sleeves rolled up, the cold
stropping its frosty blade on my spine,
I unlocked the warmth of a deer.
The sweet reek of his cedar-filled paunch
scented the air as my father,
placing his hands on mine,
guided them to the warm, wet heart.
And as we felt under the hide, touching
the lungs and the stout cord of the windpipe,
he'd tell me what they were,
for he was pleased with this first deer
his boy had killed with one shot
through a screen of greengrowth.
He'd shot so many it tickled him
to see the thrill renewed in me
as I shivered with awe
and a little regret and winced
when I caught a whiff from the gut
or felt the hot blood trickle down my arm.
And as we worked on into dusk
without even checking a watch,
I thought of that quiet moment at mass
when the altar boy and the priest
get together to wash the chalice
and return the host to its house of gold,
unconcerned with who's looking on,
heads bent, eyes lowered, making sure
they clean everything up.
Then father flung the young knub horn
across his shoulders and struck off
while I tripped along behind him

until we reached camp in the dark
where we hung the carcass to drain
and went in to warm our bellies
with coffee, fried liver, and heart.

As the Buck Lay Dead

MARSDEN HARTLEY

As the buck lay dead, tied to the fender
of a car
coming down from Matagamon way,
I saw the dried blood on his tongue, of
a thousand summer dreams and winter cogitations
the scratches on his hooves were signatures
of the many pungent sticks and branches,
the torn place in his chest was made
by a man
letting out viscerals to save weight-giving
morsels to many a greedy fox or other wild
thing,
over the glaze of his half-shut eye
hung miseries of superlative moments
struck dumb.

The Buck in the Snow

EDNA ST. VINCENT MILLAY

White sky, over the hemlocks bowed with snow,
Saw you not at the beginning of evening the antlered buck and his
    doe
Standing in the apple-orchard? I saw them. I saw them suddenly
    go,
Tails up, with long leaps lovely and slow,
Over the stone-wall into the wood of hemlocks bowed with snow.

Now lies he here, his wild blood scalding the snow.

How strange a thing is death, bringing to his knees, bringing to his
    antlers
The buck in the snow.
How strange a thing,—a mile away by now, it may be,
Under the heavy hemlocks that as the moments pass
Shift their loads a little, letting fall a feather of snow—
Life, looking out attentive from the eyes of the doe.

The Day of the Hunter

EDWARD M. HOLMES

Everyone in his home town somewhere east of the Penobscot River knew that, in or out of season, Lyle Hanscom and deer hunting were inseparable. Yet for years no one had been able to garner enough evidence to convict him. Once several casual spectators, stopping along the highway to watch three deer at the other side of a wide field, not only heard the shot that felled one of the animals, but saw a man run from a spruce grove and drag the game back into the woods. No one could quite recognize the man in the strange, drooping overcoat he was wearing, nor was anyone able to track him with success. Still, the town's rumor mill, talk of someone's cooperative dump truck—which circled the town for an hour or two with a dead deer lying in the back— and public confidence in Lyle Hanscom's unparalleled gall unofficially pinned the deed on him.

Small wonder, then, that the nearest game warden kept a sharp watch, as often as he could, on Hanscom. The time came when the officer felt he had something on his man. Somehow word had leaked to him that Lyle had sneaked home with fresh-killed meat. When the warden drove up to Hanscom's, he could see the suspect watching him from one of the front windows. Hanscom met the law at the door and admitted him without a search warrant.

"I'd like to have a look around, if you don't mind, Lyle."

"Don't mind a bit, Joey. Look all you want," Hanscom said. "There's just one thing I want to ask of you."

"Ayeah?"

"My mother in there in the bedchamber is sick. She's had a heart attack."

"Is that so? I'm sorry to hear that."

"Well, you can understand I don't want nothing done that would upset her. You can see that, can't you, Joey?"

"I got to look in that room, same as any other, Lyle."

"Oh, I know that. I just ask that you don't upset her none. Might bring on another attack."

"I'll be careful," Joey said, and began making his search of the kitchen, the three small rooms, and the attic. He apologized to

Mrs. Hanscom for intruding upon her, looked under the bed, and would have searched the closets if he could have found any. Back in the kitchen, Lyle sat in a rocking chair, smoking his pipe. "Guess I'll have to take a look in the cellar," the warden said.

"No, I guess you won't neither," Lyle said.

"How's that?"

"I let you in here nice as could be, Joey, and give you a chance to look around. You know as well as I do, I didn't have to. I even let you look in the room where my mother was laying sick, but I draw a line at the cellar. I don't want no game wardens nor nobody else poking around in no cellar of mine."

"You know I don't have to go above two miles," Joey said, "to get me a warrant."

"Then you'll just have to do it that way," Lyle said. "Call it a freak notion if you want, but I ain't giving no man permission to snoop in my cellar."

So Joey did it that way. When he came back, he presented Lyle with the warrant, and Lyle read it, every word, as slow as he could. "All right, warden, I see I'll have to let you look in the cellar if you're bound and determined to do it. You may have a mite of trouble, though: so far as I know, this house is built on cedar posts. I ain't crawled underneath lately looking for no cellar, but of course you might find one."

It *was* built on cedar posts, too, about a foot off the ground, and that was the end of that, except, of course, that Lyle Hanscom's mother has given him notice, if he ever puts a fresh-killed deer in bed with her again, heart attack or no heart attack, she will turn him over to the warden herself.

Open Secrets of Bowdoinham

STEPHEN   PETROFF

I found in thick woods the outhouse of the deer—
a small place in the trees, 6 feet by 6 feet, and
covered with hundreds of bird's egg-sized brown
deer pellets—
it was a wonderful & mysteriously musical place,
with only the scent of pine needles.

Every few years I discovered in the woods
a chicken that had escaped the chicken-house.
What strange surprise to see a chicken
among dark juniper bushes—
a chicken that has lost its human traits.
A chicken gone wild looks stern,
irritable, and dangerous.
It is so rare that a chicken
elicits such respect.

When my brother killed my mother's chickens,
he said that as he carried them
fluttering to the chopping block,
they were screaming,
"No! No! No!"

Lost hay bales that flew from the baler
& tumbled to the edge of the woods,
or dropped down gullies,
or got wedged into the
tall grass against a stone wall
turn gray and acquire
the presence of stone memorials.
Like the feral chickens, they went wild
and lost their human use.

The baling twine begins to rot
but they retain their shape through
several winters.

I remember one lost hay bale in winter,
that sat like a tombstone before a beech sapling
whose leaves had withered but not fallen.
Pale & transparent yellow leaves
crackled in the ice wind.
       (Someone had recently died & I became
       convinced that her young soul
               lived in the tree.)
The sky was heavy & gray and the only light was
shed by the deep dead beech tree.

At the edge of the woods the abandoned sheep-dip
hole is full of dead leaves & 2 feet of water.
And occasionally while walking through beds
of pine needles I will kick up the skull of a
sheep.

Death Of A Pig

E. B. WHITE

Autumn 1947

I spent several days and nights in mid-September with an ailing pig and I feel driven to account for this stretch of time, more particularly since the pig died at last, and I lived, and things might easily have gone the other way round and none left to do the accounting. Even now, so close to the event, I cannot recall the hours sharply and am not ready to say whether death came on the third night or the fourth night. This uncertainty afflicts me with a sense of personal deterioration; if I were in decent health I would know how many nights I had sat up with a pig.

The scheme of buying a spring pig in blossomtime, feeding it through summer and fall, and butchering it when the solid cold weather arrives, is a familiar scheme to me and follows an antique pattern. It is a tragedy enacted on most farms with perfect fidelity to the original script. The murder, being premeditated, is in the first degree but is quick and skillful, and the smoked bacon and ham provide a ceremonial ending whose fitness is seldom questioned.

Once in a while something slips—one of the actors goes up in his lines and the whole performance stumbles and halts. My pig simply failed to show up for a meal. The alarm spread rapidly. The classic outline of the tragedy was lost. I found myself cast suddenly in the role of pig's friend and physician—a farcical character with an enema bag for a prop. I had a presentiment, the very first afternoon, that the play would never regain its balance and that my sympathies were now wholly with the pig. This was slapstick—the sort of dramatic treatment that instantly appealed to my old daschund, Fred, who joined the vigil, held the bag, and, when all was over, presided at the interment. When we slid the body into the grave, we both were shaken to the core. The loss we felt was not the loss of ham but the loss of pig. He had evidently become precious to me, not that he represented a distant nourishment in a hungry time, but that he had suffered in a suffering world. But I'm running ahead of my story and shall have to go back.

My pigpen is at the bottom of an old orchard below the house. The pigs I have raised have lived in a faded building that once was an icehouse. There is a pleasant yard to move about in, shaded by an apple tree that overhangs the low rail fence. A pig couldn't ask for anything better—or none has, at any rate. The sawdust in the icehouse makes a comfortable bottom in which to root, and a warm bed. This sawdust, however, came under suspicion when the pig took sick. One of my neighbors said he thought the pig would have done better on new ground—the same principle that applies in planting potatoes. He said there might be something unhealthy about that sawdust, that he never thought well of sawdust.

It was about four o'clock in the afternoon when I first noticed that there was something wrong with the pig. He failed to appear at the trough for his supper, and when a pig (or a child) refuses supper a chill of fear runs through any household, or ice-household. After examining my pig, who was stretched out in the sawdust inside the building, I went to the phone and cranked it four times. Mr. Dameron answered. "What's good for a sick pig?" I asked. (There is never any identification needed on a country phone; the person on the other end knows who is talking by the sound of the voice and by the character of the question.)

"I don't know, I never had a sick pig," said Mr. Dameron, "but I can find out quick enough. You hang up and I'll call Henry."

Mr. Dameron was back on the line again in five minutes. "Henry says roll him over on his back and give him two ounces of castor oil or sweet oil, and if that doesn't do the trick give him an injection of soapy water. He says he's almost sure the pig's plugged up, and even if he's wrong, it can't do any harm."

I thanked Mr. Dameron. I didn't go right down to the pig, though. I sank into a chair and sat still for a few minutes to think about my troubles, and then I got up and went to the barn, catching up on some odds and ends that needed tending to. Unconsciously I held off, for an hour, the deed by which I would officially recognize the collapse of the performance of raising a pig; I wanted no interruption in the regularity of feeding, the steadiness of growth, the even succession of days. I wanted no interruption, wanted no oil, no deviation. I just wanted to keep on raising a pig, full meal after full meal, spring into summer into fall. I didn't even even know whether there were two ounces of castor oil on the place.

Shortly after five o'clock I remembered that we had been invited out to dinner that night and realized that if I were to dose a pig there was no time to lose. The dinner date seemed a familiar conflict: I move in a desultory society and often a week or two will roll by without my going to anybody's house to dinner or anyone's coming to mine, but when an occasion does arise, and I am summoned, something usually turns up (an hour or two in advance) to make all human intercourse seem vastly inappropriate. I have come to believe that there is in hostesses a special power of divination, and that they deliberately arrange dinners to coincide with pig failure or some other sort of failure. At any rate, it was after five o'clock and I knew I could put off no longer the evil hour.

When my son and I arrived at the pigyard, armed with a small bottle of castor oil and a length of clothesline, the pig had emerged from his house and was standing in the middle of his yard, listlessly. He gave us a slim greeting. I could see that he felt uncomfortable and uncertain. I had brought the clothesline thinking I'd have to tie him (the pig weighed more than a hundred pounds) but we never used it. My son reached down, grabbed both front legs, upset him quickly, and when he opened his mouth to scream I turned the oil into his throat— a pink, corrugated area I had never seen before. I had just time to read the label while the neck of the bottle was in his mouth. It said Puretest. The screams, slightly muffled by oil, were pitched in the hysterically high range of pig-sound, as though torture were being carried out, but they didn't last long: it was all over rather suddenly, and, his legs released, the pig righted himself.

In the upset position the corners of his mouth had been turned down, giving him a frowning expression. Back on his feet again, he regained the set smile that a pig wears even in sickness. He stood his ground, sucking slightly at the residue of oil; a few drops leaked out of his lips while his wicked eyes, shaded by their coy little lashes, turned on me in disgust and hatred. I scratched him gently with oily fingers and he remained quiet, as though trying to recall the satisfaction of being scratched when in health, and seeming to rehearse in his mind the indignity to which he had just been subjected. I noticed, as I stood there, four or five small dark spots on his back near the tail end, reddish brown in color, each about the size of a housefly. I could not make out what they were. They did not look troublesome but at the same time they did not look like mere surface bruises or chafe marks. Rather they seemed blemishes of internal origin. His stiff white bristles almost completely hid them and I had to part the bristles with my fingers to get a good look.

Several hours later, a few minutes before midnight, having dined well and at someone else's expense, I returned to the pighouse with a flashlight. The patient was asleep. Kneeling, I felt his ears (as you might put your hand on the forehead of a child) and they seemed cool, and then with the light made a careful examination of the yard and the house for sign that the oil had worked. I found none and went to bed.

We had been having an unseasonable spell of weather—hot, close days, with the fog shutting in every night, scaling for a few hours in midday, then creeping back again at dark, drifting in first over the trees on the point, then suddenly blowing across the fields, blotting out the world and taking possession of houses, men, and animals. Everyone kept hoping for a break, but the break failed to come. Next day was another hot one. I visited the pig before breakfast and tried to tempt him with a little milk in his trough. He just stared at it, while I made a sucking sound through my teeth to remind him of past pleasures of the feast. With very small, timid pigs, weanlings, this ruse is often quite successful and will encourage them to eat; but with a large, sick pig the ruse is senseless and the sound I made must have made him feel, if anything, more miserable. He not only did not crave food, he felt a positive revulsion to it. I found a place under the apple tree where he had vomited in the night.

At this point, although a depression had settled over me, I didn't suppose that I was going to lose my pig. From the lustiness of a healthy pig a man derives a feeling of personal lustiness; the stuff that goes into a trough and is received with such enthusiasm is an earnest of some later feast of his own, and when this suddenly comes to an end and the food lies stale and untouched, souring in the sun, the pig's imbalance becomes the man's, vicariously, and life seems insecure, displaced, transitory.

As my own spirits declined, along with the pig's, the spirits of my vile old dachschund rose. The frequency of our trips down the footpath through the orchard to the pigyard delighted him, although he suffers greatly from arthritis, moves with difficulty, and would be bedridden if he could find anyone willing to serve meals on a tray.

He never missed a chance to visit the pig with me, and he made many professional calls on his own. You could see him down there at all hours, his white face parting the grass along the fence as he wobbled and stumbled about, his stethoscope dangling—a happy quack, writing his villainous prescriptions and grinning his corrosive grin. When the enema bag appeared, and the bucket of warm suds, his happiness was complete, and he managed to squeeze his enormous body between the two lowest rails of the yard and then assumed full charge of the irrigation. Once, when I lowered the bag to check the flow, he reached in and hurriedly drank a few mouthfuls of the suds to test their potency. I have noticed that Fred will feverishly consume any substance that is associated with trouble—the bitter flavor is to his liking. When the bag was above reach, he concentrated on the pig and was everywhere at once, a tower of strength and inconvenience. The pig, curiously enough, stood rather quietly through this colonic carnival, and the enema, though ineffective, was not as difficult as I had anticipated.

I discovered, though, that once having given a pig an enema there is no turning back, no chance of resuming one of life's more stereotyped roles. The pig's lot and mine were inextricably bound now, as though the rubber tube were the silver cord. From then until the time of his death I held the pig steadily in the bowl of my mind; the task of trying to deliver him from his misery became a strong obsession. His suffering soon became the embodiment of all earthly wretchedness. Along toward the end of the afternoon, defeated in physicking, I phoned the veterinary twenty miles away and placed the case formally in his hands. He was full of questions, and when I casually mentioned the dark spots on the pig's back, his voice changed its tone.

"I don't want to scare you," he said, "but when there are spots, erysipelas has to be considered."

Together we considered erysipelas, with frequent interruptions from the telephone operator, who wasn't sure the connection had been established.

"If a pig has erysipelas can he give it to a person?" I asked.

"Yes, he can," replied the vet.

"Have they answered?" asked the operator.

"Yes, they have," I said. Then I addressed the vet again. "You better come over here and examine this pig right away."

"I can't come myself," said the vet, "but McFarland can come this evening if that's all right. Mac knows more about pigs than I do anyway. You needn't worry too much about the spots. To indicate erysipelas they would have to be deep hemorrhagic infarcts."

"Deep hemorrhagic what?"

"Infarcts," said the vet.

"Have they answered?" asked the operator.

"Well," I said, "I don't know what you'd call these spots, except they're about the size of a housefly. If the pig has erysipelas I guess I have it, too, by this time, because we've been very close lately."

"McFarland will be over," said the vet.

I hung up. My throat felt dry and I went to the cupboard and got a bottle of whiskey. Deep hemorrhagic infarcts—the phrase began fastening its hooks in my head. I had assumed that there could be nothing much wrong with a pig during the months it was being groomed for murder; my confidence in the essential health and endurance of pigs had been strong and deep, particularly in the health of pigs that belonged to me and that were part of my proud scheme. The awakening had been violent and I minded it all the more because I knew that what could be true of my pig could be true also of the rest of my tidy world. I tried to put this distasteful idea from me, but it kept recurring. I took a short drink of whiskey and then, although I wanted to go down to the yard and look for fresh signs, I was scared to. I was certain I had erysipelas.

It was long after dark and the supper dishes had been put away when a car drove in and McFarland got out. He had a girl with him. I could just make her out in the darkness—she seemed young and pretty. "This is Miss Owen," he said. "We've been having a picnic supper on the shore, that's why I'm late."

McFarland stood in the driveway and stripped off his jacket, then his shirt. His stocky arms and capable hands showed up in my flashlight's gleam as I helped him find his coverall and get zipped up. The rear seat of his car contained an astonishing amount of paraphernalia, which he soon overhauled, selecting a chain, a syringe, a bottle of oil, a rubber tube, and some other things I couldn't identify. Miss Owen said she'd go along with us and see the pig. I led the way down the warm slope of the orchard, my light picking out the path for them, and we all three climbed the fence, entered the pighouse, and squatted by the pig while McFarland took a rectal reading. My flashlight picked up the glitter of an engagement ring on the girl's hand.

"No elevation," said McFarland, twisting the thermometer in the light. "You needn't worry about erysipelas." He ran his hand slowly over the pig's stomach and at one point the pig cried out in pain.

"Poor piggledy-wiggledy!" said Miss Owen.

The treatment I had been giving the pig for two days was then repeated, somewhat more expertly, by the doctor, Miss Owen and I handing him things as he needed them—holding the chain that he had looped around the pig's upper jaw, holding the syringe, holding the bottle stopper, the end of the tube, all of us working in darkness and in comfort, working with the instinctive teamwork induced by emergency conditions, the pig unprotesting, the house shadowy, protecting, intimate. I went to bed tired but with a feeling that I had turned over part of the responsibility of the case to a licensed doctor. I was beginning to think, though, that the pig was not going to live.

He died twenty-four hours later, or it might have been forty-eight—there is a blur in time here, and I may have lost or picked up a day in the telling and the pig one in the dying. At intervals during the last day I took cool fresh water down to him and at such times as he found the strength to get to his feet he would stand with head in the pail and snuffle his snout around. He drank a few sips but no more; yet it seemed to comfort him to dip his nose in water and bobble it about, sucking in and blowing out through his teeth. Much of the time, now, he lay indoors half buried in sawdust. Once, near the last, while I was attending him I saw him try to make a bed for himself but he lacked the strength, and when he set his snout into the dust he was unable to plow even the little furrow he needed to lie down in.

He came out of the house to die. When I went down, before going to bed, he lay stretched in the yard a few feet from the door. I knelt, saw that he was dead, and left him there: his face had a mild look, expressive neither of deep peace nor of deep suffering, although I think he had suffered a good deal. I went back up to the house and to bed, and cried internally—deep hemorrhagic intears. I didn't wake till nearly eight the next morning, and when I looked out the open window the grave was already being dug, down beyond the dump under a wild apple. I could hear the spade strike against the small rocks that blocked the way. Never send to know for whom the grave is dug, I said to myself, it's dug for thee. Fred, I well knew, was supervising the work of digging, so I ate breakfast slowly.

It was a Saturday morning. The thicket in which I found the gravediggers at work was dark and warm, the sky overcast. Here, among alders and young hackmatacks, at the foot of the apple tree, Lennie had dug a beautiful hole, five feet long, three feet wide, three feet deep. He was standing in it, removing the last spadefuls of earth while Fred patrolled the brink in simple but impressive circles, disturbing the loose earth of the mound so that it trickled back in. There had been no rain in weeks and the soil, even three feet down, was dry and powdery. As I stood and stared, an enormous earthworm which had been partially exposed by the spade at the bottom dug itself deeper and made a slow withdrawal, seeking even remoter moistures at even lonelier depths. And just as Lennie stepped out and rested his spade against the tree and lit a cigarette, a small green apple separated itself from a branch overhead and fell into the hole. Everything about this last scene seemed overwritten—the dismal sky, the shabby woods, the imminence of rain, the worm (legendary bedfellow of the dead), the apple (conventional garnish of a pig).

But even so, there was a directness and dispatch about animal burial, I thought, that made it a more decent affair than human burial: there was no stopover in the undertaker's foul parlor, no wreath nor spray; and when we hitched a line to the pig's hind legs and dragged him swiftly from his yard, throwing our weight into the harness and leaving a wake of crushed grass and smothered rubble over the dump, ours was a businesslike procession, with Fred, the dishonorable pall-bearer, staggering along in the rear, his perverse bereavement showing in every seam of his face; and the post-mortem performed handily and swiftly right at the edge of the grave, so that the inwards that had caused the pig's death preceded him into the ground and he lay at last resting squarely on the cause of his own undoing.

I threw in the first shovelful, and then we worked rapidly and without talk, until the job was complete. I picked up the rope, made it fast to Fred's collar (he is a notorious ghoul), and we all three filed back up the path to the house, Fred bringing up the rear and holding back every inch of the way, feigning unusual stiffness. I noticed that although he weighed far less than the pig, he was harder to drag, being possessed of the vital spark.

The news of the death of my pig traveled fast and far, and I received many expressions of sympathy from friends and neighbors, for no one took the event lightly and the premature expiration of a pig is, I soon discovered, a departure which the community marks solemnly on its calendar, a sorrow in which it feels fully involved. I have written this account in penitence and in grief, as a man who failed to raise his pig, and to explain my deviation from the classic course of so many raised pigs. The grave in the woods is unmarked, but Fred can direct the mourner to it unerringly and with immense good will, and I know he and I shall often revisit it, singly and together, in seasons of reflection and despair, on flagless memorial days of our own choosing.

The Passing of Mrs. Wiggs

ROBERT   CHUTE

Mrs. Wiggs was an ugly sow
whose sunken, piggy eyes stared
unblinking through fence boards.
Boring through assumptions of safe distance.
Rat-headed, underslung, her young
hung like maggots fruiting from her side.
Even Uncle George would not go in
the pen when they were there.
But when the young were gone
he slipped a bucket over her head,
led her by tail and bucket handle
into a waiting truck. Her wild-boar teeth
were hidden and she whimpered in the pail.

Talking to the Dog

KATE BARNES

When I used to get up in the morning
And make some funny noises—
Jargon, bits of songs, nonsense—
I wasn't really talking to myself;
No, I was talking to the dog.

But now the dog is dead—
No more unkempt wolf-hound lying asleep on her back
With her legs against the wall.
I must say good-bye to her prehistoric howling,
Good-bye to the look of those
            yellow owl eyes.
I drop her unfinished dinner onto the compost pile,
I wash her bowls and put them away,
I pull the rug over the place where her bed was;
And still I think I hear her
Just stirring in the next room.

It is almost Midsummer;
The blackberries are flowering in festoons beside
            the pasture;
I will bury her ashes under the crooked pear tree
With the fruit already growing among its green leaves.
I know that for a long time I will go on
            hearing her at the door,
And for a long time I will be seeing her out of the corner
            of my eye.
When the wind tracks light through the bending grass,
For a long time I will be talking to the dog.

from *Letourneau's Used Auto Parts*

CAROLYN CHUTE

While the Babbidge family sleeps, a hoarse wind comes up. Frost forms on the old windows of the unfinished part of the house. The dogs sigh. They curl themselves up hard and small. They look like a lot of furry funny basketballs left around the dooryard.

But the little black terrier tied to the tipped-over snowmobile doesn't rest. He perches on top of the machine, his teeth bared in a little smile. His trembling is out of control ... almost mothlike.

When the little terrier wails, Blackstone doesn't raise his head from his pillow or speak, but his eyes are wide in the dark.

Then the terrier is silent a while, but the wind clashes objects around in the yard, and the trees crackle like fire.

Lillian whispers, "Poor animals. They must be freezing to death."

"Won't hurt 'em," says Blackstone. "They are made for it."

"I don't know," sighs Lillian. "They don't seem very happy."

Blackstone is silent.

Lillian thrashes the heavy blankets around a bit. She says almost cheerfully, "I don't understand why you don't fix them up some little houses...to keep them out of the weather, you know. It wouldn't take much."

"It would take *plenty*," Blackstone snorts. "Lumber costs *plenty*. I don't spend good money on a buncha damned dogs. I have a *family*."

"They must be so cold," Lillian insists.

Blackstone grunts. He reaches for her head and hair, the nape of her neck, spreading his fingers there...though he can't feel her.... His battered hands can't ever feel softness. He says, "Outdoor dogs ain't supposed to be made of. It'll ruin 'em. You want lap dogs you do one thing, you want watchdogs you do another. Those are *watchdogs* out there, Miss Lily-Ann. It may not please you, but it's got to be. Life isn't an easy road. You better face that now and get it over with. Life ain't no Walt Disney pi'ture."

The small black terrier begins yipping.

Blackstone doesn't raise his head off the pillow or shift the great bulking thickness of blankets. He just bellers. "SHUT UP AND LAY DOWN!"

There is only the roar of the wind for the rest of the night.

Dog

MITCH GOODMAN

It is meat with eyes,
it eats while it dreams,
with eagerness it eats
almost anything, it yearns
to be touched, is tame but
chained. Breaks ice crust
to drink from puddles,
                              persists:
growls in play, then
smiles. Loves us (is that
the word?) We wonder why.

Wants only one thing (it is all
one) is often hungry, rolls on
its back and shows itself shame-
lessly. Laughs, leaps, licks
faces: this is to kiss (and
we laugh, and wipe away the wetness.)

circles before it settles. Rises:
listens, hears what we don't hear;
never settles for long, still looks
for a hole in the fence, barks
in search of the others, runs away
when it can, to be on the move
and to meet the others:
alert loping, looking,
sniffing it out.

You think it doesn't see
the sunset? It does. It sighs
homeward, westward

in the reddening light
that promises another day;
waits for the night, bays
in love light of moon lust.

Lives with the wind,
with wings, petals. If the deer runs,
it will run after it. And is
dragged back. Streets and roads:
where is the wilderness?

from *The Outlaw Dogs*

C. A. STEPHENS

... A party of not less than thirty men and boys, with hounds, was made up to go in pursuit of a pack of outlaw dogs which had been killing sheep and calves in that town and vicinity. As yet the flocks in our own neighborhood had not been molested, but there was no saying how soon the marauders might pay us a visit; and a public effort had been inaugurated to hunt the pack down and destroy it.

The history of these dog outlaws was a singular one and parallels in canine life the famous story of "Dr. Jekyll and Mr. Hyde." The fact that dogs do occasionally lead double lives—one that of a docile house-dog by day, and the other that of a wild, dangerous beast by night—is well established. In this case a trusted dog had become not only an outlaw himself, but drew others about him and was the leader of a dangerous band.

A farmer named Frost, three miles from us, began to lose sheep from a flock of seventy which he owned and which were kept in a pasture that included a high hill and sloped northward over rough, bushy land to the great woods. It was not the custom there to enclose the sheep in pens or shelters, at night. They wandered at will in the pasture, and were rarely visited oftener than once a week, and that usually on Sunday morning. Then either the farmer or one of his boys would go to the pasture to give the sheep salt and count them. This was the custom among the farmers in that locality, nearly all of whom owned flocks sometimes as small as twenty, but rarely larger than seventy-five, since sheep in New England do not thrive when kept in large flocks.

Farmer Frost was not the only one who had lost sheep at this time. Six other flocks were invaded, but his loss occurred first. His son Rufus, going to the pasture to salt and count the sheep on a Sunday morning, found that two ewes and a grown lamb were missing. Later in the day the partially devoured remains of the sheep were found in the pasture not far from a brook.

"Bear's work," the farmer and his neighbors said, although an old hunter who visited the spot pronounced against the theory. But a bear had been seen recently in the vicinity; and Monday morning the Frost boys loaded their guns for a thorough hunt. Two traps were also set near the carcasses, which were left as found, to lure the destroyer back.

The destroyer did not return; the traps remained as they were set; and the youthful hunters were unsuccessful in rousing a bear in the woods. But on the following Wednesday night a farmer named Needham, living a mile and a half from Frost, lost two sheep, the bodies of which were found in his pasture, partly eaten.

It chanced that Farmer Needham, or his son Emerson, owned a dog which was greatly prized. They called him Bender. Bender was said to be a half-breed, Newfoundland and mastiff, but had, I think, a strain of more common blood in his ancestry, for there was a tawny crescent mark beneath each of his eyes. Bender was the pink of propriety and a dog of unblemished reputation.

On this occasion Bender went with the farmer and his boys to the sheep pasture, and smelled the dead sheep with every appearance of surprise and horror. The hair on his shoulders bristled with indignation. He coursed around, seeking for bear tracks, and ran barking about the pasture. In short, he did everything that a properly grieved dog should do under the circumstances, and so far from touching or eating any of the torn mutton, he plainly scorned such a thing.

The boys took Bender with them to hunt bears, as their main reliance and ally, and Bender hunted assiduously. Three or four other dogs, belonging at farms in the vicinity, were also taken on these hunts. One was a collie, another a mongrel bulldog, and a third a large brindled dog of no known pedigree. Still another half-bred St. Bernard dog set off with the others, but on reaching the sheep pasture, where they went first to get the trail and make a start, this latter dog behaved oddly, left the others and slunk away home.

Some of the boys attributed this to cowardice, and he was hooted; others suspected Roke, for that was his name, of having killed the sheep. Suspicion against him so increased that his master kept him chained at home.

No bears were tracked to their dens, and none were caught in the traps, which were also set in the Needham pasture; but less than a week later another farmer, this time the owner of the mongrel bulldog, lost three sheep in one night. As previously, the sheep were found dead and partly eaten.

If Roke's alibi had not had a tangible chain at one end of it that night, his character would have been as good as lost; for his refusal to hunt with the other dogs and the manner in which he behaved while near the dead sheep, had rendered him a public "suspect." When near the carcasses he had growled morosely, and shown his teeth. When barked at by the other dogs, he had taken himself off.

A few nights afterward Farmer Frost lost two more sheep from his flock in the pasture, and the following night Rufus watched in the pasture with a loaded gun, quite without results.

About that time two or three others watched in their pastures. Some shut up their sheep. But the losses continued to occur. Within a radius of three or four miles as many as twenty-four sheep were killed in the course of three weeks.

None of the watchers by night or the hunters by day had, as yet, obtained so much as a trace or a clue to the animal which had done the killing. They came to think that it was quite useless to watch by night; the marauding creature, whether bear, wild-cat, or dog, was apparently too wily, or too keen-scented, to enter a pasture and approach a flock where a man was concealed.

Rufus Frost, who had watched repeatedly, then hit on a stratagem. First he cut off about a foot from the barrel of a shotgun, to shorten it, and then made a kind of bag, or sack, by sewing two sheep-pelts together. Thus equipped, he repaired to the pasture after dark, and joined himself to the flock, not as a watcher, but as a sheep. That is to say, he crept into the sheepskin bag, which was also capacious enough to contain the short gun, and lay down on the outskirts of the flock, a little aloof.

The sheep were lying in a group, ruminating, as is their habit, by night. Rufus drew a tangle of wool over his head, and otherwise contrived to pose as a sheep lying down. He assumed that when thus bagged up in fresh sheepskin, the odor of a sheep would be diffused, and the appearance of one so well counterfeited as to deceive even a bear. His gun he had charged heavily with buckshot; and altogether the ruse was ingenious, if nothing more.

Nothing disturbed the flock on the first night that he spent in the pasture, not on the second; but he resolved to persevere. It was no very bad way to pass an autumn night; the weather was pleasant and warm, and there was a bright moon nearing its full.

He had kept awake during the first night, listening and watching for the most of the time, but he caught naps the second, and on the third was sleeping comfortably at about two in the morning, when he was suddenly set upon, tooth and nail, by what he believed, on first waking, to be a whole family of bears. One had him by the leg, through the bag, shaking him. Another was dragging at the back of the bag, while the teeth of a third were snapping at his face. Still other teeth were chewing upon his arm, and the growling was something frightful!

This was an alarming manner in which to be wakened from a sound nap, and it is little wonder that Rufus, although a plucky youngster, rolled over and over and yelled with the full power of his lungs.

His shouts produced an effect. First one and then another of his assailants let go and drew back; and getting the wool out of his eyes, Rufus saw that the creatures were not bears, but four astonished dogs, standing a few feet away, regarding him with doubt and disgust.

To all appearance he had been a sheep, lying a little apart from the others, and they had fallen upon him as one; but his shouts led them to think that he was not mutton, after all, and they did not know what to make of it!

Rufus, almost equally astonished, now lay quite still, staring at them. The dogs looked at each other, licked the wool from their mouths, and sat down to contemplate him further.

Rufus, on his part, waxed even more amazed as he looked, for by the bright moonlight he at once identified the four dogs. They were, alas! the highly respectable, exemplary old Bender, the collie Tige, the brindle, and the mongrel bulldog—all loved and trusted members of society. Rufus was so astonished that he did not think of using his blunderbuss; he simply whistled.

That whistle appeared to resolve the doubts of the dogs instantly. They growled menacingly and sprang away like the wind. Rufus saw them run across the pasture to the woods, and afterward, for some minutes, heard them washing themselves in the brook, as roguish, sheep-killing dogs always do before returning home.

But in this case the dogs appeared to know that they had been detected, and that so far as their characters as good and virtuous dogs went, the game was up. Not one of them returned home. All four took to the woods, and thereafter lived predatory lives. They were aware of the gravity of their offences.

During October and early November they were heard of as a pack of bad sheep-killers, time and again; but they now followed their evil practices at a distance from their former homes, where, indeed, the farmers took the precaution of carefully guarding their sheep. On one night of October they killed three calves in a farmer's field, four miles from the Frost farm. Several parties set off to hunt them, but they escaped and lived as outlaws, subsisting from nocturnal forays until snow came, when they were tracked to a den beneath a high crag, called the "Overset," up in the great woods.

It was Rufus Frost and Emerson Needham, the former owner of Bender, who tracked the band to their retreat. Finding it impossible to call or drive the criminals out, they blocked the entrance of the den with large stones, and then came home to devise some way of destroying them—since it is a pretty well-established fact that when once a dog has relapsed into the savage habits of his wild ancestry he can never be reclaimed.

Someone had suggested suffocating the dogs with brimstone fumes; and so, early the following morning, Rufus and Emerson, heading a party of fifteen men and boys, came to the Edwards farm and the Old Squire's to get brimstone rolls, which we had on account of our bees. Their coming, on such an errand, carried a wave of excitement with it. Old Hewey Glinds, the trapper, was sent for and joined the party in spite of his rheumatism. Every boy in the neighborhood begged earnestly to go; and the most of us, on one plea and another, obtained permission to do so.

All told, I believe, there were thirty-one in the party, not counting dogs. Entering the woods we proceeded first to Stoss Pond, then through Black Ash Swamp, and thence over a mountainous wooded ridge to Overset Pond.

In fact we seemed to be going to the remote depths of the wilderness; and what a savage aspect the snowy evergreen forest wore that morning! At last, we came out on the pond. Very black it looked, for it was what is called a "warm pond." Ice had not yet formed over it. The snow-clad crag where the cave was, on the farther side, loomed up, ghostly white by contrast.

Rufus and Emerson had gone ahead and were there in advance of us; they shouted across to us that the dogs had not escaped. We then all hurried on over snowy stones and logs to reach the place.

It was a gruesome sort of den, back under an overhang of rocks fully seventy feet high. Near the dark aperture which the boys had blocked, numbers of freshly gnawed bones lay in the snow, which presented a very sinister appearance.

Those in advance had already kindled a fire of drift-stuff not far away on the shore. The hounds and dogs which had come with the party, scenting the outlaw dogs in the cave, were barking noisily; and from within could be heard a muffled but savage bay of defiance.

"That's old Bender!" exclaimed Emerson. "And he knows right well, too, that his time's come!"

"Suppose they will show fight?" several asked.

"Fight! Yes!" cried old Hewey, who had now hobbled up. "They'll fight wuss than any wild critters!"

One of the older boys, Ransom Frost, declared that he was not afraid to take a club and go into the cave.

"Don't you think of such a thing!" exclaimed old Hewey. "Tham's desperate dogs! They'd pitch onto you like tigers! Tham dogs know there's no hope for tham and they're going to fight—if they get the chance!"

It was a difficult place to approach, and several different plans of attack were proposed. When the two hounds and three dogs which had come up with us barked and scratched at the heavy, flat stones which Rufus and Emerson had piled in the mount of the cave, old Bender and Tige would rush forward on their side of the obstruction, with savage growls. Yet when Rufus or any of the others attempted to steal up with their guns, to shoot through the chinks, the outlaws drew back out of sight, in the gloom. There was a fierceness in their growling such as I never have heard from other dogs.

The owner of Watch, the collie, now crept up close and called to his former pet. "I think I can call my dog out," said he.

He called long and endearingly, "Come, Watch! Come, good fellow! You know me, Watch! Come out! Come, Watch, come!"

But the outlawed Watch gave not a sign of recognition or affection; he stood with the band.

Tige's former master then tried the same thing, but elicited only a deep growl of hostility.

"Oh, you can whistle and call, but you won't get tham dogs to go back on one another!" chuckled old Hewey. "Tham dogs have taken an oath together. They won't trust ye and I swan I wouldn't either, if I was in their places! They know you are Judases!"

It was decided that the brimstone should be used. Live embers from the fire were put in the kettle. Green, thick boughs were cut from fir-trees hard by; and then, while the older members of the party stood in line in front of the hole beneath the rocks, to strike down the dogs if they succeeded in getting out, Rufus and Emerson removed a part of the stones, and with some difficulty introduced the kettle inside, amidst a chorus of ugly growls from the beleaguered outlaws. The brimstone was then put into the kettle, more fire applied, and the hole covered quickly with boughs. And now even we younger boys were allowed to bear a hand, scraping up snow and piling it over the boughs, the better to keep in the smoke and fumes.

The splutter of the burning sulphur could plainly be heard through the barrier, and also the loud, defiant bark of old Bender and the growls of Tige.

Very soon the barking ceased, and there was a great commotion, during which we heard the kettle rattle. This was succeeded presently by a fierce, throaty snarling of such pent-up rage that chills ran down the backs of some of us as we listened. After a few minutes this, too, ceased. For a little space there was complete silence; then began the strangest sound I ever heard.

It was like the sad moaning of the stormy wind, as we sometimes hear it in the loose window casements of a deserted house. Hardly audible at first, it rose fitfully, moaning, moaning, then sank and rose again. It was not a whine, as for pity or mercy, but a kind of canine farewell to life: the death-song of the outlaws. This, too, ceased after a time; but old Hewey did not advise taking away the boughs for fifteen or twenty minutes. "Make a sure job on't," he said.

Choking fumes issued from the cave for some time after it was opened and the stones pulled away. Bender was then discovered lying only a few feet back from the entrance. He appeared to have dashed the kettle aside, as if seeking to quench the fire and smoke. Tige was close behind him, Watch farther back. Very stark and grim all four looked when finally they were hauled out with a pole and hook and given a finishing shot.

It was thought best to burn the bodies of the outlaws. The fire on the shore was replenished with a large quantity of drift-wood, fir boughs and other dry stuff which we gathered, and the four carcasses heaved upon the pile. It was a calm day, but thick, dark clouds had by this time again overspread the sky, causing the pond to look still blacker. The blaze gained headway; and a dense column of smoke and sparks rose straight upward to a great height. Owing to the snow and the darkening heavens, the fire wore a very ruddy aspect, and I vividly recall how its melancholy crackling was borne along the white shore, as we turned away and retraced our steps homeward.

Ox

HENRY BRAUN

I marvel at the rope that holds me,
how it drops into its own thickness,

and the yoke too,
plant that rides me with hard thighs.

Landing on me now is the first snow,
the rain that takes time.

What season? I ask,
                    have to think,

have to begin to pull
on the syllables of winter.

For me, a field with a horse
is like a sentence with helpful punctuation.

In the Pasture

KATE BARNES

It would be impossible to draw these three work horses
Without a pencil of light
As they stand broadside to the afternoon sun
Outlined with narrow lines of fire around their vast
Chestnut forms, almost black against the dazzle.
The young mare swings her long tail from hip to hip,
And her Titian-blond mane hangs over her shoulder
Like the ringletted chevelure of a Victorian belle,
Innocent and alluring.
     Beyond her
The two big geldings, brothers and team mates,
Scratch each other's wide red backs
With careful incisors.
     Swallows fly
Over the grass, cloud shadows cross the lake
And darken the blue of the hills on the opposite shore
But in the pasture the sun is shining,
The afternoon wind has driven off the flies,
And the three big horses are all at their ease;
A small, happy society
Of souls who are gentle and do no harm,
Who live in God's pocket, who spend the long summer days
Moving from sunshine to shade and back to the sun,
Who want nothing but to be where they are.

from *The Maine Woods*

HENRY DAVID THOREAU

About two o'clock, we turned up a small branch three or four rods wide, which comes in on the right from the south, called Pine Stream, to look for moose signs. We had gone but a few rods before we saw very recent signs along the water's edge, the mud lifted up by their feet being quite fresh, and Joe declared that they had gone along there but a short time before. We soon reached a small meadow on the east side, at an angle in the stream, which was, for the most part, densely covered with alders. As we were advancing along the edge of this, rather more quietly than usual, perhaps, on account of the freshness of the signs,— the design being to camp up this stream, if it promised well,—I heard a slight crackling of twigs deep in the alders, and turned Joe's attention to it; whereupon he began to push the canoe back rapidly; and we had receded thus half a dozen rods, when we suddenly spied two moose standing just on the edge of the open part of the meadow which we had passed, not more than six or seven rods distant, looking round the alders at us.

They made me think of great frightened rabbits, with their long ears and half-inquisitive, half-frightened looks; the true denizens of the forest (I saw at once), filling a vacuum which now first I discovered had not been filled for me,—*moose*-men, *wood-eaters*, the word is said to mean,—clad in a sort of Vermont gray, or homespun. Our Nimrod, owing to the retrograde movement, was now the farthest from the game; but being warned of its neighborhood, he hastily stood up, and, while we ducked, fired over our heads one barrel at the foremost, which alone he saw, though he did not know what kind of creature it was; whereupon this one dashed across the meadow and up a high bank on the northeast, so rapidly as to leave but an indistinct impression of its outlines on my mind.

At the same instant, the other, a young one, but as tall as a horse, leaped out into the stream, in full sight, and there stood cowering for a moment, or rather its disproportionate lowness behind gave it that appearance, and uttering two or three trumpeting squeaks. I have an indistinct recollection of seeing the old one pause an instant on the top of the bank in the woods, look toward its shivering young, and then dash away again. The second barrel was leveled at the calf, and when we expected to see it drop in the water, after a little hesitation, it, too, got out of the water, and dashed up the hill, though in a somewhat different direction.

All this was the work of a few seconds, and our hunter, having never seen a moose before, did not know but they were deer, for they stood partly in the water, nor whether he had fired at the same one twice or not. From the style in which they went off, and the fact that he was not used to standing up and firing from a canoe, I judged that we should not see anything more of them. The Indian said that they were a cow and her calf,—a yearling, or perhaps two years old, for they accompany their dams so long; but, for my part, I had not noticed much difference in their size. It was but two or three rods across the meadow to the foot of the bank, which, like all the world thereabouts, was densely wooded; but I was surprised to notice, that, as soon as the moose had passed behind the veil of the woods, there was no sound of footsteps to be heard from the soft, damp moss which carpets that forest, and long before we landed, perfect silence reigned. Joe said, "If you wound 'em moose, me sure get 'em."

We all landed at once. My companion reloaded; the Indian fastened his birch, threw off his hat, adjusted his waistband, seized the hatchet, and set out. He told me afterward, casually, that before we landed he had seen a drop of blood on the bank, when it was two or three rods off. He proceeded rapidly up the bank and through the woods, with a peculiar, elastic, noiseless, and stealthy tread, looking to right and left on the ground, and stepping in the faint tracks of the wounded moose, now and then pointing in silence to a single drop of blood on the handsome, shining leaves of the Clintonia borealis, which, on every side, covered the ground, or to a dry fern-stem freshly broken, all the while chewing some leaf or else the spruce gum. I followed, watching his motions more than the trail of the moose. After following the trail about forty rods in a pretty direct course, stepping over fallen trees and winding between standing ones, he at length lost it, for there were many other moose tracks there, and, returning once more to the last blood-stain, traced it a little way and lost it again, and, too soon, I thought, for a good hunter, gave it up entirely. He traced a few steps, also, the tracks of the calf; but, seeing no blood, soon relinquished the search.

I observed, while he was tracking the moose, a certain reticence or moderation in him. He did not communicate several observations of interest which he made, as a white man would have done, though they may have leaked out afterward. At another time, when we heard a slight crackling of twigs and he landed to reconnoitre, he stepped lightly and gracefully, stealing through the bushes with the least possible noise, in a way in which no white man does,—as it were, finding a place for his foot each time.

About half an hour after seeing the moose, we pursued our voyage up Pine Stream, and soon, coming to a part which was very shoal and also rapid, we took out the baggage, and proceeded to carry it round, while Joe got up with the canoe alone. We were just completing our portage and I was absorbed in the plants, admiring the leaves of the Aster macrophyllus, ten inches wide, and plucking the seeds of the great round-leaved orchis, when Joe exclaimed from the stream that he had killed a moose. He had found the cow-moose lying dead, but quite warm, in the middle of the stream, which was so shallow that it rested on the bottom, with hardly a third of its body above water. It was about an hour after it was shot, and it was swollen with water. It had run about a hundred rods and sought the stream again, cutting off a slight bend. No doubt a better hunter would have tracked it to this spot at once.

I was surprised at its great size, horse-like, but Joe said it was not a large cow-moose. My companion went in search of the calf again. I took hold of the ears of the moose, while Joe pushed his canoe down-stream toward a favorable shore, and so we made out, though with some difficulty, its long nose frequently sticking in the bottom, to drag it into still shallower water. It was a brownish black, or perhaps a dark iron-gray, on the back and sides, but lighter beneath and in front. I took the cord which served for the canoe's painter, and with Joe's assistance measured it carefully, the greatest distances first, making a knot each time. The painter being wanted, I reduced these measures that night with equal care to lengths and fractions of my umbrella, beginning with the smallest measures, and untying the knots as I proceeded; and when we arrived at Chesuncook the next day, finding a two-foot rule there, I reduced the last to feet and inches; and, moreover, I made myself a two-foot rule of a thin and narrow strip of black ash, which would fold up conveniently to six inches.

All this pains I took because I did not wish to be obliged to say merely that the moose was very large. Of the various dimensions which I obtained I will mention only two. The distance from the tips of the hoofs of the fore-feet, stretched out, to the top of the back between the shoulders, was seven feet and five inches. I can hardly believe my own measure, for this is about two feet greater than the height of a tall horse. (Indeed, I am now satisfied that this measurement was incorrect, but the other measures given here I can warrant to be correct, having proved them in a more recent visit to those woods.) The extreme length was eight feet and two inches. Another cow-moose, which I have since measured in those woods with a tape, was just six feet from the tip of the hoof to the shoulders, and eight feet long as she lay.

When afterward I asked an Indian at the carry how much taller the male was, he answered, "Eighteen inches," and made me observe the height of a cross-stake over the fire, more than four feet from the ground, to give me some idea of the depth of his chest. Another Indian, at Oldtown, told me that they were nine feet high to the top of the back, and that one which he tried weighed eight hundred pounds. The length of the spinal projections between the shoulders is very great. A white hunter, who was the best authority among hunters that I could have, told me that the male was *not* eighteen inches taller than the female; yet he agreed that he was sometimes nine feet high to the top of the back, and weighed a thousand pounds.

Only the male has horns, and they rise two feet or more above the shoulders,—spreading three or four, and sometimes six feet,—which would make him in all, sometimes, eleven feet high! According to this calculation, the moose is as tall, though it may not be as large, as the great Irish elk, Megaceros Hibernicus, of a former period, of which Mantell says that it "very far exceeded in magnitude any living species, the skeleton" being "upward of ten feet high from the ground to the highest point of the antlers." Joe said, that, though the moose shed the whole horn annually, each new horn has an additional prong; but I have noticed that they sometimes have more prongs on one side than on the other. I was struck with the delicacy and tenderness of the hoofs, which divide very far up, and the one half could be pressed very much behind the other, thus probably making the animal surer-footed on the uneven ground and slippery moss-covered logs of the primitive forest. They were very unlike the stiff and battered feet of our horses and oxen. The bare, horny part of the fore-foot was just six inches long, and the two portions could be separated four inches long at the extremities.

The moose is singularly grotesque and awkward to look at. Why should it stand so high at the shoulders? Why have so long a head? Why have no tail to speak of? for in my examination I overlooked it entirely. Naturalists say it is an inch and a half long. It reminded me at once of the camelopard, high before and low behind,—and no wonder, for, like it, it is fitted to browse on trees. The upper lip projected two inches beyond the lower for this purpose. This was the kind of man that was at home there; for, as near as I can learn, that has never been the residence, but rather the hunting-ground of the Indian. The moose will, perhaps, one day become extinct; but how naturally then, when it exists only as a fossil relic, and unseen as that, may the poet or sculptor invent a fabulous animal with similar branching and leafy horns,—a sort of fucus or lichen in bone,—to be in the inhabitant of such a forest as this!

Here, just at the head of the murmuring rapids, Joe now proceeded to skin the moose with a pocket-knife, while I looked on; and a tragical business it was,—to see that still warm and palpitating body pierced with a knife, to see the warm milk stream from the rent udder, and the ghastly naked red carcass appearing from within its seemly robe, which was made to hide it. The ball had passed through the shoulder-blade diagonally and lodged under the skin on the opposite side, and was partially flattened. My companion keeps it to show to his grand-children. He has the shanks of another moose which he has since shot, skinned and stuffed, ready to be made into boots by putting in a thick leather sole. Joe said, if a moose stood fronting you, you must not fire, but advance toward him, for he will turn slowly and give you a fair shot.

In the bed of this narrow, wild, and rocky stream, between two lofty walls of spruce and firs, a mere cleft in the forest which the stream had made, this work went on. At length Joe had stripped off the hide and dragged it trailing to the shore, declaring that it weighed a hundred pounds, though probably fifty would have been nearer the truth. He cut off a large mass of the meat to carry along, and another, together with the tongue and nose, he put with the hide on the shore to lie there all night, or till we returned. I was surprised that he thought of leaving this meat thus exposed by the side of the carcass, as the simplest course, not fearing that any creature would touch it; but nothing did. This could hardly have happened on the bank of one of our rivers in the eastern part of Massachusetts; but I suspect that fewer small wild animals are prowling there than with us. Twice, however, in this excursion, I had a glimpse of a species of large mouse.

This stream was so withdrawn, and the moose tracks were so fresh, that my companions, still bent on hunting, concluded to go farther up it and camp, and then hunt up or down at night....

But, on more accounts than one, I had had enough of moose-hunting. I had not come to the woods for this purpose, nor had I foreseen it, though I had been willing to learn how the Indian manœuvred: but one moose killed was as good, if not bad, as a dozen. The afternoon's tragedy, and my share in it, as it affected the innocence, destroyed the pleasure of my adventure. It is true, I came as near as is possible to come to being a hunter and miss it, myself; and as it is, I think that I could spend a year in the woods, fishing and hunting just enough to sustain myself, with satisfaction. This would be next to living like a philosopher on the fruits of the earth which you had raised, which also attracts me.

But this hunting of the moose merely for the satisfaction of killing him,—not even for the sake of his hide,—without making any extraordinary exertion or running any risk yourself, is too much like going out by night to some wood-side pasture and shooting your neighbor's horses. They are God's own horses, poor, timid creatures, that will run fast enough as soon as they smell you, though they *are* nine feet high. Joe told us of some hunters who a year or two before had shot down several oxen by night, somewhere in the Maine woods, mistaking them for moose. And so might any of the hunters; and what is the difference in the sport, but the name? In the former case, having killed one of God's and *your own* oxen, you strip off its hide,—because that is the common trophy, and, moreover, you have heard that it may be sold for moccasins,—cut a steak from its haunches, and leave the huge carcass to smell to heaven for you. It is no better, at least, than to assist at a slaughterhouse.

This afternoon's experience suggested to me how base or coarse are the motives which commonly carry men into the wilderness. The explorers and lumberers generally are all hirelings, paid so much a day for their labor, and as such they have no more love for wild nature than wood-sawyers have for forests. Other white men and Indians who come here are for the most part hunters, whose object is to slay as many moose and other wild animals as possible. But, pray, could not one spend some weeks or years in the solitude of this vast wilderness with other employments than these—employments perfectly sweet and innocent and ennobling? For one that comes with a pencil to sketch or sing, a thousand come with an axe or rifle. What a coarse and imperfect use Indians and hunters make of Nature! No wonder that their race is so soon exterminated. I already, and for weeks afterward, felt my nature the coarser for this part of my woodland experience, and was reminded that our life should be lived as tenderly and daintily as one would pluck a flower.

With these thoughts, when we reached our camping-ground, I decided to leave my companions to continue moose-hunting down the stream, while I prepared the camp, though they requested me not to chop much nor make a large fire, for fear I should scare their game. In the midst of the damp fir-wood, high on the mossy bank, about nine o'clock of this bright moonlight night, I kindled a fire, when they were gone, and, sitting on the fir-twigs, within sound of the falls, examined by its light the botanical specimens which I had collected that afternoon, and wrote down some of the reflections which I have here expanded; or I walked along the shore and gazed up the stream, where the whole space above the falls was filled with mellow light. As I sat before the fire on my fir-twig seat, without walls above or around me, I remembered how far on every hand that wilderness stretched, before you came to cleared or cultivated fields, and wondered if any bear or moose was watching the light of my fire; for Nature looked sternly upon me on account of the murder of the moose.

Strange that so few ever came to the woods to see how the pine lives and grows and spires, lifting its evergreen arms to the light,—to see its perfect success; but most are content to behold it in the shape of many broad boards brought to market, and deem *that* its true success! But the pine is no more lumber than man is, and to be made into boards and houses is no more its true and highest use than the truest use of a man is to be cut down and made into manure. There is a higher law affecting our relation to pines as well as to men.

A pine cut down, a dead pine, is no more a pine than a dead human carcass is a man. Can he who has discovered only some of the values of whalebone and whale oil be said to have discovered the true use of the whale? Can he who slays the elephant for his ivory be said to have "seen the elephant"? These are petty and accidental uses; just as if a stronger race were to kill us in order to make buttons and flageolets of our bones; for everything may serve a lower as well as a higher use. Every creature is better alive than dead, men and moose and pine-trees, and he who understands it aright will rather preserve its life than destroy it.

Is it the lumberman, then, who is the friend and lover of the pine, stands nearest to it, and understands its nature best? Is it the tanner who has barked it, or he who has boxed it for turpentine, whom posterity will fable to have been changed into a pine at last? No! no! it is the poet; he it is who makes the truest use of the pine,—who does not fondle it with an axe, nor tickle it with a saw, nor stroke it with a plane,—who knows whether its heart is false without cutting into it,— who has not bought the stumpage of the township on which it stands. All the pines shudder and heave a sigh when *that* man steps on the forest floor. No, it is the poet, who loves them as his own shadow in the air, and lets them stand.

I have been into the lumber-yard, and the carpenter's shop, and the tannery, and the lampblack factory, and the turpentine clearing; but when at length I saw the tops of the pines waving and reflecting the light at a distance high over all the rest of the forest, I realized that the former were not the highest uses of the pine. It is not their bones or hide or tallow that I love most. It is the living spirit of the tree, not its spirit of turpentine, with which I sympathize, and which heals my cuts. It is as immortal as I am, and perchance will go to as high a heaven, there to tower above me still.

Erelong, the hunters returned, not having seen a moose, but, in consequence of my suggestions, bringing a quarter of the dead one, which, with ourselves, made quite a load for the canoe.

Climbing Katahdin

DANIEL HOFFMAN

Hoisting yourself
From fingerniche to toehold,
Approaching the Knife-Edge,

A deep shagged ravine gapes on the one side,
The eye of a blueberry-silver pool steep
Down the dizzydrop other,

Your breath short,
Each rib rasping,
Grasping the thinned air above the timberline,

Clinging
To the desolate rocks
Below the snowline,

You can believe
As others have believed—
This stony ridgepole bracing

Heaven the longhouse of the mountain,
Ktaadn.
You breathe his breath.

Hoisting yourself
Atop the spined ridge you'll find
On a slight plateau

Stretching toward the peak's rise
Huckleberries growing
Beside a spring!—you laugh at the surprise

Of it and chew in the icy air
Bursting berries big as birds' eggs,
Your lips and tongue relish the purple—

Then arise from feasting
On silvery frosted fruit
In the desolation

To hoist yourself,
From fingertip to toehold
Each breath grasping

As high up as the mountain allows you.

John Marin, Stonington, Maine, 1923, watercolor, 18³/₈" x 21⁷/₈",
Courtesy, Colby College Museum of Art.

Communities

"A rush of anecdote and regret."

Maine Speech

E. B. WHITE

I find that, whether I will or no, my speech is gradually changing, to conform to the language of the country. The tongue spoken here in Maine is as different from the tongue spoken in New York as Dutch is from German. Part of this difference is in the meaning of words, part in the pronunciation, part in the grammar. But the difference is very great. Sometimes when a child is talking it is all one can do to translate until one has mastered the language. Our boy came home from school the first day and said the school was peachy, but he couldn't understand what anybody was saying. This lasted only for a couple of days.

For the word "all" you use the phrase "the whole of." You ask, "Is that the whole of it?" And whole is pronounced hull. Is that the hull of it? It sounds as though you might mean a ship.

For lift, the word is heft. You heft a thing to see how much it weighs. When you are holding a wedge for somebody to tap with a hammer, you say, "Tunk it a little." I've never heard the word tap used. It is always tunk.

Baster (pronounced bayster) is a popular word with boys. All the kids use it. He's an old baster, they say, when they pull an eel out of an eel trap. It probably derives from bastard, but it sounds quite proper and innocent when you hear it, and rather descriptive. I regard lots of things now (and some people) as old basters.

A person who is sensitive to cold is spleeny. We have never put a heater in our car, for fear we might get spleeny. When a pasture is sparse and isn't providing enough feed for the stock, you say the pasture is pretty snug. And a man who walks and talks slowly or lazily is called mod'rate. He's a powerful mod'rate man, you say.

When you're prying something with a pole and put a rock under the pole as a fulcrum, the rock is called a bait. Few people use the word "difference." When they want to say it makes no difference, they say it doesn't make any odds.

If you have enough wood for winter but not enough to carry you beyond that, you need wood "to spring out on." And when a ewe shows an udder, she "bags out." Ewe is pronounced yo by old-timers like my friend Dameron.

This ewe and yo business had me licked at first. It seemed an affectation to say yo when I was talking about a female sheep. But that was when I was still thinking of them as yews. After a while I thought of them as yos, and then it seemed perfectly all right. In fact, yo is a better-sounding word, all in all, than yew. For a while I tried to pronounce it half way between yew and yo. This proved fatal. A man has to make up his mind and then go boldly ahead. A ewe can't stand an umlaut any more than she can a terrier.

Hunting or shooting is called gunning. Tamarack is always hackmatack. Tackle is pronounced taykle. You rig a block and taykle.

If one of your sheep is tamer than the others, and the others follow her, you say she will "toll" the others in. The chopped clams which you spread upon the waters to keep the mackerel schooling around your boat are called toll bait. Or chum bait. A windy day is a "rough" day, whether you are on land or sea. Mild weather is "soft." And there is a distinction between weather overhead and weather underfoot. Lots of times, in spring when the ground is muddy, you will have a "nice day overhead."

Manure is always dressing, never manure. I think, although I'm not sure, that manure is considered a nasty word, not fit for public company. The word dung is used some but not as much as dressing. But a manure fork is always a dung fork.

Wood that hasn't properly seasoned is dozy. The lunch hour is one's nooning. A small cove full of mud and eelgrass is a gunkhole. When a pullet slips off and lays in the blackberry bushes she "steals away a nest." If you get through the winter without dying or starving you "wintered well."

Persons who are not native to this locality are "from away." We are from away ourselves, and always will be, even if we live here the rest of our lives. You've got to be born here—otherwise you're from away.

People get born, but lambs and calves get dropped. This is literally true of course. The lamb actually does get dropped. (It doesn't hurt it any—or at any rate it never complains.) When a sow has little ones, she "pigs." Mine pigged on a Sunday morning, the ol' baster.

The road is often called "the tar." And road is pronounced rud. The other day I heard someone call President Roosevelt a "war mongrel." Statute is called statue. Lawyers are busy studying the statues. Library is liberry. Chimney is chimley.

Fish weir is pronounced fish ware. Right now they're not getting anything in the wares.

Hoist is pronounced hist. I heard a tall story the other day about a man who was histed up on the end of a derrick boom while his companions accused him of making free with another man's wife. "Come on, confess!" they shouted. "Isn't it true you went out with her all last year?" For a while he swung at the end of the boom and denied the charges. But he got tired finally. "You did, didn't you?" they persisted. "Well, once, boys," he replied. "Now hist me down."

The most difficult sound is the "a." I've been in Maine, off and on, all my life, but I still have to pause sometimes when somebody asks me something with an "a" in it. The other day a friend met me in front of the store, and asked, "How's the famine comin' along?" I had to think fast before I got the word "farming" out of his famine.

The word dear is pronounced dee-ah. Yet the word deer is pronounced deer. All children are called dee-ah, by men and women alike. Workmen often call each other dee-ah while on the job.

The final "y" of a word becomes "ay." Our boy used to call our dog Freddie. Now he calls him Fredday. Sometimes he calls him Fredday dee-ah; other times he calls him Fredday you ol' baster.

Country talk is alive and accurate, and contains more pictures and images than city talk. It usually has an unmistakable sincerity that gives it distinction. I think there is less talking merely for the sound that it makes. At any rate, I seldom tire listening to even the most commonplace stuff, directly and sincerely spoken; and I still recall with dread the feeling that occasionally used to come over me at parties in town when the air was crowded with loud intellectual formations—the feeling that there wasn't a remark in the room that couldn't be brought down with a common pin.

The Black Fly Festival

TIM SAMPLE

One reason Maine is such a popular spot for folks to visit in the summertime is the wonderful variety of fairs and festivals goin' on. I've been to a lot of 'em myself. I try to make it up to Eastport every year for the vacant building festival. And of course, Mother and I wouldn't miss the Wiscasset worm days. But for pure local Maine fun and good times you've got to head up to Rangeley in the spring, for the annual Black Fly Festival.

Rangeley is one of the prettiest towns in the state, and lots of folks go up in the winter for the skiin' at Saddleback Mountain. Matter of fact, years back I used to play music in the lounges up there, always hopin' I'd get hooked up with the ski crowd. You know the ski crowd? Them young good-lookin' folks from away, that drives Porsches and got money?

To tell you the truth, I never did really hook up with the ski crowd, but I ran head on into the skidder crowd, and that's a whole different crew altogether. And the skidder crowd is the one you're likely to see at the Black Fly Festival. It runs for a whole weekend with all types of events and contests, but everyone agrees that the highlight of all the activities happens on Saturday night at seven-thirty right in the center of town at the I.G.A. parkin' lot. The annual Miss Black Fly competition.

Don't get me wrong now, this Miss Black Fly competition ain't just another beauty contest. (As a matter of fact, beauty don't hardly even enter into it.) These girls are all from the skidder crowd, and they're all good strong hefty Maine girls. Last year's winner, probably weighed in at about 235 pounds, and for the talent part of the competition she carved a life-size statue of Michael Jackson out of pulp wood with her chainsaw. They made a video tape of her doin' it. Only took her about an hour and it looked just like him.

In order to get a good position to see the show, Mother and I arrived down at the parkin' lot about six-thirty, and even then you could just feel the excitement. Crowds of people from all over the place was swarmin' in. Not to mention the Black Flies. The stage was a flatbed truck hung with buntin'. They had originally planned to buy a set of them big spotlights like you see at one of them gala Hollywood movie premieres. As I say, they wanted to get 'em, but I guess the town budget wouldn't stretch that far. But they did pretty good just the same. They parked the two police cruisers facing the stage and then backed 'em up so their hind wheels were down over the curb. Then the Girl Scout troop colored each headlight a different color with magic markers. When the deputies flipped them high beams on the effect was real professional lookin'.

When seven-thirty rolled around, the three finalists walked on-stage in their swimsuits and the crowd was cheerin' like mad. The M.C. announced through a bullhorn that this was serious business. Just like the Olympics, he said. The contestants had been instructed that they couldn't use any chemicals. No Off, or Ben's 100, or old-time woodsmen's fly dope. Then he stood back and the girls posed in their swimsuits. You could hear a pin drop as the whole crowd watched. Them black flies started swarmin' somethin' fierce. Finally the girl on the left broke down and swatted one of the critters and was automatically eliminated, leavin' only two standin'. Them two battled it out for the better part of three minutes until the one on the right finally gave out and started swattin' them little demons left and right. The crowd let out a cheer as the M.C. placed the Miss Black Fly crown atop the winner, knowin' that she had passed a test of stamina, endurance, and character that few people could ever match.

Three and One, Arrowmoosic

CONSTANCE HUNTING

Too cold to swim.
June, too. We might have known.
Let's play a game.
What kind of games
you girls know how to play?
Euchre.
Hearts.
What's that game
we played in the car coming down?
The one you play by yourself?
Only game I really know how to play is euchre.
Poker?
Deuces wild.
Larry, you would say that.
Honestly, Larry, you're a scream.
Linda, you deal. You're kidding! Me?
(Curlers aglow, she deals.)
Juanita's got two kings. Juanita,
I can see your hand.
You can see my hand?
They got us beat already. Larry,
I bet you got an ace over there
you use every time.
Let's bury somebody.
Larry, let's bury Larry.
Sharon, get some water.
Don't get it in my hair.
Put your arms down by your sides,
we got to lay you out.
Don't kick it at me, chrissake.
His toes are impossible!
You didn't do

a very good job, sister, I don't think
you know what you're doing,
tell you the truth.
Linda, hold his ankles.
Sharon brings water in her cap. He pretends
terror. They must touch him. Ritual. Hey!
He resurrects,
brushes sand
like flies off his torso, legs
apart
tolerant
fully operative
(Shoot,
I'm going in).

Black Sunday

VIRGINIA CHASE

Our village was, by and large, a tolerant one. Politics offered no grounds for dissension, Republicans outnumbering Democrats fifty to one. Pornography was never an issue with us, and the obscenities that appeared in public places were generally ignored. A certain amount of vandalism, we told ourselves, had to be expected, especially on the night before the Fourth, and when swing-chairs and settees disappeared from lawns and piazzas to reappear atop some outhouse or on an island in the bay, we blamed their owners for carelessness in leaving them outside.

When feuds sprang up, as they did now and then over boundaries or lobster pots or trespassing cows, only the parties involved got much upset. For the rest of us they offered real diversion. Yet we were careful not to provoke confrontation and cheerfully acted as intermediaries when communication was necessary. All in all, we took things pretty much as they came. When a newly married couple surprised us with a baby, we were bound to do a little quick mental arithmetic, but only the gossips counted out loud. And as for the gossips themselves, we regarded them lightly.

Rowdiness, too, we accepted as a matter of course, especially at Fair time when liquor invariably leaked in (Maine was, of course, a Prohibition state), or on those nights when the steamer lay over and the boat fellows lined the drugstore steps making inflammatory remarks at those who passed. Then if things got really bad, somebody might go far enough to call the constable, who took his time coming, confident that order would be self-imposed before his arrival.

Granted there were times when our patience was strained. A thief who was caught and proved without contrition might be sent away for a few weeks to the State Reform School where it was assumed he would learn a lesson. If he didn't and was caught again, he might end up for a month or so in the County Jail where discipline was known to be casual.

Behavior which today would be termed psychotic we called "just odd." If the man who brought us our clams wanted to board up his windows and live in darkness, that was his business. If two sisters who could never agree painted half the outside of their house yellow and half green, well, that was up to them. Of course if a man chased his neighbor with a hatchet and persisted in it, he might as a last resort be sent for a spell to the asylum in Bangor while, more likely than not, his intended victim kept watch over his place and his family until the time of his release. Generally we lived and let live, even in the matter of religion.

We had two churches, the Congregationalist and the Baptist. There was inevitably some competition between them, and since my father (or more aptly his family) belonged to the former and my mother to the latter, she was careful to allot each of her children to one or the other in turn. Though the Baptists, with whom my lot fell, were the more orthodox, I met only one bigot among them. I was eight years old at the time.

Now and then the children of our Sunday School were expected to participate in the regular church service by reciting Biblical texts. When my class did so, our teacher, Miss Rendy Mason, wrote the texts on slips of paper and placed them like bookmarks in a hymnal. Then each of us drew one. The lucky drew short ones like "God is love" or, better still, "Jesus wept." These required only a spring across the platform and a mere glance at the congregation. Longer verses required a slower pace and longer exposure. So we hurried to count the words while Miss Rendy kept strict watch to be sure there was no trading.

On my Black Sunday I discovered, counting, that my verse had nine words in it. That alone was a disaster. I was upset at the start.

"For the Lord thy God," I read reluctantly, "is a jealous God."

The text was new to me, but not the word jealous. That was all too familiar, for I was a seventh child, submerged completely by my brothers and sisters. I loved them, but as I began to grow older their shadows hung perpetually over me. To their teachers (whose recollections were softened by time) they had all been models of brilliance, neatness, promptness, agreeableness, penmanship and deportment. Try as I did, I could never measure up. If I approached in one regard, I slipped badly in at least five others. Even my mother, who like other mothers of her time had never heard of sibling rivalry, often made comparisons. "Olive's neck is always clean," she would remind me. Or, "I can always count on John to remember." It was the same in the village. "You'll have to go some to catch up," one after another would tell me.

The weight of it would have been lightened had people only called me by my own name. But few, except perhaps the neighbors, did. "Mornin' Edith," someone would greet me. Or "Bless my soul if it isn't Olive!" The postmaster, when he spoke to me at all, always prefaced any remark by asking, "Which one of the Chases are you?" I told him loudly, but it never registered. The next time he greeted me it would be by the name of one of my sisters. This troubled me greatly, for though I seldom had a letter of my own—valentines and such being delivered by hand—there always lurked in my mind the possibility that I might, and I feared somehow that I would never receive it. So being sent for the mail in the morning always gave me a bad start for the day.

When I sulked and refused to say what the matter was, my mother would talk solemnly to me about jealousy. It was, so it appeared, my Cardinal Sin. Yet it persisted, aggravated by the fact that things had to be done in turn in families. That wasn't so bad if you were a second or even a third child, but when you were a seventh it was another matter. Invariably the privilege you were to receive after interminable waiting turned out to be sadly depleted or at best to arrive at the wrong season. What especially stung was that, though it was my room as much as Olive's, I had the inside of the bed. *I* had the bottom drawers just because I was younger.

That Sunday, reading my verse, it all came to a head. I was jealous. God was jealous. Yet *I* was punished for something He could get away with. *I* was bad. Yet He was worshipped. He, who had no reason to be jealous at all. No one to boss Him. No models to live up to. He could be worshipped while *I* ...

I felt myself nudged, then pushed. I do not know today what was going on within me. I only know that when I reached the platform, stumbling, I did not speak at all. I just stood there, frozen.

Miss Rendy began to prompt me in a whisper. "For the Lord ..."
It had no effect.

She tried again, louder, her lips shaping the words. But I only stood there, unable or unwilling to speak. She tried still again, leaning almost out of the pew. This time she spoke aloud. I must have looked up, for I remember my mother's flushed face, saw her lips, too, moving. I saw the postmaster, the druggist, the dressmaker, neighbors, the butcher, the fishman, the grocer. The entire village, it seemed, all in a blur. Gradually their faces merged into one face, its mouth grimacing: "For the Lord, thy God ... " They knew He was jealous, yet they were all standing up for Him, taking His part. They knew He was as bad as I was. Still they expected me to praise His name. Well, I wouldn't, now or ever again. They couldn't make me.

What must have been two or three minutes passed with no sound but the loud tick of the clock and an undertone of hoarse whispers from the congregation. "For the Lord, thy God ..." Then an impatient voice spoke. "Speak up, child," it said, "or God won't ever let you into Heaven."

That was too much for me. My rage boiled over. "If God's like that," I fairly shouted, "I wouldn't be in the same place with Him."

I closed my eyes and waited. Would He come as a lightning bolt through the ceiling and strike me dead? Or would the floor open and drop me straight into Hell? Or would the deacons rush forward and tear me limb from limb? Or would I, perhaps, like Lot's wife, be turned then and there into a pillar of salt?

But nothing whatever happened. Someone—I have never been sure who—came and led me to a seat in the wings where I sat rigid, staring at my patent leather shoes until the service was over. Then when all heads were bowed in the benediction, I raced quickly down a side aisle and through the swinging doors. Outside, I began to run, not down the road where the others would come, but toward the brook and the woods beyond where I sat on a boulder and waited. Let God get me there where no one could see.

When it became apparent that vengeance would be delayed, I got up and, walking very slowly, headed for home.

I opened the back door very quietly, intending to go upstairs. Normally I changed into my second-best dress and shoes when church was over. But that day I decided not to. I needed all the confidence my best clothes gave me. I would sit bolt upright in them and wait for what was coming. And I would sit on Olive's side of the bed.

Before I was halfway upstairs I heard my mother's voice. "We've been holding up dinner for you," she said.

Dinner was never held up for anyone except my father. I stood still, trying to take it in. Dinner waiting for me. For me, a sinner, who had expected no dinner at all ...

"Hurry," she went on, raising her voice a little. "We're all ready to sit at the table."

I went cautiously into the dining room, eyes downcast, and slipped into my chair. Brothers and sisters, coached, as I was later to learn, said nothing.

I was always served last, as a matter of course. But that day when I started to pass on the first plate, my father spoke. "Keep it," he said. "It's yours."

Gratifying though that was, I still had the village to face, and the terror of confronting God himself had faded before the terror of going for the morning mail. I would be openly reproached, I told myself. Certainly shunned.

But it didn't happen that way at all. The druggist, hurrying to open his store, patted me on the head with his paper as he passed. People who normally, if they saw me at all, greeted me with a half-wave or an automatic "Lo," smiled and said "Mornin." The doctor, coming down the steps of the post office, looked up from a letter he was reading and gave me what I was sure was a wink. But most astonishing of all was the behavior of the postmaster who, when he handed me the mail, actually called me by my own name.

The Rumor

ERSKINE CALDWELL

To George Williams went the distinction of being the first to suggest making Sam Billings the new town-treasurer. The moment he made the nomination at the annual town meeting there was an enthusiastic chorus of approval that resulted in the first unanimous election in the history of Androscoggin. During the last of the meeting everybody was asking himself why no one had ever thought of Sam Billings before.

The election of Sam to the office of town-treasurer pleased everybody. He was a good business man and he was honest. Furthermore, the summer hotel property that he owned and operated on the east shore of Androscoggin Lake paid about a tenth of the town's total tax assessment, and during the season he gave employment to eighty or ninety people whose homes were in the town. After he was elected everybody wondered why they had been giving the office to crooks and scoundrels for the past twenty years or more when the public money could have been safe and secure with Sam Billings. The retiring treasurer was still unable to account to everybody's satisfaction for about eighteen hundred dollars of the town's money, and the one before him had allowed his books to get into such a tangled condition that it cost the town two hundred and fifty dollars to hire an accountant to make them balance.

Clyde Ballard, one of the selectmen, took George aside to talk to him when the meeting was over. Clyde ran one of the general stores in the village.

"You did the town a real service today," he told George. "Sam Billings is the man who should have been treasurer all the time. How did you come to think of him?"

"Well," George said, "Sam Billings was one of my dark horses. The next time we need a good selectman I'll trot another one of them out."

"George, there's nothing wrong with me as a selectman, is there?" Clyde asked anxiously.

"Well, I'm not saying there is, and I'm not saying there's not. I'm not ready to make up my mind yet. I'll wait and see if the town builds me a passable road over my way. I may want to buy me an automobile one of these days and if I do I'll want a lot of road work done between my place and the village."

Clyde nodded his head understandingly. He had heard that George Williams was kicking about his road and saying that the selectmen had better make the road commissioners take more interest in it. He shook hands with George and drove back to the village.

The summer-hotel season closed after the first week in September and the guests usually went home to Boston and New York Tuesday or Wednesday after Labor Day. Sam Billings kept his hotel open until the first of October because there were many men who came down over the weekends to play golf. In October he boarded up the windows and doors and took a good rest after working hard all summer. It was two or three weeks after that before he could find out what his season's profits were, because he took in a lot of money during July and August.

That autumn, for the first time in two or three decades, there was no one who spoke uneasily concerning the treasurer or the town's money. Sam Billings was known to be an honest man, and because he was a good business man everybody knew that he would keep the books accurately. All the money collected was given to Sam. The receipt of the money was promptly acknowledged, and all bills were paid when presented. It would have been almost impossible to find a complaint to make against the new treasurer.

It was not until the first real snow of the winter, which fell for three days during the first week in January, that anything was said about the new town-treasurer. Then overnight there was in general circulation the news that Sam Billings had gone to Florida.

George Williams drove to the village the same afternoon the news reached him over on the back road. He happened to be listening to a conversation on the party line when something was said about Sam Billings having gone to Florida, otherwise George might possibly have waited a week or longer before somebody came by his place and told him.

He drove his horse to the village in a hurry and went into Clyde Ballard's store. They were talking about Sam Billings when George walked in.

George threw off his heavy coat and sat down in a chair to warm his feet against the stove.

"Have you heard about it yet, George?" Clyde asked him.

"Sure I have, and God never made a bigger scoundrel than Sam Billings," he answered. "I wouldn't trust him with a half-dollar piece of my money any farther than I can toss a steer by the tail."

"I heard you was one of Sam's principal backers," one of the men said from the other side of the stove. "You shouldn't talk like that about your prime candidate, George."

Clyde came up to the stove to warm his hands and light a cigar.

"George," he said, winking at the other men around the fire, "you told me that Sam Billings was your dark-horse candidate—you must have meant to say *horse-thief*."

Everybody shouted and clapped his knees and waited for George to say something.

"I used to swear that Sam was an honest man," George began seriously, "but I didn't think then that he would turn around and run off to Florida with all the town's money in his pants. At the next election I'm going to vote to tie the town's money around my old black cow's neck. I'd never again trust an animal that walks standing up on its hind legs."

"Well, George," Clyde said, "you ain't heard it all, about Sam yet. Can you stand a little more?"

"What else did he do?" George stood up to hear better.

"He took Jenny Russell with him. You know Jenny Russell— Arthur Russell's oldest girl. I guess he's having plenty of good times with her and the town's money down in Florida. I used to think that I had good times when I was younger but Sam Billings's got me beat a mile when it comes to anything like that."

George sat down again. He filled his pipe and struck a match.

"So he made off with a woman too, did he? Well, that's what they all do when they get their hands on some money that don't belong to them. Those two things go hand-in-hand—stolen money and women."

"He picked a good-looker while he was about it," another of the men said. "He'd have to travel a far piece to find a better-looker than Jenny Russell. And if he don't have a good time with her he ought to step aside for a younger man."

George grunted contemptuously and sucked the flame into the bowl of his pipe. He remembered the time when he had had an eye on Jenny Russell himself.

"I heard it said this morning that Sam was going to have his hotel property fired so he could collect the insurance on it," Clyde said from behind the counter where he was waiting on a customer. "If he does that, the whole town assessment will have to be changed so we will be able to collect enough tax money to keep the roads repaired and the schools running."

Nobody said anything for several minutes. George glared at each man around the stove. The raising of the tax-rate stared everybody full in the face.

Clyde came over to the stove again and stood beside it, warming his hands.

"My wife heard it said over the party line last night—" He paused and looked from face to face. Everybody in the store leaned forward to hear what Clyde was going to say. "—She heard that Sam Billings murdered one of those rich men from New York in his hotel last summer. I guess he killed him to get his money. He wouldn't stop at anything now."

"Well, I always said that Sam Billings was the biggest crook that ever lived in the town of Androscoggin," George said disgustedly. "The last time I saw Sam I thought to myself, 'Now, how in hell is Sam Billings going to keep the town's money from getting mixed up with his own?' I know now that I was right in thinking that. We ought to catch him and have him sent to the Federal prison for the rest of his life."

"He'll be a slick eel to catch," Clyde said. "Men like Sam Billings figure out their getaway months beforehand. He's probably laughing at us up here now, too. That's the way they all do."

"The Federal government knows how to catch men like Sam Billings," George said. "They can catch him if they start after him. But I don't suppose they would bother with him. We can send him to the State prison, though."

The men around the stove agreed with George. They said that if they ever got their hands on Sam they would do their best to have him sent to prison for as long a time as the law would allow.

A few days later George saw another of the selectmen and asked him about Sam Billings. George's plan of action was to get the Florida police to locate him and then have the sheriff send a deputy down to bring him back for trial. The selectman was in favor of getting Arthur Russell to have the Federal government go after Sam on the charge of taking his daughter Jenny out of the State. In that case, he explained to George, they could get Sam back without it costing the town any of its own money.

George was in favor of any plan just so long as Sam Billings was brought back and tried for stealing the money.

Later in the winter somebody told George that Sam had taken Jenny Russell and gone to Cuba with her. After that was generally known, there was nobody in the whole town who would take up for Sam or speak a word in his behalf. He had taken the town's money and made off with it. That was all there was to it.

"I never did take any stock in that Billings," George said in Clyde's store in the village. "He made so much money out of his hotel he couldn't be satisfied with what he had of his own, but had to go and take the town's money too. And if I was Arthur Russell I'd get the Federal law after him for taking Jenny off like he did. If she was my daughter and Sam Billings took her off to Florida for a good time, or wherever it was he went to, I'd get him arrested so quick it would scare the hide off his back."

"We made a big mistake when we trusted all the town's money to him," Clyde admitted. "It will take us ten years to wipe out that loss. He had almost a thousand dollars when he left."

"You were one of the fools that voted for him," George said. "It's a pity the voters ain't got more sense than they have about such things."

"If I remember correctly," Clyde retorted, "you nominated Sam Billings for town-treasurer."

George went outside and unhitched his horse. He drove home without answering Clyde Ballard.

Nothing further was heard either directly or indirectly from Sam during the remainder of the winter. There were no bills that had to be paid right away though, and the town was not yet suffering because the funds were in Sam's possession.

Early that spring, when Sam usually began getting his hotel into shape for the season that opened in June, everybody in town heard one day that he was back home. Sam Billings had been seen in the village early one morning hiring a crew of carpenters and laborers. He had always made repairs on his hotel property at the same time each year.

And Jenny Russell was back home too, and everybody knew about it the same day.

There was a crew of twenty men at work around the hotel Monday morning, getting it ready for the coming season. The boards were removed from the windows and doors, and a new boathouse was being built beside the landing-float in front of the hotel. All the unemployed men in town went to the hotel and applied for jobs, because everybody knew that Sam Billings paid good wages and settled promptly every Saturday night.

Sam went about his business just as he had always done each spring. No one told him of the things that had been said about him during the past winter, and he knew nothing about the charges that Clyde Ballard and George Williams and practically everybody else in town had talked about all winter.

George went to the village the first of the week and heard that Sam was back in town for the summer. He went into Clyde's store and sat down on the counter.

"Well, I guess the town's money is safe enough," he told Clyde. "Sam Billings is back home, and I hear that Jenny Russell is too."

"I heard over the party line last night that Sam bought a big hotel down in Florida last autumn," Clyde said. "He hired Jenny Russell to go down there with him to see that the chamber-maids kept it clean and orderly. Jenny Russell is a good worker, and I guess Sam figured that she was a better supervisor than he could get anywhere else. She keeps his hotel here clean and orderly all the time."

"Sure, Jenny is a good supervisor," said George. "There's no better worker anywhere than Jenny Russell. I used to think I'd hire her for my house-keeper, and maybe marry her some day. Sure, she is a fine supervisor. Sam Billings is a good business man and he knows the kind of help he needs for his two high-class hotels."

"There's no sense in worrying about the town's money," Clyde said. "Sam Billings is an honest man."

"Sure, Sam is. There never was a more honest man alive than Sam Billings. I've known Sam all my life. The town's money is just as safe with him as it would be in my own hands. Sam Billings is an honest man, Clyde."

from *Sing Peace to Cedar River*

WILLIAM CLARK

One of the hardest things to do in any small town is to escape a family reputation. That was the problem that Kenneth Gage faced. He was a hard worker and a born giver. By heritage, he had no right to be either one.

Prudence and Pearl Gage had proved that a Gage daughter, if caught early enough by a respectable husband, could be "un-Gaged" and so turned toward responsibility and virtue. But Kenneth started defying Gageness on his own hook when he was just a small boy.

Kenneth carried groceries. He helped people mow lawns. He washed milk cans for Deak Trembley.

These actions didn't indicate a desire to earn money. He was never rewarded with anything more than a cookie or a kind word. So Kenneth confused all the adults in town. They couldn't explain why a Gage would volunteer to work. Most of them figured there was something wrong with his head but a few credited him with having some ulterior motive that would eventually come out.

Actually, what Kenneth Gage had was an immense capacity for taking on himself the problems of other people. No one in Cedar River could believe this was a possible condition.

"A Gage is a Gage," said my Uncle Oscar. "Blood is blood. That's what I always say."

The men in the store assembly nodded, even though most of them believed that Oscar's blood wasn't blood at all but a solution of alcohol and red dye. They knew Oscar wasn't talking about his blood but about blood in general.

In the outside world, people can talk about genes. In the hill country the reference has always been to blood. The blood of every family line had specific character-forming ingredients.

This was a very handy belief to have. It excused weaknesses and it permitted a downgrading of accomplishment. If a man habitually let his fences deteriorate, it would be remembered that his grandfather was no great hand with fences either. Fence neglect was in the man's blood.

Ned Burns had the best corn in town, year after year, but no one had to go to the trouble of studying Ned's methods. Corn growing was in the Burns blood. No man could be upbraided for not being able to compete with what was in another man's blood.

This was such a comforting theory that children picked it up early. One of the young Nelsons tried to extend its acceptance to school, but he learned that there was a difference between folklore and academic credence.

He hadn't done his homework and he said, "I forgot, I'm absentminded. All the Nelsons are absentminded."

"That's interesting," said Mrs. Kelly. "Well, then we'll have to work hard, won't we, to see to it that you're the first Nelson that isn't."

She walloped him about five times and he decided that he could become a non-absentminded Nelson without any more work at all.

But when almost every adult in a town believes in the power of good blood and bad blood, a few defiers of the belief don't make much impression. So suspicion of Kenneth Gage's motives for helping people never did end.

"He's deep," said the men at the store. "He's got plans."

That attitude should have turned Kenneth into a challenger of his own humanitarian impulses. It didn't. He retained his concern. He kept trying to demonstrate it.

He was about 18 when he offered to help Ted Carter.

Ted was an old bachelor who lived out on the Big Brook road. He didn't have much except a garden patch, a pig, a woodlot, a horse, a cow, and a hayfield. He took sick one winter and he didn't seem to be able to gain strength through the spring and into the summer.

He came into town in mid-July, just when everyone was busy with this and that. He expressed his need for help.

"Can't pay much," he said, "but I can pay a little. Ain't looking for no charity. I got to get my hay cut and I never finished bringing out my wood before I commenced to feel poorly."

The men hesitated. If there had been drama involved, such as a sudden widowhood or a fire, they would have ganged up and helped. But this seemed more like the offer of a job and they didn't need jobs. They were all busy. They were inclined to stall.

Kenneth Gage, however, offered himself. "I'll help you out for a couple of weeks," he said, "and it won't cost you anything. I got a little time to spare. We're pretty well caught up at home."

Ted Carter thanked him, accepted his offer, and went home. That night, the men voiced their suspicions. They decided to act.

"No Gage helps a man for nothing," they said. "It ain't in his blood. Kenny is probably figuring on stealing half that wood and most of the hay. We'd ought to get over there and see that he doesn't. Any man should take time to keep decent citizens from being robbed."

So the next day, there were eight men and four horses in the Carter hayfield watching and helping Kenny. It took only three days to fill the barn. Then the men helped Kenny in the woods so they could be sure he didn't take any of the stump-piled firewood out the back way, to be added to Kenny's own winter supply.

There were so many scoot loaders and unloaders and fitters and pilers that they got in each other's way. They set up what was almost a conveyer belt from the woods to the stacks in the shed. Then, just to make sure that Kenneth wouldn't have any excuse to come back and maybe steal a few tools, they cleaned out the stable and the tie-up in good shape and spread the manure on the fallow land that would be next year's tillage.

When they left, Ted Carter said, "Thank God for my good neighbors."

Back in the store that evening, the men laughed and said, "We sure kept that Gage kid from getting away with anything."

Kenneth Gage ate supper with his sister Prudence and her husband, Tom Webster. Kenny said, "You know, those guys worked so hard that I didn't have a chance to help half as much as I meant to."

"Good solid bunch," agreed Tom. Then he shook his head at Prudence because he knew what he was sure she was going to say should not be said.

Cap't Bunker's Boy

STURGIS   HASKINS

He was different they said
    How could any boy grow up
And not lobster after school
    Or clam the weekend tides

Nobody asked the Bunker boy why
    Why he didn't fish or worm like the rest
Or why he chose the quiet beaches
    Not to work, but to walk alone

What thoughts harbored that Bunker boy
    Whose eyes looked down
Down at the earth and at his feet
    Down the bay, down the bay and away

Captain Bunker fished alone
    Kept his traps, gammed with boys his boy's age
And made no mention of a son, then or now
    It was always that way they say

Nobody said much about the Bunker boy
    A little different they thought of course
He didn't fish and that was enough
    To set a boy apart there

Nobody said much and one day he went away
    He went away to do things his way
He went away to do things his way
    And not to come back. And not to come back.

Step-Over Toe-Hold

SANFORD PHIPPEN

Even in mid-November when it was getting cold, I'd climb up the unpainted, broken-down shed stairs after supper with a flashlight to the shed chamber where I'd play for hours with my homemade television studio, so strong was the pull of my fantasy world. There I'd plan variety, dramatic, and panel shows directed by me; design miniature sets for my cardboard actors attired in their aluminum foil and crepe paper costumes. Using mostly cardboard, scotch tape, toothpicks, foil, wax paper, multi-colored index cards, cookie package dividers, bits of cloth and glass, I devised an elaborate multi-floored dollhouse. I even wrote scripts for the shows and made dressing rooms for my stars.

One night, as I was making my way across the shed, amidst cries from my mother from the adjoining pantry that it was too cold to play up there, I hesitated briefly before my father who was busy skinning out a deer he had just killed early in the hunting season. He had most of the fur coat skinned off and was cutting the meat and putting pieces of it in a big enamel pan on the floor beside him. Newspapers covered the floor. My father, as usual, had on his old baseball cap and a cigarette hanging out of his mouth. The deer, which was a pretty fair-sized buck, was hanging from a bolt on one of the middle beams across the shed ceiling. I had once tried to help my father skin out a deer, but it had made me sick to my stomach, and so he didn't ask me anymore. "Where ya going?" he asked. "Up to the shed chamber to play with dolls?"

I didn't answer him. I just went upstairs. Through the cracks in the floor I could see him hacking away at the deer; and because he was short of breath and always smoking, he'd cough and grunt. He had already suffered one mild heart attack and my mother was always worried about him. Finally, he'd holler up at me, "O.K., I'm going in now and I'm turning the light off. You come down now."

He'd give my mother the fresh meat to wrap up in aluminum foil and label and put in the freezer compartment of our old Gibson refrigerator while he and I would go into the living room and watch television. A great outdoorsman who loved fishing and hunting, my father never liked team sports; and even when my older brother and I were on teams in school, he'd never go to see us play. But he did like watching boxing and wrestling matches on television. In the mid-Fifties, there were boxing matches on Wednesday and Friday nights and wrestling bouts on all the time. Two men beating each other around a ring made sense to my father. The Wednesday night matches were sponsored by Gillette. I'd go off to bed with their jingle of "Look sharp! Feel sharp! Be sharp!" ringing in my head. After one fighter was declared the winner, my father would always say, in his dry, dead-pan voice, "What a man!"

The wrestling matches I enjoyed more than the boxing exhibitions, because I enjoyed all the show biz and dress-up that went with them. Gorgeous George was like Liberace as a wrestler and Ricki Starr wrestled in pink tights and ballet slippers. There were also crazy midgets and tough women wrestlers in spangled bathing suits. The melodrama, week after week, was, of course, unending. There was always a grudge match that would continue for weeks; the villains were ever-so dastardly and the heroes so clean-cut and full of fair play. My favorite at the time was the handsome blonde muscle man named Edouard Carpentier from Montreal who was billed as "The Flying Frenchman," because of the way he could execute back flips, drop kicks, and cartwheels mixed in with the more conventional takedowns, headlocks, and bearhugs. It was always very exciting when the "body beautiful" Frenchman tangled with the villainous Killer Kowalski, who would commit all manner of illegal atrocities against the handsome hero to the great boos and screams of the crowd. Kowalski's most punishing hold was the dreaded "claw hold," which, when applied to the other wrestler's stomach, was the end of the line for Kowalski's foe.

There were other wrestling terms, too, which were a part of the amusement: terms like "flying double arm wringer," "double hiproll," "flying head scissors," and every wrestler's specialty hold. It might be Kowalski's "claw hold" or someone else's "cobra clutch" or "congo butt" or "Italian pile driver." All of the wrestlers that we liked to watch in the '50's seemed to enjoy using airplane spins, flying dropkicks, and body scissors. And someone was always using the step-over toe-hold, a very ineffectual-looking hold, but one which was supposed to give some authority and power over an opponent. At least it held an opponent at bay until the wrestlers could think of what else to do before it was time for one or the other to win the pin.

My father also loved watching William Bendix of "The Life of Riley" and Jackie Gleason and Art Carney in the "Honeymooners" skits. He'd sit there in his rocking chair in his pajamas, sipping on his Narragansett, and laughing his head off as Gleason ranted and raved at his long-suffering wife played by Audrey Meadows. My mother hated Jackie Gleason.

When I was old enough, my father took me out in the backfield and showed me how to shoot with a rifle. When I was very little, he let me use a .22 and I would shoot at tin cans and bottles lined up on the neighbor's fence. One time I got to try his beloved .300 Savage, which literally knocked me on my rear end. The few times, however, that I went hunting with him, while I loved being in the November woods, I was scared to death, especially when the men would start drinking and then driving for a deer, racing and yelling through the woods with their loaded rifles. My father would shoot at anything. One time walking down a woods road he spotted a chipmunk and shot it. I was horrified and ran over to the bloody body. With his dying breath, the chipmunk bit me. "For Christ's sake, that'll teach ya!" my father said. "Now you'll probably get rabies or something." That same walk he shot at a loon out on the lake. The other male relatives and neighbors really respected my father's prowess with a hunting rifle. He always got his deer, and usually more than one. So, once in the woods, with an audience, it was like he had to show off. He really lived all of his life for November.

One of the last times I went hunting with him and his boss and other men friends I really embarrassed him. I got scared and hid under a log when there was a drive on; and he found me there crouching. He was disgusted, even though he never said anything.

In the hunting camp where my father would hole up for a week or two, he always seemed to play the role of cook, or "cookee," as he called it. "Cookee" was a term used on the old Maine Central steam boats that my father used to work on as a young man.

And there was fishing. My father had once caught one of the biggest bass ever recorded from East Grand Lake Stream. We had pictures of the beast all over the house and my father and uncles were always looking at the pictures and discussing the magnitude of the catch. Once, as a little fisher myself with a bamboo fishing rod, I wanted to impress the old man, so while he had gone off with his boss for an all-day fishing trip one summer day, I sat on the dock at the camp and caught about a dozen suckers, which I thought were pretty impressive-looking fish. I put them in a pail which I hid out back of the woodshed to show him when he got back. But, alas, by the time he returned, a couple of cats had discovered my cache and removed all of the suckers. Again, I had only an empty vessel to show him.

So I started taking piano lessons.

I was thirteen or so and I loved music. We had an old, untuned, upright piano with a couple of missing keys, and I wanted to know how to play it. So I talked my mother into letting me use some of my summer lawn-mowing money for the one dollar a week after school lesson. My father hated the idea and he hated my practicing. The schoolbus from Taunton Corner would drop me off at Taunton Junction, where my father worked for the Rudolph Keen Fuel Oil Company, and I would walk the mile or so down the hill, across the Taunton bridge, to West Hamlin and the big green house where Mrs. Scott, who reminded me of Loretta Young in both looks and mannerisms, would give me my lesson. Afterwards, I walked back across the bridge to the Fuel Oil Company, hung around while my father "cashed up" with Virginia, the long-time, old maid secretary and treasurer of the firm. Sometimes Virginia would give me little gifts if I had to wait for my father who was having an unexpected or late delivery. She once gave me a Planter's Peanut Coloring Book with Mr. Peanut cavorting about New York; and often she gave me money for a candy bar or a free Coke from the machine. When it was time for my father to go home, he let me sit up front with him with my red John Thompson music books while three of his greasy colleagues (everyone was greasy around the garage and trucks, of course) with their dinner pails would crowd into the back seat. There would always be a few humorous remarks about my music lessons, usually from my father. There I was embarrassing him again.

In the seventh grade, I announced one night at the supper table that I was going to become a writer. My father just looked across at me, his hair hanging in his face as usual, and said, "You'd better be a school-teacher or minister." That was a major insult since he was always saying how stupid teachers were and how ministers were either crooks or queers. In the eighth grade I announced I was going to college. My father greeted this by saying, "Ya better get that notion out of ya head. Only rich kids go to college. Unless ya haven't noticed it, we ain't rich."

All of my younger life, and even up through high school, I had very few new clothes to call my own. I always wore hand-me-downs from my brother, family friends, or the summer people. But in the ninth grade I did buy myself with my own money my first pair of new Levis, and upon seeing me in them, my father said, "Those pants are too tight about the crotch! Take 'em off!" Also, up until high school, my father gave me all of my haircuts on Sundays in our "kitchen barbershop." And he made sure he gave me a haircut, all right. When he finished with me, I looked like a skinned monkey. When I'd complain, he'd say, "Well, ya wanted a haircut, didn't ya?"

When I made the JV basketball team in high school, my father tried to talk me into quitting by telling me repeatedly that I'd "break something and be maimed for life." I think he just didn't want to have to come pick me up after practices. As a member of the cross country team, I'd often try to practice running, as I was supposed to, on the weekends; but my father made me stop. "Running down the road that way," he said, "the neighbors will think our house is on fire!"

One night I was holding the flashlight for him while he tried to fix the engine of our old 1951 Mercury. At one point, I moved the light a bit, and he yelled at me. "You think I'm stupid, don't ya?" I yelled back. "Yes, I think you're goddamn stupid if ya can't even hold a flashlight steady for five minutes," he said. I threw the flashlight down and ran into the house. Another time I swore at him at the kitchen table, and in an instant found myself on my back on the kitchen floor with my father on top of me, a cigarette dangling out of his mouth, and the ashes falling on my face. I was sixteen by then and around six feet, so I was shocked by my father's ability to take me down so fast and pin me so solidly. And I was surprised to realize how strong he was, how I couldn't move a muscle under him. "You're lucky I didn't give ya a goddamn super piledriver!" he said.

I'd watch him eat in the morning. He always made this oatmeal concoction with brown sugar, melted butter, the whole thing swimming in canned milk. At supper he loved to sop up the gravy with pieces of bread. He loved anything soggy, sweet, and fattening.

I helped him paint and shingle our house. I helped him with all the seasonal chores: banking the house with tarpaper and brush in the fall, taking the banking off in the spring, burning the backfield as soon as the snow was gone. I washed and waxed the car. As I got older, I gradually did all of the mowing, clipping and raking; and I helped both of my parents with their caretaking chores at two summer places on Taunton Point.

Once I accompanied him on one of his night fuel oil deliveries in the middle of the winter downeast to Cherryfield or Harrington or some place; and it seemed like we drove forever. Dad did sing a few of his tunes. He'd always sing the two lines or so that he knew over and over. One of them was, "I'm a poor little girl waiting for bread." He'd smoke his Camel cigarettes and keep asking me if I were too cold or too warm. He also drove that Texaco truck right in the middle of the road and at about twenty miles over the speed limit. He never drove all that fast when with Mom because she'd scream at him not to go over forty.

She'd also scream at him to cut his meat up into smaller pieces at supper and she'd scream at him when he'd come home every year drunk from his Texaco banquets.

I was thrilled to read after school one day a headline story on the front page of the Bangor *Daily News* about my father. Dad was a hero! COURAGEOUS TRUCK DRIVER STOPS BLAZE the headline read and the story went on to relate how my father had stopped a potentially explosive gasoline fire which had started at the Texaco fuel oil storage area in Bangor. When he came home that night, I congratulated him by saying, "Dad! You're a hero!" "Yeah," he said, "but you notice they forget to tell ya who started the fire." Then I noticed the ever-present cigarette dangling from his lips. "It's a wonder I didn't blow myself up," he said.

Spending a weekend home from college during my freshman year,

I was sitting across the living room from my father watching him reading a Rommel book with his W.T. Grant three dollar eyeglasses on when he looked at me and said, "Yes, I know. I'm a complete failure."

But he actually never failed to help me when I really needed help.

When the battery on my first car, a 1959 Ford Galaxie, which I bought the last semester of my senior year at the University of Maine, went flat the night before I was to start my student teaching in Bangor, he drove all the way to Orono after work to install a new battery in my car and make sure everything was going to go o.k. in the morning.

By the time I was in my mid-twenties, and Dad was nearing sixty, I realized that I didn't have much more time in which to try and become friends with him. I knew we would never be close pals, that he'd never hug me or say he loved me; but I did want him to look upon me at least once with some faint glimmer of approval.

From one of my first paychecks I sent him a ten dollar check for his birthday and it bounced. I sent him books: General MacArthur's *Reminiscences*, Truman Capote's *In Cold Blood* and other books I thought he'd enjoy and that we could talk about. Whenever I was home for occasional vacations, I'd try to get him to talk about his life working on the steamboats, working on the old lumber wharves over to Ellsworth, driving his trucks all over Maine.

One summer when I was home from my teaching job in New York, I got him to go with me for a beer and a boxing match in Ellsworth. The beer was good, and he seemed to be enjoying himself; but the boxing matches disgusted us both. The Job Corps then had an outlet in Bar Harbor and an Ellsworth boxing promoter, who also ran the movie theater, sold foundation garments, and served as the Boy Scout leader, arranged to have the Black and Puerto Rican Job Corps boys fight some Maine Indian boys in the old Grand Theatre before a predominantly white redneck audience. The promoter kept taking up a collection for the Jimmy Fund, and the boys pounded each other around the ring while the worst kind of racist comments were hurled back and forth. My father and I left early.

When he turned sixty-one, and had been holding down a regular job since he was thirteen, I asked my father about his plans. "I'm going to retire next year," he said, "and then drop dead the year after."

He sure knew how to call 'em.

We were sitting together two years later on the couch at my brother's place outside of Cape Kennedy in Florida right after Christmas 1969 when Dad suddenly said, when he and Mom were talking about visiting along the way back to Maine, "I'd like to drive up to Syracuse and see An-day's apartment and have a few beers with him."

Ah, the line I had been longing to hear all of my grown up life. My father actually wanting to do something with me in my world. I was thrilled.

But he never made it. That Christmas vacation was the last time I saw him alive. Shaking his hand just before I got into my brother's car to drive to the Orlando Airport to return to Syracuse, I sensed this was it. And so I stared back at him, standing there next to a palm tree, his hair in his face, the cigarette dangling from his lips, his hands in his pockets, his stomach hanging over his belt, unsmiling forever, as my mother beside him waved and waved goodbye.

He died of a heart attack a few days later, in a South Carolina motel on the way back to Downeast. My mother told me that he had cried uncontrollably the night before and that it had frightened her. The night that my brother called to tell me of our father's death, I did the same.

Of Small Towns

BARON WORMSER

It is not so much gossip that absorbs
Them as a fondness, to be found
Even in the children, for measuring lives:
The noting of how many years some wife
Has outlived her husband and how each of the road
Commissioner's four children quit high school
In the middle of the eleventh grade and how
It was twenty years to the day (they are
All addicted to anniversaries) that
A black spruce fell on a one-armed man.
Comparison is insistent—the father who
Is a better shot but not as good a card
Player as the son; the sister who
Writes poems while the other two clean house.
Here, people want to live to learn
Who the next President will be, how many
Games the World Series will go, whether
The trains will ever come back.
Ceremonious and dutiful to national symbols,
Too many of the sons die in the wars.
The coffins indicate that faraway
Places exist, that you can die quite forcibly
Elsewhere. Those who have hoisted themselves up
And fled will say that the finitude of
Small-town life breeds idiocy, that
The imagination turns upon itself, chews
Its substance over and over until it is worse
Than nothing. The surmises that the metropolis loves
To make, the crushes of people whose names you will
Never know, the expansive gestures made
Among incoherent buildings—all that is
Peculiarly urban and self-aware is lacking.

Instead you have a hodgepodge:
Legends hovering, dreams that lapse into
Manias, characters ransacked like cottages
In winter. Each random movement would become
An event. It is no surprise that every now
And then the attentiveness becomes too great
And some hamlet spawns a horror
Of the first degree. As is to be expected,
The *émancipé's* letters home are blunt:
"You are all like those vile canning jars,
Lidded and sealed and put away for endless winter."
And yet—it is these towns that dignify the slimmest
Of lives with a history, remembering even dogs
With an earnest pleasure, a rush of anecdote and regret.

RUTH MOORE

Sayl Comey went to school every day, but it seemed to him that things got worse instead of better. He couldn't get used to the routine, and he couldn't see any sense in what went on. In class he presented a face of bleak and absolute boredom.

Something in the sight of the big sullen fellow, sitting always on the end of his spine and the back of his neck, irritated the teachers extremely. No matter what they did to interest or amuse the class, Saylor Comey's face never changed. Miss Rayne, the English teacher, carried the battle to him the first week of school by sending him out of the room for not paying attention. Once she made him go back to the door and come in quietly because his big foot had upset a wastebasket—on purpose, Miss Rayne told herself. After that, the hatred between them was cordial and enduring.

Miss Rayne was young. Her first year out of college was rapidly proving to her that a woman's place should be in the home—as soon as she could manage it—and that no teaching job was going to take the place in her heart of being president of her sorority. She had wanted a little money of her own, and she had hoped to get through a year of teaching without being bored to death. But she had never guessed that a respectable job like this would bring her into contact with so much cheapness. And some of these kids certainly were cheap!

The freshman class was getting through the English period by reading aloud their assignment from *Macbeth*. *Macbeth* properly belonged to the juniors, but the textbooks of *Washington's Farewell Address* had not come in time for the opening of the term, and *Macbeth* was the only text on hand with enough copies to supply the whole class. Mr. Benson, the principal, had decided to start the freshmen in on it.

The class did not understand what some of the passages meant, but they felt they couldn't be blamed because, after all, *Macbeth* was junior English. Everybody found at once that there was a very good reason for turning up unprepared.

There came a day when Miss Rayne also turned up unprepared, and she did not know what some of the passages meant either. She had had a date the night before with a Coast Guard fellow, for the movies and a ride afterward in his car. When she had got home, she just had not had the energy to make out lesson plans or to read assignments and look up words. She had expected to get through the period by making the kids recite and by picking up enough information that way. She hadn't counted on nobody's knowing anything. Finally she gave up altogether and set the class to reading aloud.

"At least," she told them in an offended voice, "this will be *one* assignment you've read."

She certainly felt pretty vague today. Every once in a while her mind shied away from Shakespeare and went off on little tours of its own. George was so sweet. You had to look out for that kind of smooth, good-looking fellow, though. From far off she heard the stumbling voices hesitating over the far-off unaccustomed words.

The boy who was reading stopped suddenly. Miss Rayne's attention jerked back to the class.

"What does that passage mean, Mr. Comey?" she asked automatically.

Sayl mumbled. "Dun know."

"Please stand up, Mr. Comey, and address your comments to me, not your stomach. That's a perfectly simple passage ... if you know how to read."

The sarcasm and the tittering from the class which followed it made Sayl turn brick-red.

"Well, Mr. Comey?"

"Them three ole wimmen was cookin rotten guts in a kittle," Sayl said desperately.

The roar of laughter made Miss Rayne furious. *Macbeth* was great literature. She had read it in high school and someday she meant to sit down and read it right through again. She certainly wasn't going to listen to coarse talk about it, or anything else, not in her classroom.

"What do you mean by using language like that?" she demanded.

Sayl fell back upon the only weapon he had in situations like this, a kind of detached and supercilious silence.

"This is no place to show how ill-bred you are." Miss Rayne, getting red herself, was determined to prick him out of it this time. "You get up on your feet and apologize to me and to the class."

Sayl did not move.

"Do as I tell you, Mr. Comey."

In the pin-dropping silence the freshmen sat immovable and delighted that something interesting was at last happening in one of Miss Rayne's classes.

"Well, then, you can go up to Mr. Benson. Take him this note from me."

She sat down and wrote a sharp little message to the principal, informing him that Sayl had used disgusting language in class and had been disrespectful to her.

Sayl piled his books together and took the note. As he went out of the room he rolled his eyes at Haral and let one black eyebrow writhe upward into his tanned forehead.

Haral sniggered, and Miss Rayne fell upon him furiously.

"What are you laughing at, Mr. Turner?"

"Nothin."

"You think your friend Comey is very funny, don't you?"

The reminder of Sayl's interpretation of the three old women was too much for Haral. His repressed laughter burst out in a loud, spitting snort, and some of the other members of the class sniggered too.

"All right, Mr. Turner. Take your books and go up to see Mr. Benson. I'm sure you'll both find him very, very amusing." Miss Rayne looked over the class. "Anybody else care to go along?"

But the class looked back at her with blank, sober eyes.

Haral caught up with Sayl at the end of the long corridor.

"Teachers pet! Well, well!" commented Sayl.

They climbed the stairs to the principal's office on the second story of the building.

No one was there. Mr. Benson had a class and would not be back until the end of the period.

The bare, ugly little office held very little except Mr. Benson's desk, littered with papers and class books, his scabby varnished swivel chair, and a small bookcase crowded with dusty notebooks and a few texts. On the windowsill was a scrawny geranium growing in a pot.

"My God!" Sayl said. "Think of spendin your life cooped up in a place like this. No wonder they all look and act screwy!"

Now that Haral was in the same boat he was, Sayl felt better. The writhing embarrassment that had swept over him at being made a show of in front of the class was gone.

"That little mush-face dame has sure got it in for us," said Haral. "She's been lookin for a chance like this ever since school started."

"All she's got to do is wait," Sayl said grandly. "We'll fix her. Rayne, Rayne, gives me a pain." His eye fell on the geranium and he went over and lifted the pot scornfully off the windowsill. "Gawd, a plant in a pot! I bet he waters it every mornin and sets it in the sun, the big pansy!" An idea came to Sayl and a grin spread slowly over his face. "Watch the door, Haral, and le'me know if anyone's comin."

Under Haral's awestruck eyes he made water in the pot and set it back on the windowsill.

"Gee," he said. "She don't hold much. I got some to spare. What'll I do with it?"

"Out the window," said Haral in a kind of hoarse croak.

"What, waste it? Oh, no, my son." Sayl's roving eyes fell on the principal's neat hat hanging over his coat on a rack in the corner.

When Mr. Benson arrived at his office, Sayl was sitting in the extra chair by the desk and Haral was perched on the windowsill. Both were reading studiously in their English books and both looked very downcast indeed.

"What are you boys doing here?" the principal asked.

Sayl offered Miss Rayne's note.

"I see." Mr. Benson read the note and tossed it on his desk. "Bad language in class, eh? What about you?" he demanded, turning to Haral.

Haral looked up mournfully and Mr. Benson was gratified and surprised to see traces of tears on his cheeks.

"I ... I couldn't help laughin," he said with a hiccup.

"You think nasty talk is funny, eh?"

Haral shook his head and looked at the floor.

"You want to apologize to Miss Rayne, or quit school and clear out?"

"'Pologize," mumbled Haral.

"All right. Now, Comey, I've had my eye on you. You don't try, and you're ill-tempered. You boys who come in here from the islands, you think you can talk and act the way you're allowed to at home. Now, here in this school, we're civilized and we act like gentlemen. The quicker you learn that, the better." Mr. Benson had been striding up and down the little office, shaking his finger for emphasis. Now, as he turned he observed that his hat had fallen off the rack and lay upside down on the floor in the corner. He picked it up and hung it back over his coat with a sharp little *clap*.

Haral's Adam's apple clicked in his throat, and Sayl turned a little pale, but Mr. Benson merely went on with his lecture.

"Swearing in front of ladies is one thing that a real gentleman never does. The next slip out of you and you'll go back to Comey's Island, or whatever other foreign country you happen to come from."

Sayl's dead-pan face did not alter. When he had first come in, a going-over like this, especially the slur on his family, would have made him ready to fight. Now his one idea was to get out of here as quickly as possible.

"You fellows get back to Miss Rayne's room and apologize to her properly. And don't forget, the next time I'll take steps."

The boys went down the stairs, two at a time. In the cloakroom on the first floor they hid among the lockers and laughed until they were weak.

"He ... he ... never even noticed it," gasped Haral, rocking back and forth on the floor.

"Wait till he puts it on," said Sayl. "We hadn't better be around then, had we?"

"Gee, no. What'd we better do?"

"He can't prove nothin."

"No, but he'll guess who done it."

"You goin to 'pologize to old Rayne-in-the-face? By God, I ain't."

This was a new idea to Haral. "We got to, ain't we?" He had had in the back of his mind that they'd better go pretty soon and get this unpleasant job over.

"What you mean, *got* to?"

"We said we would."

"Sure. But what'll we say? Like's not, she'll make us do it in front of the class. Not me. Not after what ole Stinky-lid said about my family livin in a foreign country."

The descriptive nickname sent Haral off again into helpless squeaks of laughter.

Sayl himself grinned, but his mind was busy with the problem at hand. "Shut up, now, Haral, and listen. What d'you think your old man and Joe's goin to say when we tell em what he said about Comey's Island?"

Haral sobered. The insult to his home and his family appeared before him in clarity for the first time. "Why, the old skunk!" he said. "That makes me mad."

"It does me, too. I ain't goin to no school where they call my family a foreigner."

"Me neither. Le's go home and tell em. Darn if they won't be mad."

"S'pose they'll believe us?"

"Sure they will. Look, you stick that damn English book in your pocket so's we can show em how it started. By God, I looked up a lot of them words in the dictionary to see if I could make some sense of it, and I guess the' ain't very much difference between the way that feller writes and the way I talk. Only, with him you have to look it up in the dictionary," said Sayl.

They sneaked out of the cloakroom, down the stairs to the school basement, and crawled out a cellar window. By the time they had walked the half mile to the shore and had hunted up transportation to the island, they were afire with the injustice done them, and Mr. Benson's slurs on the people of Comey's Island burned in their minds with the flame of righteous and unpunishable justice.

That the man they found to take them over to the island was Perley Higgins was better luck than they had dared to hope for. Perley made a wonderful audience, and they poured the full story out to him in all detail, except the part about the flowerpot and the hat, which seemed not to have much bearing on the matter.

Perley was indignant. "Why, the domineerin old sudsbucket!" he growled. "We're jest as good people as he is, and if your folks don't go over'n tell him so, I'll go myself, by God. The' ain't a one of us over here on Comey's but what paid taxes to help maintain that high school, too.

You jest wait till I git a chance to talk to some a the Harbor fellers!"

Haral left Sayl at the cross-path that turned off toward Sayl's house, and continued on up the hill toward his own. His mind was so full of the story he had to tell his family that he did not notice Jap Comey's new fence until he walked almost into it.

The peeled spruce fence posts looked raw and yellow, and Jap and Eddy were just finishing stringing the last reel of barbed wire.

Eddy let out a yell. "Hey, look where you're goin!"

Haral backed up and stood looking at the fence, his mouth hanging open. "Well!" he said, at a complete loss. "Well!"

"And a couple a holes," mocked Eddy. "You Turners too dumb to know a good hint when you see one?"

"What's the matter with you?" said Haral. "Huh?"

"Huh?" mimicked Eddy. "Ain't they learnt you nothin but 'huh' over to the high school?"

"Shut up, Ed." Jap advanced on Haral, his dark lean face menacing. "This fence means I don't want your folks trampin acrost my land no more. After this, you got to go round it, see?"

"Oh!" said Haral. "Is that so?" He put a hand on one of the new posts and vaulted the fence. "So I heard a monkey say."

Jap started over the fence after him, but Haral ran at top speed up the path and banged in at the kitchen door. "Ma," he said breathlessly, "you see what they're doin? You see what Jap 'n Eddy's doin?"

Josie turned sharply from the breadboard, taking her hands, white with flour, out of the dough she was kneading. "Haral! For heav'n sakes, what you doin home in the middle of the week?"

"Ma," said Haral, "they're buildin a *fence* down there. Jap 'n Eddy—"

"My land, yes, I know it," Josie said. Her cheeks glowed red, making a dab of flour beside her nose stand out clearly. "Your father'll tend to them. What I want to know is, what you're doin to home *in the middle of the week?*"

Haral sat down in a chair by the door. The look he bent on his mother was concerned and serious. "Ma," he said, "Sayl and I, we just can't bring ourselves to stay at no school where they say such awful things about our folks."

"Haral!" Josie was scandalized. "What kind of a story you tryin to tell me? Have you got into a mess? If you have, don't you try to lie out of it!"

"I ain't! It's every word the truth! Mr. Benson said that we folks over on Comey's Island talked and acted nasty in our homes and that we never had no manners, and that we ain't no better'n foreigners, that's what he said! And I quit school and so's Sayl, and we ain't goin back, not to no place where they talk about our folks like that!"

Josie sat down weakly and stared at him.

"He ain't fit to be no schoolteacher, the lyin old fool!" Grammy leaped happily into the fray. "If he said that, your father'n Leonard better go right over there and beat the arse off him. Where's my money, Haral? You ain't goin to set foot inside this house till I git my money back!"

"You'll get it," said Haral. "I ain't goin back there and that's all!" He shot a quick glance at his mother and was instantly stricken to see that tears were rolling down her cheeks. "Aw..." he said. "Aw ..."

Heavy footsteps sounded on the porch and Joe Comey came in. Behind him was Sayl, scared and sobered.

"I come to hear Haral's side a this yarn," Joe said grimly. "What happened over there, Haral? What started it?"

Haral told the story from beginning to end, blessing the fore-thought that had made them bring home the English book.

"Look," he said, turning over the pages. "Here 't is. That line right there. Sayl and I both looked up the words. That one there, it means guts. Sayl never wanted to say what it meant, but Miss Rayne made him."

"Enteruls!" said Grammy, peering over his arm. "Of course it means guts. What's the matter with that woman? She a fool? You leave that book home, Haral. I want to read it."

"She sounds like one," said Josie, the light of battle in her eye. She had dried her tears, now that Haral's story was beginning to make sense to her decent and practical mind, and she was beginning to believe that he was not entirely to blame. "I want to go see them school people, Joe, before I make up my mind about this. It don't sound to me like they've done right."

"I do, too," said Joe, setting jaw. "I'll fix Benson."

"No," said Josie, thoughtfully. "I don't think you better, Joe. I think I and your mother had ought to go see him."

"Ma?" Joe stared at her. "She won't go. She don't like fights."

"It won't be a fight," said Josie. "My land, if it turns out to be a fight, Mr. Benson'd have a right to think we don't have any manners over here."

Joe grinned. "I guess you better see him, at that, Josie. My manners'd prob'ly be pretty lousy if it turns out he said what the kids said he did. We'll take you across in the boat tomorrow."

Gram lay in wait for Hardy that night and pounced on him as he came through the door.

"Haral's home," she announced with relish. "Been throwed out a school for talkin nasty. Now, Hardy, I want my money back."

"Haral?" said Hardy. "Home? What you talkin about, Marm? I paid you that seventy dollars back last Tuesday."

The debt to his mother, in fact, had been the first money that Hardy had paid out of his windfall.

Gram let out a howl. "You never! You ain't goin to cheat me out a my money, Hardy Turner, lyin and sayin you paid it! Haral's come home and he don't need it now, and you gi'me it!"

"You've forgot, Marm," said Hardy patiently. "Remember, you put up a fuss about it because it was all herrin scales? You look in your bag. You'll find it."

"It ain't. It ain't in my bag!" Gram scrabbled fiercely around in the contents of her knitting bag and suddenly subsided. "Well," she said, in an abused voice, "I paid you clean bills, and them you gi'me back has made my bag stink like a blubber barrel. Herrin scales! Pu!"

His mother could certainly put on a good show of failing faculties when she wanted to, Hardy thought. He suspected she hadn't forgotten about being paid. The point was, he had a little ahead now, and she was figuring that if she made enough fuss, he might pay her again just to keep her quiet.

He looked for the milk pail, but it was gone. Josie must be in the barn milking the cow. On the way through the shed, he met Haral, staggering under a double armload of stovewood.

Hardy said nothing, waiting until Haral had dumped his load in the woodbox and returned to the shed for another.

"Warn't expectin to see you," said Hardy.

"Well, no," said Haral brightly. "I warn't expectin to be here."

"How come you are?"

Haral broke into his story, which he told quite well now.

"That all that happened?"

"That's every single thing."

"Ain't lyin anywhere, are you?" asked Hardy, eyeing him.

"No, I ain't, Pa. That's just what happened."

"You lied pretty smooth, remember, about that fish oil."

"Ayeh. I know; but I ain't now. You can ask Benson himself, but maybe he wouldn't own up to sayin what he said." Haral looked away vaguely and began to shift his feet.

"Somebody'll have to go see Mr. Benson, you know," said Hardy.

"I know they will. Ma says she's goin." Haral began to load up another armful of wood. "I'd just as soon she would."

"Where is your mother?"

"Milkin, I guess," Haral mumbled. He cast a quick look over his shoulder at his father, but Hardy had turned away and was going on into the barn.

Josie had apparently finished milking, for the tie-up was closed for the night and the pail of milk, carefully covered, was sitting on the feed barrel. In the gloomy dusk of the barn at first he did not see her, but after a moment he made out her colored dress at the far corner by the window.

"What you doin, Josie?" he asked. "It's cold out here."

"Thinkin," she said.

"What of?" He put his big hands on her shoulders and for a moment she leaned against him. "He'll go back tomorrow, Josie."

Hardy stopped uncomfortably and stood motionless. Something was going on in Josie's mind that she was trying to find words for. He sensed a struggle, feeling the tense muscles of her shoulder under his hands.

"I'm not sure I want him to," she answered finally. "That was an awful cheap way for a man to talk, Hardy."

"Most like he was mad. You can't tell what them kids had been up to. A high-school teacher's got a lot to contend with."

"I don't doubt he was tired. The trouble is, Hardy, I ain't sure but what he said was so."

"Why ... no, it ain't, Josie."

"You know it is. I've tried to learn Haral and Mildred both their manners and to talk nice and to have sense about things. And Haral, he's wilder'n a hawk, and all he thinks about anythin is what's in it for him. And Mildred, she's a tomboy and she knows more about things she hadn't ought to than I do. I don't know what's goin to become of em, Hardy, I swear I don't."

Josie's shoulders trembled a little and Hardy dropped his hands from them in a panic. To have Josie upset by any situation shook him to his foundations. She was his refuge. He never had been, and had never thought of being, hers.

"It ain't nothin to worry about," he began. "They'll grow out of it."

"Hardy, this island ain't a good place to bring up kids. I don't know what's got into people to change em so. Look at em, backbitin and fightin with each other and gossipin, till you don't know but your best friend is your worst enemy. I've see it gettin worse and worse, and now the' ain't a one of my neighbors I'd dare to trust."

"I guess that's so." Hardy said. He moved uncertainly away from her in the darkness and sat down on a box. "But what can you do?"

"I guess you can't do anything," Josie said. "But I'm scairt for my kids, growin up dog eat dog like this."

"Leonard's all right."

"Yes, but Leonard ain't the man he could be if we lived somewheres else but here." She drew a long breath, whether of relief or sorrow he could not tell.

He sat puzzled and shaken, trying to think of something to say that would comfort her, make her be steady again.

"It's like potaters," she said suddenly. "You grow em too many years in one place and they come up scabby."

"You want to move away from here, Josie?" he asked slowly.

To his utter desolation she put her head down on her hands and cried. "No," she said, at length. "I don't, Hardy. I like this island. I'm to home here."

Josie dressed herself carefully for the trip to the Harbor the next day. She put on her best black dress and the black glass beads that had been her grandmother's. The hat that she had bought two years ago and had retrimmed twice was still in style and became her very well. When she was ready to go, she looked at herself steadily in the mirror. The neat woman who looked back at her was not Josie Turner, but the daughter of Captain Hosea Scott, of Bellport and Boston.

She had been deeply troubled at the implications inherent in Haral's story. It couldn't be, she thought, that the people over at the Harbor looked down on the islanders as they looked down on foreigners. Of course, the boys might be lying, but their story had too many logical details to be entirely made up. At any rate, Josie meant to get to the bottom of it, and she would have to do it by herself. For, as Joe had said, Sarah Comey refused to go. In fact, she obviously thought it out of the question.

"It wouldn't help matters any," she said, with a chuckle, looking at Josie with her clear blue gaze, "if I was to go in the clothes I've got."

At the school Josie waited, sensibly, until Mr. Benson came back from his lunch, and she caught him just before he left his office for his first afternoon class. He was surprised, then pleasantly flattered, to see the nice-looking, well-dressed lady in his office.

"I know you're busy," she began, "and I won't keep you long. But my boy came home from school yesterday with a queer story, and I thought I'd like to get to the bottom of it. I'm Mrs. Hardy Turner."

For a moment Mr. Benson did not make the connection. Then his jaw dropped a little. "Are you——"

Josie nodded. "Haral Turner's mother. He don't want to come back to school. His reason is that you called the people over on Comey's Island foreigners, and said that we let our young ones talk nasty in our homes. It didn't seem to me likely that you said just that."

Mr. Benson turned quite red. "Well, I—" He looked up to find her steady eyes upon his. "I don't believe I remember quite what I did say. I was ... angry. The other boy's been hard to manage."

"I ain't got any doubt Haral has, too. But no worse'n other boys, Mr. Benson. He's had a decent bringin up."

"I'm sure he has."

"Then you didn't say what the boys said you did? I'd like to have the story straight. The people over on Comey's is pretty mad about it."

Mr. Benson was caught. He thought fast. Quite a few boys from outlying islands attended his school, and if this story got around it might make trouble for him with the schoolboard. He wanted to keep his job.

"Mrs. Turner, I think the boys repeated to you what they *thought* I meant. What I intended to say to them was that they were the representatives here of their village on the island, and if they acted badly, it reflected—er—on their people."

"I see." Josie got up quietly. "Well, thank you for explainin. They didn't understand it that way."

He opened the office door for her. "Good-by, and come in again if anything seems to go wrong."

"Good-by, Mr Benson."

He watched her straight back go out of sight down the stairs and then breathed a sigh of relief. Most irate mothers who came to him were not so easy to deal with. He had not been aware of the desecration of his potted plant and his hat, and thus had no telling weapon with which to meet her. He seldom looked at the plant, and the hat, by the time he had been ready to go home, had dried sufficiently to escape his notice.

Josie went out of the high school building and down the street toward the town landing. The little weasel, she thought. Now didn't he lie out of that some slick! I ain't a one to take a part in a kid's row, but I don't think I want a man like that to educate a boy of mine.

Thanks to the weir, she and Hardy had money ahead now. There was a good high school in Bellport, and she had some cousins there. Haral could board with Deborah Scott. She hadn't wanted to send him to her family unless she and Hardy could pay a respectable sum for his board.

The Reach

STEPHEN KING

"The Reach was wider in those days," Stella Flanders told her great-grandchildren in the last summer of her life, the summer before she began to see ghosts. The children looked at her with wide, silent eyes, and her son, Alden, turned from his seat on the porch where he was whittling. It was Sunday, and Alden wouldn't take his boat out on Sundays no matter how high the price of lobster was.

"What do you mean, Gram?" Tommy asked, but the old woman did not answer. She only sat in her rocker by the cold stove, her slippers bumping placidly on the floor.

Tommy asked his mother: "What does she mean?"

Lois only shook her head, smiled, and sent them out with pots to pick berries.

Stella thought: She's forgot. Or did she ever know?

The Reach had been wider in those days. If anyone knew it was so, that person was Stella Flanders. She had been born in 1884, she was the oldest resident of Goat Island, and she had never once in her life been to the mainland.

Do you love? This question had begun to plague her, and she did not even know what it meant.

Fall set in, a cold fall without the necessary rain to bring a really fine color to the trees, either on Goat or on Raccoon Head across the Reach. The wind blew long, cold notes that fall, and Stella felt each note resonate in her heart.

On November 19, when the first flurries came swirling down out of a sky the color of white chrome, Stella celebrated her birthday. Most of the village turned out. Hattie Stoddard came, whose mother had died of pleurisy in 1954 and whose father had been lost with the *Dancer* in 1941. Richard and Mary Dodge came, Richard moving slowly up the path on his cane, his arthritis riding him like an invisible passenger. Sarah Havelock came, of course; Sarah's mother Annabelle had been Stella's best friend. They had gone to the island school together, grades one to eight, and Annabelle had married Tommy Frane, who had pulled her hair in the fifth grade and made her cry, just as Stella had married Bill Flanders, who had once knocked all of her schoolbooks out of her arms and into the mud (but she had managed not to cry). Now both Annabelle and Tommy were gone and Sarah was the only one of their seven children still on the island. *Her* husband, George Havelock, who had been known to everyone as Big George, had died a nasty death over on the mainland in 1967, the year there was no fishing. An ax had slipped in Big George's hand, there had been blood—too much of it!—and an island funeral three days later. And when Sarah came in to Stella's party and cried, "Happy Birthday, Gram!" Stella hugged her tight and closed her eyes

(do you do you love?)

but she did not cry.

There was a tremendous birthday cake. Hattie had made it with her best friend, Vera Spruce. The assembled company bellowed out "Happy Birthday to You" in a combined voice that was loud enough to drown out the wind . . . for a little while, anyway. Even Alden sang, who in the normal course of events would sing only "Onward, Christian Soldiers" and the doxology in church and would mouth the words of all the rest with his head hunched and his big old jug ears just as red as tomatoes. There were ninety-five candles on Stella's cake, and even over the singing she heard the wind, although her hearing was not what it once had been.

She thought the wind was calling her name.

"I was not the only one," she would have told Lois's children if she could. "In my day there were many that lived and died on the island. There was no mail boat in those days; Bull Symes used to bring the mail when there was mail. There was no ferry, either. If you had business on the Head, your man took you in the lobster boat. So far as I know, there wasn't a flushing toilet on the island until 1946. 'Twas Bull's boy Harold that put in the first one the year after the heart attack carried Bull off while he was out dragging traps. I remember seeing them bring Bull home. I remember that they brought him up wrapped in a tarpaulin, and how one of his green boots poked out. I remember . . .

And they would say: "What, Gram? What do you remember?"

How would she answer them? Was there more?

On the first day of winter, a month or so after the birthday party, Stella opened the back door to get stovewood and discovered a dead sparrow on the back stoop. She bent down carefully, picked it up by one foot, and looked at it.

"Frozen," she announced, and something inside her spoke another word. It had been forty years since she had seen a frozen bird—1938. The year the Reach had frozen.

Shuddering, pulling her coat closer, she threw the dead sparrow in the old rusty incinerator as she went by it. The day was cold. The sky was a clear, deep blue. On the night of her birthday four inches of snow had fallen, had melted, and no more had come since then. "Got to come soon," Larry McKeen down at the Goat Island Store said sagely, as if daring winter to stay away.

Stella got to the woodpile, picked herself an armload and carried it back to the house. Her shadow, crisp and clean, followed her.

As she reached the back door, where the sparrow had fallen, Bill spoke to her—but the cancer had taken Bill twelve years before. "Stella," Bill said, and she saw his shadow fall beside her, longer but just as clear-cut, the shadow-bill of his shadow-cap twisted jauntily off to one side just as he had always worn it. Stella felt a scream lodged in her throat. It was too large to touch her lips.

"Stella," he said again, "when you comin across to the mainland? We'll get Norm Jolley's old Ford and go down to Bean's in Freeport just for a lark. What do you say?"

She wheeled, almost dropping her wood, and there was no one there. Just the dooryard sloping down to the hill, then the wild white grass, and beyond all, at the edge of everything, clear-cut and somehow magnified, the Reach . . . and the mainland beyond it.

"Gram, what's the Reach?" Lona might have asked . . . although she never had. And she would have given them the answer any fisherman knew by rote: a Reach is a body of water between two bodies of land, a body of water which is open at either end. The old lobsterman's joke went like this: know how to read y'compass when the fog comes, boys; between Jonesport and London there's a mighty long Reach.

"Reach is the water between the island and the mainland," she might have amplified, giving them molasses cookies and hot tea laced with sugar. "I know that much. I know it as well as my husband's name . . . and how he used to wear his hat."

"Gram?" Lona would say. "How come you never been across the Reach?"

"Honey," she would say, "I never saw any reason to go."

In January, two months after the birthday party, the Reach froze for the first time since 1938. The radio warned islanders and mainlanders alike not to trust the ice, but Stewie McClelland and Russell Bowie took Stewie's Bombardier Skiddoo out anyway after a long afternoon spent drinking Apple Zapple wine, and sure enough, the skiddoo went into the Reach. Stewie managed to crawl out (although he lost one foot to frostbite). The Reach took Russell Bowie and carried him away.

That January 25 there was a memorial service for Russell. Stella went on her son Alden's arm, and he mouthed the words to the hymns and boomed out the doxology in his great tuneless voice before the benediction. Stella sat afterward with Sarah Havelock and Hattie

Stoddard and Vera Spruce in the glow of the wood fire in the town-hall basement. A going-away party for Russell was being held, complete with Za-Rex punch and nice little cream-cheese sandwiches cut into triangles. The men, of course, kept wandering out back for a nip of something a bit stronger than Za-Rex. Russell Bowie's new widow sat red-eyed and stunned beside Ewell McCracken, the minister. She was seven months big with child—it would be her fifth—and Stella, half-dozing in the heat of the woodstove, thought: *She'll be crossing the Reach soon enough, I guess. She'll move to Freeport or Lewiston and go for a waitress, I guess.*

She looked around at Vera and Hattie, to see what the discussion was.

"No, I didn't hear," Hattie said. "What *did* Freddy say?"

They were talking about Freddy Dinsmore, the oldest man on the island (two years younger'n me, though, Stella thought with some satisfaction), who had sold out his store to Larry McKeen in 1960 and now lived on his retirement.

"Said he'd never seen such a winter," Vera said, taking out her knitting. "He says it is going to make people sick."

Sarah Havelock looked at Stella, and asked if Stella had ever seen such a winter. There had been no snow since that first little bit; the ground lay crisp and bare and brown. The day before, Stella had walked thirty paces into the back field, holding her right hand level at the height of her thigh, and the grass there had snapped in a neat row with a sound like breaking glass.

"No," Stella said. "The Reach froze in '38, but there was snow that year. Do you remember Bull Symes, Hattie?"

Hattie laughed. "I think I still have the black-and-blue he gave me on my sit-upon at the New Year's party in '53. He pinched me that hard. What about him?"

"Bull and my own man walked across to the mainland that year," Stella said. "That February of 1938. Strapped on snowshoes, walked across to Dorrit's Tavern on the Head, had them each a shot of whiskey, and walked back. They asked me to come along. They were like two little boys off to the sliding with a toboggan between them."

They were looking at her, touched by the wonder of it. Even Vera was looking at her wide-eyed, and Vera had surely heard the tale before. If you believed the stories, Bull and Vera had once played some house together, although it was hard, looking at Vera now, to believe she had ever been so young.

"And you didn't go?" Sarah asked, perhaps seeing the reach of the Reach in her mind's eye, so white it was almost blue in the heatless winter sunshine, the sparkle of the snow crystals, the mainland drawing closer, walking across, yes, walking across the ocean just like Jesus-out-of-the-boat, leaving the island for the one and only time in your life on *foot*—

"No," Stella said. Suddenly she wished she had brought her own knitting. "I didn't go with them."

"Why *not*?" Hattie asked, almost indignantly.

"It was washday," Stella almost snapped, and then Missy Bowie, Russell's widow, broke into loud, braying sobs. Stella looked over and there sat Bill Flanders in his red-and-black-checked jacket, hat cocked to one side, smoking a Herbert Tareyton with another tucked behind his ear for later. She felt her heart leap into her chest and choke between beats.

She made a noise, but just then a knot popped like a rifle shot in the stove, and neither of the other ladies heard.

"Poor *thing*," Sarah nearly cooed.

"Well shut of that good-for-nothing," Hattie grunted. She searched for the grim depth of the truth concerning the departed Russell Bowie and found it: "Little more than a tramp for pay, that man. She's well out of *that* two-hoss trace."

Stella barely heard these things. There sat Bill, close enough to the Reverend McCracken to have tweaked his nose if he so had a mind; he looked no more than forty, his eyes barely marked by the crow's feet that had later sunk so deep, wearing his flannel pants and his gum-rubber boots with the gray wool socks folded neatly down over the tops.

"We're waitin on you, Stel," he said. "You come on across and see the mainland. You won't need no snowshoes this year."

There he sat in the town-hall basement, big as Billy-be-damned, and then another knot exploded in the stove and he was gone. And the Reverend McCracken went on comforting Missy Bowie as if nothing had happened.

That night Vera called up Annie Phillips on the phone, and in the course of the conversation mentioned to Annie that Stella Flanders didn't look well, not at all well.

"Alden would have a scratch of a job getting her off-island if she took sick," Annie said. Annie liked Alden because her own son Toby had told her Alden would take nothing stronger than beer. Annie was strictly temperance, herself.

"Wouldn't get her off 'tall unless she was in a coma," Vera said, pronouncing the word in the downeast fashion: *comer*. "When Stella says 'Frog,' Alden jumps. Alden ain't but half-bright, you know. Stella pretty much runs him."

"Oh, ayuh?" Annie said.

Just then there was a metallic crackling sound on the line. Vera could hear Annie Phillips for a moment longer—not the words, just the sound of her voice going on behind the crackling—and then there was nothing. The wind had gusted up high and the phone lines had gone down, maybe into Godlin's Pond or maybe down by Barrow's Cove, where they went into the Reach sheathed in rubber. It was possible that they had gone down on the other side, on the Head . . . and some might even had said (only half-joking) that Russell Bowie had reached up a cold hand to snap the cable, just for the hell of it.

Not 700 feet away Stella Flanders lay under her puzzle-quilt and listened to the dubious music of Alden's snores in the other room. She listened to Alden so she wouldn't have to listen to the wind . . . but she heard the wind anyway, oh yes, coming across the frozen expanse of the Reach, a mile and a half of water that was now overplated with ice, ice with lobsters down below, and groupers, and perhaps the twisting, dancing body of Russell Bowie, who used to come each April with his old Rogers rototiller and turn her garden.

Who'll turn the earth this April? she wondered as she lay cold and curled under her puzzle-quilt. And as a dream in a dream, her voice answered her voice: *Do you love?* The wind gusted, rattling the storm window. It seemed that the storm window was talking to her, but she turned her face away from its words. And did not cry.

"But Gram," Lona would press (she never gave up, not that one, she was like her mom, and her grandmother before her), "you still haven't told why you never went across."

"Why, child, I have always had everything I wanted right here on Goat."

"But it's so small. We live in Portland. There's buses, Gram!"

"I see enough of what goes on in cities on the TV. I guess I'll stay where I am."

Hal was younger, but somehow more intuitive; he would not press her as his sister might, but his question would go closer to the heart of things: "You never wanted to go across, Gram? Never?"

And she would lean toward him, and take his small hands, and tell him how her mother and father had come to the island shortly after they were married, and how Bull Symes's grandfather had taken Stella's father as a 'prentice on his boat. She would tell him how her mother had conceived four times but one of her babies had miscarried and another had died a week after birth—she would have left the island if they could have saved it at the mainland hospital, but of course it was over before that was even thought of.

She would tell them that Bill had delivered Jane, their grandmother, but not that when it was over he had gone into the bathroom and first puked and then wept like a hysterical woman who had her monthlies p'ticularly bad. Jane, of course, had left the island at fourteen to go to high school; girls didn't get married at fourteen anymore, and when Stella saw her go off in the boat with Bradley Maxwell, whose job it had been to ferry the kids back and forth that month, she knew in her heart that Jane was gone for good, although she would come back for a while. She would tell them that Alden had come along ten years later, after they had given up, and as if to make up for his tardiness, here was Alden still, a lifelong bachelor, and in some ways Stella was grateful for that because Alden was not terribly bright and there are plenty of women willing to take advantage of a man with a slow brain and a good heart (although she would not tell the children that last, either).

She would say: "Louis and Margaret Godlin begat Stella Godlin, who became Stella Flanders; Bill and Stella Flanders begat Jane and Alden Flanders and Jane Flanders became Jane Wakefield; Richard and Jane Wakefield begat Lois Wakefield, who became Lois Perrault; David and Lois Perrault begat Lona and Hal. Those are your names, children: you are Godlin-Flanders-Wakefield-Perrault. Your blood is in the stone of this island, and I stay here because the mainland is too far to reach. Yes, I love; I have loved, anyway, or at least tried to love, but memory is so wide and so deep, and I cannot cross. Godlin-Flanders-Wakefield-Perrault..."

That was the coldest February since the National Weather Service began keeping records, and by the middle of the month the ice covering the Reach was safe. Snowmobiles buzzed and whined and sometimes turned over when they climbed the ice-heaves wrong. Children tried to skate, found the ice too bumpy to be any fun, and went back to Godlin's Pond on the far side of the hill, but not before little Justin McCracken, the minister's son, caught his skate in a fissure and broke his ankle. They took him over to the hospital on the mainland where a doctor who owned a Corvette told him, "Son, it's going to be as good as new."

Freddy Dinsmore died very suddenly just three days after Justin McCracken broke his ankle. He caught the flu late in January, would not have the doctor, told everyone it was "Just a cold from goin out to get the mail without m'scarf," took to his bed, and died before anyone could take him across to the mainland and hook him up to all those machines they have waiting for guys like Freddy. His son George, a tosspot of the first water even at the advanced age (for tosspots, anyway) of sixty-eight, found Freddy with a copy of the *Bangor Daily News* in one hand and his Remington, unloaded, near the other. Apparently he had been thinking of cleaning it just before he died. George Dinsmore went on a three-week toot, said toot financed by someone who knew that George would have his old dad's insurance money coming. Hattie Stoddard went around telling anyone who would listen that old George Dinsmore was a sin and a disgrace, no better than a tramp for pay.

There was a lot of flu around. The school closed for two weeks that February instead of the usual one because so many pupils were out sick. "No snow breeds germs," Sarah Havelock said.

Near the end of the month, just as people were beginning to look forward to the false comfort of March, Alden Flanders caught the flu himself. He walked around with it for nearly a week and then took to his bed with a fever of a hundred and one. Like Freddy, he refused to have the doctor, and Stella stewed and fretted and worried. Alden was not as old as Freddy, but that May he would turn sixty.

The snow came at last. Six inches on Valentine's Day, another six on the twentieth, and a foot in a good old norther on the leap, February 29. The snow lay white and strange between the cove and the mainland, like a sheep's meadow where there had been only gray and surging water at this time of year since time out of mind. Several people walked across to the mainland and back. No snowshoes were necessary this year because the snow had frozen to a firm, glittery crust. They might take a knock of whiskey, too, Stella thought, but they would not take it at Dorrit's. Dorrit's had burned down in 1958.

And she saw Bill all four times. Once he told her: "Y'ought to come soon, Stella. We'll go steppin. What do you say?"

She could say nothing. Her fist was crammed deep into her mouth.

"Everything I ever wanted or needed was here," she would tell them. "We had the radio and now we have the television, and that is all I want of the world beyond the Reach. I had my garden year in and year out. And lobster? Why, we always used to have a pot of lobster stew on the back of the stove and we used to take it off and put it behind the door in the pantry when the minister came calling so he wouldn't see we were eating 'poor man's soup.'

"I have seen good weather and bad, and if there were times when I wondered what it might be like to actually be in the Sears store instead of ordering from the catalogue, or to go into one of those Shaw's markets I see on TV instead of buying at the store here or sending Alden across for something special like a Christmas capon or an Easter ham . . . or if I ever wanted, just once, to stand on Congress Street in Portland and watch all the people in their cars and on the sidewalks, more people in a single look than there are on the whole island these days . . . if I ever wanted those things, then I wanted this more. I am not strange. I am not peculiar, or even very eccentric for a woman of my years. My mother sometimes used to say, 'All the difference in the world is between work and want,' and I believe that to my very soul. I believe it is better to plow deep than wide.

"This is my place, and I love it."

One day in middle March, with the sky as white and lowering as a loss of memory, Stella Flanders sat in her kitchen for the last time, laced up her boots over her skinny calves for the last time, and wrapped her bright red woolen scarf (a Christmas present from Hattie three Christmases past) around her neck for the last time. She wore a suit of Alden's long underwear under her dress. The waist of the drawers came up to just below the limp vestiges of her breasts, the shirt almost down to her knees.

Outside, the wind was picking up again, and the radio said there would be snow by afternoon. She put on her coat and her gloves. After a moment of debate, she put a pair of Alden's gloves on over her own. Alden had recovered from the flu, and this morning he and Harley Blood were over rehanging a storm door for Missy Bowie, who had had a girl. Stella had seen it, and the unfortunate little mite looked just like her father.

She stood at the window for a moment, looking out at the Reach, and Bill was there as she had suspected he might be, standing about halfway between the island and the Head, standing on the Reach just like Jesus-out-of-the-boat, beckoning to her, seeming to tell her by gesture that the time was late if she ever intended to step a foot on the mainland in this life.

"If it's what you want, Bill," she fretted in the silence. "God knows I don't."

But the wind spoke other words. She did want to. She wanted to have this adventure. It had been a painful winter for her—the arthritis which came and went irregularly was back with a vengeance, flaring the joints of her fingers and knees with red fire and blue ice. One of her eyes had gotten dim and blurry (and just the other day Sarah had mentioned—with some unease—that the firespot that had been there since Stella was sixty or so now seemed to be growing by leaps and bounds). Worst of all, the deep, griping pain in her stomach had returned, and two mornings before she had gotten up at five o'clock, worked her way along the exquisitely cold floor into the bathroom, and had spat a great wad of bright red blood into the toilet bowl. This morning there had been some more of it, foul-tasting stuff, coppery and shuddersome.

The stomach pain had come and gone over the last five years, sometimes better, sometimes worse, and she had known almost from the beginning that it must be cancer. It had taken her mother and father and her mother's father as well. None of them had lived past seventy, and so she supposed she had beat the tables those insurance fellows kept by a carpenter's yard.

"You eat like a horse," Alden told her, grinning, not long after the pains had begun and she had first observed the blood in her morning stool. "Don't you know that old fogies like you are supposed to be peckish?"

"Get on or I'll swat ye!" Stella had answered, raising a hand to her gray-haired son, who ducked, mock-cringed, and cried: "Don't, Ma! I take it back!"

Yes, she had eaten hearty, not because she wanted to, but because she believed (as many of her generation did), that if you fed the cancer it would leave you alone. And perhaps it worked, at least for a while; the blood in her stools came and went, and there were long periods when it wasn't there at all. Alden got used to her taking second helpings (and thirds, when the pain was particularly bad), but she never gained a pound.

Now it seemed the cancer had finally gotten around to what the froggies called the *pièce de résistance*.

She started out the door and saw Alden's hat, the one with the furlined ear flaps, hanging on one of the pegs in the entry. She put it on—the bill came all the way down to her shaggy salt-and-pepper eyebrows—and then looked around one last time to see if she had forgotten anything. The stove was low, and Alden had left the draw open too much again—she told him and told him, but that was one thing he was just never going to get straight.

"Alden, you'll burn an extra quarter-cord a winter when I am gone," she muttered, and opened the stove. She looked in and a tight, dismayed gasp escaped her. She slammed the door shut and adjusted the draw with trembling fingers. For a moment—just a moment—she had seen her old friend Annabelle Frane in the coals. It was her face to the life, even down to the mole on her cheek.

And had Annabelle winked at her?

She thought of leaving Alden a note to explain where she had gone, but she thought perhaps Alden would understand, in his own slow way.

Still writing notes in her head—*Since the first day of winter I have been seeing your father and he says dying isn't so bad; at least I think that's it*—Stella stepped out into the white day.

The wind shook her and she had to reset Alden's cap on her head before the wind could steal it for a joke and cartwheel it away. The cold seemed to find every chink in her clothing and twist into her; damp March cold with wet snow on its mind.

She set off down the hill toward the cove, being careful to walk on the cinders and clinkers that George Dinsmore had spread. Once George had gotten a job driving plow for the town of Raccoon Head, but during the big blow of '77 he had gotten smashed on rye whiskey and had driven the plow smack through not one, not two, but three power poles. There had been no lights over the Head for five days. Stella remembered now how strange it had been, looking across the Reach and seeing only blackness. A body got used to seeing that brave little nestle of lights. Now George worked on the island, and since there was no plow, he didn't get into much hurt.

As she passed Russell Bowie's house, she saw Missy, pale as milk, looking out at her. Stella waved, Missy waved back.

She would tell them this:
"On the island we always watched out for our own. When Gerd Henreid broke the blood vessel in his chest that time, we had covered-dish suppers one

whole summer to pay for his operation in Boston—and Gerd came back alive, thank God. When George Dinsmore ran down those power poles and the Hydro slapped a lien on his home, it was seen to that the Hydro had their money and George had enough of a job to keep him in cigarettes and booze . . . why not? He was good for nothing else when his workday was done, although when he was on the clock he would work like a dray-horse. That one time he got into trouble was because it was at night, and night was always George's drinking time. His father kept him fed, at least. Now Missy Bowie's alone with another baby. Maybe she'll stay here and take her welfare and ADC money here, and most likely it won't be enough, but she'll get the help she needs. Probably she'll go, but if she stays she'll not starve . . . and listen, Lona and Hal: if she stays, she may be able to keep something of this small world with the little Reach on one side and the big Reach on the other, something it would be too easy to lose hustling hash in Lewiston or donuts in Portland or drinks at the Nashville North in Bangor. And I am old enough not to beat around the bush about what that something might be: a way of being and a way of living—a feeling."

They had watched out for their own in other ways as well, but she would not tell them that. The children would not understand, nor would Lois and David, although Jane had known the truth. There was Norman and Ettie Wilson's baby that was born a mongoloid, its poor dear little feet turned in, its bald skull lumpy and cratered, its fingers webbed together as if it had dreamed too long and too deep while swimming that interior Reach; Reverend McCracken had come and baptized the baby, and a day later Mary Dodge came, who even at that time had midwived over a hundred babies, and Norman took Ettie down the hill to see Frank Child's new boat and although she could barely walk, Ettie went with no complaint, although she had stopped in the door to look back at Mary Dodge, who was sitting calmly by the idiot baby's crib and knitting. Mary had looked up at her and when their eyes met, Ettie burst into tears. "Come on," Norman had said, upset. "Come on, Ettie, come on." And when they came back an hour later the baby was dead, one of those crib-deaths, wasn't it merciful he didn't suffer. And many years before that, before the war, during the Depression, three little girls had been molested coming home from school, not badly molested, at least not where you could see the scar of the hurt, and they all told about a man who offered to show them a deck of cards he had with a different kind of dog on each one. He would show them this wonderful deck of cards, the man said, if the little girls would come into the bushes with him, and once in the bushes this man said, "But you have to touch this first." One of the little girls was Gert Symes, who would go on to be voted Maine's Teacher of the Year in 1978, for her work at Brunswick High. And Gert, then only five years old, told her father that the man had some fingers gone on one hand. One of the other little girls agreed that this was so. The third remembered nothing. Stella remembered Alden going out one thundery day that summer without telling her where he was going, although she asked. Watching from the window, she had seen Alden meet Bull Symes at the bottom of the path, and then Freddy Dinsmore had joined them and down at the cove she saw her own husband, whom she had sent out that morning just as usual, with his dinner pail under his arm. More men joined them, and when they finally moved off she counted just one under a dozen. The Reverend McCracken's predecessor had been among them. And that evening a fellow named Daniels was found at the foot of Slyder's Point, where the rocks poke out of the surf like the fangs of a dragon that drowned with its mouth open. This Daniels was a fellow Big George Havelock had hired to help him put new sills under his house and a new engine in his Model A truck. From New Hampshire he was, and he was a sweet-talker who had found other odd jobs to do when the work at the Havelocks' was done . . . and in church, he could carry a tune! Apparently, they said, Daniels had been walking up on top of Slyder's Point and had slipped, tumbling all the way to the bottom. His neck was broken and his head was bashed in. As he had no people that anyone knew of, he was buried on the island, and the Reverend McCracken's predecessor gave the graveyard eulogy, saying as how this Daniels had been a hard worker and a good help even though he was two fingers shy on his right hand. Then he read the benediction and the graveside group had gone back to the town-hall basement where they drank Za-Rex punch and ate cream-cheese sandwiches, and Stella never asked her men where they had gone on the day Daniels fell from the top of Slyder's Point.

"Children," she would tell them, "we always watched out for our own. We had to, for the Reach was wider in those days and when the wind roared and the surf pounded and the dark came early, why, we felt very small—no more than dust motes in the mind of God. So it was natural for us to join hands, one with the other.

"We joined hands, children, and if there were times when we wondered what it was all for, or if there was ary such a thing as love at all, it was only because we had heard the wind and the waters on long winter nights, and we were afraid.

"No, I've never felt I needed to leave the island. My life was here. The Reach was wider in those days."

Stella reached the cove. She looked right and left, the wind blowing her dress out behind her like a flag. If anyone had been there she would have walked further down and taken her chance on the tumbled rocks, although they were glazed with ice. But no one was there and she walked out along the pier, past the old Symes boathouse. She reached the end and stood there for a moment, head held up, the wind blowing past the padded flaps of Alden's hat in a muffled flood.

Bill was out there, beckoning. Beyond him, beyond the Reach, she could see the Congo Church over there on the Head, its spire almost invisible against the white sky.

Grunting, she sat down on the end of the pier and then stepped onto the snow crust below. Her boots sank a little; not much. She set Alden's cap again—how the wind wanted to tear it off!—and began to walk toward Bill. She thought once that she would look back, but she did not.

She didn't believe her heart could stand that.

She walked, her boots crunching into the crust, and listened to the faint thud and give of the ice. There was Bill, further back now but still beckoning. She coughed, spat blood onto the white snow that covered the ice. Now the Reach spread wide on either side and she could, for the first time in her life, read the "Stanton's Bait and Boat" sign over there without Alden's binoculars. She could see the cars passing to and from on the Head's main street and thought with real wonder: *They can go as far as they want . . . Portland . . . Boston . . . New York City. Imagine!* And she could almost do it, could almost imagine a road that simply rolled on and on, the boundaries of the world knocked wide.

A snowflake skirled past her eyes. Another. A third. Soon it was snowing lightly and she walked through a pleasant world of shifting bright white; she saw Raccoon Head through a gauzy curtain that sometimes almost cleared. She reached up to set Alden's cap again and snow puffed off the bill into her eyes. The wind twisted fresh snow up in filmy shapes, and in one of them she saw Carl Absersham, who had gone down with Hattie Stoddard's husband on the *Dancer*.

Soon, however, the brightness began to dull as the snow came harder. The Head's main street dimmed, dimmed, and at last was gone. For a time longer she could make out the cross atop the church, and then that faded out too, like a false dream. Last to go was that bright yellow-and-black sign reading "Stanton's Bait and Boat," where you could also get engine oil, flypaper, Italian sandwiches, and Budweiser to go.

Then Stella walked in a world that was totally without color, a gray-white dream of snow. *Just like Jesus-out-of-the-boat*, she thought, and at last she looked back but now the island was gone, too. She could see her tracks going back, losing definition until only the faint half-circles of her heels could be seen . . . and then nothing. Nothing at all.

She thought: *It's a whiteout. You got to be careful, Stella, or you'll never get to the mainland. You'll just walk around in a big circle until you're worn out and then you'll freeze to death out here.*

She remembered Bill telling her once that when you were lost in the woods, you had to pretend that the leg which was on the same side of your body as your smart hand was lame. Otherwise that smart leg would begin to lead you and you'd walk in a circle and not even realize it until you came around to your backtrail again. Stella didn't believe she could afford to have that happen to her. Snow today, tonight, and tomorrow, the radio had said, and in a whiteout such as this, she would not even know if she came around to her backtrail, for the wind and the fresh snow would erase it long before she could return it.

Her hands were leaving her in spite of the two pairs of gloves she wore, and her feet had been gone for some time. In a way, this was almost a relief. The numbness at least shut the mouth of her clamoring arthritis.

Stella began to limp now, making her left leg work harder. The arthritis in her knees had not gone to sleep, and soon they were screaming at her. Her white hair flew out behind her. Her lips had drawn back from her teeth (she still had her own, all save four) and she looked straight ahead, waiting for that yellow-and-black sign to materialize out of the flying whiteness.

It did not happen.

Sometime later, she noticed that the day's bright whiteness had begun to dull to a more uniform gray. The snow fell heavier and thicker than ever. Her feet were still planted on the crust but now she was walking through five inches of fresh snow. She looked at her watch, but it had stopped. Stella realized she must have forgotten to wind it that morning for the first time in twenty or thirty years. Or had it just stopped for good? It had been her mother's and she had sent it with Alden twice to the Head, where Mr. Dostie had first marveled over it and then cleaned it. Her watch, at least, had been to the mainland.

She fell down for the first time some fifteen minutes after she began to notice the day's growing grayness. For a moment she remained on her hands and knees, thinking it would be so easy just to stay here, to curl up and listen to the wind, and then the determination that had brought her through so much reasserted itself and she got up, grimacing. She stood in the wind, looking straight ahead, willing her eyes to see . . . but they saw nothing.

Be dark soon.

Well, she had gone wrong. She had slipped off to one side or the other. Otherwise she would have reached the mainland by now. Yet she didn't believe she had gone so far wrong that she was walking parallel to the mainland or even back in the direction of Goat. An interior navigator in her head whispered that she had overcompensated and slipped off to the left. She believed she was still approaching the mainland but was now on a costly diagonal.

That navigator wanted her to turn right, but she would not do that. Instead she moved straight on again, but stopped the artificial limp. A spasm of coughing shook her, and she spat bright red into the snow.

Ten minutes later (the gray was now deep indeed, and she found herself in the weird twilight of a heavy snowstorm) she fell again, tried to get up, failed at first, and finally managed to gain her feet. She stood swaying in the snow, barely able to remain upright in the wind, waves of faintness rushing through her head, making her feel alternately heavy and light.

Perhaps not all the roaring she heard in her ears was the wind, but it surely was the wind that finally succeeded in prying Alden's hat from her head. She made a grab for it, but the wind danced it easily out of her reach and she saw it only for a moment, flipping gaily over and over into the darkening gray, a bright spot of orange. It struck the snow, rolled, rose again, was gone. Now her hair flew around her head freely.

"It's all right, Stella," Bill said. "You can wear mine."

She gasped and looked around in the white. Her gloved hands had gone instinctively to her bosom, and she felt sharp fingernails scratch at her heart.

She saw nothing but shifting membranes of snow—and then, moving out of that evening's gray throat, the wind screaming through it like the voice of a devil in a snowy tunnel, came her husband. He was at first only moving colors in the snow: red, black, dark green, lighter green; then these colors resolved themselves into a flannel jacket with a flapping collar, flannel pants, and green boots. He was holding his hat out to her in a gesture that appeared almost absurdly courtly, and his face was Bill's face, unmarked by the cancer that had taken him (had that been all she was afraid of? that a wasted shadow of her husband would come to her, a scrawny concentration-camp figure with the skin pulled taut and shiny over the cheekbones and the eyes sunken deep in the sockets?) and she felt a surge of relief.

"Bill? Is that really you?"

"Course."

"Bill," she said again, and took a glad step toward him. Her legs betrayed her and she thought she would fall, fall right through him— he was, after all, a ghost—but he caught her in arms as strong and as competent as those that had carried her over the threshold of the house that she had shared only with Alden in these latter years. He supported her, and a moment later she felt the cap pulled firmly onto her head.

"Is it really you?" she asked again, looking up into his face, at the crow's-feet around his eyes which hadn't sunk deep yet, at the spill of snow on the shoulders of his checked hunting jacket, at his lively brown hair.

"It's me," he said. "It's all of us."

He half-turned with her and she saw the others coming out of the snow that the wind drove across the Reach in the gathering darkness. A cry, half joy, half fear, came from her mouth as she saw Madeline Stoddard, Hattie's mother, in a blue dress that swung in the wind like a bell, and holding her hand was Hattie's dad, not a mouldering skeleton somewhere on the bottom with the *Dancer*, but whole and young. And there, behind those two—

"Annabelle!" she cried. "Annabelle Frane, is it you?"

It *was* Annabelle; even in this snowy gloom Stella recognized the yellow dress Annabelle had worn to Stella's own wedding, and as she struggled toward her dead friend, holding Bill's arm, she thought that she could smell roses.

"Annabelle!"

"We're almost there now, dear," Annabelle said, taking her other arm. The yellow dress, which had been considered Daring in its day (but, to Annabelle's credit and to everyone else's relief, not quite a Scandal), left her shoulders bare, but Annabelle did not seem to feel the cold. Her hair, a soft, dark auburn, blew long in the wind. "Only a little further."

She took Stella's other arm and they moved forward again. Other figures came out of the snowy night (for it *was* night now). Stella recognized many of them, but not all. Tommy Frane had joined Annabelle; Big George Havelock, who had died a dog's death in the woods, walked behind Bill; there was the fellow who had kept the lighthouse on the Head for most of twenty years and who used to come over to the island during the cribbage tournament Freddy Dinsmore held every February—Stella could almost but not quite remember his name. And there was Freddy himself! Walking off to one side of Freddy, by himself and looking bewildered, was Russell Bowie.

"Look, Stella," Bill said, and she saw black rising out of the gloom like the splintered prows of many ships. It was not ships, it was split and fissured rock. They had reached the Head. They had crossed the Reach.

She heard voices, but was not sure they actually spoke.

Take my hand, Stella—

(do you)

Take my hand, Bill—

(oh do you do you)

Annabelle . . . Freddy . . . Russell . . . John . . . Ettie . . . Frank . . . take my hand, take my hand . . . my hand . . .

(do you love)

"Will you take my hand, Stella?" a new voice asked.

She looked around and there was Bull Symes. He was smiling kindly at her and yet she felt a kind of terror in her at what was in his eyes and for a moment she drew away, clutching Bill's hand on her other side the tighter.

"Is it—"

"Time?" Bull asked. "Oh, ayuh, Stella, I guess so. But it don't hurt. At least, I never heard so. All that's before."

She burst into tears suddenly—all the tears she had never wept— and put her hand in Bull's hand. "Yes," she said, "yes I will, yes I did, yes I do."

They stood in a circle in the storm, the dead of Goat Island, and the wind screamed around them, driving its packet of snow, and some kind of song burst from her. It went up into the wind and the wind carried it away. They all sang then, as children will sing in their high, sweet voices as a summer evening draws down to summer night. They sang, and Stella felt herself going to them and with them, finally across the Reach. There was a bit of pain, but not much; losing her maidenhead had been worse. They stood in a circle in the night. The snow blew around them and they sang. They sang, and—

—and Alden could not tell David and Lois, but in the summer after Stella died, when the children came out for their annual two weeks, he told Lona and Hal. He told them that during the great storms of winter the wind seems to sing with almost human voices, and that sometimes it seemed to him he could almost make out the words: "Praise God from whom all blessings flow/Praise Him, ye creatures here below . . ."

But he did not tell them (imagine slow, unimaginative Alden Flanders saying such things aloud, even to the children!) that sometimes he would hear that sound and feel cold even by the stove, that he would put his whittling aside, or the trap he had meant to mend thinking that the wind sang in all the voices of those who were dead and gone . . . that they stood somewhere out on the Reach and sang as children do. He seemed to hear their voices and on these nights he sometimes slept and dreamed that he was singing the doxology, unseen and unheard, at his own funeral.

There are things that can never be told, and there are things, not exactly secret, that are not discussed. They had found Stella frozen to death on the mainland a day after the storm had blown itself out. She was sitting on a natural chair of rock about one hundred yards south of the Raccoon Head town limits, frozen just as neat as you please. The doctor who owned the Corvette said that he was frankly amazed. It would have been a walk of over four miles, and the autopsy required by law in the case of an unattended, unusual death had shown an advanced cancerous condition—in truth, the old woman had been riddled with it. Was Alden to tell David and Lois that the cap on her head had not been his? Larry McKeen had recognized that cap. So had John Bensohn. He had seen it in their eyes, and he supposed they had seen it in his. He had not lived long enough to forget his dead father's cap, the look of its bill or the places where the visor had been broken.

"These are things made for thinking on slowly," he would have told the children if he had known how. "Things to be thought on at length, while the hands do their work and the coffee sits in a solid china mug nearby. They are questions of Reach, maybe: do the dead sing? And do they love the living?

On the nights after Lona and Hal had gone back with their parents to the mainland in Al Curry's boat, the children standing astern and waving good-bye, Alden considered that question, and others, and the matter of his father's cap.

Do the dead sing? Do they love?

On these long nights alone, with his mother Stella Flanders at long last in her grave, it often seemed to Alden that they did both.

from *The Walk Down Main Street*

RUTH MOORE

Carlisle had been up at the gym all day, not so much helping as waiting around for Debby to get through. He had started out with the others, but the work of putting up the decorations for graduation was mostly on stepladders; fellows with two sound legs kept going ahead, past him, and doing it. Not that they were mean at all. It was always, "Oh, hey, Carl, let me do that," or "Hi, fella, get down before you fall down"; all nice and helpful. By lunchtime he was sulky and sick of the whole thing.

If they'd just pass it over, shut up; let him do what he could; but no, they had to keep bearing down.

A crip; a gimp; they thought they had to take care of him. So he took to hanging around on the outskirts of things, and they all, even Debby, seemed to take it for granted that he was better off out of the way.

He went over and leaned against the doorjamb, watching the noisy crowd down by the stage, where they were fixing lilacs around the American flag. Nobody missed him. He had to go down to the lavatory, sometime; that took effort, going up and down stairs; he might as well start now, be back to take Debby to lunch.

Every time you went out of or into the gym, you passed by the glass-enclosed cases where the basketball trophies were kept. There were quite a lot of small ones—area and regional awards—but only two big silver basketballs, the awards for the State Championships, 1948 and this year. Carlisle paused by the case. He often did, nowadays, when no one was around to kid him for looking in at his own photographs, or whatever they thought he might be doing.

Quite a few photographs had been set along the shelves among the trophies—group pictures of teams from way back when, shots of individual players, shots of the high spots in various games. Taken mostly by newspaper photographers, they were fine, clear, dramatic pictures. There was one that was a honey, of the monumental pile-up of Boone players and himself, on the night when he'd first hurt his knee.

"Look at that!" people had said, peering in at this photo. "Look at that! Isn't that awful, the way they tried to cripple him!"

Yare, Carlisle thought. They sure did. Did a better job than they knew.

Not at the time, though. Heck, at the time, he didn't know, himself, that he'd been hurt. Got rolling so fast that he didn't feel any pain.

If only he'd been able to get going like that in that last Boston game. If only he could have started to ramble.

If he'd just been able to reach out and lay hold of that light feeling he'd always had in a big game, as if his feet were off the floor and he was traveling on air, nothing could stop him; if he could have got back that terrific thing that happened to him in the Boone game. He'd been counting on that; and nothing.

Maybe the different kind of auditorium, the Boston Garden, so much bigger than he was used to, had something to do with it; or the cheering-section, which had been tremendous and all hostile, except for one pitiful little patch of home-town fans, a bug in a bottle, not making much noise.

He'd felt jerky from the beginning, feet heavy, wrists stiff. And his leg, from mid-calf to mid-thigh, where the novocaine had taken hold, had seemed to be not there at all. The others on the team felt just as wonky as he did; he could tell.

But mostly, the opposing team had been hotter than a pistol that night; maybe they were always hot, it seemed as if they might be. Their game was easy, slick, smooth, almost professional; and two of them, those colored fellows ... wow!

When the newspaper pictures came out, there'd been a hooraw around the town at home here—real-gone speeches down at the poolroom, centered around the insult to "our nice, clean, white, American boys." So on. A lot of crap. But it was all long gone. Nobody thought about it now, or if anyone did, all he remembered when he saw you gimping around, was that you'd lost their game for them, lost their money.

At first, the team had heard plenty about that. Every time one of them went anywhere, some joker made a crack, until they were all ready to fight.

If I'd stayed around town, hadn't had to go away to the Clinic before it all died down, Melly Hitchcock wouldn't have been the only one got a sock on the nose.

So now they all saw you, gimping around.

Oh, yare, got crippled up, playing ball.

The idea seemed to be that you'd been numb to let it happen.

Nobody cared what you thought now; or what you did, just so you stayed in the background, kept out of the way so people wouldn't have to look at you. Half the time, they just looked away when they saw you coming. So all right, so nobody gave a damn.

Ma, in Boston. When you'd think that the least she could do was worry some, what did she do? Tooted off all over town, bought new clothes. Made a fine use of the occasion to get herself married to Charles Kendall.

Oh, it was all right with him if she got married. Charles was a nice guy, had some dough. But it just went to show. A guy's whole life was shot to hell. What chance did he have now to be anything but a damn bum? So things went right along just the way they always had gone, nobody so much as turned his head.

Since he'd got back, he couldn't even get right with Debby. She seemed to think he could do different.

Do *something*, she said.

Didn't say much, but you could tell she was blaming you all the time.

Work, she said. Dig into the books, honey, we'll go to college together next fall, if only you'll try to catch up. College! Who wanted that egghead stuff, now?

So all right, let her stick up the damn lilacs around the picture of Abraham Lincoln, along with the guys who had two good legs and could climb a stepladder.

He stood leaning against the glass showcase, staring in.

No more ball. No more ball, forever. Because if his knee ever did heal so it wouldn't be stiff, what kind of condition could he keep himself in, how could he ever get back what he'd had? The only thing he'd had. So what else was there?

To hell with it. A bum. A goddam useless bum.

He heard a noise behind him, spun around.

What a cluck! Let someone catch him gawping in here at his own pictures!

He opened his mouth, getting ready to put in first, to let off a mouthful before whoever it was could start ribbing; but the fellow who had come into the building from the front door was nobody he'd ever seen before.

He was a tall, sloppy young man, in an old pair of khaki pants and a black leather windbreaker, slouching along, hands in his pockets, bareheaded, so that you could see how the hair had receded a little from his temples. A middle-aged guy. Thirty, anyway. He had a potbelly, and he wore a pair of old, beat-up, basketball shoes.

The fellow said nothing. He gave Carlisle a short, sidewise stare, and ranged alongside, looking in through the glass at the trophies in the case.

Carlisle turned and had started to move away, when the newcomer spoke.

"Well, well," he said softly. "Whaddya know!"

"What?" Carlisle said. "Did you say something?"

"Yare. I had a bet on, with myself. I lost."

"A bet?" On ball, that was nothing new.

The fellow said no more for a moment. He stood looking into the case. Then he went on.

"That was some game, you know it? So-ome game! Jesus, it was ten years back, and them pictures make it like it was last night. Look, that Charlesville forward—in about three seconds, he's going to stick out his foot and I'm going arse-over-bucket. Wonder what ever happened to him—God, I'd like to know if he lived to grow up before someone clobbered him for good."

He came to a stop, and stood looking.

"I bet they'd yank my pictures out of here, flush 'em down the john," he said. "They didn't, they left 'em in. Whaddya know?"

Carlisle came back. He looked at the fellow curiously. "Pictures?" he asked.

"Sure. Them photos, there. Those. That one."

He laid a finger on the glass, pointing.

"And drill my name off of that silver ball, by God," he said. "And there it still is. How about that?"

Carlisle stared at the photograph.

The tall boy. Snub nose, black wavy hair, brash, cocky tilt to his head. You-go-to-hell written all over him. About like anyone you knew of his age, only more so. Somebody you'd look at twice if he came up against you in a game. Arthur Grindle.

Holy old smoke, who would have known?

"Okay, you can quit looking," Grindle said, coldly. "It's me. You can tell it around town, so the women can lock their doors and keep the kids off the streets. Art Grindle. I just got home."

Carlisle turned red, aware that he had been caught staring, mouth open, jaw dropped. He swallowed with embarrassment, wondering what to say. What did you say to a man just out of jail?

"Oh," he managed feebly. "Well. Hi."

Grindle looked at him.

"Don't bust a gusset, kid," he said. "I didn't come in here to talk to you or anyone else."

He turned back, silently, to his contemplation of the trophies in the case.

Why, gee. Seems the first place the guy headed for, after all those years in jail, he came up here to see the basketball trophies, to find out if his photos and his name were still there.

"Hey," Grindle said, suddenly, looking at him and then back at Carlisle's own photographs. "You're McIntosh. Old Shirttail."

"Yare," Carlisle said. "Yare, I am."

"What's with the crutches? How'd you get hurt?"

"Bad knee."

"In a game?"

"Uh-huh."

"Was that what ailed you that last game in Boston? The Boone game, you was hotter than a pistol."

Carlisle stared. "How did you get to—" He stopped. The words "see it" died in his mouth.

Grindle shrugged. "They got all kinds luxuries down in the pokey," he said. "TV, newspapers, books, even a copy of *Mein Kampf* in the library. We watched the games. That Boone game, I got pretty excited. You went on a whingding, made some of the handsomest shots I ever saw. And then, down in Boston—"

"Don't tell me, let me guess. You'd never know I was the same guy."

Here it was for probably the thousandth time. Though this guy at least remembered the good game.

Grindle nodded. "An off-night," he said. "I knew it! The same as us, the year we went down. We got so hyped up to win the state that we went right up over the top and down the other side. Never could get back up there again. Us, we never even made the semi-finals, got clobbered the first game we played in Boston. An off-night. That how it was?"

"Yup."

"So ever since all you've heard is how lousy you were," Grindle said. "You heard how the referees were all on the other team's side; and how the rules out there are different, so no wonder you lost; but mostly, you were lousy, it was your fault, you couldn't play ball. That's what you heard in this town, when you got back."

"You forgot the two 'jigs,'" Carlisle said. "The ones they had on their team, 'so what was the matter, couldn't they find enough white boys?'"

Grindle said nothing. He stood looking in at his own photographs, his own name on the big silver ball of 1948.

"Ah-h-h," he said suddenly. "This goddam town! I'd like to see it burnt down. I'd like to see it hit with a hydrogen bomb, blow the crap to hell out of it." He swallowed as if he had a lump in his throat, as if it tasted bad and wouldn't go down. "They got the idea a hundred years back that they're the top, they're the best there is—made them, threw away the model. Nothing could happen to make them feel different, or that anybody else in the world amounts to anything; they're the end. Which end? I ask myself."

"What did you come back for then?" Carlisle asked.

Gee, this guy. The way he talked! Made you hot under the collar.

"Don't think I'm here to stay," Grindle said. "I wouldn't die here, for fear somebody might find me dead in this place. I had to come, my old man's died, and there's some crap about his estate—the few cents he had left he didn't spend trying to keep me out of jail. Oh, I could stay. Crawl around, take guff. Watch people go into a huddle every time I went by on the street, having it over about the jailbird, putting a rock on the top of the cookie can. Because that's all they got, cookie cans. Maybe after another ten years, if I didn't get out of line anywhere, I'd be a citizen in the town again. But, say I was? Say I got it all back, tomorrow? What's it worth, what they think? It ain't worth my time; or any man's time."

He swung around, flinging out a hand, thrusting his face forward. Carlisle got a whiff of his breath, foul with old whiskey smell and something else like garlic or onions; the bared strong teeth were yellow and two of the front ones were missing.

Grindle jerked a thumb at his crutches. "So you're lame," he said. "Give your all. Like me." He turned back to the showcase again. "When that picture was taken, my whole foot was numb. I still got a couple toes ain't right. But did I care? I still never wanted to do a thing but play ball."

"People always said you were good enough for the pros," Carlisle said, and stopped; because this, when you knew why Grindle had never gone to play ball with the pros, was the wrong thing to say.

"Do they, now?" Grindle said. "Why, God bless their little pointed heads! If you want to know, I wasn't, not in a million years. Geest, I beat myself out, the whole summer after I graduated. But the pros, they're college grads mostly, and all about seven feet tall. I wasn't tall enough, but if I could go to college, play on a college team for awhile, I figured I might get good enough. I couldn't pass exams for college on what I learnt in this joint, and they weren't so free with their scholarships then. So Pop said he'd send me a year to prep school. Hell, I never even knew enough for prep school, I couldn't read the damn textbooks. I got bounced out after half a term.

"So I come home," Grindle went on. "I hung around and played on the town team, but Pop wouldn't stand for me doing nothing, said I better enlist. Well, that was forty-nine and the War was over, some fun; but I figured the Army might have a ballteam I could get onto. So I was planning to leave the next day, and that night I had Pop's car and a date in Fairport, the last chance I had to say good-by to my girl. Only no gas. And no dough, because Pop was sore anyway over my using the car so much. Feller in the gas station wouldn't trust me, hell, he knew Pop was good for it, that was only his night for being a bastard. A few months back, this guy at the gas station, he would've *give* me the gas and a slap on the back, I could have had the cupola off the damned old Town Hall. So we lost a ballgame, so now I was a bum, couldn't even organize five gallons of gas. This guy, he give me the ripe old bull about what bums all us young kids was. So I blew. I out of the car and let him have it, knocked him to hell down. I was so mad I never stopped, I thought, Blast him, I'll get my tankful out of it, so I filled 'er up."

He glanced around, saw that Carlisle was listening, big-eyed, open-mouthed.

"I can see you're kind of taken with my tale," Grindle said.

"Yare. I socked a guy, too."

"Did you, now? Knock him down?"

"Uh-huh."

"Then the only difference between me and you is that your guy didn't kick off, ain't it the truth? I got into the car and drove over to Fairport, said good-by to my girl. Hell, I never even knew I was into anything. I never slugged the guy with a club, the way they said I did. Only my fist. He must've hit his head when he fell, because I just socked him on the nose. Just once. But the next morning, in the jail, somebody hands me a newspaper. There I was in the headlines. 'Youthful Thug Robs Gas Station, Kills Attendant,' it says. You know, they tried to shove me as far as they could see me go, but they couldn't make first degree stick, so I got manslaughter. I was a good boy in jail, settled down and learnt to be a first-class mechanic; for nine years."

"Oh," Carlisle said. "That's how it happened."

His mouth felt dry. He ran his tongue over his lips, trying to moisten them, thinking, What if Melly Hitchcock had banged his head? He could have, when he went down ...

"Well, that's my side of it," Grindle said. "I dunno why I bother to tell it to anybody here in this town. If you'll believe it, you're the first one ever did. About five hundred old bats come down on me like a ton of bricks, like they do on any kid steps out of line. Hell, when he's little, he's cute, he's a dear baby, nothing's too good. But let him get to be fourteen, he's an outlaw, a thug. All it is, he's trying to learn something, get the works of things through his head, but it makes a stranger out of him, even to his own folks. Everybody's scared to death of him, and the way they use him, well they may be."

Grindle shoved his hands into his pockets, shrugged himself deeper into his leather jacket. He stared into the glass case. "Old James Goss, he used to be the principal here, is he still around?—part of the crap he dished, culture, he said, it's what a man can get to make him different from the animals."

"He's still here," Carlisle said. "He's around."

"Be darned! Darned if I wouldn't like to see the old coot. We fought a running battle him and me for four years. Well, down there I read in the newspapers and magazines, them all yakking about you kids and the hell you raise, rock'n roll, it's a dance, so they call out the cops. It was the same kind of warmed-over old crud. Made me wonder if anybody over thirty, except Adolf Hitler, ever liked kids."

"Arthur Grindle," said James Goss's voice, unexpectedly, cordially, behind them. "I wondered if that might not be you."

He had come out of his office, noiselessly along the corridor, on his rubber soles.

"How are you?" he said, holding out his hand.

Grindle shook the hand. "Old Wheels," he said.

James smiled "That's right. I—har—believe they still call me that."

"Nosing in," Grindle said. "Just like old times. Turn around quick, who's behind you? Old Wheels."

James nodded. "One of the—har—unsavory aspects of my job," he said. "To be where not expected."

"How much did you hear this time? Enough to heave me out of the nice, new high-school building on my ear?"

"I never saw reason for that, Arthur. I might have been ready to, in the—har—old days. You were a problem. I haven't heard much—only your remark about Adolf Hitler. Which puzzled me."

"Why?" Grindle asked.

He grinned, not nicely, rocking back and forth on his heels, his chest out. "You was always crowding my tail to read," he went on. "Read, you said. Read, read, read."

"And you remember it."

"I remember it. I read, all right. Everything I could get my hands on. About the War. About Hitler. Some damned old do-gooder stuck a copy of his book in the jail liberry."

"And what did you make of *Mein Kampf*?" James asked.

"You can ask me. I never got through it, it was too tough. I still don't read good, I only read more. But I got enough to know. That guy, he had it made. Guys like me, kids, anybody didn't have any place, he give them all something to do made them feel they was somebody. I wish I'd been there. I'd have been his topkick. I'd sure like to hit into this town some dark night, with a bunch of them Black Shirts. I'd make it fit to live in. It's the only way you could."

"Arthur," James Goss said. "I know you. I suspect you have lain awake nights getting that speech ready to deliver here in this town, to me, to anyone you could find to listen. I congratulate you on your delivery; I think you may have learned some of it from me. If you had ever made as careful a preparation of any assignment for Public Speaking, I should have been a happy man. But your ideas are nonsense. I am not going to argue them. You know quite well what Hitler was; what happened to him."

"Pep talk. Tie a can to it."

"No, I will not! Hitler is in the past, thank God, so the verb you used should be 'gave,' not 'give.' And the nominative pronoun 'they' takes the plural. 'They were somebody.' Second: A man does not wait for, nor does he wish, to be given anything by anyone, and surely not by a megalomaniac dictator, for the sole purpose of creating a black disgrace upon history. A free man and a fighter finds his own place, his own job. He cannot become somebody unless he does it for himself. You are now free and you are a fighter as I—har—have reason to know.

Now you—tie a can to it. Do you need a job?

"Big words you still got. A job—in this town?"

"In any town."

"Look, I'm going so far away from here—I'm walking just once more down the Main Street of this town. To the bus."

"Can I do anything? A letter of recommendation?"

"I'm a mechanic. At least, they learnt me that down there."

"Taught," James said. "'They *taught* me that down there.' I'm sorry, Arthur. But culture is still—"

"—all a man has to make him different from the animals." Grindle lifted a hand. "I'll be going. So long, Mr. Goss."

"Good luck, Arthur," James said. "If you come back with your Black Shirts, I expect you won't find me hard to wipe out."

"Ah-h-h, no, Mr. Goss," Grindle said. He looked shocked. "Not you, Mr. Goss. Old poops like you don't do no harm."

He turned and went down the corridor, his feet making a slight shuffling sound on the hard tile floor. The revolving door swung behind him; the sloping shoulders in the battered jacket passed out of sight down the steps.

James stood in front of the glass case, looking in.

Carlisle had stepped back into the corner by the end of the case. Knowing that the sound of his crutches on the floor would call attention to him, he was embarrassed to go away. He waited, hoping Mr. Goss would just shut up and go back into his office.

But James stood there, looking in at the photograph of the snub-nosed, black-haired boy, with the basketball brashly poised on the palm of his hand.

"'I am a part of all that I have met,'" he said suddenly, softly, under his breath.

Horrified, Carlisle watched him fumble in his pocket, pull out a handkerchief, and wipe away tears which had begun to trickle down his cheeks.

Why, the old slob's crying! he thought, and one of his crutches slipped on the floor, with a rubbery sound.

James's gaze swept over him, blindly. "Har—"he said. "You see how the man of culture—har—produces in emergencies at least an apt quotation," and he turned away, walking with his forward motion on the balls of his feet, went into his office and closed the door.

Left alone, Carlisle stood by the trophy case; after a moment, he stepped in front of it and stood looking in.

That guy, Grindle, he thought. So he's what happened to the basketball star.

In the case, the black-haired boy met his eye. You-go-to-hell. So how are you any different?

Carlisle lifted a hand to him. "You and me both, bud," he said, under his breath.

Used us. Squeezed us dry and dumped the pieces.

If he had never been convinced before, he was now.

It wasn't anything we did. It was what was done to us. So you got jail, I got crutches. And who gives a good goddamn?

Mr. Flood's Party

EDWIN ARLINGTON ROBINSON

Old Eben Flood, climbing alone one night
Over the hill between the town below
And the forsaken upland hermitage
That held as much as he should ever know
On earth again of home, paused warily.
The road was his with not a native near;
And Eben, having leisure, said aloud,
For no man else in Tilbury Town to hear:

"Well, Mr. Flood, we have the harvest moon
Again, and we may not have many more;
The bird is on the wing, the poet says,
And you and I have said it here before.
Drink to the bird." He raised up to the light
The jug that he had gone so far to fill,
And answered huskily: "Well, Mr. Flood,
Since you propose it, I believe I will."

Alone, as if enduring to the end
A valiant armor of scarred hopes outworn,
He stood there in the middle of the road
Like Roland's ghost winding a silent horn.
Below him, in the town among the trees,
Where friends of other days had honored him,
A phantom salutation of the dead
Rang thinly till old Eben's eyes were dim.

Then, as a mother lays her sleeping child
Down tenderly, fearing it may awake,
He set the jug down slowly at his feet
With trembling care, knowing that most things break;
And only when assured that on firm earth

It stood, as the uncertain lives of men
Assuredly did not, he paced away,
And with his hand extended paused again:

"Well, Mr. Flood, we have not met like this
In a long time; and many a change has come
To both of us, I fear, since last it was
We had a drop together, Welcome home!"
Convivially returning with himself,
Again he raised the jug up to the light;
And with an acquiescent quaver said:
"Well, Mr. Flood, if you insist, I might.

"Only a very little, Mr. Flood—
For auld lang syne. No more sir; that will do."
So, for the time, apparently it did,
And Eben evidently thought so too;
For soon amid the silver loneliness
Of night he lifted up his voice and sang,
Secure, with only two moons listening,
Until the whole harmonious landscape rang—

"For auld lang syne." The weary throat gave out,
The last word wavered, and the song was done.
He raised again the jug regretfully
And shook his head, and was again alone.
There was not much that was ahead of him,
And there was nothing in the town below—
Where strangers would have shut the many doors
That many friends had opened long ago.

Not For Hire

EDWARD M. HOLMES

When Lew Medric, after years of wandering, searching for the right place in the country or in the city and never finding it, returned to the island of his childhood, he was fifty-nine, single, and—like many at the close of the Great Depression—very nearly penniless. He had tried living with his widowed sister ashore at Black Harbor, but she had burned his dungarees, had insisted he buy new ones, had growled about his pipe, and, most excruciating insult, had refused to eat his butchered pig.

"I like to get my pork," she said daintily, "from the butcher shop."

"How in hell do you think the butcher come by it?" he asked, and, without waiting for a silly or irrelevant answer, traded the pork, ham, bacon, and lard for a leaky dory, and rowed the four miles to the island, bringing with him a rifle, a bag of clothes and tools, a dog, a hen, and a tomcat. The day after he moved into the old house that had been his father's, the dog killed the hen and he shot the dog.

Although the island held a score of houses, widely separated, only his and ours were lived in. Kathy and I were concerned at first about his getting enough to eat, for in early April fish had not yet come inshore from deep water; but there was a dignity in the sharpness of his eyes, an independence in his carriage that forbade the offer of help. Like some other Yankees, he had much in common with the cat.

He ate gulls' eggs, clams, and mussels until there were fish. He dug clams to sell to the Black Harbor canning company at fifty cents a bushel. With the cash from twenty bushels a week he bought chewing tobacco, seed potatoes, fish lines, and hooks. He refused to accept credit, yet by June he had built and was hauling ten lobster traps, for which he had bought the laths, twine, nails, and buoy paint. He used second-hand warps left discarded on Black Harbor wharves by fishermen who hauled with power winches and could no longer trust old rope. He cut bows, sills, and hoops in the island woods. He combed the shore for lost buoys, wrecked traps, and lumber to repair the barn and house.

Late in the fall he stored on the bank twenty-five traps. He had seven bushels of potatoes and a keg of salted mackerel in the cellar, purchased grain in the barn, flour in the house, and ten hens and a rooster in the henhouse. A shotgun stood beside his rifle on the rack, and, lest there be any doubt, a sign hanging over the two read: THESE GUNS ARE LOADED.

His was no idyllic life; it was filled with long, lonely, tedious labor and sweat. Like others, he was the slave of his stomach, of the need for bodily warmth, but of no one, and of nothing else. That winter he cut a year's supply of wood (two month's work), set a few deadfalls for mink, built twenty more lobster traps, and in spite of freezing gales that cut through clothing like a lashed whip, dug in the clam flats.

Long since, of course, Kathy and I had become acquainted with our neighbor. He was always willing to do a favor, but would never ask one. (When Kathy was sick, it was Lew who rowed ashore to get help, fighting wind and ice for two hours to do it.) He would always pause in his work but seldom come to visit. He would accept a cake or home-baked bread, but always returned it in fish, clams, or eggs. He might give his labor, but it was not for hire.

When war shortages appeared, the life of towns in the form Lew disliked most came to see him: "He comes out here in a powerboat," Lew told me, "and he understands I got livestock. 'Let me see it,' he says.

"'Why should I let you see it? You act like you already owned it,' I said.

"'I'd like to buy some, live weight.'

"'Is that so?' I said, but he set there and talked anyway until finally I said: 'I will show you the pigs. I might sell a pig.'

"But he wouldn't offer enough for either one, and he didn't want no sheep, only lambs. Mistake I made was letting him get a sight of the cow. 'Ah-h,' he says, 'beef, that's what I'm after.'

"'She ain't for sale,' I said. So he looks her all over.

"'I'll give you a hundred dollars for that cow,' he says, all joyous.

"'You won't do no such a damn thing,' I said.

"'You never paid nothing like that for her,' he says.

"'That may be or it may not,' I says. 'What I paid ain't no business of yours.'

"He scratched his hair then like he couldn't drive out the bugs. 'You are a hard man to trade with,' he said.

"'I never asked for no trade,' I said.

"'Well,' he says, 'I will give you a hundred and twenty-five for her.'

"'She ain't for sale,' I said.

"'Do you mean to say that you—'

"'Where would I get me another cow?' I said.

"'Think of the money,' he says.

"'I already thought of it,' I told him, 'and I can't eat that: it ain't like milk, or eggs, or meat.'

"'Well, sir,' he says, all feathered out, 'there won't be nothing in it for me, nothing but the work that is, not a cent. I'll take her just to accommodate my customers, and I'll pay you a hundred and fifty dollars.'

"'She's not for sale,' I said. I thought he was going to blow up right there in the barn.

"'What will you take for her then?' he said.

"'Will you pay a hundred and seventy-five?' I asked him.

"'Yes,' he said.

"'She's not for sale. I just wanted to see how big a damned fool you were,' I said."

Three weeks later the cow was sick. It was Lew's judgment that any animal should be tolerable around a place and useful (at least to itself) or else dead. When he felt the cow was past recovery, without hesitation, without sentiment or apparent regret, he killed her and threw away the meat.

No one, of course, can completely avoid commerce, and Clyde Hamor, a Black Harbor fisherman, finally bought Lew's pig. He came to the island, looked at the pig, paid the price, and took away his purchase, but two days later he was back, suggesting a ten-dollar rebate. "When I butchered, he didn't weigh out as well as I thought," Hamor said.

"Is that so?"

There was a long silence.

Thoughtfully, Lew rubbed his thumb around the top edge of his boot. Then he went into the next chamber for the vacuum bottle and from it extracted the thin roll of savings. As a man might take the dried skin from an onion, he peeled a ten-dollar bill from the bunch. The rest were ones. "All right, providing you answer one question," he said. "Suppose you'd gone and found that pig weighed out a lot more than you thought, would you have come out here to pay me ten dollars extra?"

The two eyed each other like belligerent roosters.

"You know damned well you wouldn't. You'd have gone all over town bragging to every one what a good trade you'd made, and I know it. Now, take that cash and get out."

The bill fluttered from his hand to Hamor's feet. Taut-lipped, Hamor scuffed at the money with his boot and stamped out. It lay on the floor two days before Lew would pick it up.

But a trade did not always have to go like that. The winter he learned, casually, that I wanted to sell my sheep, he came to the house after dark, muffled in an archaic, mothy overcoat, and held out toward me his hand, doubled up. "Do you know what I've got here?"

I did not.

"Three sheep."

I held out my hand. "Pass them over." He dropped the bills into my palm and I shoved them crumpled and unexamined into my pocket. "They're yours," I said. He was pleased that I had not counted the money and sat down to talk. He had paid me, of course, the price I had asked and a little to boot.

That kind of trading was possible because we were neighbors and friendly, but distant businesses were frequently in for a going over, something like this:

Dear Mr. Clarke Davis:
I have tried your Hasso Dip you advertised so much, and you can have it. After one trial my sheep had more lice than they had to begin with. Tobacco juice works better . . .
Or:

Dear sir,   May 1, 1946
I paid for a brahma rooster and you sold me a damned capon. If he don't crow in another week I will chop his head off and throw him on the manure heap . . .

Dear sir,   May 10, 1946
You write me brahmers mature slow and I must be patient, but he don't crow yet. You say if I am not satisfied, you will send me the best rooster you have on the farm, only I must pay the express. When you sold me this rooster you said *he* was the best on the place. What the hell do I want with the second best?

His real scorn, however, was vented on an inflationary seller of shoats:

Dear sir,
I enclose two dollars more which you say you must have before you send the pigs I bought. Why the hell do you fellows to New York state care so much about a dollar one way or another? You say pigs is high this year, but you are wrong. Pigs is right where they was last year. It's your prices that's high.

L. Medric

After he had the headache, Kathy and I were understandably anxious about him. We had found him bending over his kitchen sink, blood coursing out of his nose as if from a tap. All three of us thought he would bleed to death, but after two hours it did stop. Kathy, performing what I looked upon as the impossible, persuaded him to lie down, rest, and be taken care of for a few hours.

He told us about the long, intense headache that had come first, about its suddenly stopping and the almost instantaneous rush of blood. He was under no illusions about his physical state. "One more shock," he told us, "and it wants to be a damned good one."

"You mustn't talk like that," Kathy said, but she couldn't help what a man thought, nor keep his eyes away from the gun rack, so when that calm spring morning came, and the gunshot, we should not have been surprised or frightened, yet we were. We ran toward his house, hoping we were wrong, hoping we were foolish, but the pile of dirt in the field was new and obvious. I told Kathy not to look but she did, turning away, white, while I retched and felt sick.

There is no beautiful way to do a thing like that, but at least this was precise, neat, complete. Every corner was square; the walls were plumb; the breadth and length, generous; and he lay at the bottom of it very straight, one hand still clutching the screwdriver that touched the trigger, the muzzle cradled beside him in his other arm.

"Like everything else he did," Kathy said.

I did not mind Kathy's crying; she had a right to weep. As we were walking away toward the shore and the boat, I looked back. His spade was standing up, defiantly, stuck high in the pile of dirt.

"If there had been any possible way to do it," I told her, "he would have shovelled in the earth."

Richard Cory

EDWIN ARLINGTON ROBINSON

Whenever Richard Cory went down town,
We people on the pavement looked at him:
He was a gentleman from sole to crown,
Clean favored, and imperially slim.

And he was always quietly arrayed,
And he was always human when he talked;
But still he fluttered pulses when he said,
"Good-morning," and he glittered when he walked.

And he was rich—yes, richer than a king—
And admirably schooled in every grace:
In fine, we thought that he was everything
To make us wish that we were in his place.

So on we worked, and waited for the light,
And went without the meat, and cursed the bread;
And Richard Cory, one calm summer night,
Went home and put a bullet through his head.

Summer Person

GLENNA JOHNSON SMITH

When Mrs. Ashley walks across a room
she leaves an almost-fragrance
so quickly blown away
it may be just a trick of memory,
a dream perfume.

      (White sheets blowing on a clothesline—
      the crumpled death of roses—)

Her tennis dress new-fallen on the bed
the saffron satin robe
shrugged off before her bath
hint the same bouquet.

The local high school girl,
lady's maid by summer,
breathes in the haunting message.
She longs to hold it
for a moment in her hands.

Eagerly and fearfully
while Mrs. Ashley's out to tea
the girl opens cut glass jars
to find the secret source.
But no bottle, tube or vial
contains the subtle essence.

The women of the village
smell of fried potatoes, onions,
Fels-Naptha soap and sometimes sweat
from scrubbing floors and making jam
in mid-July.

(Cashmere Bouquet and Coty's Talc
are saved for Saturday night.)

Perhaps only summer ladies
perspire sun and wind
and dying roses.

Island Girl

CATHARINE S. BAKER

This island hasn't got room for us any more. I saw it coming, and now it's here. They own the view, and the fact that we and our generations were here first is no more account than seagulls screaming. I'm not talking about the christly ferry lines, either. My family has always had boats and gone off the island when we wanted to. But now we can't go on the island. It don't belong to us no more. I'd like to burn those castles down, and their signs and fences. They will shame you in front of any passing dog, like you was one.

Take the other day—I was home by four because I skipped lunch, and I says to my daughter, "Tammy, let's take a hike up to the graveyard. I got this plastic arrangement for Gram's grave. It's nice out. Do you good."

"Naah. Karen said she'd call me. We might go up to the store."

I counted the petals on one of the yellow roses with the edge of my fingernail. I thought of several things I might say, any of which would have been an improvement on what I felt like saying. I rejected "She said that two days ago and you still ain't seen her." Also "Get off your fat butt before you need a block and tackle." I tried, "Hon, you look pale. There's a good breeze up there. When you're expecting, you have to take care of yourself." It sounded like something someone else would say, but oddly enough it worked. Probably just the sort of thing mothers say in those afternoon shows. She's gotten into those.

So we went, waddle waddle. She's wearing her brother Fred's old woods jacket and I've got my parka I used to get fir tips in. It's clear, bright and lonely. All the alder leaves have curled. They don't turn colors, just roll up brown like someone had started in making cigars and given it up as unprofitable. The smell of the fields is, well, bitter somehow. I know how a hayfield should smell, we made pretty fair hay when I was a kid, but these little meadows down here have all gone to rank weeds, redtop, asters, goldenrod, and dogbane. All you can say is it smells like fall.

The little birds that are in the fields in summer have gone. Someone forgot to tell the old hawk, though. Sharpshins, sharp eyes aglitter on the dead spruce at the end of our road. Tammy got spooked and threw a rock.

"Someone tell you hawks eat people? That's vultures, and they have to be dead. The people, I mean."

"I know, I know. He was giving me the evil eye. I do not need the evil eye on me. I need good luck charms," and she started singing this rock-and-roll song about the evil eye lady who has charms to sell. I've heard it.

"Well, for good luck you can't beat a double-ring rock. We should stop down to the beach. It's not far." God, it's like a million miles, back to when she and Fred would be down there hunting magic rocks. They would always manage to fight over one, many as there are on that stone beach. We made our way through the blackberry canes and alder trash. The path used to be a kid highway. Now the summer people have it all to themselves, with their Dobermans and their Private Property No Trespassing signs every six inches. They're gone now, though. All you'll meet is their donkey-man, guard dog Mallory, checking it out, and that's pretty rarely.

So we went down onto the beach, to the edge of the shingle, and hunted up a good rock. I love the feel of a beach pebble. When I first went over to work at the Mart, I always kept one in my apron pocket to rub and feel when I was getting lectured to by the French poodle there, Mrs. Collins of Customer Relations. It helped a good deal. I thought maybe Tammy could use one. She used to be the biggest collector of trash you ever saw. Doing her wash was life endangering, with the stuff in the pockets. You'd put your hand in and wish you hadn't. She was much worse that way than either of the boys.

She was poking and stooping, with grunts, when I heard a halloo. I stopped in my tracks, I didn't like the sound. I looked all around me to see where it had come from. Damned if someone wasn't yelling and waving from the porch of one of those new summer places that isn't a cottage but built where one was. Cars were in the drive. They hadn't gone home. They were staying down, might be living there if you can call that living—all so neat, no wash out, just walls of glass. They didn't want us in the view out their windows, I could tell. I decided to ignore the whole thing.

"Tammy, let's go up the beach a bit."

"Ma, who is that yelling? I didn't know anybody was still down here. Whoever it is, he's mad." She was right about that.

"Don't pay them any mind. We aren't hurting the beach any, walking on it." But she was nervous now, she gets self-conscious around strangers. You'd think it was the old days when a girl that was pregnant was never seen outdoors. I didn't want to shame her. So I kept walking, eyes sharp for a lucky stone, and she came along, muttering to herself.

But we wasn't fast enough. Damned if this old carcass doesn't come right down on us, down his seawall or whatever, even though we were well on our way and out of his.

"You people are on private property, are you aware of that?"

I wasn't going to answer someone who used that tone with me. I knew where I was, knew a hell of a lot more about it than he did. He thinks his beach is cast in bronze; I know how much it's moved and will move in the next storm. I kept going.

"This isn't a public right-of-way, if it ever was. This land is posted and belongs to the Association."

This land comes and goes of its own free will.

"If you people don't depart immediately the way you came, I will have to document this intrusion for my lawyer." I spun around then. It wasn't enough that he was running us off and Tammy was starting to cry because she was humiliated by it, but he was going to take pictures. I swear, there he was with a camera. I couldn't stand there for that.

I yelled at him, "You think because you have money that you own this. Well you don't. My people dug clams here and had clam feeds and beached their boats and spread their nets and made weirs and walked on this beach before your kind ever heard of this island. This don't belong to you or anyone else but the tide. And I'll leave the way I please."

He started coming closer, he had his camera up to his face, I could hear him taking pictures of me shouting, and Tammy trying to hide her face because she wished she'd never been born. I know I shouldn't have done it, but he was trying to trap me, he kept moving closer with no eyes but his camera like a mask, he wasn't human. I know I shouldn't have but I had that lucky rock and I threw it and hit that camera. I am a good hand chucking rocks. It broke something, I can tell. He ran and screamed for help. We hustled off the other way.

I had left my arrangement for the grave up in the alders; and I meant to go fetch it and get on my way. Tammy wasn't having any more. She wanted to go home. "I ain't coming out for a week. Ma, they are going to send the sheriff after you."

"Perhaps they are. It's all on film. Nothing to hide any more. I guess I'll just go on. They want us all in the kennel, come out for dog duty when they whistle—nice dog, come clean up this mess. Well, I'm fed up to the eyelashes. Let him drag the whole shebang and shingle into the courts. They say every dog can have its day. I guess I'll have mine before we're done."

I was talking to myself by now. Tammy was doing her best to hustle back up the road to home. She had got an airing, all right. I imagine she thinks I arranged it all to make her feel like a freak, and she has enough troubles. I went on up to the graveyard on the Head. There really is a good breeze there. The old folks liked a view, too. They don't have no objection to sharing it, though.

I set there awhile on the stone wall, looking down the lane all grown up with weeds. They only mow for the hearse to come through, which is often enough the way the old island people are dying off. The young have gone to the mainland for work, and then when they want to come back to live they can't afford the land they left. Pretty soon the whole place will be like that little old graveyard—fenced off, with little markers for where the people used to be. I get real cheerful after a spell of sitting up there.

I started down, thinking what I could do for Tammy to make her feel like she had a right to be walking around inside her skin. It doesn't help to have a loudmouth mother, not when your personal preference would be invisibility. She's always been that way, too. It's not being pregnant with no engagement ring; that's just the latest in a long string of disasters styled with her in mind, the way she sees it. She'll probably get in high gear now about going ashore to live with her father's sister, where no one knows her. That's the whole problem, though. They aren't the least interested in having her. She won't fit in with their life style, they said. She's just an island girl, doesn't know how to mix with people she didn't grow up with.

I scooted on home, crosslots through the pasture. They're schooling in the channel, all right, them sharks. I told Tammy later, getting supper, the island isn't big enough, even with the tide out all the way. But I will have my day, all right. I will show my face. Just you wait and see.

The Glow of Copper

CHRISTOPHER FAHY

A slash of light made Hattie Slocum pull over. She shifted to neutral, kept the engine running, and stared across the windblown field to the house.

She spit on her palm and rubbed at a greasy smear on the pickup's window. It didn't budge, so she rolled the window down. The glass wobbled and squeaked.

She was wearing Alfred's heavy shirt, and fastened the highest button against the cold. The shirt wasn't so good anymore. The black checks were black as ever, even blacker, but the white ones were yellow as an old dog's teeth. The bottom two buttons were gone, as well as the ones on the cuffs, and the wool was full of holes from those goddamn rats. She reached through the hole above the left pocket, felt around in her gray work shirt, and located a Chesterfield. She stuck the cigarette in her toothless gums, struck a match and lit up.

Last week of September, and already cold. She only had two cords of wood, that foolish Cubby—

There—on the edge of the eave—she saw it again: that shine, the glint of sun on metal. She squinted. New shingles. They'd put on a whole new roof—and had flashed it with copper!

The summer people had promised to live there year 'round, not just in season, and they'd kept their word, but look what they'd done to the place! Every time she went by—which was once every couple of months—things had changed. The summer before, they had torn out the bamboo, cut the puckerbrush, put in a big new kitchen window and painted the trim. In the fall, storm windows and doors had gone up, and spring brought skylights, a new electric service, new clapboard on the south....

And now the roof. Hattie had seen that roof done twice before in her life. Once when she was a girl, when Daddy and Uncle Van had done it with cedar shingles, and the time she and Alfred did it with asphalt—when? Right after Korea, wasn't it? It had to be, they were back from Bath Iron Works. My god, that long ago. It was due, all right: the open chamber had leaked some bad the last few years, and the ceiling was damn near wrecked.

The cold wind rippled the field, sending waves toward the house. Good Jesus, copper, Hattie thought. She and Alfred had flashed it with galvanized metal sheets from the printer, stuff he was throwing out. They used feedbags under the shingles instead of tarpaper, too. When you didn't have money, you learned to make do. She took a warm drag on her Chesterfield, thinking of Alfred. Ought to quit these filthy things, she thought, but doubted she ever would.

Buddy, her youngest, had asked: "Don't you want to go in and see what they done to the place? It must be tore up something wicked, they took eight dump trucks out of there." "No," Hattie had answered, "I want to remember it like it was.—Like when me and Oscar and me and your daddy lived there."

Just seeing that garden spot was hard enough, and god only knew what she'd find if she went inside. She and Alfred had grown enough food for a dozen people in that plot: squash and potatoes and turnips and carrots and cabbage enough to last all winter packed away in leaves down cellar—and now there was a big two-car garage standing right where the corn had been! It was built on damn good dirt, they used to shovel out the stable there. There were lots of flowers next to the house where the bamboo used to be, but these people didn't grow food. Didn't *have* to grow food.

The pickup wheezed and died. Hattie crushed out her cigarette and turned the key. The engine protested, sputtered, caught. She pumped the gas.

"Hi! How are *you*?"

Hattie jumped. Through the window she saw the rosy, square-jawed face she sometimes saw in dreams. How the hell had she let him sneak up like that, was she losing her mind? She forced a smile. "Well, hi! Pretty cool for September, ain't it?" She felt her pulse speed up.

"Frigid," the man said, blinking. He was wearing a brown felt hat, a sort of derby, and a thick red flannel shirt like they sold at Bean's. It looked brand new.

"Got your wood in?" Hattie asked.

The square-jawed man hesitated a second, then said, "All set."

"You heat with just wood or you use coal too?"

"Mostly wood—but we put in a furnace. See the chimney?"

Hattie looked at the house again. Two flues. She hadn't noticed that, her eyes must really be going. "Oh, that's good," she said.

"The way wood's escalated in price, you probably don't save much over oil these days."

"I guess that's true," Hattie said, thinking: True if you *buy* your wood. She remembered that time they ran out: she was sick all fall and Alfred was working in Bath and the kids hadn't cut enough for the kind of winter they had. It was gone by the middle of March, and the cold came down real hard. She burned cardboard boxes, she burned a chair, and then there was nothing left to burn and it dropped to zero inside. She walked up and down the road holding Buddy, the baby, in her arms, till the sun came up. Sick as she was, she walked for hours. It was the only way she could think of to keep Buddy warm.

The man—what the hell was his name?—said, "You have time to stop in?"

Hattie nudged the accelerator, shaking her head. "No, I gotta get home," she said. "Got tons to do around the place."

"Just for a minute?—Just to see how we've fixed things up."

The engine died again and Hattie thought *damn*. This truck had cost her half of the money these people had paid for her house, and now it was stalling out. In the silence she felt herself starting to sweat.

"Cackie hasn't seen you in ages," the man said. "She'd love you to visit."

Cackie. Catherine, her real name was, it was on the deed. Cackie was a foolish, rich woman's nickname. "I better get back," Hattie said, "my truck's actin' up. I better get Buddy to check it out."

"How *is* Buddy?" the man said brightly. "I saw him at Grossman's once, oh, maybe six months ago."

"He's fine," Hattie said, and wondered: Had they seen Buddy's name in the paper last week? Operating under the influence, driving to endanger ...

"Why here's Cackie now," the man said.

Good god, she was already halfway across the field. Tall, golden, sleek, and looking like she owned the whole damn world.

The hay was up to her waist. If Hattie still owned the house that hay would have been cut twice by now, but these people didn't have horses, didn't have animals at all, that's what Luke had said. The barn where her Sally and Toby had lived was used for storage now.

Shielding her eyes with her hand and smiling, Cackie came up to the truck. "Why Hattie, it's *so* good to see you," she said. "But I feel so *guilty*. We've been meaning to have you to dinner for over a *year*. *Impossible* to believe so much time has gone by. Can you join us for lunch?"

Hattie's work pants were splattered with dirt and grease. Straw stuck out of her sleeve. "No, I have to get home," she said.

"Steamed mussels," Cackie said. "Am I tempting you?"

Steamed mussels. Depression food, that's what they used to eat in the days of no money. "Sounds good," she said, "but I gotta go bank that trailer of mine. Won't be long before snow, by the feel of it."

"Well stop in for just a minute, then. You just *have* to see what we've done." She smiled again. "Come on."

Hattie protested again that she had to get back. But the next thing she knew she had opened the pickup's groaning door and was hunching out of the cab and limping along beside Cackie, who said, "We'll walk up the drive, it's easier than going through the field."

The drive had been scraped and leveled and topped with crushed stone. There hadn't been any sinking up to your hubcaps in mud *this* March. "We *love* this field," Cackie said. "In the spring it's just gorgeous, and even now, as dry and brown as it is, Fred and I both think it's *terribly* attractive."

Fred, that was his name, thank god the woman had mentioned it. "This field fed a lot of animals," Hattie said.

"I imagine it did," Fred said.

The sparkling white chips of stone crunched under Hattie's boots. Must've cost a goddamn arm and a leg to have this laid down, she thought. When she looked at the house again, she thought: it seems bigger, but why? The way the eaves were painted blue, that kind of blue they used in Camden and Wiscasset, maybe that was doing it.

"Do you like our new roof?" Cackie asked.

"Oh yes, it's *elegant.*"

Fred laughed. "I don't know if I'd go *that* far."

"I think the copper flashing really *is* elegant," Cackie said; and looking at Hattie, she added, "We love the glow of copper."

"So don't I," Hattie said, thinking: and the glow of gold ain't hard to take either.

Cackie frowned, but kept smiling. "We wondered why the old roof was done in three colors," she said. "We'd never seen anything quite like that before."

Hattie cackled. "Oh, that was my idea. I said to Alfred, 'We put on a roof that's red, white and green, nobody's ever gonna miss *our* place.'"

"Ah-ha," Fred said. "So that was it."

No, Hattie thought as she limped along, that *wasn't* it. They had bought Ralph Watkinson's leftover shingles cheap, *that* was it. They'd never had enough money to buy all one color.

The wind rolled through the hay again, and Hattie thought of Toby. Nicest horse in the world, that Toby, but he got the heaves. No money for the vet when he first took sick, and after he got the heaves he was finished. He was buried right next to the barn ... The barn! She laughed sharply and said, "Will you look at the barn!"

It was covered with cedar shingles. Hard to see from this far away, but they looked like selects—or first clears at the least. First clears or selects on a barn!

Fred said, "What a project. The whole south wall was rotted out, I had to have it totally rebuilt."

"Don't surprise me none," Hattie said. "It was gettin' some bad when I was here. That place was made out of secondhand lumber to start with, you know. Me and Alfred tore apart an old chicken coop up to Montville, hauled it down in a trailer and put up that barn. We lost get lightnin' rods. They say it never strikes the same place twice, but I don't believe it, do you?"

Cackie's smile was broad this time. "No, I don't," she said.

They had reached the house. It wasn't a long walk, really, but Hattie's bum hip—the one she broke at Star Rope nine years ago—was throbbing bad. She was sixty-eight, and thought as she caught her breath: it's better to live on the road at my age, not up a dirt drive. Especially in spring, if you can't afford gravel and have to park down at the end and hike in because of the mud. But she missed the place. She really did. When she looked around at all that these people had done, her heart ached.

They had torn out the bridal wreath by the door—the one that Suzie had planted when she was a kid—and the lilac that Daddy had planted. It looked funny without them, wrong. They had put in all different things—azaleas, it looked like, laurel, too, and that other plant with dark green leaves that the doctor had around his house, roto-some-thing. All the bamboo was gone. Well, good riddance to that. But of course it wasn't really good riddance, you never wiped out bamboo, no matter how smart or how rich you were. She could see a few of its dark red spears at the base of some laurel. Let it go for a couple of months and they'd have a jungle again.

The catwalk up to the front door was gone, replaced by brick. Not chimney brick—*new* brick. "I always wanted to do that," Hattie said, "get rid of them boards, but what looked like a little rock under there was a boulder! How'd you move it?"

Fred said, "Weldon Farris bulldozed it out. He's been such a help."

Hattie stared at the bricks and said, "Well, that's nice to hear."

She had lived next to Weldon Farris all her life. When times were rough after Oscar died—back when pulpwood sold so cheap that even if she sawed all day she couldn't make enough to pay her taxes and feed everybody too—Weldon hadn't offered to help. He hadn't offered to help because he wanted the town to take her house so he could buy it cheap. He didn't want the house, he wanted the land—the field and the well. He'd have torn the house down if he'd got it. But he didn't get it: she married Alfred, then the war came along and there was work. Thank god for World War II. Then three years ago when the house got so rundown she had to move into the trailer, Weldon made her an offer on it. She refused, although she couldn't pay her taxes, and the summer people had come along and she'd sold it to them for less. Weldon had always sucked up to summer people, so it seemed only right that he had them for neighbors now. Anyway, he was an atheist, and he deserved it.

"Shall we go inside?" Cackie said.

Hattie's stomach sank. She limped onto the granite step—they hadn't changed that, at least—and crossed the threshold.

She laughed, though she felt so turned around she was dizzy. The stairs were still in the same spot, right in front of her, but now they were covered with carpet. The bannister was gone, replaced by a wall and a modern railing. Her kitchen was now a dining room with a round oak table and six oak chairs; sun from the picture window fell in a brilliant bar at the foot of the table, right at the edge of the oriental rug. And the new kitchen—was in Daddy's room! They had torn down the wall and put the kitchen in there!

Feeling slightly sick, she said, "Don't that window look great. It's so *light* in here."

"Opening up that wall has made *such* a difference," Cackie said. "It lets in so much warmth in the winter months."

"Well I guess prob'ly!" Hattie said. "I always wanted to put in a window like that myself, bought a used one down to Eggle's in Owls Head, stuck it out behind the barn and before I could fix it a storm cracked a branch off the popple tree and smashed it to bits."

"What a shame," Fred said. "But we've found it doesn't pay to use old windows, you can't get them really tight."

"I guess that's true," Hattie said. She took a deep breath and said, "These the same old floors?" They used to be gouged and splintery, all the paint worn off. Now they were smooth and dark and glossy, with a prominent grain.

Cackie nodded. "We had Mr. Ransome sand and finish them. They came out quite well, don't you think?"

"Oh, *beautiful*," Hattie said.

She looked back at the kitchen, and her stomach contracted again. When the lightning killed Daddy she'd closed the door on his room and never let anyone use it for thirty years and now—the sink was right where Daddy's bed had been! She looked away—and noticed the beams overhead. "Well by god would you look at that!" she said. "I seen one of them once when I put up the celotex back in the fifties, but who ever thought they could turn out so nice?"

"Freddy's terribly clever," Cackie said. "Once we tore out that cardboard stuff—"

"The celotex?"

"Oh, is that what it's called? When we tore that out and exposed the beams, Fred instantly saw their potential. He hired some high school students to sand them down, then finished them with oil and turpentine."

"They look fine," Hattie said. "Real good." A huge refrigerator, new electric range, dishwasher ... "Well," she said, "I gotta go."

"Oh you have to see the rest of the place," Cackie said. "It'll only take a minute."

"This way," Fred said, turning back toward the stairs, and Hattie followed.

More polished floors, another oriental rug, more beams, huge sliding glass doors to a deck. The paintings on the wall had frames with little lights on top, like the paintings in that Farnsworth Museum that Clara had dragged her into.

"What did you use this area for?" Fred asked with a quizzical smile.

"This was the old kitchen," Hattie said. "—Before we drilled the well. When we got the well we tried to pipe the water in, but it froze 'cause there ain't no cellar under here. So we moved the kitchen to the other side, where it was when you bought the place, and turned this into the woodshed."

Cackie and Fred exchanged glances. "We insulated the crawlspace," Cackie said. "—With urethane."

Hattie nodded. What was this woman trying to tell her—that she was a fool? She had banked with hay—and the pipe had split—but hay was free.

"We blew cellulose into the walls, even though we tore them down and put up plasterboard," Cackie said. "Fiberglass batts are too labor-intensive."

Hattie figured that meant they were too much work. Summer people were sort of allergic to work.

Her head was swimming. She could hardly remember the way things used to be. Oscar had died here, right where the summer people's piano was standing now. She had wrapped his bad tooth in adhesive tape so the pliers wouldn't crack it up, but the damn thing shattered anyway, and what with him yelling and squirming around, she couldn't get all of it out. The pus went down into his lungs and my god he got hot, but Dr. Welsh said if they didn't pay up for Suzie's whooping cough he wouldn't come. The bedroom was freezing cold, so they'd moved Oscar into the kitchen, right next to the stove, but he'd died all the same.

"With the wall opened up, the view is superb," Cackie said. "So peaceful."

"Yeah," Hattie said, and her voice sounded distant and thin. She looked through the sliding glass doors at the spot that used to be her riding ring and a shock went through her. "My apple trees," she said.

Cackie tilted her head. "It was dreadful to have to cut them down," she said, "but they were right in the line of our view. Unfortunate."

"I guess," Hattie said.

Those trees had been Gravensteins, wonderful keepers, apples you couldn't buy in any store. For years they had been the only fruit they ate all winter, and now they were gone. She and Alfred planted them back when Buddy was just a baby, and Cubby fell out of one once and broke his wrist. They must have been thirty years old. Good trees like that, cut down for a view.

Fred led the way through the door that used to go out back. Now it led to a hall, a bedroom with a gigantic closet and a downstairs bath. The shower was fiberglass, and the sink—dark blue—was set in a tan formica vanity. "Blue," Hattie said. It just slipped out, she hadn't meant it to.

"Isn't that color delightful?" Cackie said.

Hattie hesitated. "Well," she said, "I always liked a white bathroom myself."

At the head of the stairs was another, larger, bath with another fiberglass tub and shower and a *yellow* sink. How dirty *were* these people, anyway? Hattie thought. She always sponged down once a week and took a real bath once a month in the kitchen tub. Who needed more than that?

A washer and dryer sat against one wall, and the dryer was going— on a windy, sunny day like this! There was something wrong about that. She nodded at the washing machine. "Them automatics ain't all they're cracked up to be," she said. "I'll stick with my wringer. I like to be able to wash my clothes for as long as I want."

Cackie smiled her maddening smile and said, "But you can do that with an automatic, too, you simply reset the timer."

Hattie felt herself blush. "Oh really?" she said. "I didn't know that."

The south bedroom had been transformed. She and all of her kids had been born in that room—all except Chuckie, that is, who had given her so much trouble. Hattie had always found if she stared at the dark brown stain where the chimney leaked, the pain didn't hurt so bad. Now the stain—the whole ceiling—was gone, and Hattie felt mad as hell, though she couldn't say why. After all, it was their house now. In the north bedroom she said, "You sure got a lot of closets. I only had that tiny one downstairs."

"I guess we're pretty thingy people," Fred said.

When she was carrying Chuckie she had that growth on her neck, and the bigger she got, the bigger the damn growth got. If she had it off her baby would be retarded, Dr. Lord told her, but letting it go would kill her for sure. So she had it off, of course—and Chuckie *was* retarded, just like Dr. Lord had said, even though she had him in the hospital.

Well, not *retarded* exactly, he just couldn't read real good, but boy could he drive a car! She figured the growth was punishment for fooling around with Harlow, but then again Suzie wasn't really Oscar's and she'd turned out fine, got half way through eleventh grade. God must've been looking the other way that time. Or maybe He only let you make one mistake.

Fred opened the door at the end of the hall. Hattie's heart felt thick.

The room looked twice as large as she remembered it, with a blue flowered print on the walls, two skylights, and wall-to-wall carpet, all white. "My god," she said.

"My study," Fred said.

"Why, who would've guessed ..." Her voice trailed off.

"Isn't it handsome?" Cackie said. "Fred loves the quiet here, and the light. What was it you used to call this room? You told us once."

"The open chamber," Hattie said.

Cackie nodded. "The open chamber. And what did you use it for?"

"Just storage," Hattie said—which was another lie. They'd kept a commode in here for when it got too cold and snowy to use the backhouse, and they'd hung the winter wash in here.

Through the window, the field shone and shook in the sun. In the bathroom, the dryer hummed.

As they went downstairs again, Cackie said, "It's certainly not a spacious house, but it's fine for just the two of us. Fixing the open chamber and building the new addition have helped a lot."

"I raised ten kids here," Hattie said.

"With your father's room closed off? And the open chamber used for storage? Amazing."

"We managed," Hattie said. At the foot of the steps she squinted at Cackie. "You people are gonna have kids, right? Didn't you tell me that?"

Cackie glanced at her husband, then smiled again. "We're not sure yet. Fred has his business, I have my photography ..."

"Yeah," Hattie said. When they'd come to her about buying the place, she had asked the same question and they'd told her, Yes, they were sure they would want to have children one of these days.

"And of course we have our cats," Cackie said.

"Of course," Hattie said, and thought: You call two animals having *cats?* She herself had sixteen cats, with more on the way.

They took her out back to show her the deck. The sheds where she'd kept her goats and pigs and tools had been torn down. And the blueberry field—had been plowed under! It was nothing but lawn! "The blueberries here, my god, we got quarts and quarts ..."

Cackie said, "From those tiny little plants?"

"Best berries on the peninsula," Hattie said. A sudden knot hardened and burned in her ribs.

Around front Fred said, "*So* good to see you again. You'll have to come back when the landscaping's finished."

"Oh, yeah, I'll do that," Hattie said. "Thanks for showin' me through."

As she limped down the drive, the knot in her side made her catch her breath. She stopped, lit a Chesterfield, sucked it, exhaled. Smoke streamed away on the wind as she walked again.

Cubby was right, she thought, she should never have sold the place to these people. They had wrecked everything she and Oscar and

Alfred had done. They had promised they wouldn't tear the place down, and they hadn't, but they hadn't kept anything either: not the roof, the walls, the cement steps Oscar had poured, the sheds ... And they'd lied about having kids. She coughed deeply, bringing up phlegm, which she spat at the field.

The pickup's door creaked loudly as she hauled herself inside. She sat there, smoking, staring at the house.

The pain had moved higher, was close to her heart, and she thought: Oh these people were clever, all right, with their college degrees—cutting down apple trees it took thirty years to grow, plowing under the best blueberries in Maine, building a garage on the richest soil you'd ever want to find. Yeah, that was real clever.

What a fool she had been. Cubby warned her, but she hadn't listened. She had sold the house for damn near nothing because these people had said they would care for the land, have kids ... Well, that was summer people for you, you couldn't trust them.

The copper flashing sparkled like a river full of coins. A blast of wind sent a shiver down Hattie's back.

The wind had been like this in fifty-three, that time when Luke was playing with matches. They hadn't cut the field a second time that year because the tractor broke, and my god did it burn! They'd only had three brooms and it was beating them, but luck—for once—had been on their side: the wind had changed, and the blaze took the chicken coop, sparing the house.

Hattie turned the ignition key and the pickup started. She revved the engine, thinking, Don't stall on me now. Don't you *dare* stall on me now. She looked at the house that was no longer hers, put the truck in gear, took a final drag on her cigarette, then flicked the butt into the field.

There was smoke for a minute, a sudden small flash, then the wind fanned a circle of copper into the hay.

Oh you're clever, all right, Hattie thought as she pulled away. And you're probably lucky, too. Well, let's just see.

Letter From Maine: How I learned to love junk cars

JACK ALEY

High on the ridge behind my house in Maine, just where our ski touring trail crosses the locals' snowmobiling circuit, are the remains of a very old pickup truck. There's not much left of the Chevy Apache. The price of scrap has been pretty good in recent years.

There remains, however, the bare suggestion of the cab, a bit of firewall and dashboard and a tatter of seat. The odometer, which stopped at 42,106, is the only real reminder of the derelict's original function.

The Chevy up on the ridge is one of the last wrecks on my land. Almost ten years ago, when I bought the thirty acres and the sad, drooping Cape, it was one of many. I had laid claim to a veritable outdoor museum of American automotive memorabilia, the existence of which I knew figured in the low price I paid for the property.

Back in the spring of 1974 the junkers didn't excite my imagination the way the Chevy Apache has on much more recent winter afternoons. In fact, I hated the sight of them. I wanted them gone. And that is why I had a problem with Charlie.

Charlie is a native and he is my neighbor. He is a medium-sized bull of a man with a thick neck, thick arms and thick, graying hair cropped short and flat. He doesn't wear down parkas or Bean boots and he doesn't say very much. Charlie is not exactly a menacing man but I would never want to trifle with him.

Charlie is also the man who sold me my piece of Maine countryside and the 29 (I counted them dolefully) junk cars and trucks that were thrown in. The bleak February afternoon Charlie first showed me around the place, he mentioned that at one time he had had more than 100 wrecks out back. The hint of pride in his voice suggested he remembered those days fondly. Inwardly, I shuddered.

I'm not sure how I knew I just couldn't tell Charlie right out that the junkers had to go. I just couldn't say, "You know, Mr. Pratt (I called him Mister for at least two years), those goddamn wrecks are a perfect symbol of what I wanted to shove out of my life when I decided to move into the country." Instead of telling Charlie man to man that the junkers had to go, I cravenly wrote a provision to that effect in the sales agreement. The wrecks were to be removed by September, six months after the signing, or the contract was void. Charlie read the provision and signed without comment. He needed the money to finance the mobile home he was going to put in a couple of hundred yards down the road. I don't think the plans had formed in his mind yet for the auto body shop.

Slowly during the course of the summer, the wrecks began to disappear. Once or twice a week, one of Charlie's relatives would show up in a pickup truck and spend the morning cutting up a wasted Bonneville or Fairlane into marketable scrap. But the progress was slow and along towards fall I was getting impatient.

It's awfully easy to feel a little paranoid from time to time if you are a certain kind of newcomer to Maine and are surrounded by xenophobic natives. They don't have to (and seldom do) say anything, but if general disapproval and a certain disdain can be exuded, they exude it. They tend to distrust people from away, especially if those people exhibit the strange behavior of former city dwellers or (even worse) college graduates.

It appears that a lot of natives figure if you drive a small foreign car you are somehow un-American. Or if you own down jackets and boots with Vibram soles, you've got more money than you need. Or if you have a long beard and long hair, you're a pinko. Or if you jog after work, the work you did all day wasn't worth doing in the first place.

Native Charlie pretty much had me on all counts when I moved into his old house, and he moved into his new trailer. My old Peugeot sure was foreign enough. I had an orange down ski parka and a nifty pair of boots with Vibram soles I bought from a German boot maker with a shop on Colfax Avenue in Denver. My beard was long and scraggy and my hair was probably thirty times longer than Charlie's butch. Regularly in the evenings I'd don my pair of New Balance running shoes and shuffle on down the road past Charlie's new abode. And I was even pretty sure Charlie knew I listened to "funny" music when I gardened or labored at gutting the house of absolutely everything Charlie had left behind.

During those first months, Charlie never asked for or gave me the time of day. He acknowledged my presence with perfectly expressive silence.

So when September finally rolled around, it was with considerable ambivalence (call it fear if you want to) that I approached Charlie to remind him that all the wrecks hadn't been removed and the deadline was near. Charlie didn't tell me to go to hell in so many words. He just gave me a bulldog look in the eye and growled real low: "I'll get to them when I get to them." The end of that conversation came with the firm slamming of Charlie's trailer door.

Charlie pretty much kept his word. He did get to them when he got to them. Through the fall one of Charlie's brothers or sons or nephews (but never Charlie himself) occasionally would show up with their torches and reduce another wreck. They never got them all, but I never summoned up the courage to bring up the subject again. I've still got the Chevy Apache up on the ridge and the green bed to a dismembered Ford and dozens of rusted gas tanks littered around in the woods. My land hasn't been returned to anything like a pristine state. But it does look much better now, at least to me. I imagine Charlie thinks it looks pretty naked.

Every spring, when I turn over the half acre of ground I claimed for a garden, I find subterranean reminders of the junkyard I took over in 1974. There is still some pretty choice stuff buried shallowly in the ground. I've got a nice little collection of radiator caps, fan belts and hub caps. The first few springs I unearthed such things, they made me as mad as had their parent eyesores. I'd dig up a tailpipe or radiator hose, mutter something damning about the "native mentality" and heave the part into the growing heap behind a stone wall.

In recent years, however, the detritus I've collected from Charlie's junkers has bothered me less for some reason. In fact, when I dig up another part (I found a distributor cap just last month), I sometimes find myself thinking about Charlie more than the Industrial Age run amuck. Charlie and his wrecks have begun to connect. I'm beginning to find in the offal of Detroit a means through which I can understand my native neighbor a little better. He was here first, after all. And he's not just going to disappear.

Charlie and I, it has slowly dawned on me, literally don't see the same thing when we look at a junk car or truck. I see a provoking symbol. Charlie sees a resource and a promise in part fulfilled. To Charlie, the wrecks represent mobility and hardwon freedom from the legacy of living in a hard, poor land. They are his chunk of the American dream. No better part of it ever showed up in Charlie's part of Maine.

Sure, the totaled sedans and pickups aren't worth much in themselves, but Charlie can take parts of them to make some other vehicle function again. He's able to drive and sell patched and rebuilt vehicles, and that fact alone has whisked him into a semblance of the Modern Age. He doesn't have to walk anymore or be drawn by a beast like he did when he was a kid. Charlie has surpassed his ancestors.

So what right did I, an overindulged college kid from an affluent suburb of Chicago, have to tell Charlie that his junkers were not aesthetic? For that matter, what did I know, what would I ever know, about the hard necessity of heating with wood and growing one's own food and walking winter miles to rude schools without gymnasiums or hot lunch programs?

Tearing up Charlie's house has, with time, produced some other revelations, too. When I bought it, I hated everything in it at first sight. I spent the first six months carting loads of linoleum and sundry other floor, wall and chimney coverings to the dump. Charlie and the native dwellers who preceded him successfully had covered up every natural substance in the place. Whereas I, in my hellbent return to the "basics," coveted wooden walls and floors and bare brick chimneys, Charlie had wanted to banish all that from sight. All that natural stuff reminded him of just one thing: earlier times, harder times, times when rough wood and raw brick were all people had to build their rude homes. When things like linoleum and enamel paint in many colors came on the market, they looked pretty damned good to Charlie. They were colorful and easy to clean and they covered up the past. Charlie had wanted such things badly. And that took a person like me a little time to begin to understand. But I think I have begun to understand.

Charlie and I get along fairly well now. I think the episode with the junkers is almost forgotten. We'll probably never be real friends. There's too little common ground for that. But we can talk about the weather and taxes and how much wood we're burning.

I sense that, at the very least, Charlie doesn't mind me anymore. I have learned to keep my mouth shut. That was important. And over the years, Charlie's seen me build up a garden and cut my winter's wood a year ahead just like you're supposed to do it. Charlie is like a lot of natives. He doesn't give a damn what you say, but he'll watch what you do and note how long you hang in there doing it. He'll form an opinion very slowly.

A few summers ago, Charlie and his wife showed up one evening to ask if I minded very much if they cut some shrub roots so they could transplant them around their trailer. It gave me a very curious kind of pleasure to say, "Yes, please go right ahead."

That same summer, I started bringing Charlie a little produce from the garden after he changed a couple of tires for me and never charged me for the service. He liked new potatoes and beets and tried butter-crunch lettuce for the first time in his life.

Two winters ago, Charlie plowed out my driveway after the first storm. He's been plowing it regularly ever since. He never asked if I wanted him to do it and has never asked for any money. By then I knew better than to be very effusive in my thanks, so I just got into the habit of bringing him over a beer once in a while.

Last Christmas, I dropped off a half case of Old Milwaukee down at Charlie's trailer. He'd already plowed me out several times. Charlie and his wife were just sitting down to their holiday dinner of boiled lobster when I knocked at the door. Charlie asked me if I wanted to come in for a beer, but I'm pretty sure he was relieved when I said I had to get right back home. I doubt I'll ever be invited to Charlie's house for dinner. I also doubt I'll ever invite him to mine.

I never said anything when Charlie built his auto body shop replete with a mercury vapor light directly across the road from my house. It's a real eyesore and a constant source of flatulent noises. But I've learned to live wth it.

For his part, Charlie never said anything when I turned in the old Peugeot for a slightly less old Volvo. Sometimes, he even waves to me when I'm grinding out the last yards of a long run in my New Balance running shoes. But then I don't run nearly as much as I did when I moved in eight years ago. I'm pretty sure Charlie has noticed that as well.

A Sharing of Silences

RICHARD ALDRIDGE

West Point, Maine

late fall, the summer people gone

into the village store I go

six fishermen are sitting round
just talking joking supper done

because I have stuck out
now seventeen Maine winters

still have the wife I started with

have had their children now and then
up at the high school off in town

they let me in a little
by not going quiet like wind dying down
or worse just up and easing out

and yet their talk takes on
the slightest shade of guardedness

because I do teach English
after all   which means of course
good grammar is my holy flame

and too (they hear) write poems
and such   so who knows what
I might go off and copy down

if they could only understand
the only words I care to find
are those the counter image of

the windworn creases in their brows
the bark-like hardness of their hands
the upright carriage of their pride

and those are not for finding

AUTHOR BIOGRAPHIES

RICHARD ALDRIDGE, 1930-

Richard Aldridge, born and brought up in New York City, began coming to Maine at the age of three as a summer camper. He graduated from Amherst College and from Oxford University. He has had four books of poetry published and edited *Maine Lines*, an anthology of contemporary Maine poetry published in 1970. For twenty-three years he taught secondary English in Bath. Presently he lives and works in the coastal township of Phippsburg, which has been his home in Maine since 1958.

About poetry he says: "The most important thing in life to any person is another person, not a whole number of other people. That is why poetry will always fill a vital place—in essence, it is an art where three really is a crowd. You should be able to hang around with a good poem just as you do with a good or best friend. As with a best friend, a poem you really like will have said something to you in a way that touches bottom, while at the same time it will just be there, on call any time. If it could see and think, it would observe you growing and changing and reaching all the time. And you, coming back and back to it from time to time, will see new angles and depths and reaches that you never quite knew were there at first acquaintance."

JACK ALEY, 1944-

"After college and graduate work in English and after a long, eye-opening third-class tour of the world, I moved to Maine in 1971 to work for the Associated Press. For three years, I honed my basic skills as a writer in the pressure cooker of wire service reporting.

"In 1974, when I was 29, I left the AP for the 'boonies' of my adopted state to begin homesteading, restoring an old house and writing about other things than fires and schoolboy basketball. In my poor, rural town, I quickly sensed the huge gulf and enormous tensions that often existed between newcomers like myself and the hardworking natives who were my neighbors. As a writer, I felt compelled to explore this conflict. "In 'A Letter from Maine,' I described my relationship with Charlie, one that began with suspicion and mistrust and slowly evolved over many years into a fragile friendship. Charlie may have learned to see a few things my way. But, in the end, I suspect I learned to see more things his way."

CATHARINE BAKER, 1950-

"I really have been a writer most of my life, when I think of it. Do you count all those 'comic books' I drew before I could write, and stapled together for Christmas presents to my dad? How about the long, handwritten stories I piled up for my sixth and seventh grade teacher? I learned to write more carefully in high school and college; there the story line didn't count for much if you had endless paragraphs, chronic parentheses and epidemics of semicolons. But I didn't have anything much I felt I had to tell anyone.

"Not until I lived for four or five years on a farm in Washington County, alone most of the year, five miles from the post office and twenty-five miles from town. I had to do everything for myself, I had to make friends with people who didn't need me at all, and I found out what loneliness does to people. I delivered the mail, and met people who were lonelier than me. I talked to myself and the farm animals a lot. I told myself stories, and when I came back [to Damariscotta] from Downeast I found I still had all the stories. Most of them are about other people who have to do something with their lives, something they'd rather not.

"I've written stories about the mother of a pregnant teenager, a man who has to haul cattle to the slaughterhouse, a mail lady who doesn't want to know about sexual abuse on her mail route, and a neighbor of a crazy lady who abuses kids and animals, and I'm writing a novel now, about a young married woman in Aroostook who puts an ad in the *Maine Times* personals column and gets involved in a murder."

KATE BARNES, 1932-

"Although I was born in Boston, I came to Maine when I was two weeks old with my parents, the writers Henry Beston and Elizabeth Coatsworth. I went to school here as well as in other places. I started writing when I was little, mostly because it was what everyone was always doing in our family. It was a case of 'monkey see, monkey do.'

"When I was little I liked poetry about horses best, but I gradually came to like a lot of other poetry as well. If you find even one poem you really like, you can always expand from there. I loved our home farm and took it for granted that the rest of the world was as beautiful as Maine was. Now I know that's not so!

"After living away from Maine for many years, I have returned, to a ridge of blueberry fields and woods in Appleton. My four children are all grown up and my companions are a big dog named Osa and a buggy horse named Blackberry. Like my parents, I find Maine a more natural place to write than any other. I never wake up in the morning without being happy to be exactly where I am."

LURA BEAM, 1887-1978

Lura Beam spent the first twelve years of her life in Marshfield, Maine, a town of 227 inhabitants near Machias, of which she wrote, "I was related to one household in every three." The daughter of a sea captain, she also moved out into the world, studying at Barnard College and the University of California at Berkeley. She then taught black high school children in the South for the American Missionary Association at a time when public education for blacks ended with the seventh grade. She was to write about this experience decades later during the civil rights movement, when her "memory began to recover the past." She wrote, "I worked in the only zone where the lights grew brighter, in education." In her later life she pursued other projects in education, the arts, and health education.

Beam had learned from her childhood reading, including Sarah Orne Jewett's *The Country of the Pointed Firs*, "that my own surroundings could be the stuff of poetry." Just before she revisited Marshfield in 1953, she mapped its houses and their former residents from memory, and was able to remember "every house and 216 people." That visit prompted her to write *A Maine Hamlet*, a recreation of her childhood environment whose "fascination ... is in its difference from contemporary culture.... The hamlet impressed me in childhood as a place of wonder and beauty. It held all the world of pity, terror, love, faith, fate."

FRED BONNIE, 1945-

Fred Bonnie was born in Bridgton, Maine, the third son of Dr. F. Leroy Bonnie, an optometrist, and Helen Louise Gilmore Bonnie, a housewife and later proofreader for the *Portland Press Herald*. Bonnie began his education in a two-room school house in North Bridgton. When his father died in 1954, the family moved to Portland. He attended public and parochial school and graduated in 1964 from Cheverus High School. In 1971, he graduated with honors from the University of Vermont.

"Growing up in Maine had a lot to do with my becoming a writer," Bonnie says. "As a child, I was indoctrinated with the Natives-versus-Outsiders frame of mind. Complaining about the outsiders has become the state sport. In Portland, I was exposed to a broad range of human types. Portland is small, but has some people most of us would call weird. A port city tends to have street people, some interesting, some just pitiful. But decades before the street people gained national news attention, they were common in downtown Portland.

"As a part-time dishwasher in a downtown restaurant when I was in high school, I observed at close range the types of people John Steinbeck and Erskine Caldwell were writing about during the 1930s and 40s. I write about people trying to deal with life. I've always sympathized with underdogs. I hope I always do."

PHILIP BOOTH, 1925-

"I grew up skiing and fishing and going to school in New Hampshire, and coming to my Maine grandmother's house in Castine in the summers. I grew up learning to row and sail and know almost every island and lobsterman in this part of Penobscot Bay. I went away into the Air Corps, and college and later became a teacher out in Syracuse. But I've always brought my own children back to this same house in this much changed town where I live.

"What I write often begins with an image from my Maine experience, but as I write I explore what I feel that image (and the further images it generates) may come to, my imagination often takes me (and the poem) well beyond its Maine sources.

"Since a poet often finds that the finished poem displaces the experience which moved him to write, it's often hard for the poet to say how a poem came into being. But I do, even with the writing far behind me, still know something about the way 'How To See Deer' began. And about the way writing it led me to see that the poem was not just about deer.

"After a year when I saw fawns all summer, and does and bucks all through hunting season, I realized sometime the next September that I hadn't, for months, seen even one deer. As I started the poem that 'How To See Deer' finally became, I think, looking back that I was trying to write myself instructions on where and how to look for deer, instructions on how to recover some of my previous year's experience. I think I may have envisioned the poem as a kind of ironic Field Guide. But as I got into writing the poem, I found it wanting to move (and my wanting to let it move) in another direction. I found myself revising *as I wrote*, until I saw that my revisions were not focused on looking for deer, but were looking into what I might, in the abstract, now call something like 'access to vision'... I found myself finding, as I wrote, that the poem was looking into what I barely knew I was searching for: not deer but ways of being, ways of learning."

HENRY BRAUN, 1930-

"I have published one book of poems, *The Vergil Woods*, and have another manuscript, *Peculiar Enlargements* ('Ox' is in it), ready for publication. I taught at the University of Maine at Orono (1963-1964) and for the last two decades at Temple University in Philadelphia. I retired early from Temple last year in order to have more time for my own work. We will, very likely, come to live permanently on our farm in Weld. I have given readings and conducted creative writing workshops at many high schools and universities in Pennsylvania and Maine. I also conducted several workshops at the Maine State Prison in Thomaston. I am married to the artist Joan Braun. We have two grown daughters and a very new grandson.

"Our Maine address—with its big mail-loving container—is Box 84, Weld, Maine 04285. The phone there is 585-2218."

ERSKINE CALDWELL, 1903-1987

Caldwell spent his childhood in a succession of small towns throughout the rural south. A free-spirited and energetic boy, he "roam[ed] the town from morning till night," and was willing and able to pick up any sort of work to put change in his pocket. Before he became self-supporting as an author, he worked as, among other things, "a mill laborer, cotton picker, cook, waiter, taxicab driver, farmhand, cottonseed shoveler, stone-mason's helper, soda jerk, [semi-]professional football player, bodyguard, stagehand in a burlesque theater, and a hand on a boat running guns to a Central American country in revolt."

Caldwell quit college twice, the second time to support his new wife Helen by working as a cub reporter and book reviewer. A few years later, he moved with Helen and their two children to a farmhouse in Mount Vernon. "One of the principal reasons for selecting Maine as a place to live," he wrote, "was that I wanted to go as far away as possible in order to have a perspective of the scenes and circumstances of life in the Deep South." His attempts at farming were followed by a brief, unsuccessful venture as the owner of a bookstore in Portland.

For the rest of his eighty-four years Caldwell continued his pattern of restlessly moving from place to place, writing, often with humor, about the "hard ugly facts of poverty, illness, and degeneration," and finally acquiring substantial fame and fortune.

"What I have resisted doing as a writer was knowingly falsifying the anguish or the jubilation of men and women who had been brought to life and were captives in a story of mine."

WILLIAM CARPENTER, 1940-

"I grew up in Waterville during the days of Elvis Presley, hung out at street dances and in the darkness of Foxie's pool room, then managed to escape over to Dartmouth College in New Hampshire. I lived in Minneapolis and Chicago for ten years, doing graduate work, teaching, and coming to Maine only in the summer. Then I heard about a new experimental college starting up in Bar Harbor and took a job there teaching literature. I sailed the coast and fixed up an old house in Southwest Harbor with my family; and somewhere in the process I started writing poetry myself. Now I divide my time between teaching, writing and traveling. I've lived in Mexico and Italy, and I spent the winter of 1988 in India. My house is an old summer cottage overlooking the Penobscot River that used to be a speakeasy in the Prohibition days. Maine is full of stories like that; life here is just as strange and surprising as it is anywhere else in the world. Sometimes I write about exotic places, but most of my work comes from what I see and hear right around home. Many of my poems, like 'Fire,' are about edges and boundaries. Maine is full of boundaries—the land and the ocean, the past and the present, wealth and poverty, civilization and wildness. For that reason I can't think of a better place to write."

SAMUEL DE CHAMPLAIN, 1567 or 1570-1635

As a young man Champlain joined the French army, where he served King Henry IV as an officer for five years during France's protracted religious wars. After the victory of the royal armies, he had no inclination to settle down to a sedentary life. With the king's support he embarked on a series of voyages to North America, pledging on his return to "make a truthful report of them to His Majesty." So began his life as an explorer, chronicler, and cartographer, Geographer Royal to the King.

His third voyage, in 1604, under the captaincy of Sieur de Monts, brought him to Nova Scotia to establish a settlement at Saint Croix Island. That September, on an independent expedition down the coast of Maine, he travelled up the Penobscot River in search of the mythical Northwest Passage to China, and continued down the coast as far as Pemaquid. On subsequent voyages he continued south as far as Cape Cod.

Champlain carefully observed, and faithfully recorded, his natural surroundings and the customs of the native Americans. Unlike several English explorers of the time, he respected the Indians and came to be trusted by them. Upon this trust he was able to found and sustain the city of Quebec, the heart of France's settlements in the New World, to whose growth and defense he devoted the remainder of his life. His accounts of his voyages are an important source of information about Canada and Maine in the early seventeenth century.

VIRGINIA CHASE, 1900-1987

Born at the turn of the century in Blue Hill, Chase had a protected yet adventurous childhood. Her father, a lawyer and judge, was a strict man given to fancies. He persuaded the state to rehabilitate a set of government buildings on Widow's Island for convalescent mental patients by vowing to send his own children there. Virginia spent weeks every summer on the island, now called Chase Island, with the women patients, seeing them as strange only in that they let her go barefoot and seemed to have "forgotten that children should be seen and not heard." When she was seven her father bought an old hotel in Blue Hill with a clientele of "drummers, travelling-show actors and actresses, Evangelical preachers...as well as tourists." There was much for a child to observe, and her father taught her to be observant. "What did you see today that you never saw before?" he would ask when he came home from court.

Chase dropped out of the University of Orono after her father's death left her family without money for school. At eighteen she became principal for a year of the Steuben school in Washington County. Later she began a lifelong career of teaching in high school and college. After she began to write in the 1930s, her childhood and her experience as a teacher became the subject matter of her short stories and four novels, two of which are set in Maine. Her life came full circle when she moved back to Blue Hill with her husband to undertake blueberry farming ("never seriously") in the 1960s.

ROBERTA CHESTER, 1938-

"My earliest recollection of making poems is an image of myself in the back of my father's blue Chevy when I was about three or four and we were driving down the ramp on the Jersey side of the Hudson River on our way into the Lincoln Tunnel. I remember singing little rhymes to myself and being absolutely delighted and surprised with my own creativity. I think they were rhymes about bears, but I'm not sure about that. I do know that if my parents in the front seat or my little brother next to me were listening, their pleasure was not nearly as great as mine, because what I felt then was the joy of discovering I could invent something with words. What I was experiencing was a feeling of intense amusement.

"I guess I feel that same sort of pleasure whenever I write. Language has infinite possibilities and entertaining them as I construct a poem is the way I define 'fun.' Even the hard work of revising and polishing and trying one word after another till the effect is right is enjoyable, and sometimes hours pass without my being conscious of the time at all. There have been times when my own children have had to remind me to 'come back from outer space' because poems that are in the process of entertaining their own possibilities are hard to postpone.

"Now that I live in Maine, the intense beauty of the Maine landscape has been a constant inspiration. I can't think of a better place to be a poet than Maine, where each of the seasons arrives with so much passion that all of our senses are awakened. If we're poets we have to respond."

"History"—In Eastern Europe around the turn of the century, many Jewish communities were attacked and massacred by gangs of their countrymen, often with the complicity of the government and the army. These "pogroms" were largely responsible for the large-scale Jewish immigration to the United States during those decades. Restrictive rules against the Jews, which might authorize the confiscation of property or conscription into the Russian army, were announced by the posting of a "white paper/ in the marketplace."

"Succoth"—Succoth is a harvest holiday celebrated by living and eating in huts open to the stars and colorfully decorated with fruits and vegetables. It follows the Jewish new year's holiday of Rosh Hashanah and the fast day of Yom Kippur, which is announced by the blowing of a ram's horn ("shofar")—a season for atoning for the sins of the past and making resolutions for the year to come. A "shul" is a Jewish house of worship, also called a temple or synagogue. Challah is a large, braided bread accorded a place of honor during traditional "Shabbas," or Sabbath, meals.

CAROLYN CHUTE, 1948-

Chute grew up in the Pond Cove section of Cape Elizabeth, at the time a rural area. She found no outlet for her creativity in school. "In the first grade I saw a teacher grab a kid who was acting up and stuff her between the wall and the piano. The teacher stuffed paper in the kid's mouth and wrapped her in masking tape. I remember thinking, 'I don't like this happening.' I knew right then I would never raise my hand or open my mouth anymore in a public place as long as I lived."

It took her many years to change her mind. She left school, married and pregnant, at sixteen, divorced eight years later, and found herself caught in a cycle of poverty. She worked low-wage jobs such as picking potatoes and scrubbing floors to support herself and her child. Eventually, she earned her high school diploma, began taking courses at the University of Maine, and became the Gorham correspondent for the *Portland Evening Express.*

Since childhood, writing had been a refuge for her, and a means of control. She had been working for years on a novel, one that would be nearly two decades between its start and its completion. Several established writers recognized her talent when she attended the Stonecoast Writers Conference at U.S.M., and encouraged her to publish her work. The novel, *The Beans of Egypt, Maine*, appeared in 1985.

In *The Beans* and in *Letourneau's Used Auto Parts*, her second novel, Chute writes about rural poverty in Maine. Her directness and strong imagery have won her work passionate admirers and detractors. Chute says simply that she writes about people she knows and loves. About her writing she says, "I cook it till it's done. Until it's just right, it's just lousy."

ROBERT CHUTE, 1926-

"My family ran a summer hotel, so in the summer I associated with 'city folks,' mostly adults. In the winter in Naples, Maine, they rolled up the sidewalks. I was two and a half miles from what passed for a town, nine miles from a movie, no TV, no VCR, not even a bicycle. Church on Christmas and Easter. I had to amuse myself—even instruct myself: no lectures on 'the facts of life,' no 'peer group.' Teenagers and pre-teens hadn't been invented yet. I walked a mile to a one-room school, where Miss Pitts was my teacher through seven grades. Books and the woods, the library and the countryside, were my salvation. Six books was the town library's limit, so every week, in the winter, I took out six books. Kipling and A.A. Milne became my poetic models. Love of books led me to writing at age thirteen. Time spent alone in the woods, by the lake, led me, later, to become a biologist. My thanks to the Naples library and to Miss Pitts, who, when my lessons were done early, sent me down to the swamp in Leavitt's woodlot behind the school to collect pollywogs and salamanders."

"January, 1724" and "The Last Moon" are from a poem sequence called *Thirteen Moons*. Most of the poems in the sequence are, as "January, 1724," in the voice of the French Jesuit priest and scholar Sebastian Rale, who lived among the Norridgewock Indians for thirty years, during which time he produced an Abenaki-French dictionary. [The priest sees the sunset in terms of images of his European upbringing, whereas his Abenaki companion sees it in terms of his life as a hunter.] Rale was hated and feared by the English settlers of the Province of Maine, who considered him an agent of France and an instigator of Indian rebellion. The English raided the Norridgewock settlement four times between 1705 and 1724, once burning the village to the ground. In August of 1724, Rale and many Indians were killed in the final raid on the village. *Thirteen Moons*, though written in English, was published in a bilingual edition, English and French, in recognition of Sebastian Rale's importance in the history of French settlement of North America. We hope one day to see the sequence translated into the tongue of the native Americans in whose voice it also speaks.

WILLIAM (BILL) CLARK, 1913-1988

Though he was actually a native of upstate New York and didn't settle here until 1956, Bill Clark's life and writing were to become totally identified with rural Maine. One of his seven published volumes is titled *Maine Is My Heart*. He graduated from Colby College, earned an education degree from the State University of New York, then began a first career teaching English that was eventually to lead him back to Maine, as a teacher at York High School, then at the University of Southern Maine.

Clark was not a person who lived exclusively in books. During World War II, he was a gunner in the Navy. Two of the ships he was crewman on were torpedoed; in one of those sinkings, he was the only survivor. He worked as a sawmill operator, logger, and carpenter, and originally conceived of his newspaper column, "Logrolling," as a way of promoting "better use of forest products." The column quickly expanded in scope and audience, however; it was moved to the editorial page, and Clark used it as a forum for his stories, and for his views on life and politics. He valued traditional ways and rural common sense, and could be bitingly satirical about the practices of urban dwellers and city-educated "back-to-the-landers."

His stories, which were later published as collections, were set in the fictional town of Cedar River. Cedar River is peopled with rural characters much like those who inhabit any part of the state where people still sustain themselves by working directly with nature. Clark himself moved to such a town, Caratunk, in 1971, and was its first selectman for several years.

Author Biographies   443

ELIZABETH COATSWORTH, 1893-1986

Coatsworth was born in Buffalo, New York. When she was a little girl she was shy and always had a hard time speaking up. She began writing stories and poems for fun when she was in school. She said that many of her friends wrote far better than she did, that the difference was that she kept going.

After college and graduate study she traveled in the Orient, North Africa, and Europe. At first a poet and writer of short stories, she turned to children's stories after she married the naturalist Henry Beston. Still later she wrote novels and essays. Her life was "one of books, travels, children, household and writing, and [I] have never gone to a meeting if I could help it." She moved to Maine with her husband, at first living there only in the summertime, but after about twelve years stayed there summer and winter.

She and her husband lived for more than forty years on an old farm in Nobleboro which they called "Chimney Farm." There she wrote the majority of her more than one hundred books, many of which concern themselves with the elements of life in and around the farm, such as their friends' wooden houseboat and their neighbor's little steers. She died there at the age of ninety-three and is buried in the farm graveyard at the edge of the fields.

Coatsworth believed that most children write naturally, but that as they get older they lose the gift unless they have a chance to keep writing.

ROBERT P. TRISTRAM COFFIN, 1892-1955

One of seven children in a close family, Coffin spent his early childhood on his parents' salt water farm on Great Island in Harpswell. The easy familiarity the Coffin children developed with nature there became the basis for Coffin's poetic sensibility. Watching a buck deer escape two chasing dogs by swimming across a bay, "the sun sparkling on the water in his wake," years later inspired the poem "Crystal Moments," in which he writes of a kind of natural beauty one sees "only once or twice this side of eternity."

Coffin wrote his first poem at eight; he often improvised verses satirizing local events or characters, including himself. An excellent but mischievous student, he once fulfilled an assignment in recitation by getting up on stage and saying,

"Speaking pieces hard and tough,
Speak two lines and that's enough."

In truth, however, he wrote continually and fluently. While a student at Bowdoin College, he was already earning money publishing poems in papers and magazines.

He graduated from Bowdoin first in his class. He had been class poet, art editor of the college literary magazine, and editor-in-chief of the college newspaper. A year later, he went to Oxford University on a Rhodes Scholarship. In answer to an application question about the extent of his previous travel he had written, "To Lewiston on the north, Portland on the west, East Harpswell on the east, and South Freeport on the south." The scholarship committee may have felt it was time for him to see the world.

Coffin taught at several colleges and universities, including his alma mater. He published forty books in his lifetime, garnering innumerable honorary degrees and other awards for his poetry, novels, and non-fiction writings, including the Pulitzer Prize; for forty years he was an active and important contributor to the literary life of America.

LEO CONNELLAN, 1928-

"I never wanted to do anything else but write. I was born in Portland on November 30, 1928 and we moved to Rockland in 1930. When I was a little kid and growing up, I'd read something and I'd think I'd notice something the writer missed, something I could do that would make what I was reading better ... I'd think about baseball games and football games and how no matter what you do in them that's outstanding, it's gone and forgotten as soon as the game is over, but if I could write something the very best I could, it would always be there to read and never vanish in memory. A wonderful English teacher, Mrs. Ludwig of Rockland High School, encouraged me and sent poems of mine to the national contest run by Scholastic Scope. Poems of mine won two years in a row. I was the only poet in Maine besides Edna St. Vincent Millay to win....

"My mother died in Rockland in 1936 when I was seven. In June every summer we'd drive up from Rockland to this side of the Bath bridge and take the road down to Five Islands, where my mother's people had a summer place. My aunt Madge, who somehow seemed the human being who got stuck with everybody's kids, would tell me that if I didn't eat up all the blueberries I picked she'd make us some pie and muffins. Her muffins were the best I ever ate anywhere. She wasn't my mother and I'd lost mine, but one day, as I worked on my book of poetry, *Death In Lobster Land*, I suddenly thought about her. I thought how unconscious children are of what waits in life 'out of the woods' and how much children take for granted, so I wrote 'Blueberry Boy' for my aunt Madge because I wouldn't want to go to my grave without ever having tried to write it. I wanted 'Blueberry Boy' to mention and remember a woman who was already in her late seventies when I was nine or ten years old, who gave me love as if I was one of her own children."

PAUL CORRIGAN, 1951-

"My first poems were based on recollections of the summers that I spent with my family at our camp on a northern Maine lake. This was no ordinary escape to a comfortable summer home accessible by the family station wagon over a pleasant gravel road. We carried all our provisions in pack baskets over a three-mile trail in order to reach the run-down cabin that my father had fixed up for us. My brother, sisters, and I had that corner of the lake all to ourselves with a breathtaking view of Mount Katahdin rising a mile above us in the distance. Deer, moose, and an occasional bear would wander into the campyard at night. When we weren't fishing or swimming, my brother and I read avidly or listened to the Red Sox game on the portable radio. What I got in return for the lack of modern conveniences and the isolation was an experience of vast importance, especially for me as a writer. From those summers I received an early, first-hand acquaintance with the Maine woods—a locale that has been a source of inspiration for my writing ever since."

REBECCA CUMMINGS, 1944-

"When I was growing up and dreaming of perhaps becoming a writer, I thought that the experiences a writer chooses to write about must be out of the ordinary. Every book I read—and I read constantly—had exciting people, exotic places, and strange events. Because I thought my life was so uneventful, I didn't think I had anything to write.

"One day a few years ago, I was making a turnip pie, which is a main-dish pie made from pork and turnip wrapped in a bread crust. We of Finnish heritage love the pie; just the thought of it, warm from the oven, is enough to make me hungry. As I was making the pie, kneading the bread dough, I became acutely aware of my rhythm, the elasticity of the dough, and smells and texture. My mind wandered, and I started to think about what might happen if someone who hadn't had it before ate too much. Suddenly, I had a story! I couldn't wait to get that pie in the oven so that I could write it.

"As you can see, although it's taken me quite a few years, I have finally come to realize that what is everyday to one person is unusual and interesting to another. We all have our stories.

Cummings' Finnish heritage in western Maine extends back to all four of her grandparents. She grew up surrounded by the Finnish language, foods, and traditions. Travel has also been an important part of her life. She served for three years as a Peace Corps volunteer in Thailand, taught for two years in a private school in Brazil, and has traveled through Southeast Asia, South America, and Europe. Although she has not written about her experiences as a traveler, she feels that, having been a "foreigner" herself, she better understands the emotions of the immigrant.

MARGARET DICKSON, 1947-

"I was born in Lewiston, Maine , and have lived in Maine almost all of my life. I went to Bates College. Three books of mine have been published by Houghton Mifflin; a fourth one has been bought by Bantam Books. Some short stories and poems have been printed in magazines, and I've written a play that won a national prize. Some of my work is available in other countries.

"Even so, I feel I'm always in a magic between the things I know, and the things I still have to learn. Long ago I attended classes given by John Tagliabue, a world traveler. I had always believed in a special spirit that touches and unites people all over our state, throughout our country, and everywhere in the world. From John and his wife and their United Nations of Poetry I learned that global awareness and concern does indeed begin in individual creative hearts. I believe that today, and it helps me find where I'm going.

"In my lifetime I've also been lucky to know—as Marl does in the segment of *Octavia's Hill* in this volume—friends who stand by me whether I'm covered with grime, or with glory. To me this means that no matter how strange we seem to each other, we're always looking for the sort of friendship that Marl and Ol' Sears share."

LEW DIETZ, 1906-

"I was born in Pennsylvania, educated in the New York City area and escaped to Maine in 1931—still young enough to be adopted by the state that would be my home for over fifty years. In that span of over a half-century I've managed to write eighteen books, including a history of the Camden-Rockport area, and a hundred or more short stories and articles. Along the way, I worked in state politics, served on the Maine Arts Commission and helped to establish *Down East* magazine.

"In my writing I've drawn primarily on my experiences in Maine's great out-of-doors. My book (with Harry Goodridge) *A Seal Called Andre* is a reflection of my life-long love for animals. My books for young people include the Jeff White books (adventure stories set in Maine's North Woods), *Full Fathom Five, Pines for the King's Navy, Savage Summer,* and *The Year of the Big Cat.* The last novel, which was produced by Disney as a TV motion picture some years ago, was inspired by my years of hunting and fishing in the St. John River Valley and the fifteen years I spent covering the state for *Field and Stream* magazine.

"The question that young people ask me most frequently is how did I learn to write and what does it take to become a writer. I tell them my interest in writing was awakened by reading and I learned to write by writing and writing some more. There is no other way."

ABBIE HUSTON EVANS, 1882-1983

As a teenager, Evans moved with her family from her native Bristol, an area her mother's family had settled in 1730, to Camden. She realized she wanted to be a poet when she heard her father read William Wordsworth's "Ode on Some Intimations of Immortality" one Sunday in his sermon at the church where he was pastor. Fate set back her plans, however, when she was eighteen; an illness that threatened her eyesight kept her from reading and writing for ten years. She spent a great deal of that time outdoors, in particular walking the Camden Hills with a young friend who had been her pupil in Sunday school, Edna St. Vincent Millay.

Evans entered Radcliffe College at twenty-eight, and graduated Phi Beta Kappa. She worked as an English teacher, a Red Cross volunteer during World War I, and a social worker among the families of miners and steel-workers. She eventually went back to teaching, in Philadelphia, coming back during the summers to Maine.

Recognition as a poet came slowly to her. She remained in relative obscurity until the 1960s, when she received an honorary doctorate from Bowdoin College and several poetry prizes. Her *Collected Poems*, published in honor of her ninetieth birthday, at which time she was still writing, has received wide acclaim.

Evans said of the Maine countryside, "It's the kind of place I would have made, had I been God." She studied the natural world so as to understand the place of the human spirit within it, and to understand the relationship of any small part of it to the universe at large.

CHRISTOPHER FAHY, 1937-

"I learned to read at the age of four and couldn't get enough of it; I was possessed by words. My parents gave me a subscription to *Jack and Jill* magazine, and I devoured every issue as soon as it came out. I memorized the poems in it and tried to write my own. For a long time, I assumed that everyone wanted to write. What else was worth doing? Except possibly acting or drawing cartoons.

"In second grade, something terrible happened: I was fitted with glasses and told I'd go blind if I didn't stop writing and reading. Scared, I gave up the writing but couldn't stop reading. I sneaked books into my room and read comics at the homes of friends. My eyes got worse and worse, but the ban was lifted when I was twelve. So I drew my own comic books for a while, but didn't start writing again until after college. That was long ago, and I feel as if I'm still catching up.

"When I moved to Maine, I bought a vacant old wreck of a house with smashed-out windows, splintered doors, and rotted clapboards. As I fixed it up, the big tough toothless woman I'd bought it from came to visit from time to time, but would never set foot inside. Why not? I wondered. What would her feelings be if she did? Thinking about this led to 'The Glow of Copper'."

TOM FALLON, 1936-

"'How the devil did you write 'Work Piece'?' How could I make something positive out of my unintellectual, unimaginative, uncreative work experience in a Maine factory? It was getting me down—I hated this stupidity for eight hours every day, six days a week, week after week after week—the same simple physical work performed over and over and over again was getting me down! How could I get 'on top of it'— how could I make something positive out of something I was beginning to hate so very much?...

"I was very fortunate to see a Channel 10 program about the contemporary American composer, Steve Reich, and his 'minimalist' music. Here was a classical musician using repetitions of sound with only very slight variations....

"Here was a key for my literary form!

"Repetition. Minimalism!

"Repetition of words and phrases to express the reality of paper mill work—to create the reality of factory work in America....

"After I had finished 'Work Piece,' I felt better. I had created something positive. I had created a 'minimalist' literary piece. I had created something positive from a bad human experience—I had created. I had not let a negative human experience overcome me, change my attitude toward life, make me bitter, as so many other people had become bitter about the continuing negative experience of their lives. And I continued to work in the paper mill...."

Fallon lives and works in Rumford. A prolific writer, his most recent book is *The Man on the Moon*. He describes himself as a "questioner. I continuously ask questions about society, art, and life."

MITCHELL GOODMAN, 1923-

"I've lived two different lives, one in the big city (New York), the other here on a back road in Temple. I've married twice and had two sons, one in the city, the other here on this old sidehill farm with woods all around us. For forty years I've been a writer. For the last twenty-five years I've been a political activist as well: a radical dissenter working in a community we call The Movement to bring more social justice, more equality, more kindness and generosity into a society now dominated by big corporations and big money.

"Out of these different lives have come prose and poetry that reflect my love of the earth and its creatures and my anger toward those who would destroy them—whether it be with guns, chemicals, chainsaws or nuclear weapons.

"I was born five years after World War I. The common blood-red thread running through my life is war, holocaust, militarism and the social injustice that underlies them. My strongest response to that heritage is my novel, *The End of It*, which has been called the best book about war written by an American. It is a book full of death and violence, but in the end it is about the experience of being alive."

BETSY GRAVES, 1962-

"I grew up in Orono, across the river from the University of Maine. Orono isn't your average Maine town; the University creates certain opportunities and problems that are different from those in places like Dexter or Howland. However, I was just as ready to leave after high school as anyone else in a small Maine town, even though part of me loved the state and wanted to stay. All through college in Connecticut I struggled with homesickness for a place that I both loved and hated. After graduation and a brief stint in New York City, I decided to come back. Today I'm very glad I made that decision.

"Returning to Maine also meant returning to writing, which I'd been interested in all through school, but had abandoned in college. I began *Past the Shallows* in the summer of 1987, remembering a camp we'd had in Aroostook County when I was a kid. One scene led to another, and I am still working on the novel.

"Writing *Past the Shallows* has helped me to understand that creating a story requires time, patience, and the ability to listen. Though I usually write first drafts of scenes in one sitting, without worrying too much whether or not they're 'good,' I change things in my work almost every time I reread it. When I revise, I constantly ask myself, 'Would this person really say that?' and 'Is this the right word, or do I mean something else?' The main thing I try to remember is to be true to the characters, and trust that they'll lead the story where it's supposed to go."

LAWRENCE SARGENT HALL, 1915-

"I've never lived long far from salt water. I'm a New Englander by birth and a Mainer by adoption and preference; was an undergraduate at Bowdoin, have taught English there and at Yale, Columbia and Delaware; was an officer in the Navy in WWII; have lived on Orr's Island since 1952 when I bought and operated an old boatyard for a decade. I live in a house I designed and built myself on the shore of Harpswell Sound. My only fresh-water adventure was a lonely cruise down the Mississippi River in a Banks Dory rigged for sail, which I subsequently took Downeast on a cruise protesting against oil company schemes for refineries on the coast. I wrote 'The Ledge' for the same reason most writers write, including Hawthorne, on whom I'm currently doing a book—out of fascination with the experience of humankind living on this planet.

"Frequently I'm asked whether my story was based on fact, as if fact would make it more true. It would not, of course. It would just make it more factual. Fact is often insignificant, and always, if it enters in, only a trigger of fiction. Fiction, serious fiction, is more true and therefore more significant because it reveals beyond what perhaps happened what could, or would, or should happen. People who ask me how come I thought I knew what actually happened on that ledge that winter when nobody in reality knew, are asking the wrong question."

HELEN HAMLIN, 1917-

Helen Hamlin was born in Fort Kent, into a family that has lived in Aroostook County for generations. She spent her childhood between Fort Kent and the Fish River chain of lakes, where her grandfather had a camp. A graduate of the Madawaska Training School for teachers, she taught school at Churchill Lake near the headwaters of the Allagash. She is the author of two books, *Nine Mile Bridge* and *Potatoes, Pine Trees and People*.

"It is only natural that a person's childhood environment should always remain the most glamorous and most interesting phase of one's life, and I am no exception. Growing up in a town like Fort Kent, with a generous dose of Grandpa's rich woods lore of old Aroostook, and in a mixed French and English household, has done more than just build a collection of reminiscences. It has left a distinct love and admiration for a land, and no other place can ever seem as attractive."

MARSDEN HARTLEY, 1877-1943

Marsden Hartley was born in Lewiston of English parents. His mother died when he was eight, and he spent his childhood in poverty, becoming a factory worker at fifteen. After moving to Cleveland, he began to study painting, and soon won scholarships to continue these studies. Literature was also important to him, particularly the work of the Transcendentalists. Throughout his life he would try to incorporate spiritual values into his creative work.

Pursuing a double career as a poet and painter, Hartley associated himself with the literary and artistic avant-garde. Like several other modern artists, he found religious sources in nature and in tribal cultures that lived close to the land, among them the American Indians of New Mexico. He lived in Europe through much of the 1920s, which was for him a period of experimentation in both of his art forms.

Hartley moved back to New England in the 1930s, and spent most of the last years of his life in Maine. Here he seemed to rediscover "the spiritual presence of place itself." He wrote of his childhood, of the sea, of life and death, with all the precision of an artist painting a difficult but beloved landscape.

EDWARD M. (TED) HOLMES, 1910-

"I grew up in a New Jersey suburb where most workers boarded trains to New York City at eight each morning and returned on the five-fifteen. Dull, I called it, slavery. All they did was make money. So at sixteen I became deckhand on a schooner on Long Island Sound: an education, but it didn't last. Society insisted I finish school. Later I sailed to Europe on a French liner, playing drums in a pick-up jazz band. Great, but I could''t make a living at it. I tried New York as store salesman, as Wall Street runner, but quit to become seaman/stage-carpenter on a floating theater. The theater failed. I became a news reporter for a suburban paper (another education), and later, business manager of a health co-op in Maryland.

"In 1939 my wife and I moved to Maine. I was a lobster trucker, clam digger, organizer of co-operatives, shipyard worker (first in Manset, then Boothbay), mate on cruise schooners from Camden, high school principal in Princeton, and finally high school and then college English teacher. Officially retired, now 78, I live in Winterport on the Penobscot River, and teach two Honors classes at the University of Maine.

"'Not for Hire' is fiction, but like a great deal of fiction, it stems from the writer's experiences and observations of others. In the 1940s my wife and I lived for more than three years on an island in the Mount Desert Island region. Much of that time we had only one neighbor, whom I have called Lew Medric. The portrait of him here, based for the most part on his anecdotes about himself, is I believe accurate, except for the end of the story. That was my addition, but it fitted his character."

LUCY HONIG, 1948-

"I seem to have inherited a city-country split from my parents: when they met, my mother was a New York City factory worker, my father was an upstate farmer. I grew up on a farm and couldn't wait to move to a big city; after college I got a job in Paris, then New York. That was enough big city for me! When I moved to rural Maine I thought I'd stay there all my life, but after ten years the city lured me back, and now I live in New York again. Of course I dream of the quiet beauty of Maine, and I'm sure I'll return.

"I'd written some fiction before I moved to Maine, but I believe Maine really made me a writer. Living on a farm in Washington County I didn't see many people, so I thought a lot about the few I did see, what they were doing and what made them tick. When I shoveled in my garden, I'd remember all the conversations I'd heard and all the things I wished I'd been clever enough to say. As I pulled weeds, I'd mull over ideas for stories, and in the clear Maine air people's motives and desires somehow seemed clear, too. It was in my Maine garden that I began to get deep inside my characters. I've always wanted my readers to feel the characters' feelings, too, not just look at them from outside.

"In all my writing I'm concerned with people who struggle to make a living and who don't fit into the 'average American family' mold—maybe because the people I've liked most never quite fit in as much as others thought they should. In writing about people's hardships, about their deepest and sometimes most confusing feelings, I hope to show that there is always a possibility for change: that people can learn and grow, that individuals can make a difference in the world around them."

CONSTANCE HUNTING, 1925-

"As a very young child, I was read to a great deal, both poems and stories. I suppose it was my enjoyment of being read to that led me to write my first poem when I was seven. Ever since, writing has been the core, the source of my existence. Writing is arranging the world, in words. Every person's writing is different from any other's, because each person sees the world through a unique set of eyes. My poem 'New England' came to me one early morning in Washington County near the sea. It came just as you read it. Other poems must go through many changes before they become their real selves. Maine is important to me as a writer; its atmosphere seems to allow the freedom to try things, to explore possibilities. If one thing doesn't succeed, try another!

"I guess you could say that I'm a literary person. I teach Creative Writing at the University; I edit *Puckerbrush Review*; I have a small publishing house, Puckerbrush Press; I review Maine books for public radio. But I also like to go to our woodlot and help get ready for that long Maine winter. Maine makes us believe in weather. And that in turn makes us believe in Maine."

SARAH ORNE JEWETT, 1849-1909

"Wild but shy" as a child, Jewett preferred learning through travel and conversation with her father and grandfather and the books in her South Berwick home to going to school. Four years at the Berwick Academy, from which she graduated at sixteen, was her entire formal education. At about that time she decided that she would be a writer: "I determined to teach the world that country people were not awkward and ignorant as city people seemed to think. I wanted the world to know their grand, simple lives. So far as I had a mission when I first began to write, I think that that was it."

Before she was twenty she began publishing stories in *The Atlantic Monthly*. She continued to write for forty years, composing in all over a hundred fifty stories, publishing ten volumes in her lifetime. Her works were consistently set in rural and small town Maine and told of ordinary people going about the ordinary business of their lives. She made that seem important.

On the surface, Jewett's own life was uneventful. She never married, and lived out her life in the family home in South Berwick. However, she spent months each year among her literary friends in Boston, and corresponded extensively.

On her fifty-second birthday, shortly after receiving the first honorary doctoral degree given to a woman by Bowdoin college, she was thrown from her carriage. Injuries to her head and spine left her partially paralyzed and without the strength to write. During the last years of her life she met and entertained many among the next generation of women writers. Write about what you know was her advice to them.

RITA JOE, 1932-

Rita Joe is a Micmac, mother of eight, and grandmother of eighteen. She is author of two books, *Poems of Rita Joe* and *Song of Eskasoni*.

When her children were in grade school, around twenty years ago, they would bring homework from school, and she saw what she believed to be derogatory information about native people. She would think to herself, "If history were written by Indians, it would be different." She began to write poetry that was published in the *Micmac News*. Encouraged by the many letters that she received from readers, she continued to write about the positive side of Native Indian life. Rita Joe lives on a reserve of 2050 people in East Bay Nova Scotia where she sees and writes about the beautiful things that happen there. The Micmac people are native to eastern Canada and northeastern United States.

JOHN JOSSELYN, 1608-1675

John Josselyn was an aristocratic, but impoverished, Englishman who, from 1638 to 1639, and again from 1663 to 1671, visited his elder brother Henry, a colonial administrator who lived at Black Point, Scarborough, in the Province of Maine. A natural historian, Josselyn's careful accounting of the region's plant and animal life was for a time given great authority among the scientists of Britain's Royal Society. He identified accurately over 100 different kinds of plants, flowers, herbs, shrubs, and trees native to the state, illustrating many of his descriptions with line drawings. His accounts of native American society and behavior are unusually sensitive and sympathetic among settler narratives.

Josselyn recorded in his diaries more than he saw, however, so he also has some claim to the title of Maine's first folklorist. He included in his catalogue of New England creatures the lions, sea serpents, and mermen of local legend. He recorded the way of life of the early settlers of Maine, their medicinal cures and stories, not attempting to judge their efficacy or truth. For him, America was a paradise on earth, a garden of Eden in which all things were possible, if not always understood. He once mistook a wasps' nest for a pineapple, and paid for the mistake with an upper lip that "'swelled so extreamly' that his friends could recognize him only by his clothes."

After his prolonged second voyage he returned to England to write his two books, *New-Englands Rareities Discovered* (1672) and *An Account of Two Voyages to New-England* (1674), and to fulfill "the French proverb, 'Travail where thou canst, but dye where thou oughtest, that is, in thine own Countrey.'"

STEPHEN KING, 1947-

Stephen King was born in Portland in 1947.

He started writing for pay as a sophomore at Lisbon High School, after having gotten in trouble for writing a satirical newspaper. His guidance counselor suggested that he use his writing talents constructively, and the young King was given a job writing about sports for the *Lisbon Enterprise* at 1/2¢ a word.

Since then, King has authored over twenty books, under his own name, and under the pen name Richard Bachman. His first novel, *Carrie*, was published in 1973.

A graduate of the University of Maine, King lives in Bangor with his wife, the novelist Tabitha King, and their three children.

GARY LAWLESS, 1951-

"I grew up in Belfast, and wrote my first poems there. I started writing poetry in high school, when I discovered that it was all right to write about your own life, what you saw and heard around you. I found that poetry rises out of the world around us, and belongs to everyone. The first poet to show this to me was Gary Snyder. I went to Colby College and studied East Asian literature, because I especially enjoyed the way that Chinese and Japanese poets brought the natural world into their writing. After graduating, I asked Gary Snyder if I could come to California to live and study with him. I lived there for almost a year, but I missed Maine. I came back to work here in a bookstore. That was fifteen years ago, and now I co-own a bookstore, am editor and publisher of Blackberry Books, and have had seven collections of poems published. I live in Nobleboro, caretaking the farm of writers Henry Beston and Elizabeth Coatsworth. I doubt if I'll ever leave Maine. There is so much to write about here, so much to move us, to see and hear."

DENIS LEDOUX, 1947-

"There seemed to be a given when I grew up about people always coming back to Maine from wherever they had gone, and that proved true for me, too.

"I studied at Catholic University in Washington, D.C. and afterwards for a few years I traveled. Then, according to some inner clock, it began to be time to return and I did, but most of my peers, most of my cousins, did not.

"Maine for me wasn't so much the hills and the rivers and the long cold winters.

It was the home of the Franco-American community I had been born into. My family has lived here for four generations, and that makes me very much a Maine writer, but I think of myself primarily as a Franco-American artist. It was here somehow that the amalgam of the French-Canadian and the American that I needed existed. In time I settled in Lisbon Falls, a half mile from where I grew up, with Martha Blowen and our two children, Zoe and Maxim.

"I've taught a number of years at both the high school and the university levels and I've done quite a bit of freelance non-fiction. I've found living in Maine (in my part of it at least) is difficult for a writer. I have often wondered if my writing life would have been easier if I had not come back.

"My stories usually begin with an image or a sentence that recurs insistently. 'Germaine' began when, in my mind's eye, I saw a woman crying, thinking, 'There's nothing left!'

"As I focused on the woman and her sorrow, I realized that she was leaving something. What? Obviously, she had a great attachment to whatever it was.

"I came to realize that she was leaving her home and her homeland. She was migrating to another country where what she knew wasn't what she would have to know."

KATHLEEN LIGNELL, 1942-

A native of California, Lignell currently lives in Orono, where she works as a writer, editor and literature instructor at the University of Maine. Her most recent book is a novel, *The White Buffalo*.

"One day I was sitting in my friends' camp in Carrying Cove, which is out in South Lubec at the end of the road of America, where the fog comes blasting in every afternoon all summer long. We were sitting there watching the fog roll over Grand Manan and pretty soon we couldn't see that Canadian island anymore. And then we watched the lighthouse at West Quoddy Head disappear in the fog, and soon we were wrapped in a white shroud of fog ourselves. All that fog made us go into ourselves and start to tell stories. I hadn't lived in Maine long, and my friends had grown up in Lubec, and they began to educate me about my new home territory. One told me the way it was—and still is—in the sardine packing houses in town. The whistle goes off early in the morning, and the women know the sardine carriers have brought in fish to be slit and canned. It's hard work for these women, and they are paid by the piece, not on an hourly wage. The next day, I went over to the wharf to see for myself. My friend took me through the entire factory, not hiding any of the stench and wounded hands and raw fingers from my eyes. I went home and went about my business. And then about a week later, I heard the whistle blow early in the morning, and I got up with those women who were putting on their old clothes and tying bandanas around their heads, and as they punched their timecards into the clocks, I sat down and wrote 'In the Sardine Factory.'"

HENRY WADSWORTH LONGFELLOW, 1807-1882

Longfellow, probably Maine's most famous writer, was born in Portland in a house that is now open as a museum to visitors. He graduated from Bowdoin College in the same class as Nathaniel Hawthorne, and stayed on as professor of modern languages. In addition to his teaching duties, he also served as Bowdoin's librarian.

Two extended trips to Europe influenced Longfellow the writer as well as Longfellow the academic. He acquainted himself with European legends and verse forms. He came back from the second trip to a teaching post at Harvard University.

Longfellow was an outgoing man who described "the true poet" as someone who views life and nature "in the spirit of love." Tragedy dogged his personal life, but did not embitter him or alter his fundamentally optimistic world view. His first wife died after suffering a miscarriage; his second wife burned to death before his eyes when a dress she was wearing caught fire from a candle she was using to melt sealing wax. The full beard that is so much a part of the older Longfellow's image in our minds covered facial scars left by the burns he suffered trying to douse that fire.

Longfellow's fame was built on the rhythms and imagery with which he was able to bring to life historical incidents and legends, early American characters and scenes. His poetry shaped our view of ourselves as a people. For the better part of a century no student got through an American high school without reading, and memorizing passages from, his long narrative poems "Evangeline," "The Song of Hiawatha," and "The Courtship of Miles Standish."

JOHN MCPHEE, 1931-

John McPhee writes, "I decided I wanted to be a writer when I was twelve years old because I thought it would be easy. Mistake number one." The son of a medical doctor on the faculty of Princeton University, he went to the Princeton public schools and to the university and still lives in Princeton. It was his father's summer job at a camp that focused on ecology and the out-of-doors that "began an affection for the woods—backpacking, and especially canoeing—that eventually led to Maine, Canada, and Alaska. Much of my work as a writer is traceable to those experiences.... Long ago," McPhee continues, "I developed a very strong affection for the Maine woods—for all of Maine as well. This has caused me to seek to do [writing] projects there. These have included 'Heirs of General Practice,' 'The Survival of the Bark Canoe,' 'The Keel of Lake Dickey,' and 'North of the C.P. Line.'"

Despite the fact that writing isn't as easy as McPhee anticipated, he has done a great deal of it, and that most successfully. The author of twenty books, he is a long-time staff writer for the *New Yorker* magazine and a professor of journalism at Princeton. Among his many awards are honorary doctoral degrees from Bates and Colby Colleges.

EDNA ST. VINCENT MILLAY, 1892-1950

Millay, who preferred being called "Vincent" to "Edna," was born in Rockland and moved with her family to Camden when she was twelve. Her divorced mother had little money to support herself and her three daughters with, but managed always to bring books and music into their lives. Millay began to write poems and stories.

After graduating from Camden High School, where she edited the school magazine, Millay had no money to go to college. That might have been the end of her formal education but for a party at Camden's Whitehall Inn at which she read her now-famous poem "Renascence." Among the audience was a woman from New York who recognized her talent and sponsored her undergraduate study at Vassar College.

Millay was attractive, magnetic, and saw herself as a free spirit. She moved to Greenwich Village, became friendly with a wide circle of artists, continued acting, wrote poetry and plays, and supported herself largely by writing stories for magazines under a pen name. By the time she was thirty-one she had become a foreign correspondent, published three books of poetry, and been awarded a Pulitzer Prize. The next year she met and married a wealthy man twelve years older than she. In 1933 they bought Ragged Island in Casco Bay, and returned to it each year as a retreat.

For two decades Millay was a poetry superstar, going on reading tours, involving herself through her writing and speeches with women's rights and other political causes. Her straightforward, passionate poetry, written in traditional forms, won her tremendous popularity. She spent the last years of her life in isolation, suffering a nervous breakdown in the late 1940s. Her husband died in 1949; she died the following year at fifty-eight.

RUTH MOORE, 1903-

Moore was born on Gott's Island. She lived on the island until she went to high school in Ellsworth. After graduating from college in New York State she had a number of jobs: teaching school, running a ranch in California, and working as an editor at *Reader' Digest.* She says that she learned how to construct a novel while working there, where her job was to condense and simplify other people's novels.

Moore was forty when her first book was published. She returned to Maine when her second novel, *Spoonhandle,* was made into a movie by Twentieth Century Fox. She has lived in Maine ever since, and has published fourteen novels, a book of ballads, and a book of poems. All of her work centers on Maine coastal community life. She has said that "the only thing I really try to do is not to tell a lie about a place. If I'm describing something, I know what I'm describing. I just tell the truth about what there is.... My object is to interpret this region realistically. After all, I grew up in it."

SAMUEL FRENCH MORSE, 1916-1985

Morse was born in Danvers, Massachusetts, studied at Dartmouth College, and worked around New England, teaching at the University of Maine, Colby, Trinity, Mount Holyoke, and Northeastern. He travelled to India, New Zealand, and Japan. He died in Boston. When he lived in Maine, his home was at Hancock Point. He was there enough to keep a garden, and in it, some unusual plants not native to Maine. He liked to tell their names, and where they'd come from, which adventurer had brought them back, what nursery stocked them. He liked just as well, while walking visitors around the point, to name and place the natives—plants and birds, the islands—in Frenchman's Bay. Not born in Maine, he knew the word "native" meant different things, including the mysterious Red Paint People, long extinct and the Micmacs, who persist.

ELISABETH OGILVIE, 1917-

"Maine made a writer out of me. I'd always loved reading stories and making up my own, ever since I could first remember, but the passion to get into print didn't hit until I was just fifteen. My family went back to visit a place where I'd spent summers when I was two or three. I still retained bright bits of enchanted memories of this island twenty-five miles off the coast, and the reality didn't let me down.

"That fall I wrote a story about it which was published in the high school magazine. This came out three times a year and had a big literature section, and believe me, I was hooked!

"I was not able to go college, but I had moral support from my family, and a good tough grounding in English and literature from high school. So I dug in. Anyone who wants to be a writer must write, just as a pianist must practice. I've written millions of words which no one else has ever seen, besides the many that were sent out and came back with rejection slips.

"I went back to the island every summer. My Maine summers kept the furnace stoked, so to speak, and I actually began my first novel there, about the island and a family of my own creation. It became Bennett's Island, the setting for many of my adult books and a few for younger readers. 'Scobie' was inspired by a story I heard out there about a man who actually lived in an old boat and kept a little pig for a pet. He too disappeared, with his pig, over the horizon.

"Now I live most of the year on another island, closer to the mainland, but I still have ties to the far-out island. Bennett's Island and its people exist for me and many readers, for which I'm thankful."

STEPHEN PETROFF, 1951-

"Three hundred years ago my relatives lived on Topsham Heights. One of my ancestors was proprietor of the first grocery store in Harpswell in the 1760s. Two of my cousins fought at Gettysburg. Not a one of them was named Petroff. Petroff came to America in 1917. My mother's family came from Red Beach. My father grew up in Cundy's Harbor, but I was born in Hunter Field, Georgia, because my father was in the U.S. Army. Because of this, my girlfriend thinks I'm an out-of-stater. But I was always taught that my hometown is Bowdoinham, Maine. That's where I live, right now.

"In 1967 I decided to become a painter/poet, so I apprenticed myself to Tuli Kupferberg, a poet and singer and cartoonist in New York City. He gave me a mimeograph machine, and I handed out poems for free in Tompkins Square Park. Then I taught myself oil painting by studying old masters in museums here and there.

"I returned to Maine in 1974, and have been painting and writing ever since. In the meantime, women have loved me, ART EXCITES ME EVERY DAY, and I have had the most wonderful life imaginable. And, best of all, I have children. They live and breathe and make Everything believable.

"'Open Secrets of Bowdoinham' is a sequel to a long and VERY SECRET poem called 'Secrets of the Town of Bowdoinham.' The original is a big tapestry-poem which lists a great many incredible and wonderful things that happened in my town during my childhood. The last time I checked, six people must die before my poem can be published. (Otherwise, I'd get in trouble.) I wrote 'Open Secrets of Bowdoinham' when I realized that many 'small' things had happened there, too, which were just as significant as the great, dreadful, front-page Secrets. In fact, those 'little things,' having to do with hay-bales, and chickens lost in the woods, may be more important after all."

SANFORD PHIPPEN, 1942-

"I grew up in Hancock, a small, rural coastal town next to Ellsworth and across Frenchman's Bay from Mount Desert Island. Hancock has a summer colony, Hancock Point, where I used to work as a boy mowing lawns, delivering milk and eggs, and helping my parents and relatives caretake a number of summer places. Several of the summer people I worked for were writers, one of whom was Mrs. Jo Fulton, a prolific 'hack' writer who would send me to the post office with her manuscripts for mailing to various national publications. As a boy of twelve and thirteen who liked to read, I was very impressed by her manuscripts, typewriter, and large library.

"Near where I lived at Gull Rock on the east side of Hancock lived Mrs. Durand, known to the literary world as Ruth Sawyer, who published a children's book called *Maggie Rose* when I was in grammar school. It was about Hancock and people I knew and went to school with. I was very impressed by that book, seeing how the life around me became art. Everyone all over town seemed to be reading and discussing it. In the seventh grade, I won a book report prize for my report on a book about Abraham Lincoln. The prize was three dollars; and I was presented the prize by Mrs. Durand. I was in the seventh grade also when my Ellsworth dentist, Dick Adams, pulled me out of the dentist's chair one day so I could catch a glimpse of E.B. White walking down Main Street.

"Hancock was and is a great storytelling town full of legends and myths of sea captains, fishermen, farmers, Nazi spies, summer people, steamboat and train workers, famous names, and town characters. I see now clearly that it was a great place for a budding writer to grow up."

SYLVESTER POLLET, 1939-

"Once upon a time I was a Boy Scout in Woodstock, New York, keeping a record of each new bird I could identify for sure. Eventually I got the bird-study merit badge, and my resolution to keep those records up-to-date for life went the way of most resolutions. But that's not the same as saying I lost interest—I didn't.

"It must have been about the same time that I came upon the nature poetry of Chinese and, particularly, Japanese writers, like Basho and Issa. The way they could do so much with so few words fascinated me (it still does) and I suppose one consistent effort in my writing has been to try to learn to approach their clarity of image, but in ordinary local situations and language. 'Poem for St. Francis,' for example, is my attempt to record, and maybe to understand better, something I saw happen at the birdfeeder behind my house.

"What else would be useful to know? I live in the woods in the far northwest corner of Ellsworth, in a house my wife and I built ourselves. I've lived in Maine since 1971, and I'm staying. The last few years, I've been teaching writing and doing editorial work at the University of Maine. My ambitions are to get my firewood in earlier next year, to improve my French, to write more, and to learn more about sailing. Oh yes, one more thing: the hawk was a female sharp-shinned hawk."

GERARD ROBICHAUD, 1908-

Born in St. Evariste de Bauce, a small town in Canada's Quebec Province, Gerard Robichaud moved as a small boy with his family to Lewiston. After graduating from high school there, he studied for the priesthood at a seminary in Quebec. He began to develop his writing at the seminary, composing vignettes and essays in French.

Robichaud left the seminary and his ambitions for the priesthood, a decision he says "changed my life completely," and returned to the United States. Because he had been raised within a Franco-American community, he did not learn to speak or write English until this point in his life, when he was nearly twenty. He spent several years in New York, absorbing what it had to offer as a cultural center, then served in the U.S. Army during World War II in the Pacific. There he entertained his fellow soldiers with stories, some sad, some happy, of his childhood in Lewiston.

After leaving the service, Robichaud studied writing at Columbia University, and began to consider a career as a writer. It was only, however, after publishing several works that "didn't grab me" that he discovered what he wanted to write about. At the suggestion of his wife, who, like his Army buddies, loved listening to his childhood reminiscences, he began to write about the Franco-American community within which he grew up. "That's when I came home," he says. "Lewiston gave me such treasures. I walked away from it completely, and then I came back."

Robichaud recently moved back to Lewiston to live, and to work on a sequel to his novel *Papa Martel*, from which "The Bad One" was taken. He describes the process of preparing to write the new novel as one of "listening and hearing and listening and hearing.... My best stories of Lewiston are yet to be told."

EDWIN ARLINGTON ROBINSON, 1869-1935

He called himself at one point "a failure from the beginning." It is no wonder, perhaps, that Edwin Arlington Robinson peopled his poetry with tragic failures. His home town of Gardiner, where his family moved shortly after his birth in Head Tide, provided the model for "Tilbury Town," in which his famous characters, among them Richard Cory (based on a Gardiner attorney who died a destitute drunk) and Mr. Flood, led their self-isolated lives. Many of his poems are short character studies that convey in a single incident or a dramatic monologue the essence of a life.

Robinson was a mediocre student at both Gardiner High School and Harvard University, which he left before graduating when the family finances collapsed. Both his mother and his father soon died. Robinson spent the next several years in a "hand to mouth existence" in New York, working as a timekeeper on a subway construction crew, struggling to write at night. His first volume of poetry, *Children of the Night*, earned him little recognition.

But Theodore Roosevelt, then governor of New York, came upon a copy of Robinson's book and responded enthusiastically. Roosevelt wrote to Robinson, extending him encouragement and the offer of a job as a clerk in the New York Customs House, which would leave him more time in which to write. He kept this job until he was able to support himself as a writer.

By the 1920s Robinson had become a pre-eminent American poet. He won three Pulitzer Prizes and an honorary doctoral degree from Bowdoin College. He remained until his death, however, a retiring person who avoided personal publicity.

TIM SAMPLE, 1951-

"If anyone had told me a few years back that I would someday be known as a 'writer,' I'd probably have said, 'Not likely, chummy!' Then an interesting thing happened. After years of 'making up' stories, telling them on stage and recording them on albums, someone asked me, 'Do you write your own material?'

"I had to think for a moment, but the answer was, 'Yeah, come to think of it, I guess I do write most of it.'

"'The Black Fly Festival' first came to me during a performance with Marshall Dodge at the Theatre at Monmouth in the summer of 1981. It was one of the first of the Sample and Dodge shows and we were pretty short on material. When the audience hollered for an encore we didn't have anything prepared. They definitely wanted more. Marshall whispered, 'What're we gonna do?'

"'Let's just go back out there,' I said, 'You ask me a question and I'll make up some ridiculous answer, and we'll take it from there.'

"We walked on stage; the audience settled down. Marshall turned to me and asked, 'So, Tim, been to any interestin' festivals lately?'"

MAY SARTON, 1912-

"I began writing poems for the fun of it when I was nine or ten years old, maybe because my mother read poems to me every night before I went to sleep, so poetry was an important part of my life from the start.

"My father was Belgian and my mother English so I am a naturalized American—we were driven out of Belgium by the Germans in 1914. I am very glad to be an American. It is the best country there is for a serious writer. I knew I belonged to the U.S.A. when I bought an old farmhouse in Nelson, New Hampshire. Owning thirty-six acres of woods and meadows was an adventure. Attending town meetings, I learned how democracy works. But when, fifteen years later, friends offered to rent me a house right on the ocean in York, Maine, I could not resist, as I have always dreamed of ending my life by the sea. I am very happy here with my Himalayan cat Pierrot and my miniature dachshund Grizzle. I am now seventy-six with forty-six books published and have just finished a long novel which will be out next year. Mine has been a life of hard work and great joys."

LEE SHARKEY, 1945-

"Maine is a state where anything is possible, so long as you are willing to do it yourself. I moved here in 1971, and in the years since have built my own house, learned to grow my own food, raised a child, and taught myself to hand set and print books on a hundred-year-old printing press named Pearl. I have taught writing to students, teachers, prisoners, and mental patients. Being the local poet has given me access to a range of people and places I would otherwise never have encountered.

"'exercise' is from my most recent book of poetry, *first moments*. It was written in the spring of 1983. That was the season I realized I had never cried over the Nazi Holocaust or the dropping of the atom bombs on Hiroshima and Nagasaki. I was pushing forty and had never stopped to mourn the loss of innocence those double monsters of destruction have made our birthright. It scared me to realize that I had so insulated myself. I began to let the pain come in, cried for months at the drop of a hat—a child's face was enough to set me off— and little by little the pain took the shape of dreams and poems. As an 'exercise' I brought the threat of nuclear destruction we all live under down to the level of personal loss by imagining what is to me the most unspeakable horror, the death of my own child.

"Why put myself through the pain of such an 'exercise'? I don't really know, other than to say that to be numb to the realities of life is in itself a form of death, and there'll be plenty of time for that after we die. I do know I came out the other side of my season of despair both stronger and more vulnerable, and I hope something of the same happens to those who allow themselves to feel their way through the poem."

SUSAN HAND SHETTERLY, 1942-

"My husband and I live in the woods because we learn vital things here: to cut firewood, to grow food in our garden, to recognize change when it comes and the cycles that bring returning events, such as mud season and January thaw and summer warblers.

"When I was a young girl in my parents' home in suburban Connecticut, my father used to read me poetry. He would stretch out on the couch and prop his head up. He tilted his glasses against his nose. It was always night, as I remember, the windows dark; in winter a fire sometimes crackled in the fireplace, throwing shadows out onto the floor. I sat in a chair across from my father as he read from the book that his mother had read to him. He read me long poems and short poems. His relaxed voice went on and on, carrying the cadences of his favorite verses as if he were really carrying something that had weight and value.

"Wilderness and poetry. They mean a great deal to me today. I write about wild places and wild animals because people stray from the connections that make them whole—and I want to pull them back. We have stacked so much clutter between us and the sound of the wind. I am worried that we will cease to hear the wind—won't listen to the small birds that migrate in the dark high over our heads on clear September nights. I don't want us to forget how to live on the earth."

DOROTHY SIMPSON, 1905-

"My family lived on a small island—365 acres—twenty-five miles at sea, and all my grown-up male relatives were fishermen. I had the sea in my blood too, and as a youngster I felt sure I could earn my living from fishing when I grew up. When I realized such a thing could not be, I decided to write about the sea and islands and fishing people. I thought I had to start out with short stories, so for twenty-five years I wrote them and sent them away and they came back. I kept all this a secret, I didn't want to be laughed at.

"As a child I never thought we were poor just because there was no way to get the extras that were not needed to hold body and soul together. When I earned a nickel or dime for running an errand I bought notebooks, and eventually began filling pages with descriptions of the sea and sky, which were so tremendous and all-encompassing. I copied favorite chapters and verses from borrowed books into notebooks; meanwhile I was loving the island and its life, studying its people and trying to understand them completely.

"I live on another island now, very close to the mainland—nearly the size of my childhood island—and it gives food and shelter to deer, racoons, porcupines, skunks, and woodchucks, as well as grouse, pheasants, mourning doves and woodcock. I love the state of Maine, especially the coast, and wouldn't want to live anywhere else. It is more than rocks, rivers, lakes, forests, fields and mountains, with the ocean rising and falling against its broken outside edge. We all have dreams, and one of mine is that Maine can be forever a place that puts a spark into the hearts of its people which can never be snuffed out, and will spring into flame whenever there is a need."

EDMUND WARE SMITH, 1900-1967

A Connecticut native with a love for adventure and the out-of-doors, Smith once ran away from prep school and rode the rails in a freight train. He survived the incident to continue his education at Antioch College, where he and a friend started a successful restaurant as part of the school's work-study program.

For the next decade he worked for *National Sportsman* and *Hunting and Fishing* magazines, and after that as a freelance writer. During his lifetime he wrote some 600 short stories and a single novel, *Rider in the Sun*.

Smith moved to Maine with his second wife in 1945 and built a cabin on the shores of Matagamon Lake the next year. James Ware Smith describes his father and stepmother's life in the cabin as one of "peaceful serenity ... conducive to writing." He continues:

"He didn't like to wear a suit, but on occasion he was forced to comply with society. While wearing a suit, he would get away with wearing Maine moccasins—or sometimes slippers. His quiet, private and casual life was undoubtedly invaded too many times when he was in the limelight. However, there were many friends in the Damariscotta area, where he and Mary moved around 1956. He and some of these pals formed a group called Jake's Rangers. Jake was Maurice Day, an artist and photographer. Their trips through the Maine woods were memorable times for my father."

GLENNA JOHNSON SMITH, 1920-

"I grew up in a Maine coastal village, Ashville, and I have spent my adult years in Easton and Presque Isle. Perhaps I started writing young because I was an only child in a quiet, reserved household. Often I spent time outdoors alone, comfortable with the fields, the hills, and the bay. I'd sit on a big rock with my tablet and write to help me make sense of my sometimes frightening world and the people in it. In the years when I was a farmer's wife, mother of three young sons, and a schoolteacher, I had little time for writing. Now that the sons are grown and I no longer live on the farm, I am still a schoolteacher who hunts for the quiet spaces. Although I have swapped the tablet for a word processor, I still feel akin to the Maine countryside, whether it be the wide, rolling potato fields of Aroostook County or the shores of Frenchman's Bay, and I write for nearly the same old reasons: to try to understand the perplexities of my world and the changing seasons of my life."

SEBA SMITH, 1792-1868

Smith taught school around his hometown of Buckfield before entering Bowdoin College in 1815. After graduation and another brief stint at teaching, he traveled to England, then settled down to a career as a journalist in Portland. One of the newspapers he founded, the *Portland Courier,* carried his humorous letters from a fictitious "Major Jack Downing of Downingville." These and other writings from the pen of Downing brought Smith a national reputation. He was one of America's first political satirists, caricaturing "the problems and squabbles of Jacksonian democracy" and the independent and ornery Yankee, of whom his creation Jack Downing is a perfect example.

The economic panic of 1837 forced Smith and his family to relocate to New York, where he continued his career in journalism until his retirement in 1860.

ELIZABETH GEORGE SPEARE, 1908-

Elizabeth George Speare was born in Melrose, Massachusetts. She earned a B.A. and an M.A. from Boston University, and taught high school English for four years. She is the author of numerous books, two of which have earned the Newbery Award.

"I have lived all my life in New England, and though I love to travel I can't imagine calling any other place on earth home.

"Gathering the material for a book takes me a year or more. While I am taking pages of notes in libraries and museums the story is growing in my mind. When I finally begin to write, I know in general what my characters are to do and how their story will end, though many surprising changes always occur on the way. I work very slowly, doing only a few pages a day, trying to make each sentence say exactly what I mean. Sometimes I reach a blind spot, a sort of gulf, and for weeks I cannot see how I can possibly get my characters across to the other side where I want them to be. But sooner or later almost by magic a bridge appears. Some bit of history, some ancient custom, or perhaps just the sort of person one character has turned out to be suggests a way, and presently we are all safely across."

C.A. (CHARLES ASBURY) STEPHENS, 1844-1931

Stephens was born in Norway, Maine, a descendant of one of its founding families. Norway was then farm country surrounded by wilderness, and Stephens spent his childhood years working on the family farm and in the woods, hiking and camping, hunting and fishing. He went to school "when money and time made it possible." He nevertheless was accepted to Bowdoin College, and managed to graduate in two years at the top of his class.

A professor at Bowdoin encouraged him as a writer, but he was unsure about making a career of writing until he met Daniel Ford, the publisher of *Youth's Companion,* a popular periodical for children. Stephens sold Ford his first two stories for fourteen dollars; thus his career was launched.

Stephens contributed to *Youth's Companion* for over sixty years. His writing consisted of lightly fictionalized reports on his travels through North and Central America, the West Indies, and Europe, and stories about his childhood experiences in Maine. He was convinced that "children preferred stories which they believed to be real," so he made his writing as realistic as possible. For this reason his stories are a valuable source of information about life in nineteenth-century New England.

When Daniel Ford wanted someone to report knowledgeably on medical affairs for *Youth's Companion,* he encouraged Stephens to go through medical school. Stephens did so, and developed in the process an abiding interest in biology. After graduating in 1887, he built a laboratory near his home in Norway to research the causes of old age, and wrote about his theories and research, as well as childhood reminiscences, until his death at age 86.

JOHN TAGLIABUE, 1923-

"I sort of danced and acted my way into poetry. In elementary and high school I enjoyed acting, dancing, reading, and wrote some poems and stories. But it was after my give and take with some inspiring teachers and poems in college that I began to write my thousands of poems (and a few short plays, essays, and many travel journals). Travelling in books too—finding phrases, thoughts, images—helped excite some of my teaching and much of my writing. I started teaching in Beirut, in 1945; since then I've also taught in Italy, Japan, Greece, Spain, Brazil, and recently in the People's Republic of China.

"My wife and I came to Maine in 1953; that's when I started teaching at Bates and though I've taken off often for short or long trips, most of my years have been spent here and most of my poems written here. 'I'm not a regionalist,' Robert Frost said, 'but a realist. I write about realms of the spirit.' And so do I—naturally affected by my moods, the weather, scenes, events tragic or comic in my life. All along it has been my love of language, words, sounds, phrases, images, making connections that has helped keep the writing going; often a form of exuberance. The need to respond to moments via rhythm and cadence and song and dance in words has helped increase my feeling for reality; often my poems search and celebrate communion and 'original unity.'"

HENRY DAVID THOREAU, 1817-1862

Thoreau was born and raised in Concord, Massachusetts, and spent much of his childhood wandering the woods and fields of that town. His schooling was interrupted by ill-health and family financial problems, but he graduated from Harvard University as an honor student.

Highly principled, Thoreau quit his first teaching job rather than be forced to inflict corporal punishment on his students. He then established a private school in his home, one which anticipated twentieth century "progressive education." Some years later he went to jail rather than pay a poll tax that he believed supported the institution of slavery in the South.

Thoreau wrote constantly, keeping a daily journal from his young adulthood until shortly before his death, defining the principles he lived by in notes for lectures which he then developed into essays. One of the Transcendentalist writers, he was always searching for the larger meaning behind any natural or human occurrence. The woods of Maine held such meaning for him.

Although he thought of himself as a poet, we know Thoreau for his essays and for two books that grew out of his journal keeping, *Walden* and *The Maine Woods*, a storehouse of careful observations of the natural world. He was working on his *Maine Woods* papers at the time of his death from tuberculosis in 1862. His last words were "moose" and "Indian."

E. B. (ELWYN BROOKS) WHITE, 1899-1985

White was a successful and well-loved essayist for the *New Yorker* and *Harper's* magazines, and the author of several collections of essays. His clear, witty, informal style has made him a favorite among armchair readers and professors of English alike. *Elements of Style*, a writer's handbook which he co-authored with William Strunk, Jr., has become a standard in college composition courses.

White grew up in New York State and began his career in New York City, but Maine was always a part of his life. He spent summers as a child in the Belgrade Lakes region. He and his wife, also a writer, moved to an old farmhouse in North Brooklin, overlooking Blue Hill Bay, in 1938. Many of his essays, such as "Maine Speech" and "Death of a Pig," describe with warmth the characters and characteristics that make up Maine.

MARGERY WILSON, 1943-

"I was born and brought up in a place very different from Maine—Brooklyn, New York. For the first seventeen years of my life, I lived in an apartment, went to six-story brick schools (and rode on subways to get to them), cheered for the Brooklyn Dodgers (and hated the Yankees), and played stickball out in the street.

"But I went to college in Maine, and met my husband there; so when we were able to find work here, we were very happy to return. I teach English now at the University of Maine, and I write about the rural life I see around me, as well as about other Maine writers.

"My husband and I have raised all five of our children here, on our farm in Troy. They grew up milking cows, cleaning out pigpens, and driving our team of draft horses. But there's one way in which my childhood and theirs is exactly the same: they hate the Yankees, too."

ROBLEY WILSON, JR., 1930-

"Sanford is my home town, and I still consider it home—even though I haven't lived there since 1950, and even though I don't approve of the changes that 'progress' has made there. The older I get, the more I feel a strong necessity for roots, and I'm grateful for mine in Maine. I've lived in the Midwest for thirty years, but I've never been comfortable so far from the ocean. I can't remember when I didn't want to be a writer, though for a long time (certainly all through high school) I wanted to be a sportswriter; that seemed the best possible career for a (sigh) Red Sox fan. In fact, I didn't actually publish my first poem until I was thirty years old, my first story until a couple of years later, my first book until I was 47. Writing is not an art for the impatient. I've made a so-so living from teaching, but if I had my life to do over, I think I would gamble and only write.

"'A Stay at the Ocean' is simply a what-if story. What if the tide went out and never came back? The story sets out to answer the question (that kind of question is often called 'the premise') by focusing on an ordinary tourist family from Ohio. It describes their response to the disappearing of the ocean, and the responses of others, and then it arrives at the obvious final answer to the what-if: if the tide goes out, it must come back. What makes the story work, if it works at all, is the horror—both the family's and the reader's—of realizing the obvious answer too late. The hard thing about writing this kind of 'premise' story is making the impossible seem believable. But that's the fun of it, too. I hope that once you accept the premise, everything else appears perfectly possible."

BARON WORMSER, 1948-

"I moved to Maine with my wife in 1970 and have lived in Maine since then. I am grateful for the chance to live here. The weather, the people, and the landscapes have an unmediated quality which I prize. It seems to me that a writer should live on the earth rather than in his or her head. Close contact with a natural and a social world makes a person aware that all actions have consequences. And that is what my writing is all about—consequences."

ACKNOWLEDGEMENTS

IDENTITY

"Whale!" from *New England Short Stories*, copyright 1974, by Yankee, Inc., published by Yankee Books. Reprinted by permission.

"Blueberry Boy," from *New and First Collected Poems*, copyright 1989, by Leo Connellan, published by Paragon House Publishers. Reprinted by permission.

"A White Heron," originally published in 1925 in *The Best Stories of Sarah Orne Jewett*, by Houghton Mifflin Co.

Excerpt from *Octavia's Hill* by Margaret Dickson. Copyright© 1983 by Margaret Dickson. Reprinted by permission of Houghton Mifflin Company.

"John and Emma Carpenter," from *Aldenville*, copyright May 1988, by Glenna Johnson Smith, published by Hummingbird Press (1989). Reprinted by permission.

"My Lost Youth," originally published in *The Courtship of Miles Standish*, 1858, by Ticknor & Fields.

"Scobie," from *Woman's Day* Magazine, copyright August 1951, by Elisabeth Ogilvie, published by *Woman's Day* Magazine. Reprinted by permission.

"The State Meet," from *Too Hot and Other Maine Stories*, copyright 1987, by Fred Bonnie, published by Dog Ear Press. Reprinted by permission.

"The Bad One," from *Papa Martel*, copyright 1961, by Gerard Robichaud, published by Doubleday. Reprinted by permission.

"Renascence," by Edna St. Vincent Millay. From *Collected Poems*, Harper & Row. Copyright © 1921, 1928, 1934, 1948, 1955, 1962 by Edna St. Vincent Millay and Norma Millay Ellis. Reprinted by permission.

"Past the Shallows," by Betsy Graves. Printed by permission.

"Silhouettes," from *Collected Poems* , copyright 1950, by Abbie Houston Evans, published by University of Pittsburgh Press. Reprinted by permission of the publisher.

"The Ledge," originally published in *The Hudson Review* , XI no. 4, Winter 1958-59, copyright 1960 Lawrence Sargent Hall. Reprinted by permission.

"exercise," from *first moments*, copyright 1987, by Lee Sharkey, published by Puckerbrush Press. Reprinted by permission.

ORIGINS

"A Poem About The Red Paint People," from *The Changes*, copyright 1964, by Samuel French Morse, published by Alan Swallow. Reprinted by permission.

"Champlain Navigates the Penobscot," translation originally published in *Voyages of Samuel de Champlain*, Charles Scribner's Sons in 1907.

Excerpt from *John Josselyn, Colonial Traveler*, copyright 1988, edited by Paul J. Lindholdt, published by University Press of New England. Reprinted by permission.

"English and Indians Have It Out at Pemaquid," originally published in Boston in 1736, printed for William Dodge.

"We Are the Stars Which Sing," from *Passamaquoddy Texts*, J.D. Prince, 1921, G.E. Stechert & Co.

"The Stars" by Jerome Rothenberg, *Technicians of the Sacred*, copyright 1968, J.R. Doubleday & Co.

"January, 1724" and "The Last Moon," from *Thirteen Moons/Treize Lunes*, copyright 1982, by Robert M. Chute, published by Penumbra Press. Reprinted by permission.

"The Coming of Glooskap," originally published in 1893 in *The Life and Working Traditions of the Red Man*, by Joseph Nicolar.

"Gluskap Fashions the Animals" and "Gluskap Goes to France," from *Gluskap the Liar and Other Indian Tales*, copyright 1966, Cumberland Press. Reprinted by permission.

"Koluskap and the Wind" and "When Koluskap Left the World" by Wayne Newell and Robert Leavitt. Copyright Indian Township School Committee. Reprinted by permission.

"The Witch of Harpswell," anonymous.

"Jack Downing's Visit to Portland," from *The Life and Writings of Major Jack Downing of Downingville*, 1833.

"Lost Graveyards," Elizabeth Coatsworth. Reprinted by permission.

"Turnip Pie," copyright 1987, by Rebecca Cummings, published by Puckerbrush Press. Reprinted by permission.

XXIII from "The Clear Blue Lobster-Water Country," from *New and First Collected Poems*, copyright 1989, by Leo Connellan, published by Paragon House Publishers. Reprinted by permission.

"Germaine," copyright 1987, by Denis Ledoux. Published in *Puckerbrush Review* by Puckerbrush Review; in *le Canado-Américain* by l'Association Canado-Américain; and in *RAFALE* by F.A.R.O.G. Forum. Reprinted by permission.

"History" and "Succoth," from *Light Years*, copyright 1983, by Roberta Chester, published by Puckerbrush Press. Reprinted by permission.

"Remembering the First 'Newcomers,'" from *The Waldo Independent*, copyright March 3, 1988, by Margery Wilson, published by The Waldo Independent, Inc. Reprinted by permission.

"Micmac," from *The Changes*, copyright 1964, by Samuel French Morse, published by Alan Swallow. Reprinted by permission.